D0408380

AMERICAN WOMEN
AND
WORLD WAR II

HISTORY OF WOMEN IN AMERICA

AMERICAN WOMEN
AND
WORLD WAR II

Doris Weatherford

CASTLE BOOKS

This edition published in 2008 by
CASTLE BOOKS ®
A division of Book Sales, Inc.
114 Northfield Avenue
Edison, NJ 08837

This edition published by arrangement with and permission of
Facts On File, Inc.
460 Park Avenue South
New York, NY 10016
USA

Copyright © 1990 by Doris Weatherford

All rights reserved. No part of this book may be reproduced or utilized in any form or by any means, electronic or mechanical, including photocopying, recording, or by any information storage or retrieval systems, without permission in writing from the publisher.

For information contact:

Facts On File, Inc.	Facts On File Limited
460 Park Avenue South	Collins Street
New York, NY 10016	Oxford OX4 1XJ
USA	United Kingdom

Library of Congress Cataloging-in-Publication Data:

Weatherford, Doris.
    American women and World War II / Doris Weatherford.
        p.   cm. – (History of women in America)
    Includes bibliographical references and index.
    1.   World War, 1939-1945 – Women – United States.
    2.   Women – United States – History – 20th Century,   I. Title. II. Series.
D810.W7W43 1990
940.53' 15042' 0973 – dc20

89-71489
CIP

A British CIP catalogue record for this book is available upon request from the British Library

ISBN-13: 978-0-7858-2490-9
ISBN-10: 0-7858-2490-1

Printed in the United States of America

FOR MY MOTHER

LEONA BARGE

WHO LIVED THROUGH THIS WAR

AND MUCH MORE

CONTENTS

INTRODUCTION

War holds many ironies, and among them is its liberating effect on women. Although any society at war must subject its members to greater regimentation, to loss of accustomed freedoms and to altered life-styles, it will allow—even encourage—women in wartime to do things that are closed to them in peace.

Women were of course present at America's birthing, but—occasional Molly Pitchers and Betsy Rosses aside—their chief task in America's first war was to run the farms most soldiers left behind. Probably expressing the thoughts of many others, Abigail Adams spoke of her unpleasant responsibilities in contrast to the excitement of the faraway places that John was seeing. Writing at one particularly trying time, she said:

> Since you left me I have passed through great displeasures of both body and mind ... You may remember Isaac was unwell when you went from home ... I was seized with the same disorder in a violent manner ... The next person in the same week was Suzy ... Our little Tommy was next, and he lies very ill now ... Yesterday Patty was seized ... Our house is a hospital in every part; and what with my own weakness and distress of mind for my family, I have been unhappy enough. [1]

Like thousands of her female contemporaries, Mrs. Adams battled sickness and death; she heard the roar of cannons and the march of soldiers near her; she saw firsthand the consequences of war. But for most of the seven-year revolution and for most women, the days of fear and excitement were few and the days of hard work, high prices, drudgery and loneliness were many. The tasks women performed in maintaining farms and businesses were largely thankless. The Revolution had little emancipating effect on these women who protected hearth and home, and indeed, some legal rights were lost in the passage from colonialism to statehood.

Eighty-five years later there was a second and deadlier war. This time, women not only tended farms, plantations and businesses, but they also were a part of factories that sprang forth to supply war needs. Moreover, when blood began to flow in torrents from Civil War battlefields, women entered that masculine ground. The idea that men were not merely cannon fodder, that governments had a responsibility to seriously try to bind up the wounds they had caused, began with Clara Barton and her followers. The battlefield work of these women was dangerous and exhausting, but perhaps the hardest thing for them to face was that, although wounded soldiers might have considered them angels of mercy, the public at large had difficulty distinguishing them from the traditional camp followers. This was an age when a great many people preferred to allow men to die rather than subject the innocence of womanhood to the sight of male bodies. In their insistence on saving lives, women not only reformed governmental attitudes toward soldiers, but they also established a new field of occupation for women.

The right to be a nurse was perhaps the only concrete gain that women obtained from the Civil War, for the courts held that although the 15th Amendment, added to the Constitution as a result of the war, spoke of "the right of citizens of the United States to vote," obviously women were not intended to be included under the meaning of "citizens." Abigail Adams had written during the Revolution:

In the new code of laws which I suppose it will be necessary for you to make, I desire you would remember the ladies and be more generous and favorable to them than your ancestors. Do not put such unlimited power into the hands of the husbands. Remember, all men would be tyrants if they could. If particular care and attention is not paid to the ladies, we are determined to foment a rebellion, and will not consider ourselves bound by any laws in which we have no voice or representation.[2]

Though her intellectual descendants continued to work for female enfranchisement for decades after the Civil War, the plea went unanswered until the end of our third major war.

World War I brought a hysteria of patriotism to the Western world; women were not excluded. The spirit of the times was such that women wanted to "do their part" and men could not consistently refuse their aid. Moreover, the long and bloody stalemate of battle mounted such a costly toll of lives that, especially in Europe, the industrial labor of women became essential. Women worked in munition plants and on public transportation, drove ambulances, nursed on and off the battlefield and served with distinction as translators and telephone operators at the front.

While most of this work was civilian and often volunteer, the first timid steps were taken during the last months of the Great War to make women a part of the U.S. military itself. Desperately needing clerical help, the Navy researched enlistment law and found no legal barrier to the admittance of women. Almost 13,000 women enlisted in the Navy and Marine Corps on the same status as men. Uniformed in ankle-length skirts and martial blouses, these "Marinettes" were pictured drilling with rifles and bayonets, though their work was largely with the typewriter and laundry. The contributions to victory of women in all of these fields at last brought the vote. War had finally accomplished for women what peace and reason had failed to do.

Their goal of three-quarters of a century achieved, women—like men—relaxed in the 1920s. Important social changes were occurring: Burdensome dresses were shortened and lightened; heavy hair was bobbed; women indulged equally with men in the formerly forbidden vices of alcohol and tobacco; "Freudian" freedom became the byword of bedroom and back seat.

The bubble burst in the 1930s, and "Depression" aptly referred to the mental state of millions of women, as well as to the economy. Women who had optimistically prepared themselves for careers in the bright days of the twenties now went to the end of the unemployment line. State laws were passed barring married women from jobs, and "a woman's place is in the home" became the common litany.

The next decade brought another war, and just as women had been confined to the home in the 1930s, they were coaxed out of it in the 1940s. America was to become the "arsenal of democracy"; President Roosevelt called for an impossible number of planes and ships and weapons, and women—the last "labor reserve"—would have to make them. Millions responded to the appeal and left their kitchens for defense plants. They found better jobs than they had ever had before—or would have again.

Thousands of other women enlisted with their brothers in the branches of the military opened by the crisis, and they found experiences unlike any known by American women before. Serving in hundreds of occupational slots all around the globe, they endured both the danger of battlefields and the boredom of clerical work to bring the victory. Countless other women did during the war what women have always done in running homes and rearing children, but they did it in circumstances that were altered—almost always for the worse—by war.

This book is a look at the lives of American women during World War II and how they fought the battles of war, whether on the home front or the front lines.

SOURCE NOTES

1. Letter from Abigail Adams to John Adams, September 8, 1775. Charles Francis Adams: *Familiar Letters of John Adams and His Wife Abigail Adams*, originally published in 1875; reprinted Freeport, New York: Books for Libraries Press, 1970, p. 94.
2. Ibid, March 31, 1776, p. 149.

AMERICAN WOMEN
AND
WORLD WAR II

PART I

BE A NURSE AND SEE THE WORLD

1

MILITARY NURSES IN BATTLE

The turkey on Christmas Day, 1941, went uneaten; the potential diners at Sternberg General Hospital in Manila were far too busy dodging bombs. For sleepless days and nights since Pearl Harbor, Army nurses had driven themselves to care for the wounded who crowded the corridors of the hospital and overflowed into temporary annexes in night clubs, colleges and business buildings. Because medical corpsmen were staffing ambulances, nurses found themselves doing heavy and loathsome work: "We had to cut off clothing soaked with blood and stiff from burning, and that took so long that we couldn't get to many of the men even to give them emergency treatment."[1] But now that particular stage of the horror was over. They were preparing to evacuate. Manila was falling to the Japanese.

Manila had been an outpost of American influence since the Spanish-American War of 1898, when the United States liberated the Philippine islands from Spanish rule and put them under its own semicolonialist umbrella. Though Japan's expansionist plans had been clear for a decade, U.S. bases throughout the South Pacific in 1941 were not at all prepared for the Japanese attack in early December. The women of the Army Nurse Corps assigned to the Philippines (like their male military colleagues elsewhere) were in a state of disbelieving shock when the bombs began to fall.

Most of their patients would be left behind in Army hospitals to become prisoners of war, for the rule of the Army is to live to fight another day, and the nurses were part of that Army. Hurriedly they packed a few belongings and slipped to the docks, hiding from the bombs that rained from planes overhead, waiting for the boats they hoped could take them to safety. The quiet, snow-covered towns of North America and the happy family scenes of Christmas seemed impossibly distant.

Most of the nurses were sent to Bataan, a name that later became synonymous with starvation and agonizing death but then sounded hopeful. They thought they would be there only a few weeks before a victorious U.S. military arrived. Instead, they found themselves running a "hospital" that spread out for miles in the jungle, living with snakes and rats and monkeys that stole the little food they had. Months later, the nurses again evacuated in terror. "Little did I dream," said one Army nurse, "that we would be always hungry, always frightened. That we would grab shovels and help dig foxholes so we would have some shelter to crawl into when the dive-bombers came. That we would all suffer malaria and dysentery and diarrhea. It was a good thing for all of us that we had no idea what we were getting into."[2]

It was not supposed to be like this. The Army Nurse Corps (ANC) had been, in the twenties and thirties, a very pleasant life.* A military nurse's pay was far better than that of the average civilian woman; her room, board and laundry were taken care of for her; she was assured of free medical care, graduate education and liberal retirement benefits. The opportunity to travel attracted many: "Almost any Nurse Corps veteran has memories of service in the Philippines, Alaska, Hawaii, Panama or China."[3] They worked eight-hour shifts except in emergencies, and, since they were treated as officers, their free time was their own for recreation. Because they were greatly outnumbered by men, there were hordes of admirers available for dates.

Yet despite the seemingly country-club sound of this life, something in it had taught these women discipline and fortitude, for they faced the dangers and deprivations of Manila and Bataan and Corregidor and not one of them cracked. Physical exhaustion became the overwhelming factor in their lives. At Camp Limay on the north end of Bataan, said a Navy nurse, "Everybody worked from seven in the morning until ten at night, and then tried to break away and get some sleep. We had seven operating tables, two doctors and a nurse and two Corpsmen to a table, and we were kept going. Wounded men would be waiting in lines of stretchers for us to get to them."[4]

Accustomed to a ratio of one nurse to 10 patients, these women found themselves attempting to care for 200 or 300 apiece by the time Bataan fell. Beds were dismantled to accommodate two patients—the mattress on the ground for one and the blanket-covered springs for another. "Days and nights were an endless nightmare," one woman recalled, "until it seemed we couldn't stand it any longer. Patients came in by the hundreds, and the doctors and nurses worked continuously under the tents amid the flies and heat and dust. We had from eight to nine hundred victims a day."[5]

Eating became the second major problem, the center of thoughts and day-dreams. Two "meals" a day were all that these hard-working people could get, with breakfast no more than some fritters or a little oatmeal and supper usually consisting of a stew and rice, the stew having been made of carabao, horse or mule meat. Once, some unusually good stew was enjoyed; a little later, nurses noticed that their pet monkey Tojo no longer frolicked through the camp. "When

---

* The ANC was created by Congress in 1901 in response to the work women did as volunteers in the recently ended war with Spain.

the soldiers went on half rations in January, so did the nurses," testified the head of the Nurse Corps. They "learned to look forward to rice cooked with raisins as a staple dish . . . At the end, a full day's ration consisted of a few slivers of mule meat served with a half cup of rice."[6]

Other shortages existed. One nurse in charge of almost 300 patients reported that she "had only six medicine glasses, fifteen thermometers and a single teaspoon."[7] Because there were not enough beds even for patients, nurses slept in "frail triple-deckers fashioned of bamboo and rattan . . . unsheltered except for trees."[8] Mosquito netting was probably the most prized commodity next to food and was similarly scarce. The nocturnal raids of malaria-spreading pests did almost as much harm as the daytime attacks of Japanese planes, and only exhaustion made sleep possible. Supplies of essential medicines such as sulfa, quinine for malaria, and gangrene serum dwindled and disappeared. Nurses and doctors donated their own blood.

In the midst of all these shortages, one of the nurses whose Christmas leave had been canceled, received, by some improbable means, a package from home. With anticipation such as she had never felt before when opening a present, she dug down through the tissue paper and pulled out a lacy veil attached to a large picture hat.

Although the nurses sometimes felt that no one understood their situation, and although hunger gnawed at them and death surrounded them, morale remained good. Even when the hospital (which was clearly marked with Red Crosses) was twice directly bombed, killing over 100 patients, the reaction was anger, not despair. The nurses' morale was improved by that of their patients; all testified that the men, despite pain, were cheerful. "You'd be amazed," said one, "about how little people complain, especially soldiers, and about how much punishment a human body can take."[9]

Nurses in turn cheered their patients with personal contact as well as professional care. "We tried to make ourselves as presentable as possible. We had been able to bring along some rouge, powder, lipstick and our toothbrushes. Every day we took our baths and washed our coveralls in the nearby creek. . . . The men whom we cared for used to tell us we were the most beautiful things in the world."[10]

On those occasional evenings when there was leisure, they would gather around an old field organ that the chaplain had found. The songs of home sounded strange yet comforting in the darkness of a bombed jungle. "We were terribly frightened," said one nurse, "and we longed for peace and home, but none of us ever broke down and indulged in hysterics. It meant a great deal to the wounded and sick men to have American women to give them the expert care their mothers and wives would have wanted for them."[11]

As important as morale is, however, it alone does not win wars. The last horse and mule had been eaten, and shells were landing closer and closer. On the night of April 9, when the Japanese were only a few hundred yards away, the nurses

4

were ordered to evacuate. "The road was full of civilians, women and children crying. Nurses were riding out on all kinds of conveyances—ambulances . . . garbage trucks, anything. Some of them had to walk . . ."[12] Surrounded by the noise of gunfire, watching the sky flare as ammunition dumps were blown up, the nurses proceeded to the docks, only to find that for some it was too late. The last boat had gone. Too tired to panic, they huddled into a tunnel and discovered, to their great joy, a cache of food left by the Navy. Hash, peaches and tomato juice had never tasted so good!

Morning roll call found that some nurses had shoved off in rowboats, determined to get to the island of Corregidor on their own. As the day grew older, "a small steamer came in and fifteen of us swarmed aboard. There was the drone of planes and the steamer drifted swiftly . . . trying to dodge. Half an hour later it steamed back to the dock and more women got aboard, just in time. A few minutes later . . . the Japs blasted the piece of roadway to bits."[13]

Corregidor is a giant rock. Its deep tunnel hospital provided relative safety and comfort, though the noise as bombs hit the rock above and reverberated below could be shattering. April 29, the Japanese emperor's birthday, was a severe test of nerves; bombing began at 7:30 A.M. and never stopped all day. Over 100 explosions per minute were counted. The real heroes, of course, all nurses agreed, were the men who "were up topside, manning our guns and the field-hospital stations. They had to stay there and take it."[14]

Nevertheless it wasn't pleasant below. "The air was thick with the smell of disinfectant and anesthetics and there were too many people. Several times the power plant . . . was hit and the electricity was off for hours. It was pretty ghastly in there feeling the shock of the detonations and never knowing when we would be in total darkness."[15]

Late in April, when it was obvious that American defeat was near, some of the nurses were evacuated in dangerously overcrowded craft through perilous seas and air to the safety of Australia. They ate, slept, and came home to a hero's welcome. The first American women to be decorated for bravery in this war, they received citations in the beauty of a White House summer reception.

But many of their colleagues spent their summer—and the next three years— in the heat of a Manila prison camp, for all had not been so lucky. While 21 nurses escaped from Corregidor, 66 were captured.[16] "On the morning of May seventh, in the middle of a difficult operation," said one, "I heard a scuffling noise and glanced up. In the door stood a Japanese soldier with his bayonet fixed. This was the first Jap I'd seen, and my heart popped into my mouth. We were his prisoners."[17]

Nurses had heard horrifying stories of what the Japanese did to Chinese women whom they had captured, but though they expected the worst, no one reacted hysterically. The Japanese, as it turned out, were shocked to find women there and had no instructions as to how to deal with them. Perhaps because the women were white, perhaps because they were physically larger than Asians, the nurses found themselves surprisingly well treated.

For almost two months, life on Corregidor was reasonably decent, and the hospital staff continued their work as best they could under the circumstances, for there was little food, almost no medicine and bad water. Bloody dressings had to be reused. Under constant bombardment, nurses went for days without seeing sunshine or breathing fresh air. But then they were separated from their patients.

The nurses were interned at a camp in Manila along with over 3,000 American and British civilians, including at least 500 women, who were unfortunate enough to be in that part of the world when it fell. This, according to one nurse, "was the worst news we had heard. We were in the Army, and our duty was with our medical units and our wounded men in the military camps."[18] On June 25, another said, "They separated us from the boys. We called them 'our boys' because most of us nurses were in our late 20s or early 30s, and the wounded were mostly kids. They put the boys on ships and left them there alone, in the heat and the dark without food or water, all night. We could hear them crying for help. It was the worst night during the whole experience."[19]

During the next three years, the women lived at Santo Tomas, the former grounds of a university, but living conditions were never satisfactory. Ironically, they got worse as American victory—and Japanese defeat—grew nearer. Those who had been there since the fall of Manila had found a considerable amount of freedom in the first months, but that did not continue as the number of prisoners increased. Overcrowding soon became severe; one nurse said that there were "usually six women under each shower at once,"[20] for there were three showers and five toilets to serve 500 women.

Again, they lived in the expectation that help would come, the civilians naturally being more hopeful than the nurses who had already experienced siege. As the months turned into years, they learned to cope. Sympathetic Filipinos risked their lives to bring news of the other camps, and once more the women learned that by comparison they were doing fine. At one military camp, there were more than 5,000 graves; at the civilian prison, death was rare. They did what they could to help the soldier prisoners, sending money underground that they hoped could buy some man a bit of safety.

As the war grew worse for the Japanese, these civilians too began to suffer. They stood in a line two-blocks long to get their ration of rice and *tilanum* (a spinachlike vegetable). Day after day, they ate the same food, and there was never enough of it. People were reduced to eating anything they could find— dogs, frogs, even rats. "What saved many lives," reported a nurse corps lieutenant, "was the arrival of the Red Cross ship early in 1944." Even though the Japanese took some of the bounty, prisoners received kits containing medicines,

6

vitamins, coffee, canned butter, cheese, dried fruits, canned meat and cigarettes. The lieutenant said that she and her bunkmate "stretched our kits for almost a year, allowing ourselves half a thin slice of canned meat each day with our rice and spinach. We ate our last meat on Christmas Day."[21]

Hope for liberation became real in the fall of 1944, when American planes finally appeared over Manila skies. The precisely placed bombs that dropped around—but not on—the prisoners indicated that U.S. Intelligence had done its work well. On December 24 there was a special treat—Christmas cards descended from the air, bearing greetings from President Roosevelt and a promise that the end of the war was near. A few days later, the Japanese confirmed the promise when they began to burn official papers and prepared to save themselves. Ironically, after their long wait, more lives would be lost in the fighting for liberation than had been lost during captivity. By February 3, 1945, just over three years after their trial began, these American women, weaker in body but infinitely stronger in spirit, were free.

Those held in captivity on the Philippine islands might have, in dark moments, felt that the world had forgotten their existence; but meanwhile, the war was going on. All over the globe, other Army and Navy nurses were doing their part, assisted by a military bureaucracy that came to understand, after Bataan, that nurses were not ethereal angels of mercy, but human beings who had to have some of the same training that was given to male recruits to help them save their own lives. The nurses' white uniforms were replaced by dark-green Army fatigues. At training centers in the United States, nurse recruits learned that the war might often require them to set up a 500-bed hospital, treat patients for a day and a half and then dismantle the hospital to follow the line of battle and be where the wounded were. Women in these mobile units obviously had to be physically fit, and in a four-week crash course, the Army saw that they were.

They went on 20-mile hikes, each carrying a 30-pound pack, mess kit and gas mask, and a helmet that weighed almost four pounds. They learned to pitch tents, chlorinate water and camouflage themselves; they learned how to make a bed pan from newspaper, and a stretcher from trousers. They breathed enough mustard gas and other lethal chemicals to learn to identify them. They went through a tear-gas chamber and put out some incendiaries. But the real test of training was the 75-yard infiltration course, where nurses crawled on their stomachs through a "no-man's land of trenches and barbed wire with charges of dynamite going off to the side, in front and back of them and machine-gun bullets singing a few inches over their heads."[22] They did it successfully, and at Camp Young, Arizona, a nurse held the speed record on this tough assignment—the 75 yards in 7 minutes.[23]

Conditions in some of the training centers were almost as bad as those in the war camps, with the all-important exception of battle. At the Desert Training Center on the border of Arizona and California, for instance, nurses trained with almost 200,000 others in 130-degree heat that simulated North Africa. They lived with poisonous reptiles and severe sand storms; they tried to keep a sterile hospital while wind blew down the tents. It might be argued that those extra months of adverse conditions led sooner to combat fatigue, but the Army believed that realistic preparation and a toughening-up process were essential.

Certainly, the experience of the earliest women to be involved in this world war told them they would have to be tough. Long before there was any training, even before the United States entered the war, there were women who felt they could not sit by while their country debated whether or not to enter the fray. Some joined the British services; others, and especially nurses, entered the life-giving ranks of the Red Cross. By the summer of 1941, more than 60 U.S. women were working at Red Cross centers in England. Not all of them had pleasant trips over.

The *Maasdam*, a Dutch ship that had eluded German capture when Holland fell, began sailing for the British; on it were 17 American Red Cross nurses. It was a stormy night in late June 1941 when the torpedo hit. "I felt rather than heard the explosion," reported a Washington, D.C. woman. "I ran for my lifeboat. I knew what to do and I did it instinctively." Two Massachusetts nurses had a harder time; their lifeboat collided with the side of the ship and splintered. Immediately, the water rushed in. "First it came up to our knees, then up to our waists. . . . Soon we were completely submerged."[24] The inadequate boat capsized, and the choice was between clinging to it or swimming through the cold, dark waters in the hope of finding safety. By one means or another, all but two of the *Maasdam* nurses saved themselves and eventually made their way to England.

A few days later, a second vessel, torpedoed without warning, sank within eight minutes. This time seven nurses and their housemother went down to the deep. The German submarine that had attacked them came to the surface, and whether from chivalry or not, offered to take aboard the women. The officers of the torpedoed ship immediately rejected the proposal, believing the perils of a lifeboat a better risk for the women than becoming German prisoners.

At first it seemed that optimism was justified, for on the very day of the sinking they sighted a convoy, but their distress rockets went unseen. They drifted, attempting feebly to sail toward Greenland, fearing the storms, cold and hunger that could snuff out the lives aboard the frail craft. "Our feet were never dry during this time," said one survivor. "We started away from the ship with one hard tack each. Later this was cut to one-half. At noon each day, the captain opened a can of meatballs, divided equally among us. We were given about five ounces of water each over a period of twenty-four hours."[25]

They were finally rescued after 12 days and 11 nights adrift. Later they found out that others of their shipmates had an even worse experience. Two young women from New Jersey and New York had shared a lifeboat with two British and five Norwegian sailors, and they only barely survived their 19 days in the North Atlantic. These women had spent their time caring for the injured men, tearing up their clothes to bandage the frostbitten feet of the sailors. Their "few biscuits and little water were soon exhausted and—the rains did not come."[26] The two Englishmen died, and the others were semiconscious when they were at last rescued.

These committed women worked in England for a half a year before their nation followed them into the war. "The night the news of the Jap attack at Pearl Harbor came in," said one, "we went over to the recreation hall and curled upon the floor to listen to the radio. At two o'clock in the morning we heard the President's speech. Afterward, when the short wave brought us 'The Star Spangled Banner,' we all stood up. We felt so full of emotion we had to gulp and blink our eyes to keep it from spilling out."[27] Six months later, half of these nurses had traded their Red Cross uniforms for that of the Army Nurse Corps and were bound for North Africa. Although as nurses they were officially in a protected status, they traveled on military ships and were therefore open prey—and again, some of them were torpedoed.

When the troops poured out of their ships onto the beachheads of North Africa, over 200 U.S. nurses moved with them. At Oran and Arzew, they waded ashore, bullets and bombs exploding around them, and immediately set up their life-saving hospitals. They ripped up their underclothes to make bandages in the heat of the first emergency; they fed C-rations from their own packs to patients suffering from shock. Casualties streamed in; for a week the nurses worked 24-hour days, catching short naps fully dressed on the ground nearby. As the fighting line moved up or retreated, the nurses and their mobile hospital units followed.

"In the February push," said the chief of North African nurses, "several of our units were trapped by the Germans in front of the lines. The officers wanted to send the nurses back and let the men take their chances of getting through safely, but the nurses volunteered to stay. They were the last ones to come back."[28] A group at Kasserine Pass became isolated, and it was there that First Lieutenant Mary Ann Sullivan earned the Legion of Merit for her valor. Somehow, the unit got out, though there were German guns at both their front and their rear. Meanwhile, Sullivan's emergency treatment saved lives.

In the months that followed, nurses marched with soldiers as one African city after another fell, but none without a bloody fight. The nurses operated while planes strafed and bombed. They slept in mud-covered tents and on the bare ground. They gave their own blood. Some gave their lives. When the victory was complete, they went along again as Italy was invaded.

The physical preparation that the Army had given them proved valuable, but it is much harder to teach management of emotions than to give training in calisthenics. Nurses who dealt with death every day had to teach themselves to be strong in this area. They learned, coped and very seldom broke down. "War," said one, "is now to us an Awful Actuality and not something we hear about on the radio. Our friends are being killed—these gay young lads we danced with last week; these fine young men who told us their plans for the future, 'when this is all over and the world has stopped being mad.' We don't discuss their deaths; we pat each other on the shoulder and say, 'Well, he's had it.'"[29]

Despite their bravery, nurses were getting surprisingly little publicity in the United States. Perhaps they were simply overlooked in the massiveness of the war; perhaps it was thought that accounts of the danger would damage recruiting efforts. *National Geographic*, for example, expressed astonishment when, six months after the fact, they accidentally learned that women had been present at the African invasion.[30] The first woman correspondent to cover the Italian campaign was also somewhat surprised and similarly impressed by the nurses. "I can see scores of them," she said as she looked out from her tent, "clad in soldier's pants, clumping through the soggy Italian loam in G.I. shoes, busy, tired, intent."[31] They were up at dawn, she wrote, and worked at least 12 and sometimes 20 hours a day. What sleep they got was often to the sound of guns.

In the spring of 1944, the Surgeon General of the Army took time to praise those nurses of the Italian front. He singled out an Iowa first lieutenant, whose convoy was several times attacked by submarines; she served through the bloody battles of Tunisia and landed with the infantry on Sicily, pushed on through Palermo and was bound for the Italian peninsula when her ship was bombed. "Wet and bedraggled, wearing nothing but pajamas and tennis shoes," she got ashore and was again at work. "It was enough to try the strongest man," the general concluded.[32]

He spoke of another nurse who had been through action so severe that some of her colleagues believed she was succumbing to combat fatigue. Yet when she was caught alone with only wounded men and medical corpsmen around when the Germans bombed the plainly marked hospital, killing three nurses outright, she immediately covered the dead, began treating the wounded and restored order. A third nurse cited was a Maine woman who had injured her back when her ship lurched in a storm. She didn't tell anyone because she didn't want to be taken out of action, and with the other nurses made the landing jump into water over her head, a 55-pound pack on her sore back. She worked, nursing the wounded men of Italy until her spinal cord refused to be pushed any longer and paralyzed one leg. "There was no fear in the eyes of any of these women any more—only pity and kindness and certainty," declared the Army's Surgeon General. "They have conducted themselves as coolly as the most hardened veterans."[33]

As these women pushed up through Italy, their colleagues began working down from France. On D-Day-plus-four, Army nurses waded ashore in Normandy and slept that night on the hard-won beach. In hospitals so close to the front that sometimes they had to help bury the battle dead before they could set up their beds, they repeated the experiences of their sisters farther south, only in a colder, wetter and more miserable climate.

All over the world, in Arctic cold and tropical heat, Army and Navy nurses fought death.[34] In the South Pacific, they were generally stationed far back from the line, for the War Department refused to take the chance that they might be captured by the Japanese—despite the fact the Corregidor nurses had two years earlier declared that their experience led them to prefer Japanese capture to German. In many posts, the nursing was routine and life was dull, but whatever the assignment, around the globe from Africa to India to Australia and back to the shores of the U.S., American women—usually young, often unsophisticated—were becoming acquainted with the world, death and suffering.

While Army nurses worked on land, Navy nurses often served at sea on hospital ships. The work of the average Navy nurse was quite different from that of her colleagues in the Army, for she was a teacher and administrator as well as a nurse. This was because she was not allowed to served on combat ships, but rather remained behind the fighting line on hospital ships. Emergency medical treatment for wounded sailors was given to them by medics, who were taught by Navy nurses. "The instruction of hospital corpsmen . . . is probably the most important single duty of the Navy nurse," said a War Department official.[35]

Despite the Navy's emphasis on safety for its women, there were dangers that even the Navy acknowledged: nurses were issued ID tags made of nonmeltable material, in the event that the ship burned; they were forbidden to own cameras or keep diaries, to prevent interesting information from falling into enemy hands; radios could not be played because submarines might spot their waves; full-length mirrors were banned, because they would likely shatter if bombed. "Gas masks and steel helmets [were] as much at home as powder puffs" in their quarters.[36]

Like the Army nurse, the Navy woman was greatly outnumbered by the men around her, but for the Naval member the quarters were much closer. On most ships, there were only a handful of women and several hundred or even thousands of men. Behavior, therefore, had to be circumspect. Nurses could invite only officers to their quarters, and them only in a group. "Pairing off" was forbidden. On the other hand, this same shortage of women meant that corpsmen on the hospital ships did most of the dull routine, while the nurses were more nearly administrators. In the Navy Nurse Corps (NNC), nurses had the opportunity to ignore the bedpans and be truly professionals.

Another type of hospital ship was born in World War II, but it moved through the air, not water, and with it came one type of overseas nurse who got a disproportionate share of newsprint because her work was graphically new. Some of the new flight nurses were veteran airline stewardesses (only certified nurses were hired as stewardesses in the infant days of flying); many others, however, had never set foot in a plane before.

Although an aircraft could drop deadly bombs, it could also save lives that would have been lost in earlier wars. In the mountains of Burma and the islands of the South Pacific, the mule-packs that carried the wounded—which might have taken weeks to travel bumpy roads—were now replaced by swift silver birds that brought casualties to clean hospital beds within hours. On board was a smiling American woman, probably the first soldiers had seen in many months.

A flight nurse had an extraordinary responsibility and, young though she usually was, she had grown up fast. She saw men at their goriest, with faces half shot away, gaping stomach wounds with intestines spilling out, their bodies dirty, mutilated and bloody. She sometimes had psychoneurotic cases on board, shell-shocked men whose behavior could not be predicted. Her trips were occupied by a busy routine of giving hypodermics and oxygen and plasma, of washing and bandaging and holding cigarettes for men with no hands. In an emergency, she was on her own; her work demanded much more independence than nurses generally exercised, and she often did a doctor's duty. Yet, during 13 months of operation in the South Pacific, these young women moved out 37,000 men and lost just one patient.

A flight nurse could never feel safe, because the same planes that carried out the wounded also brought in fresh troops—and so the planes could not bear the Red Cross. The flight nurse was therefore exposed to as much danger as if she were in combat. This factor, however, did not seem to daunt volunteers for flight nursing, and applications for the specialized training required poured into the School of Air Evacuation at Bowman Field, Kentucky. There the women learned the effects that flying had on the body—that men with certain types of wounds should not fly above a certain altitude and that the dosage of some drugs had to be increased or decreased to compensate for the effects of altitude. The course also demanded tough physical education, including parachute drill, simulated bombing and strafing, fully clad swimming and dodging live machine-gun fire.

The work was dangerous and demanding, but some play also came with it. The trip from Guadalcanal to New Caledonia, for example, took two tiring, unnerving days, but then the nurse got two days off for swimming and dancing. Every three months, a flight nurse could go to New Zealand for 10 days and reacquaint herself with hot baths and telephones. At the end of a year, she was entitled to a long leave at home. As a forerunner to the Rest and Recreation combatants would receive in later war, it was indicative of the privileged status of flight nurses.[37]

In flight nursing, in health-care administration on board Navy hospital ships, and in the battlefront emergency hospitals of the Army Nurse Corps, U.S. women assumed new responsibilities in new settings. From the starvation of Bataan and the captivity of Corregidor to the bombing of North Africa and from the shelling of Europe to the isolation of Alaska and the disease of the tropics, the American nurses did their duty well and willingly.

SOURCE NOTES

1. D.D. Engles, "I Was Married in Battle," *American Magazine* (October 1942): p. 112.
2. Ibid. For further information on the U.S. Army and Navy Nurse Corps in the Philippines, see LaVerne Bradley, "Women in Uniform," *National Geographic* (October 1943): p. 445; N. MacLennon, "Army Nurse," *New York Times Magazine* (September 21, 1941): p. 12.
3. Julia O. Flikke, *Nurses in Action* (New York: Lippincott, 1943), p. 200. In addition to Flikke, who was head of the Army Nurse Corps, serious students might see also Lt. Col. Pauline E. Maxwell's 1976 13-volume unpublished history of the ANC, on file in the Center of Military History, Department of the Army, Washington, D.C.
4. Mark Murphy, "You'll Never Know," *New Yorker* (June 12, 1943): p. 42.
5. Eunice C. Hatchitt, "Bataan Nurse," *Collier's* (August 1, 1942): p. 50.
6. Flikke, *Nurses in Action*, p. 174.
7. Ibid.
8. Murphy, "You'll Never Know," p. 42. See also Melville Jacoby, "Taking Care of the Wounded on Bataan's Front," *Life* (February 16, 1942): p. 13, and, by the same author, "Bataan's Nurses," *Life* (June 15, 1942): p. 16; and "Nurses on Bataan," *American Magazine* (September 1942): p. 4.
9. Murphy, "You'll Never Know," p. 42.
10. Engles, "Married in Battle," p. 112.
11. Ibid., p. 116.
12. Ibid., p. 114.
13. Hatchitt, "Bataan Nurses," p. 50.
14.
Eunice F. Young (with Frank J. Taylor), "Three Years Outside This World," *Saturday Evening Post* (May 5, 1945): p. 18. See also "Heroic Nurses of

Bataan and Corregidor," *American Journal of Nursing* (August 1942): p. 896, and Juanita Redmond: *I Served on Bataan* (Philadelphia: J.B. Lippincott Company, 1943).

15. Frances Long, "Yankee Girl," *Life* (September 7, 1942): p. 82.
16. Flikke, *Nurses in Action,* p. 187.
17. Young, "Outside This World," p. 18.
18. Ibid.
19. Tad Bartimus, "Yesterday's 'Angel' Recalls Bataan," Associated Press syndicated article (December 1980). Interview with Dorothy Armold of Topeka, Kansas. Mrs. Armold, then Dorothy Scholl, was in the Army Nurse Corps and spent 33 months as a prisoner of war.
20. Long, "Yankee Girl," p. 82. See also a novel based on this prison camp by a journalist interned there, Shelley Smith Mydans: *The Open City* (New York: Doubleday, Doran and Company, 1945).
21. Young, "Outside This World," p. 92. See also Dorothy Davis, "I Nursed at Santo Tomas, Manila," *American Journal of Nursing* (January 1944): p. 29, and, in the same publication, Alice Clarke, "Thirty-Seven Months as Prisoners of War" (May 1945): p. 342.
22. Eleanor Darnton, "The Army Nurse Trains for Battle," *New York Times Magazine* (October 24, 1943): p. 18. See also "Army Nurses Toughened Before Leaving for Duty," *Science News Letter* (June 19, 1943): p. 390; "Nurses' Training—And How!," *Popular Mechanics* (September 1944): p. 80.
23. Faye Marley, "Training Nurses for War," *Hygeia* (November 1943): p. 823.
24. "Nurses Tell Story of Torpedoed Ship," *New York Times* (July 6, 1941): p. 14.
25. "4 Nurses Landed; Tell of Torpedoing," *New York Times* (July 23, 1941): p. 14.
26. Helen Fornay Folks, "Be a Nurse and See the World," *Independent Woman* (October 1941): p. 300.
27. P. Martin, "Angels in Long Underwear," *Saturday Evening Post* (July 31, 1943): p. 10.
28. Ibid. See also "North African Nurses," *Saturday Evening Post* (July 31, 1943): p. 9.
29. Flikke, *Nurses in Action,* p. 154.
30. Bradley, "Women in Uniform," p. 445.
31. Doris Fleeson, "Within the Sound of the Guns," *Woman's Home Companion* (January 1944): p. 4.
32. Norman T. Kirk, "Girls in the Foxholes," *American Magazine* (May 1944): p. 94. See also "It's Rugged for War Nurses, Too," *New York Times Magazine* (December 3, 1944): p. 18; Ruth Y. White, "At Anzio Beachhead," *American Journal of Nursing* (April 1944): p. 370.

33. Ibid.

34. See W.J. Granberg, "Where Blows the Williwaw: Alaska's Nurses," *American Journal of Nursing* (September 1942): p. 30; also in the same publication, Josephine Hohf, "Somewhere in Australia" (January 1945): p. 42; "Army Nurses at Leyte" (January 1945): p. 44; Anna Lisa Moline, "U.S. Army Nurses in Russia" (November 1945): p. 29; Mary H. Staats, "Navy Nurses in the Solomons" (December 1945): p. 1012; and Olivine B. St. Peter, "In the Southwest Pacific" (December 1945): p. 1012. See also Mei-yu Chow, "Nurses for China's Army," *Independent Woman* (March 1944): p. 366; "Life Visits U.S. Army Nurses in New Caledonia," *Life* (October 5, 1942): p. 34; Lawrence C. Salter, "Epics of Courage," *Hygeia* (February 1944): p. 116; and Ernest O. Hauser, "Shock Nurse," *Saturday Evening Post* (March 10, 1945): p. 12.

35. Flikke, *Nurses in Action*, p. 217. See also Sarah Lorimer, "Life Line," *Reader's Digest* (September 1943): p. 45; Doris Schwartz, "Nursing Aboard a Hospital Ship," *American Journal of Nursing* (December 1945): p. 996.

36. "Meet Ensign Dorothy Weyel," *Ladies Home Journal* (January 1943): p. 69.

37. For additional information on flight nurses, see Marion Porter, "Nurses with Wings," *Collier's* (April 22, 1944): p. 22; Sylvia Van Antwerp, "The Most Rewarding Work," *New York Times Magazine* (August 15, 1943): p. 18; Shelley S. Mydans, "Flight Nurse," *Life* (February 12, 1945): p. 45; George Mason: "Flight Nurse," *Flying* (May 1944): p. 55; Alfred Toombs, "Flight Nurse," *Woman's Home Companion* (December 1943): p. 36; "Flying Nurses Aid U.S. African Campaign," *Life* (April 19, 1943): p. 41.

2

CALLING ALL NIGHTINGALES

The recreational breaks given to flight nurses were atypical in World War II, but were a forerunner of recruitment techniques in the future. Perhaps the reasoning was that some privileges had to be granted to attract nurses, because they could not be drafted as men were. Recruiting enough of them was a continual problem throughout the war. Those women who did volunteer were worthy of the greatest respect, but as they plodded through their 20-hour days they couldn't help but wonder what was wrong with their sisters. They could tolerate cold C-rations and damp tents, but why wasn't there just a little time for a good sleep and for holding a soldier's hand?

Even before the United States entered the war, there was a shortage of nurses. Programs initiated under President Roosevelt in the thirties expanded public health awareness and, as the economy boomed because of fighting in Europe, people began to enter hospitals for attention to ills that would have been ignored in an earlier era. Already in 1941, months before Pearl Harbor, some hospitals closed wings because there were no nurses to work in them, and some doctors urged women to have babies at home because hospitals were overcrowded and short of nurses.[1] There were almost 10,000 hospital vacancies for nurses in 1941, to say nothing of the many other positions nurses fill.[2] And of course in addition to these civilian needs, the military was beginning to recruit in preparation for war. In 1940, there were a mere 700 in the Army Nurse Corps; by April of 1941, the Corps was taking in nearly that many in a single month.[3]

The Public Health Service wanted 55,000 new nursing students in 1942; the next year, the quota was raised to 65,000.[4] The National Nursing Council for War Service, in cooperation with women's magazines, tried to locate and retrain the 100,000 women who had graduated from nursing schools but were no longer in the labor force;[5] the Red Cross and the Office of Civilian Defense pleaded for another 100,000 volunteers to become aides at their local hospitals.[6] By 1944, the nation needed 66,000 nurses for the military and almost 300,00 for civilian duty—100,000 more than were available.[7]

Once again history was repeating itself. During World War I, there had been a tremendous shortage of nurses, and when the killer flu epidemic of 1918

16

struck, "the civilian population often couldn't get a nurse for love or money."[8] The problem was that, except in these dire emergencies, the population was not willing to offer either love or money. As one sociology publication acknowledged, "nursing was looked down upon by some middle class mothers as not quite a nice sort of job, and nursing is thought of as being on the career level of glorified domestic service."[9] So much for love; as for money, it had long been accepted that nurses were woefully underpaid. All writers on the subject agreed that one of the prime reasons for the nursing shortage was that, as the war economy expanded, nurses left their profession for industrial jobs. Despite years of education and experience, they found they could earn more as defense-plant trainees.

For the student nurses, the situation was even more frustrating. A high school graduate could go into industry and immediately earn high wages. Why then should she go to nursing school and work for a hospital three years for nothing and pay tuition besides? Although the military took young men and gave them free training for all kinds of jobs, if a woman wanted to join the Army or Navy Nurse Corps, she had to first become a registered nurse at her own expense. Representative Frances Bolton of Ohio worked hard to introduce some justice— as well as practicality—into the situation. She pushed for a program that would train at the government's expense students who agreed to serve in some type of necessary nursing for the duration of the war plus six months. Congress had, to be sure, already admitted the need for assistance to nursing education by appropriations of about $5 million in 1941-42 to the Public Health Service to be granted to nursing schools.[10] Both the amount and the technique of distribution proved inadequate, though, as recruiting goals were not met. The Bolton Bill intended to revitalize the area by (1) ensuring that some money went directly to the student instead of just the institution, and (2) creating a Student Nurse Corps, complete with a street uniform, that would give a young woman a sense of being part of the war. The bill encouraged early entrance into service by providing incentives to schools for offering accelerated courses, and it also tried to attract older nurses by providing assistance for refresher courses and post-graduate study.[11]

In May of 1943, Congress unanimously passed the bill, setting a precedent for federal aid to education and offering new opportunities for thousands of young women. State departments of education created programs and publications to encourage high school counselors to persuade girls (always the sex stereotype is assumed) to take advantage of the bill and enter nursing school.

While the statute was a genuine advancement for women—and perhaps one of the first Congressional appropriations to more-or-less directly aid the feminine sex—many of the arguments used by recruiters for nursing were disappointingly traditional. Counselors told students that there was no better training for a wife and mother; even *Independent Woman*, the magazine of the Business & Professional Women's Clubs, stressed as a positive that "the marriage rate is

17

higher among nurses than among women of any other profession."[12] Government publications aimed at high school girls pointed out realistically enough that nursing was ideal work for women because it was one of the few areas where they would not have to worry about giving up their jobs to returning veterans.[13]

The efforts of those who tried to persuade young women to become nurses were hampered, however, by the widespread public perception that student nurses were slave labor for hospitals. As long as a young woman was forced to spend her time carrying bedpans and trays, arranging flowers and changing sheets, it was hard to convince her that she was entering a scientific profession, much less that she was helping to win the war. Yet plainly all of these routine tasks had to be performed. The solution was, of course, to provide nurses with aides.

The Red Cross developed an 80-hour course, complete with exams, to acquaint volunteers with their duties as aides, thus relieving the hospital staff of the teaching job and giving the aide some confidence in her ability. Red Cross uniforms (though they had to be purchased by the unpaid worker) made women feel that they were something more than domestic drudges and told the world that they were doing their bit in the war.

Again, however, quotas went unmet; the 1942 goal for aides was only about two-thirds filled, despite publicity that stressed the need and glamorized the position.[14] Astute observers noted that many of the women who responded were committed to other jobs; many aides had put in a full day at the office or factory before doing evening duty at the hospital. Some of them were very faithful to their unpaid commitment; they did difficult and dirty work, often under trying circumstances.

Public attention was also given to teaching women home nursing. Perhaps because people remembered the fatal flu of 1918 and associated it with war, it was felt that every woman should know the essentials of caring for her sick family. It seemed to be assumed that women are the natural disease fighters of the species, and in a time when medical professionals were scarce, they should be prepared to take over. The Red Cross again came through with a course, and the public response was good. Even while the nation was still officially at peace in 1941, there was a 40% increase in certificates awarded for attendance at these classes.[15]

But obviously there was a certain measure of dilettantism in these efforts; they did not strike at the heart of the problem or lessen the long days of nurses in Italy and Africa. For the complicated surgery required by a man who had been hit by a grenade, a great deal more than a Red Cross course was required. While thousands of nurses with sufficient education and experience did volunteer, by 1945 most of those who were inclined to do so were already in the service, and recruitment became more and more difficult. So then, in the winter of what would turn out to be the last year of the war, the nation reluctantly began to talk of drafting nurses.

NAVY NURSES, HELD AS PRISONERS OF WAR SINCE EARLY 1942, TALK WITH AN ADMIRAL
AFTER LIBERATION OF THEIR LUZON INTERNMENT CAMP IN MARCH 1945.
NOTE HOW THIN SOME OF THEM ARE.
OFFICIAL U.S. NAVY PHOTOGRAPH; COLLECTION OF ADM. T.C. KINKAID.

THIS PHOTO OF AMERICAN PRISONERS OF WAR WASHING THEIR HAIR WAS FOUND IN A
JAPANESE BARRACK ON LEYTE ISLAND AFTER THE U.S. LIBERATED THAT AREA.
NATIONAL ARCHIVES.

ARMY NURSE CORPS MEMBERS BEING AWARDED BRONZE STARS AFTER THEIR
LIBERATION BY AMERICAN FORCES IN FEBRUARY 1945. THEY HAD BEEN CAPTURED ON
BATAAN AND CORREGIDOR ALMOST THREE YEARS EARLIER.
U.S. ARMY CENTER OF MILITARY HISTORY.

NURSES TRAINING PRIOR TO D-DAY AT THE AMERICAN SCHOOL CENTER,
SHRIVENHAM, ENGLAND, 1943.
U.S. ARMY CENTER OF MILITARY HISTORY.

LIVE AMMUNITION AND DYNAMITE CHARGES WERE USED IN ARMY NURSE
CORPS TRAINING, CAMP BLANDING, FLORIDA, 1943.
U.S. ARMY CENTER OF MILITARY HISTORY.

A UNIT OF BLACK NURSES PREPARING TO GO ASHORE AT GREENOCK, SCOTLAND.
U.S. ARMY CENTER OF MILITARY HISTORY.

THESE NURSES OF THE 13TH FIELD HOSPITAL WERE THE FIRST TO LAND IN THE
INVASION OF NORMANDY; PHOTO TAKEN ON JUNE 15, 1944, AT OMAHA BEACH.
U.S. ARMY CENTER OF MILITARY HISTORY.

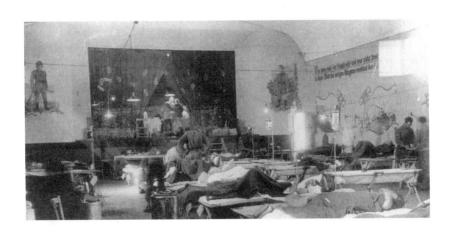

SURGERY CONDUCTED ON THE STAGE OF A FORMER SCHOOL AUDITORIUM;
60TH FIELD HOSPITAL, ST. MAX, FRANCE, OCTOBER 1944.
U.S. ARMY CENTER OF MILITARY HISTORY.

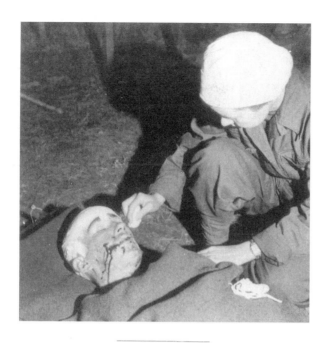

WOUNDED POW BEING TREATED BY AN ARMY NURSE AT 110TH
EVAC HOSPITAL. LUXEMBOURG. OCTOBER 1944.
U.S. ARMY CENTER OF MILITARY HISTORY.

CHRISTMAS CAROLING AT THE 19TH FIELD HOSPITAL. ANDIMESHK. IRAN, 1943.
U.S. ARMY CENTER OF MILITARY HISTORY

NAVAL FLIGHT NURSE, WITH PATIENTS ABOARD PLANE, GOES
OVER MEDICAL CHARTS WITH A PHARMACIST'S MATE, MARCH
1945. THE WOMAN PICTURED, JANE KENDLEIGH, WAS THE FIRST
NAVY FLIGHT NURSE TO SERVE ON A BATTLEFIELD.
OFFICIAL U.S. NAVY PHOTOGRAPH.

A FLIGHT NURSE AND AIR EVACUATION TECHNICIAN CHECK OUT EQUIPMENT FOR A
FLIGHT FROM A WESTOVER, MASSACHUSETTS, AIR BASE. SUCH PLANES FLEW
PATIENTS FROM ALL OVER THE WORLD TO U.S. HOSPITALS.
SMITHSONIAN INSTITUTION PHOTO NO. 34589AC.

NURSES IN FRONT OF THEIR "COPLEY PLAZA" BARRACKS AT
THE 13TH STATION HOSPITAL, TOWNSVILLE, AUSTRALIA,
JANUARY 1943.
U.S. ARMY CENTER OF MILITARY HISTORY.

INTERIOR OF NURSES' QUARTERS AT THE 29TH GENERAL HOSPITAL
IN THE SOUTH PACIFIC, FEBRUARY 1944.
U.S. ARMY CENTER OF MILITARY HISTORY.

A WASHINGTON DEPARTMENT STORE DISPLAY ENCOURAGING
WOMEN TO BECOME STUDENT NURSES, MAY 1943.
U.S. OFFICE OF WAR INFORMATION; LIBRARY OF CONGRESS.

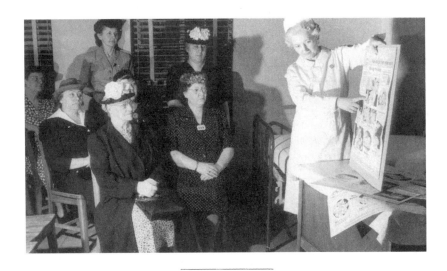

A RED CROSS HOME-NURSING CLASS HELD IN A BROOKLYN CHURCH, JUNE 1944.
U.S. OFFICE OF WAR INFORMATION; PHOTO BY HOWARD HOLLEM. LIBRARY OF CONGRESS.

In his State of the Union speech on January 6, 1945, President Roosevelt called for amendment of the Selective Service Act to "provide for the induction of nurses into the Armed Forces."[16] He pointed out that the Army and Navy needed 20,000 more nurses and that recruiting goals were not being met; that 11 hospital units had to be sent overseas without nurses; that in Army hospitals within the United States, the nurse-patient ratio was 1 to 26 instead of the recommended 1 to 15. More than a thousand nurses were hospitalized, many of them due to exhaustion.

"It is tragic that the gallant women who have volunteered for service as nurses should be so overworked," the President declared. "It is tragic that our wounded men should ever want for the best possible nursing care." Since the voluntary system was not producing the required number of nurses, he concluded that there was no option except to draft: "The need is too pressing to await the outcome of further efforts at recruiting."[17]

The public agreed; a Gallup poll revealed that 78% believed there was indeed a shortage of nurses in the armed forces, and an overwhelming 73% approved of a draft.[18] Apparently when the tradition of protection for women was placed against the need of wounded men for nurses, tradition was quick to go.

Representative Andrew May of Kentucky led the fight in Congress to break precedent and draft women. His bill, HR 2277, received thoughtful consideration; the committee hearings went on for two weeks, and the House as a whole debated the matter for a good portion of three days. Yet, as was the case with the Austin-Wadsworth bill to conscript women for industrial jobs,* little attention was given to the tremendous change this was in the historical status of women. There was almost no mention of home and family and none of the expected platitudes; most Congressmen stated their regret that a draft had to be resorted to, but their regret focused more on the fact that the draftees were *nurses* rather than that they were women.

Representative Reed of New York was typical when he refused to vote for the bill, not because women were being drafted for the first time in U.S. history, rather because the draft was limited to nurses. He said, "I will not . . . place this proposed indictment against the nurses . . . If adopted, it will be a blot on their record forever afterward."[19] Many agreed that it was wrong to single out nurses, who had already shown more patriotism than most groups. The position of the American Nurse Association and the National Nursing Council was to "approve, in principle, federal Selective Service legislation."[20] They went on to urge passage of a National Service Act to cover all women so that nurses would

---

* See Chapter 8.

not be singled out, but Congress, unwilling to rehash the debates of 1942 and 1943 in this area, did not consider this recommendation.

Opposition was for reasons other than the fact that females were being considered for the draft. There were the usual Republican charges that it was a power grab by Roosevelt; there were fears that drafting nurses would discourage young women from entering the profession. There were vehement (and probably justified) attacks on the War Department for mismanagement of recruiting. There were legitimate complaints that male nurses and black nurses were underutilized. (The Navy did not even agree to take black nurses until 1945; the Army accepted only 330 of the 9,000 black graduate nurses in the country.[21]) A few Congressional representatives even had the decency to criticize themselves for not passing the Bolton Bill until mid-1943.

Generally, the debate centered on technicalities; that women would have to be drafted was accepted by most, and the main object of their attention was exactly how this conscription should be implemented. Beginning date, geographical quotas, appeal procedures, commissions—these were the kind of topics that absorbed debate time. Although the votes on amendments were close, the final draft of the Nurses Selective Service Act of 1945 passed 347-42, with 43 abstentions.[22] Most of the House apparently agreed with Representative Michener who acknowledged, "It is hard to vote for legislation of this kind," but who went on to predict that "this bill will pass the House overwhelmingly." He summarized the views of most in Congress when he said, "No one wants to draft women nurses unless it is absolutely necessary . . . Yet I feel it is my duty and my responsibility to do each and every thing within my power to keep faith with our wounded."[23] Chivalry was of little importance when compared with life and health.

The bill was passed by the House in early March; in early April it was reported out favorably by the Senate Military Affairs Committee, their only important amendment being to strike the exemption the House had given to married women. In early May, however, the Army entered Berlin and the war in Europe was over. The Nurses Selective Service Act became one of many contingency plans that was now no longer needed, that could be forgotten in the rejoicing.

But it is important to remember—as generally we have not—that women came within a hair of being drafted in World War II. The House had passed the bill by a large majority; the Senate committee had reported it favorably; the President certainly would have signed it. All indications are that if the European war had lasted another month or two, women would have been drafted. Contrary to the picture painted by opponents of the Equal Rights Amendment in the 1970s, there is no Constitutional protection of women from conscription, and all in Congress who were involved in this debate (on those rare occasions when constitutionality was considered) agreed that they had the authority to draft both women and men. And they almost did.

During the debate on drafting nurses, Congress criticized the Army and especially the Navy Nurse Corps for underutilizing many who would have gladly volunteered for service, but who did not fit into the neat categories so important to military bureaucrats. Male nurses were not automatically commissioned as were female nurses; women over age 45 were officially excluded, and many over 30 reported that they were unofficially excluded; blacks were generally unacceptable. A Congressman from Ohio declared: "I have letters from many Negro nurses in my district and state, college graduates who are desirous of serving their country and their fellowmen in this hour of crisis. Yet they are not permitted to do so for one reason or another. Their applications have been on file for a long time."[24]*

Discrimination against blacks was the most morally offensive mismanagement, but the worst quantitative waste among nurses was the military's dedication to the single state of its women. The Army realized that it would have to accept married nurses in late 1942, but the Navy was more recalcitrant. Not until 1944, when 80% of all separations from the NNC were forced into resignation by the regulations on marriage, did the Navy finally permit its nurses to wed. Still the victory was an incomplete one, for only nurses already in the NNC were allowed to marry; the applications of married women who wanted to join were rejected. Congress showed more human understanding in this area and fought for greater use of married women by including in HR 2277 a provision that married couples could not be arbitrarily separated in war zones, as was the common practice.

But probably the most outrageous of all talent wastage was the refusal to use women doctors. Again, the intervention of Congress was necessary to make the military use what was available to them.[25] The first women doctors were not commissioned until the middle of the war, after Congress passed an act specifically approving such in April 1943. Though fewer than 100 women doctors entered the Medical Corps, those who did had been so thoroughly sifted through screens of prejudice that they were the best. The Surgeon General of the Army later testified that they "built up an enviable record of exceptionally high professional standards . . . In the face of considerable prejudice women have demonstrated their skill."[26]

---

* This is only one factor that discouraged young black women from making the commitment to nursing school. An article designed to recruit them (published in a black magazine the same month that the war ended) reported cheerfully that "there are 50 schools that accept Negro students" and "approximately 2,000 Negro girls enrolled in schools of nursing" during the last year—of 61,471 enrollees, or a mere 3%. See "Professional Training for Nurses," *Service* (September 1945): p. 14.

Several women's magazines helped the female doctors fight for their right to join the Army. *Women's Home Companion* was especially vehement, editorializing that "any woman who can get to be a practicing physician or surgeon in this country at all is something of a superwoman." They pounced on the War Department's lack of logic in worrying that women doctors were too emotional or that male patients would be embarrassed by women doctors, pointing out that nurses dealt constantly and effectively with the same cases. "Our chief allies," they declared, "suffer from no such self-imposed handicaps."[27] *Time* made the same point, citing the 85% female enrollment in Russian medical schools.[28]

U.S. medical schools were little influenced. Harvard finally opened its doors to women in the crucial last year of the war, but rays of hope were hard to detect. Though enrollments fell as men went into the service, most medical schools adhered to a 5% quota for women, and most hospitals refused to accept them as interns for postgraduate specialties. Although job opportunities for doctors had never been so good, the attitudes of medical schools created a situation in which few women were available to take advantage of them, and many communities went without doctors.

Discrimination reached an "all-time high" as the Army and Navy began contracting for a percentage of medical school vacancies and "filling them with soldiers and sailors whose education won't cost them a cent."[29] A young woman who wanted to join the Medical Corps had to pay thousands of dollars for her own education and, until the middle of the war, fight for the right to serve, while her male classmates, already commissioned officers, had their education completely subsidized. The only way a woman could get a free education was to settle for the lesser goal, take advantage of the Bolton Act, and become a nurse.

While the war did disappointingly little to improve the status of women doctors, for nurses it was truly a career boom. First of all, the war—like all wars in U.S. history—accelerated the breakdown of class structure, making the soldier from Appalachia equal to the one from Beacon Hill, and nursing reflected this change. Nursing schools before the war had "emphasized the individual care of the patient . . . to the exclusion of a great uncared for public."[30] Professional medical care and routine hospitalization were not a part of life for most people prior to the war; treatment was sought by the majority only in emergencies. Nurses, therefore, were trained to deal with their most likely clientele—the wealthy—who expected a nurse to be more like a servant with properly subservient attitudes than a professional with independent judgment.

As soldiers and their families back home began to assume their right to decent health care, the sheer quantitative increase in patient load focused public attention on nursing and gave the profession an importance it never had in the past. When the government was willing to educate thousands of young women at public expense, nursing reached a level of status never before achieved by any occupation dominated by women.

Their strength was increased by numbers, and qualitative changes followed quantitative. Nursing schools raised standards and improved curricula. Nurses moved out of the hospital-owned "nursing homes" in which they had been pre-viously cloistered, and a life-style that had greatly resembled that of nuns was replaced by more individualism and freedom. The married nurse, a rarity before the war, became commonplace. Bed and board would no longer suffice as payment; nurses would no longer live confined to a hospital atmosphere all of the time.

Pay rose, and menial duties were dropped. Women who had spent their lives emptying bedpans and folding linens found that in the military they could actually use their scientific education and that they could supervise men who did the routine chores. Women who went away as "just a nurse" came home as lieutenant or captain; they had traveled around the world and proved to all doubters that they could survive and perform under the most hellish of conditions.

The Army's Surgeon General conceded that he had been criticized for sending women so far forward. But the criticism did not come from the women: "There isn't one at the front," he said, "who would quit if she could. Not a nurse has been returned from the fronts who hasn't begged, sometimes with tears in her eyes, to go back."[31] These women did not want to go to kill and destroy, but wanted rather to do what women have done from time immemorial—to heal and cure. They did not have to go; as one grateful soldier wrote in *Stars and Stripes*, "You could be home, soaking yourself in a bathtub everyday, putting on clean clothes and crawling in between clean sheets at night."[32] Instead, many of them wore blood-stained olive drab and slept in the mud.

Most of the nurses did not see their activities as significant in a historical sense; the selflessness of nurses' training was so inbred that they made little attempt during or since the war to draw attention to their record. The result is that they have largely been forgotten, and debate today about the possibility of women in combat generally takes place in a vacuum that is ignorant of the precedents. The prediction of the government official who presented citations to Bataan nurses has not yet been fulfilled: his forecast was that, added to the "traditions of the Minutemen of Lexington and the defenders of the Alamo, . . . we now have the nurses of Bataan."[33]

SOURCE NOTES

1. "Need for Nurses," *Time* (October 13, 1941): p. 81. See also "Where Nurses Are Needed," *Survey Midmonthly* (November 1941): p. 330.
2. Folks, "Be a Nurse," p. 300.
3. Flikke, *Nurses in Action*, p. 10.
4. "Nightingales Needed," *Time* (December 28, 1942): p. 55. See also James A. Hamilton, "Trends in Hospital Nursing Service," *American Journal of*

Nursing (September 1942): p. 1034, and E. Gordon, "Needed: 50,000 Nurses," *New York Times Magazine* (April 12, 1942): p. 10.

5. "We are Trying to Find One Hundred Thousand Women," *Good House-keeping* (December 1942): p. 14; "Calling All Nurses," *Independent Woman* (May 1943): p. 138.

6. George Baehr, "More Hands for the Nurse!" *Hygeia* (February 1942): p. 92.

7. "Patients Are Turned Away Because of Nurse Shortage," *Science News Letter* (August 28, 1943): p. 136.

8. Folks, "Be a Nurse," p. 302.

9. Edith M. Stern, "Nurses Wanted: A Career Boom," *Survey Graphic* (February 1942): p. 79.

10. Alma C. Haupt, "Bottlenecks in Our War Nursing Program," *American Journal of Public Health* (June 1943): p. 666; Dorothy Schaffter, *What Comes of Training Women for War* (Washington: American Council on Education, 1948), p. 165.

11. See "Nurse Training Program," *Congressional Record—House*, 78th Cong., 1st sess., 1943, Vol. 89, pt. 2, p. 2776 ff.; Vol. 89, pt. 4, p. 4461. For additional background, see Roosevelt and Hickok, *Ladies of Courage* (New York: G.P. Putnam's Sons, 1954, p. 173 ff; J.W. Mountain, "Nursing—A Critical Analysis," *American Journal of Nursing* (January 1943): p. 29.

12. "Calling All Nurses," p. 140.

13. From *Education for Victory* see, "Nursing is War Work With a Future" (April 15, 1943): p. 22; "Cooperate in Meeting Nurse Shortage" (May 15, 1943): p. 18; "Nurses-to-Be and the Victory Corps" (January 15, 1943): p. 5; "Toward Solving the Nursing Problem" (April 1, 1943): p. 27. See also Edith H. Smith, "Educators Look at Nursing," *American Journal of Nursing* (June 1943): p. 573; and in the same publication, Lucille Perry, "The U.S. Cadet Nurse Corps" (December 1945): p. 1027.

14. "Call for Aides," *Newsweek* (February 8, 1943): p. 46. See also L.M. Miller, "Nurses Aides Prove Their Worth," *Reader's Digest* (October 1942): p. 95; "Aides Relieve Nurse Shortage," *Life* (January 5, 1942): p. 32; Louise M. Hopkins, "Your Hospital Needs More Nurse's Aides," *Reader's Digest* (March 1945): p. 89.

15. Lewis H. Bowen, "On the Home Front," *Hygeia* (August 1941): p. 628.

16. *Congressional Record—House*, "State of the Union Speech," 79th Cong., 1st sess., 1945, Vol. 91, pt. 1, p. 93.

17. Ibid.

18. George H. Gallup, *The Gallup Poll: Public Opinion, 1935-71* (New York: Random House, 1972), p. 485. Poll date was February 2, 1945. See also "What's Wrong with the Nurses?" *Time* (April 9, 1945): p. 21; Josephine Nelson, "Nurses for Our Fighting Men," *Independent Woman* (Febru-

ary 1945): p. 34; "Armed Forces Need More Nurses," *American Journal of Public Health* (January 1945): p. 80.

19. *Congressional Record—House*, "Nurses Selective Service Bill of 1945," 79th Cong., 1st sess., March 6, 1945, Vol. 91, pt. 2, p. 1805.

20. "The Proposed Draft of Nurses," *American Journal of Nursing* (February 1945): p. 87; see also in the same journal "ANA Testimony on Proposed Draft Legislation" (March 1945): p. 172; and "Nurse Draft Legislation and the ANA—A Summary" (July 1945): p. 546.

21. *Congressional Record—House*, March 5, 1945, "Nurses Selective Service Bill of 1945," pp. 1727 and 1733.

22. Ibid., March 7, p. 1877.

23. Ibid., March 7, pp. 1866-67.

24. Ibid., March 6, p. 1809. See also "The Negro Nurse," *Opportunity: Journal of Negro Life* (November 1942): p. 332; and, in the same publication, Estelle Massey Riddle, "The Negro Nurse and the War" (April 1943): p. 44.

25. See "Commissioning of Female Physicians and Surgeons," *Congressional Record—House*, Report by Mr. Sparkman and the Committee on Military Affairs, 78th Cong., 1st sess., March 24, 1943, H. Rept. 295, p. 1; "Commissioned War Jobs for Women Doctors," *Monthly Labor Review* (July 1943): p. 33; "Victory Long Overdue: Commissioning Women Physicians in Medical Corps," *Independent Woman* (May 1943): p. 132; "Prescription for a Woman Doctor," *New York Times Magazine* (May 2, 1943): p. 18; "Let Women Doctors Serve Too," *Saturday Evening Post* (February 20, 1943): p. 100; "Equality for Women Doctors," *Time* (April 26, 1943): p. 46.

26. Schaffter, *Training Women for War*, p. 123.

27. "Women Doctors at War," *Woman's Home Companion* (June 1943): p. 4.

28. "Daughters for Harvard," *Time* (October 9, 1944): p. 90. Also on this subject, see Susan B. Anthony II, *Out of the Kitchen—Into the War* (New York: Stephen Day, Inc., 1943), p. 188 ff.

29. "Aesculapius's Stepdaughters," *Newsweek* (July 5, 1943): p. 106.

30. "Transitions in Nursing as a Result of the War," *The Army Nurse* (February 1945): pp. 8-9.

31. Kirk, "Girls in the Foxholes," p. 94.

32. Letter to the editor in *Stars and Stripes*, reprinted in the *Congressional Record*, 79th Cong., 1st sess., Vol. 91, pt. 2, March 7, 1945, p. 1869.

33. "Heroic Nurses of Bataan and Corregidor," *American Journal of Nursing*, p. 898.

PART II

THE MILITARY WOMAN

3

DUTY CALLS—WOMEN ENTER THE MILITARY

This is no service of officers' wives . . . When you remember that an airplane can streak inland from the sea at a speed of three hundred miles per hour or more, you'll see that speed of operation . . . is necessary . . . Women volunteers must work slickly and accurately . . . This is an army job, and a mighty important one.[1]

These words were written in the early stages of American involvement in the war, at the beginning of 1942. Just weeks earlier, the United States had been shocked to its depths by Pearl Harbor. Appalled by the disastrous attack there, people were fearful that they might again be caught unaware—that Japanese or German planes could slip unnoticed into the thousands of miles of air space above U.S. coasts and bomb our very shores. Britain had been rained with bombs for two years; only the complacently thoughtless believed that it couldn't happen here.

And so the 6,000 women who patriotically staffed aircraft spotting stations as volunteers were to be militarized. It was thus that a permanent place for women in the U.S. military began.

That anyone would have ever assumed mobile aircraft warning stations ought to be staffed by volunteers now seems rather amazing, for in addition to the responsibility involved, the work was tedious and lonely. Yet after the Depression years of the thirties, women's time and labor was sufficiently undervalued that 6,000 worked without pay. On the floor of the House, Representative Edith Nourse Rogers said of them:

They have done a fine job, and the War Department* and the country at large are exceedingly grateful to them. It is pointed out, however, that it is vital to efficiency

---

* It wasn't until after World War II that the name was changed to the Department of Defense, rather than War, and it became commonly known by the shape of its headquarters building—the Pentagon.

and safety that the Army have military control over such employees . . . It is a
service in which speed is the prime essential—where a matter of a few seconds
may mean the difference between life and death. In Great Britain it has been
demonstrated time and again that women are faster, more alert, in this work than
is the case with their brothers . . . We all remember Pearl Harbor and we all
remember that there was no one at the aircraft warning station . . .[2]

Protection from incoming enemy planes was the immediate rationale behind Congressional establishment of the Women's Army Auxiliary Corps (WAAC), but from the beginning, it was assumed that more functions would be assigned. The WAAC, Representative Rogers argued, "would make available . . . the work of many women who cannot afford to give their services without compensation."[3] The era of the volunteer was beginning to end; the paramilitary model was making the transition to a genuine military organization. The limited job function of plane spotting would give way to hundreds of varieties of important work within the armed forces.

From America's long-ago mother country came the example of British women. By the time the United States entered the war, Britain not only had female military organizations, but women had long been subject to a draft for either military or essential industrial service. A few prescient U.S. women, who saw the Nazi threat prior to their compatriots, crossed the seas and joined the British WAAF, WRENS, and ATS.* Literally fighting for their lives, the British understood that none of their citizens, male or female, could afford the luxury of nonparticipation. And, though, because of their communist system, they were less often praised, the same was true of our female allies in Russia.

Beyond those examples, there was also the previous war, only two decades earlier and still fresh in the memories of decision-makers in this one. Nearly 13,000 U.S. women served with the same status as men in the Navy and Marine Corps during World War I. After Navy lawyers found no specific bar to female enlistment, these "Yeomen (Female)" became an army of primarily headquarters clerical workers. In addition, over 1,000 U.S. women went overseas as civilian contract employees, where they worked as translators, telephone operators, and in other employment for the American Expeditionary Forces. Though they shared the same hardships as men overseas, the women, as civilian employees of the Army, received no hospitalization or other benefits.

War Department experts, evaluating the role of these women in what was then known as the Great War and planning for the future, made several reports during the twenties and thirties that were routinely ignored. The most far-reaching, the Hughes study, recommended that women "be accorded the same rights, privileges, and benefits as militarized men."[4] Its fate was to be buried so deeply

---

* WAAF was the Women's Auxiliary Air Force; WRENS was Women's Royal Navy Service; and ATS stood for Auxiliary Territorial Service.

that the Hughes plan was not located in War Department files until late 1942, long after the WAAC had been created.

Several Congressmen, led by the indefatigable Representative Rogers, believed establishment of the WAAC was the way to prevent future inequities and inefficiencies. Support of the War Department, however, meant the difference between success and failure of the idea. The military leadership sat on the first bill Rogers introduced back in May of 1941, with one staff report acknowledging grudgingly that perhaps the War Department should develop a plan for a female corps "so that when it is forced upon us, as it undoubtedly will be, we shall be able to run it our way."[5]

Pearl Harbor, of course, changed everything—three weeks later, on Christmas Eve, the Secretary of War made a few minor changes in Edith Rogers' bill and sent it on with his recommendation. Chief of Staff General George Marshall added a letter of support, including his opinion that "there are innumerable duties now being performed by soldiers that can actually be done better by women."[6] By March, hearings had been held and House Resolution 6293 establishing the Women's Army Auxiliary Corps had been unanimously recommended by the House Committee on Military Affairs.

That didn't mean there was no opposition. A change of such magnitude in the status of women could hardly pass without objection. Representative Hoffman of Michigan spoke for the status quo, complaining to the House: "Take women into the armed services in any appreciable number, who then will manage the home fires; who will do the cooking, the washing, the mending, the humble, homey tasks to which every woman has devoted herself?"[7] Congressman Somers from New York branded it:

> ... the silliest piece of legislation that has ever come before my notice in the years I have served here. A woman's army to defend the United States of America. Think of the humiliation. What has become of the manhood of America, that we have to call on our women to do what has ever been the duty of men? The thing is so revolting to me, to my sense of decency, that I just cannot discuss it.[8]

Most Congressmen couched their opposition in more sophisticated terms, raising technical questions regarding discipline and courts-martial; the term of service and whether or not a volunteer could subsequently resign; whether benefits were best placed under the Veterans Administration or the Federal Employees Compensation Act; and attempts to ban overseas assignments. Some speakers indicated that while they were personally opposed, they nevertheless felt pressured to vote for the bill, lest they be accused of harming the war effort. Several representatives correctly perceived that the auxiliary status of the Women's Army Auxiliary Corps would lead to difficulties, but Representative Rogers, knowing that the Army would not go any further on these points, skated over these truly problematic intellectual minefields with great parliamentary skill. She was ably assisted in debate by several men, including Committee Chairman May. Washington women and the leadership of national women's organizations stood firmly together; no woman spoke publicly against the bill.* The final vote (249 to 83, with 96 abstentions) was a solid victory for Edith Rogers.

When the Senate took up the bill almost two months later, opposition was probably stronger than in the House but was less expressed. Debate was shorter, and unfriendly amendments on racial discrimination, overseas duty and, bizarrely, a ban against cremation of WAAC bodies were quickly struck. The leadership insisted over and over again that it was the Senate's duty to pass the bill exactly as the War Department wanted it and not to cause delay by amendments that conflicted with the House version. The membership agreed, but only barely. One-third of the Senators did not go on record either for or against, indicating by their apathy a lack of enthusiasm. The final vote was 38 in favor, 27 against—a mere 11-vote margin. Three days later, on May 15, 1942, President Roosevelt signed the bill, and the Women's Auxiliary Army Corps was underway.

By the time the Senate took up the WAAC bill, the House had already passed legislation creating the WAVES. The Navy, in planning for its women's organization, sought to avoid the negative publicity that the Army was already experiencing with its "Wacks"; the Navy created a good acronym first and then built explanatory and never-used words around it. WAVES were "Women Accepted for Volunteer Emergency Service."

They also learned from the difficult questions dealing with the "auxiliary" status of the WAAC. From the first, it was announced that women would have "full military status with complete equality with men in the Navy."[9] In addition to learning from the Army's mistakes, the Navy had its own past as a guideline, for it had been a clever legalism on the part of the Navy, and its correlated branch, the Marines, that militarized women as Yeomen (F) and Marinettes in World War I. News articles reminded the public of that history, while pointing out that the WAVES as "a definite part of the Navy itself (neither a corps nor an auxiliary) is precedent-breaking."[10]

Officially established by July 30, 1942, enlistment standards for WAVES were appreciably higher than for WAACs. While WAACs were required only to be over 21 and of good health and character, WAVES had to possess "a college degree, or two years of college work plus at least two years' professional or business experience applicable to naval jobs . . . Especially wanted: women

---

* Representative Jeanette Rankin of Montana, who had been elected to the House before most women had the right to vote and who was the only Member of Congress to cast negative votes on declaring both World Wars, did not speak in the debate. Her final vote was for the WAAC, when presumably her feminist principles overcame her pacifist ones.

who majored in engineering, astronomy, meteorology, electronics, physics, mathematics, metallurgy, business statistics and modern foreign languages."[11] Despite Naval publicity on the equality of its men and women, not only did WAVES have to meet these higher educational standards, they (like women in the WAACS) had to be older than male enlistees. Moreover, Congress succeeded in banning overseas service when enacting the WAVES legislation.

The other Naval branches took a leisurely approach in following the example of the WAAC and WAVES. The Coast Guard's SPARS finally came into existence on November 22, 1942. Like the WAVES, the acronym was of prime importance and the reasoning behind it secondary. SPARS stood for the Coast Guard's motto, *Semper Paratus*—Always Ready. Enlistment standards were lower than those for the WAVES; only high school or equivalent business experience was required. The SPARS enactment was precedent setting, for this was the first time women had served in the Coast Guard in enlisted or commissioned capacity.

The Marines, who had led the way in uniforming women in World War I, were the greatest laggards in the second war. Despite their previously good experience and the urgent need after Pearl Harbor, the Marine Corps did not open its doors to women until more than a year after U.S. involvement in the war. When they did, though, it was with a typically Marine no-nonsense attitude. *Newsweek*, the worst media offender in playing games with the WAAC name, wrote: "Once and for all, the Marine Corps announced firmly, its new women's reserve will be called—not Wams, not Marinettes, but simply Marines."[12] The WAAC, by this time, had already formed an organization; developed officers, set up three boot camps and dozens of specialist schools; and sent its first units to North Africa. However, with the Marine action, as of January 28, 1943, all branches of the U.S. military finally included women.

"May 22, 1942, will surely go down on the record," predicted the *Christian Science Monitor*. "It was the day that women joined up with the Army . . ."

From long before dawn until well after dimout, 440 recruiting stations throughout the nation were struggling to keep pace with the avalanche of patriotic response unloosed by the call for 540 women candidates for officers training . . .

Here were no excitement seekers looking for a thrill. These are no glamour girls in search of the spotlight. They were in earnest, all of them, motivated by a common, sober impulse—to help with the war.

They represented a cross section of American society, without a section missing. There were solemn Negro girls followed by smartly dressed society debs . . . "I have five brothers in the service already," said one. Still another: "If a man can give up his life for his country, certainly a woman can give up her time."[13]

Though the newspaper went on to express astonishment that married women could enlist without the consent of their husbands,* its treatment was more serious than that of other publications. *Time* for instance, wrote that:

> *Bemused Army recruiting officers gave out 13,208 long, pink application blanks, explained 13,208 times that an applicant must be between her twenty-first and fiftieth birthdays (no, she must not fib about her age), must be between five and six feet tall, must weigh between 105 and 200 pounds, must have a high-school education.*
>
> *. . . Women were so eager to sign up that many went without breakfast. Bosses waited in vain for secretaries, nurses arrived late and breathless at hospitals, dishes went unwashed and floors unswept . . .*
>
> *The staccato questions and treble chatter in the 440 recruiting stations got on officers' nerves . . . Said [an] officer: "They're just as tough to handle in this recruiting office as they are in civilian life."* [14]

Despite nervous officers and media amusement, the point was strong: In one day, over 13,000 women had applied for just 450 announced slots as officer candidates. Whether they were motivated by patriotism, employment security or a desire for a new type of life, eager enlistees stampeded recruiting offices in the first days. By summer's end, over 110,000 application forms had been given out. One of the earliest WAACs wrote, "Girls and women stop me all the time to ask if I think they should enlist. Before I can give my carefully prepared little answer, they launch into a discussion of what they know about the WAACs, and how their families feel, and what their general attitude toward the war is. Walking down the street has become a great adventure."[15]

The WAVES, though set up with the obvious intention of being an elitist group, quickly filled its initial ranks. Despite discouraging recruitment of women with esoteric skills—"supervisors of cable, telegraph, telephone and radio commercial offices, . . . licensed radio operators, ultra-high frequency engineers, lexicographers, amateur cryptanalysts"[16]—the Navy was flooded with applications. To prevent unseemly crowds at recruiting stations, the Navy insisted that potential WAVES write for applications, and thousands did.

The Marines "hit their January enlistment goal on Thanksgiving Day: 12,023 women, including 515 officers."[17] When 1,000 of them later were asked their motivation, most cited patriotism or some personal variation thereof. The second largest group sought individual gain, for "many had never had a chance

---

* This is probably less a liberated philosophy on the part of the military than it is a concession to bureaucratic reality. Presumably, some of the most likely recruits would be married, childless women whose first objective in winning the war would be to bring their husbands home sooner; to delay their enlistment while the mails searched for an overseas husband would be counterproductive for all concerned.

33

to go to college and expected the service, in effect, to complete their education." "These women were sober and practical, with a mere 63 saying they joined the Marines for "the novel and adventurous."[18]

But early enthusiasm faded. Throughout 1942, there were stories of the opening of new training camps and assignment stations and the interesting types of work that were being opened to women, but by mid-1943, a sour note began to be heard. Most women, it seemed, were no more willing than most men voluntarily to entrust their fate to the vagaries of military life in wartime.

By the end of 1943, those who intended to volunteer had done so. *Time* wrote two days after Christmas:

> The bitter truth was out: recruiting for the WAC* has been such a failure that officials last week admitted they were hopeless of filling their quota, figure they will be lucky to keep even a trickle of recruits coming in. War Department officials are afraid they may have got all the women volunteers they ever will get. WAC aim for 1943 was an enrollment of 150,000. Present strength: a little over 60,000.
>
> WAVES, who did just a little better than their quota, have also been getting a cold shoulder in recent months . . . SPARS and Marine Reserves reached their smaller goals some time ago. But in recent weeks their recruiting has also been hamstrung.[19]

The need was real; women had proven their worth to such an extent that the demand was now far greater than the supply. Initially skeptical Army officers soon clamored for more. The first WAAC companies assigned to the Army Air Force** were so impressive that the "AAF with less than three months' experience in the use of Waacs, discussed with [WAAC] Director [Oveta Culp] Hobby the possibility of obtaining 540,000 more."[20]

By May 1943, the news media was somewhat acknowledging its sins of the past. Speaking of the women "who had endured the cheap jokes and poor public relations of the WAAC's early weeks," *Time* wrote: "The Army has learned the desirability of its soldiers in skirts, not merely as ersatz men but for their own sakes and skills . . . One replacement group of 56 replaced 128 men."[21] Operational requests for WAACs totaled a half-million, 375,000 of which came from the more progressive Army Air Force.[22]

Talk of a million-plus WACs was ludicrous in reality, for the WAC was not anywhere close to meeting its Congressionally authorized quota of 150,000. With approximately 60,000 enlisted at the end of 1943, it was at only 40% of its goal. The WAVES, SPARS, and Marines appeared to be doing better simply because their leadership (with the benefit of WAC experience) had set realisti-

---

* The WAAC (Women's Army Auxiliary Corps) became the WAC (Women's Army Corps) on July 2, 1943. This transformation is covered in Chapter 6.

** The Air Force did not exist as a separate entity until after the war.

cally obtainable goals. The WAAC actually had more applicants in its first *day* than the entire strength of the SPARS for the four years of the war, but because it had assigned itself much higher goals, it was judged a failure. WAC Director Oveta Culp Hobby took a more complex and realistic view than that of the hysterical media which condemned her, the WAC, and women in general. "Nothing," she said reasonably, "leads me to believe that we are going to get a volunteer army of 400,000 or 500,000 women. We've never been able to get a volunteer army of men that big."[23]

It didn't keep her from trying. Women's clubs and organizations were brought into the enlistment effort; local recruitment drives were held complete with experienced WACs; General Marshall called on the nation's governors to help; there were even specific drives held for Chinese and Japanese Americans. Past mistakes were acknowledged; the advertising agency that had encouraged the "glamour girl" approach of the early days, resulting in a public and press that viewed women in the military less than seriously, was fired.

The Army Air Force, impatient with results, was given permission to run its own, separate recruitment effort. Under Colonel Betty Bandel, the top WAC officer assigned to the AAF, "the plan enabled the Air Forces to appeal to women directly, promising them job assignments of their choice and assuring them that every effort would be made to assign them to a station of their choice."[24] The results showed that women knew what they wanted and took their careers far more seriously than the advertising men had ever suspected.

The Air Transport Command, for example, "held out the prospect of eventual assignment to one of its far-flung bases around the world, and within less than a year the ATC raised its WAC strength from 500 to 5,500"[25]—a 1,000% increase. The "Air WACs" (as they began to be known, despite official War Department disapproval of this term) demonstrated that a progressive approach by a military that took women's aspirations seriously could find volunteers. The 27,047 they enlisted in a 14-month recruitment drive* was more than all other branches combined-but still far short of the 46,000 goal they had set for themselves. "I never saw anything as tough," one AAF officer said of WAC recruiting:

> *When our team hit one Florida city, we closed the place—actually got the mayor to close schools and stores so everyone would come to our parade and rally. We got important speakers, generals, war heroes. Better than 50 planes flew overhead forming the letters WAC. That night we had a big dance for prospects, with good-looking pilots as dates. Results? We didn't get one Wac in that town. Some of the local girls put in applications to please their escorts, but withdrew them the next day.*[26]

---

* From October 15, 1943, to December 31, 1944.

The Air Corps was learning a bitter lesson: There was a limit to women's history of volunteerism. Despite the military's genuine if sometimes misguided efforts, the number of women in the ranks remained minuscule compared with that of men. But most of those millions of men were not there by their own choice. By February 1943, the United States was drafting 12,000 men—a whole division—every day. When men with physical limitations and those holding jobs vital to the war were eliminated, there was no choice except to begin the drafting of men with dependents—or women.

As early as September 10, 1942, a Gallup poll showed tremendous support for drafting women. The question asked was: "The Army can either draft 300,000 single women, aged 21-35, for the WACs for non-fighting jobs, or it can draft the same number of married men with families for the same work. Which plan would you favor?" An overwhelming 81% said that women should be drafted; only 13% said the married men. Women were stronger in support of drafting women than men were: 84% of the women, regardless of marital status, supported this draft; the vote of men was 78%.[27]

Gallup asked the question again over the next months and found support that ranged from 73% to 78%.[28] Consistently, three-quarters of the American public supported drafting single women over married men. Indeed, the very absence of a female draft became a reason that many women gave for their failure to enlist. What evidence was there, they asked, that the need was real or that the Army truly wanted them if they were not subject to a draft the same as men?

Despite the apparent popularity of drafting single women, neither Congress nor the War Department ever seriously considered drafting women for military units other than the nurse corps. (Though *Time*, in another of its hyperbolic mood swings, wrote that Secretary of War Stimson's "recommendation" was for "compulsory service.")[29] The nation's elected representatives knew their constituents well enough (or thought they did) to set aside polling results as simplistic questions that ignored the complexity of reasons why women didn't join.

Some were patriotically valid. Millions of women working in defense plants saw their contribution there as far more worthwhile; surely a woman riveting planes or tanks was as valuable as one pounding a typewriter in a general's office. Moreover, they frequently needed the good money that defense plants paid, because soldiers' allotments often were inadequate to the needs of families. Women found themselves with new financial responsibilities; when men left their jobs for a private's pay, someone had to meet the mortgage, look after elderly parents and provide for the young. Even single women often found that they could not afford to enlist; with rising prices and without their brothers' incomes, many single women had to provide for families.

Moreover, government agencies, including the military, recognized the value of women working in defense plants. The Marine Corps, for example, suspended a Macon, Georgia, recruitment drive for women when it recognized that this was interfering with industrial needs.* Competition for available women became so keen that " in the summer of 1943 the Secretary of War and the Secretary of the Navy signed a joint agreement for the recruiting of women, designed to protect the labor supply of industries critical in the prosecution of the war."[30]

Further agreements with the War Manpower Commission, the Office of War Mobilization and other agencies were designed to set rules making the fight for women a fair one. Indeed, these rules became so restrictive that they nearly created a "draft" in reverse. A woman, for example, could not leave federal employment to join the military without a release from her employer; nor could a woman from "war industry" join without a similar written release. WAC recruiters were not to accept women employed in agriculture at all.

The message was clear that women's labor was valuable in places other than the military. This encouraged many women (who after all had long experience in personal time management via housework) to take a practical approach that looked askance at male military games. One older WAAC trainee summed up this view when she said of the regimentation in arranging items in her barrack footlocker, "I love all this, but really, it's more trouble than running a whole household."[31] How, women asked, could perfecting one's bedmaking technique to suit Army standards possibly shorten the war? The military's arbitrary ways were inherently irrational, many women thought, and there was no reason to encourage them by voluntarily assenting.

"Why," questioned one, "should I respond to reveille at 5:30 A.M. when it isn't essential to my job? . . . Why put myself in a position to be restricted to quarters because some GI Jennie left a cologne bottle in the washroom?" [32] This woman was doing her share as a civilian employee of the Army, a serviceman's wife, and a USO volunteer; why, she quite reasonably wondered, should grown women voluntarily revert to the position of children who could be punished even for offenses they didn't personally commit. The military's ways might make sense for teenage boys but not for mature women.

The military's reputation for not necessarily putting talents and abilities to the best possible use also hurt recruitment efforts. Despite ads for linguists and lexicographers, women knew, because of the experience of their men, that there was always the possibility they would end up in charge of latrines. The WAC in particular suffered from this. While WAVES, SPARS, and Marines were able to establish somewhat specialized images, much of the public continued to

---

* Of course, a likely situation here is that business leaders were fearful that the Marines would attract enough women to create a labor shortage that would result in higher wages in this nonunion area.

believe that the WAC wanted women for kitchen and laundry duties. After all, the earliest advocates of the WAAC talked of needing women for those jobs that they did "better than men," those for which they were "naturally suited." Even Air Force officers—the most progressive branch of the Army—persistently recommended that WACs take over mess duty, presumably providing home cooking.

There were other reasons for low enlistments. Women who understood that the need was for their clerical skills resented the physical demands of marching and KP. They were wary of a caste system that told them with whom they could and could not socialize. Often a woman's family disapproved of such independence and risk; sometimes her church objected to this fundamental change in women's historic role; very frequently her man refused assent. Censors who read soldiers' mail and were interviewed on the subject could not report any instance of a man encouraging a woman to enlist, while many opposite cases were cited.

Studies showed that negative attitudes were most likely among husbands and lovers who had not been in combat. Those with experience in battle knew the appeal for recruits was serious; nurses who had escaped from the horror of the Philippines were appalled by the apathy of Americans at home. "Nothing," said one, "on Bataan or the Rock shocked us as much as what we have found back home."[33]

But by the beginning of 1944, many Americans believed that victory was at hand and that it was only a matter of time before the war would be over. The slow progress through Europe after D-Day and the maniacally, suicidally stubborn resistance of the Japanese in the Pacific should have increased enlistment levels, but somehow the reality of the pain their men were enduring was not being brought home to American women.

During 1942 and 1943, the media poured forth a flood of stories about how women could contribute to the war effort, and by 1945 they were giving great quantities of advice about veterans and their readjustment, but during 1944 there was a noticeable decrease in attention to women and the war. Many exciting articles that could have been written in 1944 about the wonderful things military women were doing, especially in Europe and the Pacific, went unwritten. Whether this opportunity was lost because of excessive military censorship or because editors thought that their audiences were not interested in reading such stories is unclear. The point is that it became easier for women to ignore the war and the appeal for enlistment.

Although magazine stories on women in the military were lacking, they were far more visible than advertising sponsored by the WAC itself. The WAVES, SPARS, and Marines ran virtually no ads in women's magazines. These magazines provided the best possible contact with women in a time before television, and yet this market was left almost totally untapped. Public relations people frequently arranged for tours of institutions by reporters, but the substance of the articles was left to the reporters' discretion. Often authors emphasized the trivial and missed the serious points that should have been made; keeping up morale with a light-hearted approach seems to have been the greatest objective of most publications. Articles aimed at women remained relentlessly perky in tone throughout the war.

Another recruitment mistake, especially at the beginning, was an apparent belief that the military could exercise the same "selective service" with women volunteers that they did with male draftees. Throughout the war, every service eased enlistment standards downward. Even before their first classes began, the WAAC reversed itself and allowed 50-year-old women to join (the original age limit was 45). The WAVES, who at first accepted married women only if their children were over 18 and if their husbands were not in the military, soon changed their regulations to allow marriage to men in the Army, Marines, or Coast Guard, but not the Navy. By the fall of 1943, that requirement was dropped, too. Other excessively strict requirements, such as superior eyesight, were eliminated.

Near the end of the war, some training courses were shortened, and some assignments were reshuffled for maximum utility. Traditionalism gave way to realistic need, for instance, when in May 1945 General Marshall assigned the WAC to form over 100 medical units; the flood of returning soldiers who needed medical care overtook the previously sacrosanct line between the WAC and the Army Nurse Corps.[34]

Though the WAVES and SPARS lowered their entrance age to 20, all of the women's services insisted that their enlistees be older than male enlistees. There was virtually no discussion of changing these rules; that their women be at or near legal adulthood seemed given as a law of nature. This was perhaps the most foolish of deterrents to enlistment, because a young woman had to wait three years after high school to enlist and obviously would find other things to do in the interim. Boys, of course, were subject to the draft at 18 and could enlist with parental consent at 17.

High schools introduced military prep courses for boys, but girls were discouraged from taking up space in them. Guidance counselors were warned that girls "interests would not be well served" by their enrollment, and that "they might even reduce the effectiveness of these divisions for the male participators."[35] Only vague advice was offered to female students: "A high-school girl who thinks she may want to enlist at 20 or 21 can best prepare herself . . . by selecting the subjects and continuing the preparation she would pursue if anything happened to keep her from such enlistment . . ."[36] The double standard that applied to men and women regarding age was extremely inconsistent. Boys went into the military younger, but had to be older to marry or accept other adult responsibilities. Girls could marry younger, but do nothing else.

The most immoral of the military's recruitment failures, however, was its discouragement of black volunteers. Oveta Culp Hobby, from her earliest days as Director of the WAAC, tried to be as fair to black women as current standards would allow, but the unintended result probably was to damage the image of the Corps in comparison with other women's services. "Mrs. Hobby faces difficulties," *Newsweek* acknowledged in May 1942 as the WAAC got underway. "The first was the accusation of racial discrimination in the appointment of a Southerner as director. She quelled it with the announcement that Negroes would be recruited in proportion to their numbers in the population."[37]

As promised, the first WAAC officer class to graduate contained 36 blacks (almost the same 10% they represented in the population), but this bright beginning was not maintained. Ultimately the wartime "peak strength" of black WACs was about 4%,[38] for reasons that Hobby's staff always believed were the result of the comparatively high educational and skills requirements of the Corps versus the lower educational and employment opportunities available to blacks at the time.

While black women (like black men) in the Army were almost always segregated in barracks apart from whites and grouped into "all-Negro platoons" who ate at separate tables, at least the Army accepted them as recruits. The Navy did not enlist the first black woman until after October 1944, less than a year before the war ended.

It was not as though potential recruits had not presented themselves; nor was the Navy unaware of the issue. In 1943 alone, New York blacks registered four separate protests noteworthy enough to get space in the *New York Times*. Their advocates in Congress had pushed legislation banning racial discrimination since the beginning of the war. Finally, enough pressure was brought that the WAVES announced—more than two years after its formation—that "Negro women . . . would be accepted . . . Negroes will be trained and even billeted with whites . . ." And yet these proud plans called for fewer than a dozen ("probably five to ten")[39] black officers, at a time when there were nearly 80,000 WAVES.

The Coast Guard and Marines had waited to follow the Navy's "lead." After the announcement in regard to the WAVES, the Coast Guard, which *Time* termed "usually the most liberal branch of the service with regard to Negroes," adopted a similar plan for the SPARS. "The Marine Corps," it added, "had all the women marines it needed . . ."[40]

In addition to all of the burdens Colonel Hobby and the WAC had to bear because they were the first to experiment with this profound change in women's roles, they also carried the onus of being the first (and for most of the war, the only) service to take a chance on black women. Though unacknowledged, Hobby's policies of at least some opportunity for blacks doubtless harmed recruitment of whites into the WAC. Racial prejudice was still genuine in the U.S. during the 1940s. Even among northerners who considered themselves Roosevelt liberals (even in FDR's government itself), most whites were patronizing towards blacks, seeing them as not quite up to the standards of whites, not yet capable of taking on serious positions of responsibility. The average American family would not encourage their young woman to enlist in an organization where she might have to study in the same classroom as a black, where she might even be outranked by one. Promoting people that were thought of as inherently a servant class was perceived as another evidence of Mrs. Hobby's misguided social experimentation.

Congress watched; some agreed; virtually all understood the unspoken message. If three of the four female branches of the military would not accept black women—not even for laundry or kitchen duty—then the military's needs must not be all that great. The United States was not like Britain; it was not in a fight for actual survival, and it seemed likely that things would get better instead of worse. There would be no draft of women.

While quotas for the WAC and other women's services went unfilled, there was one other women's organization affiliated with the military that had exactly the opposite situation: Over 25,000 women filed applications for the WASP (Women's Airforces Service Pilots); a mere 1,830 were allowed to serve. The situation had a complicated history, beginning, like everything else, at Pearl Harbor.

"I knew I was going to join the Women's Auxiliary Ferrying Squadron," wrote Cornelia Fort in mid-1943, shortly before the bomber she piloted fatally crashed, "But I never knew it as surely as I did in Honolulu on December 7, 1941."

> At dawn that morning I drove from Waikiki to the . . . civilian airport right next to Pearl Harbor, where I was a civilian pilot instructor. Shortly after six-thirty I began landing and take-off practice with my regular student. Coming in just before the last landing, I looked casually around and saw a military plane coming directly toward me. I jerked the controls away from my student and jammed the throttle wide open to pull above the oncoming plane. He passed so close under us that our celluloid windows rattled violently and I looked down to see what kind of plane it was.
>
> The painted red balls on the tops of the wings shone brightly in the sun. I looked again with complete and utter disbelief . . .[41]

Other civilian planes did not return that day. When Cornelia Fort got back to the mainland three months later, she—like thousands of other women pilots—searched in vain for an opportunity to best use her skills for victory. Like others, she found that all she was allowed to do was teach young men who were learning to fly, for the skies had been closed to civilian pilots, and all women were civilians.

A couple of dozen American women had long ago flown to England and joined the British "ATA Girls," the Air Transport Auxiliary. By September

1942, ATA pilots, one-quarter of whom were women, had already flown over 30,000,000 miles and delivered 100,000 aircraft from the factories where they were made to the air bases where they were needed. One of the earliest U.S. veterans in this work, Pauline Gower, remembered her arrival in England in the winter of 1940:

> I began to worry . . . the Minister for Air. I kept at it until, finally, we were accepted into the ATA—myself and eight others. We were, quite frankly, unpopular at the start and we had considerable prejudice to break down during the winter of 1940 . . .
>
> Now, after three years of ferrying millions of dollars' worth of the most valuable aircraft in the world on terms of absolute equality with the men, we have actually a smaller accident rate than they have. That is a source of great pride to us and particularly to me.
>
> We spent the whole of that first winter—and it was one of the most bitter on record—ferrying Tiger Moths all over the country. We could not have had a more severe test. Tiger Moths have open cockpits . . . None of us will ever forget the pain of thawing out after such flights.
>
> . . . The women's services were not in the working order they are today. No special sleeping or washing or comfort facilities—just bleak, cold airfields and when we got back to base, we had to lug our parachutes one and one-half miles to billets! I believe the rigors of that unforgettable winter left its mark on several of our band.
>
> From Tiger Moths we were promoted to Miles Magister trainers and from these to Miles Masters and Oxfords but we were sternly precluded from flying all operational types of aircraft. We accepted the situation and plugged away at our job . . . By June, 1941, we were allowed to ferry Hurricanes and Spitfires and by the beginning of 1942, we were flying . . . bombers. Women now fly any one of the 120 different types of aircraft ferried by ATA on precisely the same footing as men.42

In the United States, things were different. War Department planners, already in the 1930s, had considered the use of women pilots and been rebuffed. The Chief of the Air Force thought it "utterly unfeasible," terming women "too high strung for wartime flying."43 Newsweek reported on December 1, 1941 (six days before Pearl Harbor) that "aviation authorities have taken a sternly masculine attitude toward air-minded women . . . On the ground that men are more suitable for flight training than women, the Civil Aeronautics Administration last July put a stop to women's participation."44

Women, however, did not quietly acquiesce. Membership in the Women Flyers of America, Inc., increased by 900% during 1941. As of the middle of that year, there were over 2,700 U.S. women who were licensed as pilots, able and willing to fly. They "badgered the authorities in Washington, they set up their own training groups, they argued that, when pilots were so urgently needed, they should be given a chance . . . And for a long time, all they got was a pat on the back for their patriotic eagerness, the grudging admission that possibly they could do the job, and questionnaires to fill out."45

Finally in September of 1942, Nancy Harkness Love, a veteran pilot who had flown planes to the Canadian border during the days of U.S. neutrality and the wife of the Air Transport Command's Deputy Chief, was able to quietly announce the formation of the WAFS—the Women's Auxiliary Ferrying Squadron. With headquarters at an Army air base near Wilmington, Delaware, the WAFS began with 40 women pilots.*

All candidates for the WAFS had to be commercially licensed pilots with at least 500 hours in logged flying time, 200-horsepower rating, and cross-country experience. These requirements, *Flying* magazine acknowledged, "were forbiddingly high, and the War Department has stressed repeatedly that the whole subject . . . was experimental."[46] WAFS were civilian employees hired on three-month contracts; they were not uniformed and not officially part of any military organization, though they operated from an AAF base. They were neither fish nor fowl; they were simply women who loved to fly, needed to fly, and wanted to do so for their country.

Meanwhile, Jacqueline Cochran, a famed aviator who had beaten men in well-publicized races and held five national and international speed records, was also at work. As the first woman to ferry a bomber across the Atlantic to England, Cochran recruited American women to fly for the ATA. She had already written to Eleanor Roosevelt in 1939 attempting to plan a place for women pilots in the war she foresaw. Like so many other planning efforts, it had been ignored. The confused result was that, almost simultaneously with the formation of Love's WAFS, came the beginning of the WASP (Women's Airforces Service Pilots) under Cochran's direction.

Based first at Howard Hughes Airfield near Houston and later at Avenger Field at Sweetwater, Texas, the WASP differed in concept from the WAFS. While WAFS pilots were so highly experienced that they began to fly immediately after a short course in Army procedures and paperwork, WASPs were less experienced, though certainly better qualified than male cadets whom the military trained from scratch. Women lucky enough to get into the WASP training program first had to have gained—at their own expense and despite restrictions on civilian flying—at least 200 hours of certified flight time.

Love and Cochran supported each other's efforts, and, especially at first, there was no direct conflict between the WAFS and WASP, for each was simply a group of civilian employees with a different geographical base and a different job description. As women began to graduate from the WASP training program, however, and as duties expanded beyond the ferrying of planes from one location to another, the missions of the two overlapped more and more. Finally General Henry ("Hap") Arnold, Chief of the Air Corps, sent down an order that

---

* Another 10 worked as administrators.

he "would not have two women's pilot organizations in the AAF—that they had to get together."[47]

The WASP was the result, officially announced on August 5, 1943, as the two merged and Cochran became director.* Except in specialized aviation publications, there was little public attention. They were still civilians, and military leadership was still reluctant to even acknowledge this experiment with women. Many potential applicants literally went from airport to airport, trying to find someone who knew something about the program and how they could join it. Far from recruiting women, WASP leadership was so keenly aware of the potential jealousy of male would-be pilots that they kept publicity to such a minimum that some people believed that existence of the WASP was a military secret.

Their paramilitary status remained, and WASPs had to fight daily to prove the worth of women pilots, but they had begun to make an impact. In every branch of the U.S. military, women were making a place for themselves.

SOURCE NOTES

1. Keith Ayling, *Calling All Women* (New York: Harper and Brothers, 1942), p. 140.
2. *Congressional Record—House*, "Women's Army Auxiliary Corps," 77th Cong., 2nd sess., March 17, 1942, Vol. 88, pt. 2, p. 2583.
3. Edith Nourse Rogers: "A Woman's Army?" *Independent Woman*, February 1942, p. 38. See also by Rogers, "The Time Is Now," *Woman's Home Companion*, August 1943, p. 24; Alice L. Manning, "Should Women Be Enlisted?" *Independent Woman*, July 1941, p. 212; and "Women Want to Join the War but Run into Some Skepticism," *Newsweek*, January 12, 1942, p. 23.
4. Kathleen Williams Boom, "Women in the AAF," in *The Army Air Forces in World War II*, Wesley F. Craven and James L. Cate, vol. 7, (Chicago: University of Chicago Press, 1958), p. 504, citing G-1 Staff Study, "Participation of Women in War," G1/8604-1, 21 Sept. 1928.
5. Mattie E. Treadwell, *The Women's Army Corps* (Washington: Office of the Chief of Military History, Department of the Army, 1954), p. 17, citing Memo, Brig. Gen. Wade H. Haislip, G-1, for C/S, 29 Apr. 1941, G1/15839-10.
6. *Congressional Record—House*, "Women's Army Auxiliary Corps," p. 2582. See also "She-Soldiers," *Time* (January 12, 1942), p. 57; "Wacks and Warns in Prospect for Petticoat Army and Navy," *Newsweek* (March 30, 1942): p. 33.

---

* Love was made the chief WASP executive assigned to the Ferrying Division of the Air Transport Command.

7. Ibid., p. 2593.
8. Ibid., p. 2606
9. "WAVES," *Time* (August 10, 1942): p. 71; see also "Permanent WAVES," *Newsweek* (August 10, 1942): p. 31.
10. Joy Bright Hancock, "The WAVES," *Flying* (February 1943): p. 182. See also by the same author, *Lady in the Navy: A Personal Reminiscence* (Annapolis: the Naval Institute Press, 1972).
11. "WAVES,"p. 71; see also "Education Directly Related to Duties of WAVE Personnel," *Education for Victory*, vol. 3, no. 19 (April 3, 1945): p. 20.
12. "Devil Dames," *Newsweek* (February 22, 1943): p. 37. For a summary of the formation of all of the women's military units, see Elizabeth M. Culver, "Women in the Service," *Annals of the American Academy of Political and Social Science*, Vol. 229, p. 63.
13. Josephine Ripley, "Women Everywhere Answer Ready! When Uncle Sam Calls the WAAC," *Christian Science Monitor* (June 20, 1942): p. 2.
14. "WAAC's First Muster," *Time* (June 8, 1942): p. 71. See also R. Black, "We're in the Army Now," *Independent Woman* (July 1942): p. 198 and "WAAC: U.S. Women Troop to Enlist in Army's First All-Female Force," *Life* (May 7, 1942): p. 26.
15. Elizabeth Pollock, *Yes, Ma'am,* edited by Ruth Duhme (New York: Lippincott, 1943), p. 170.
16. Nona Baldwin, "America Enlists Its Women," *Independent Woman* (September 1942): p. 265.
17. "Leathernecks," *Time* (December 27, 1943): p. 69.
18. "Why Women Enter the Service," *Science News Letter* (March 4, 1944): p. 146.
19. "In This Total War," *Time* (December 27, 1943): p. 63.
20. Boom, "Women in the AAF," p. 510; see also Treadwell, *Women's Army Corps*, p. 95.
21. "Stepsister Corps," *Time* (May 10, 1943): p. 55.
22. Boom, "Women in the AAF," p. 508; citing Memo, Classif. & Repl. Br. AGO for Col. Catron, 21 Oct. 1942; Rpt., Clasif. & Rpl. Br. AGO for WAAC Hqs., 25 Nov. 1942; and Biennial Report of C/S to S/W, 1 July 1943–30 June 1945.
23. "In This Total War," p. 63.
24. Boom, "Women in the AAF," p. 515.
25. Ibid.
26. Treadwell, *Women's Army Corps*, p. 245; quoting Capt. Dewey Couri, February 1944.
27. Gallup, *The Gallup Poll*, p. 406.
28. Ibid., pp. 412, 420, and 435. See also Alice Manning, "Women Accept Their Responsibilities," *Independent Woman* (March 1944): p. 72; and

"AAUW Recommends Drafting Women for the Armed Forces," *School and Society* (April 8, 1944): p. 244. Both polls were mail ballots and showed that the leadership of the Business and Professional Clubs and the American Association of University Women supported drafting women.

29. "In This Total War,", p. 63.
30. Boom, "Women in the AAF," p. 509. See also Treadwell, *Women's Army Corps*, pp. 172 and 246–49.
31. "Meet Officer Candidate Mary Johnston," *Ladies Home Journal* (January 1943): p. 73.
32. Ruth Peters, "Why I Don't Join the WACS," *American Mercury* (September 1944): p. 296.
33. Elizabeth R. Valentine, "Our Nurses on the World's Fronts," *New York Times Magazine* (September 13, 1942): p. 53.
34. "WAC Medical Aides," *Hygeia* (May 1945): p. 326; see also J. Noel Macy, "Negro Women in the WAC," *Opportunity: Journal of Negro Life* (Winter 1945): p. 14.
35. "Future WAAC's, WAVES, Spars, and the High-School Victory Corps," *Education for Victory*, vol. 1, no. 23 (February 1, 1943): p. 18.
36. Ibid.
37. "Mrs. Hobby's Wacks," *Newsweek* (May 25, 1942): p. 32; see also "Negro Women and the WAAC," *Opportunity: Journal of Negro Life* (April 1943): p. 54, and Ina M. McFadden, "Women on Their Own," *Pulse* (February 1943), p. 4.
38. Treadwell, *Women's Army Corps*, p. 596; see also pp. 590 and 619.
39. "Negro WAVES," *Time* (October 30, 1944): p. 72.
40. Ibid.
41. Cornelia Fort, "At the Twilight's Last Gleaming," *Woman's Home Companion* (July 1943): p. 19.
42. Pauline Gower, "The ATA Girls," *Flying* (August 1943): p. 30; see also "ATA Girls," *New York Times Magazine* (August 9, 1942): p. 9.
43. Boom, "Women in the AAF," p. 528, citing Lt. Col. Betty Bandel, "The WAC Program in the AAF," p. 3, and USAF Historical Studies, No. 55: "Women Pilots with the AAF, 1941–44," p. 8.
44. "Feminine Flyers," *Newsweek* (December 1, 1941): p. 45. See also a general history of women in aviation, Charles E. Planck: *Women With Wings* (New York: Harper & Brothers, 1942).
45. Russell Birdwell, *Women in Battle Dress* (New York: Fine Editions Press, 1942), p.190.
46. Rowland Carter, "The Ladies Join the Air Forces," *Flying* (December 1942): p. 88. See also "WAFS," *Time* (September 21, 1942): p. 58; E. Evans, "The Sky Is No Limit," *Independent Woman* (November 1942): p. 326; "Mrs. Love of the WAFS," *Newsweek* (Septermber 21, 1942): p. 46; "Here Come the WAFS," *Time* (June 7, 1943): p. 60; H. Taylor, "WAFS

Fly for the Army," *Scholastic* (May 17, 1943): p. 10; "Women's Ferrying Squadron Planned," *Education for Victory*, vol. 1, no. 12 (November 2, 1942): p. 14; and Dickey Meyer (Georgette Louise Chapelle), *Girls at Work in Aviation* (New York: Doubleday, Doran & Company, 1943).

47. Boom, "Women in the AAF," p. 529.

4

YOU'RE IN THE ARMY
NOW—LIFE IN THE CAMPS

Still in civilian clothes, Jane Pollock, a WAAC recruit enroute to basic training, found herself already under strict command. The lieutenant who traveled with the young women assigned their sleeping berths in the train and monitored their behavior: "There is a bar car," she said. "You may go there, but please drink soft drinks or only beer. Be careful of strangers . . . "[1]

Once at camp, the first order of business was getting out of heels and dresses and into a uniform. A reporter, posing as a "synthetic WAAC" for *Newsweek*, detailed:

> *At the clothing warehouse, we were measured for fit. In one hand, we clutched "civies." With the other we contorted our perspiring bodies into skirts, shirts, bilious cotton stockings, and olive-drab underwear. I insisted I wore a size 10; the Army insisted I wore a size 12. In less than an hour we were tightly sealed and delivered Waacs, checked out of the warehouse in shirt, skirt, and tie harness, with regimental headgear . . . Though I felt strait-jacketed in my uniform, I discovered that the regular Waacs love them.*[2]

No other thing about women in the military so captured the public's notice; media attention to women's uniforms was interminable. "As to the all-important uniform," *Time* wrote in May of 1942, "prospective WAACs signed with relief to find that the Army does not intend to design it. Miss Dorothy Shaver, vice president of Manhattan's Lord & Taylor, has charge of that momentous problem."[3] *Reader's Digest* reported, among other things, that WAAC gloves were made of "the finest leather and would cost $12 or more in the stores."[4] *The Nation*, despite its long history of thoughtfulness, believed its readers wanted to know that "each issue included three brassieres, two girdles, cotton and flannelette pajamas, a clothesbrush, rayon panties, wool panties, three slips, four dress shields, four pairs of cotton stockings, an apron..."[5] Even *Current History* felt compelled to record for posterity details such as that WAAC slips were "of a new attractive shade the color of Boston coffee." Their concern with women's underwear even extended to announcing that the maximum time permitted for a WAAC to don her girdle was "one and one-half minutes" and that said girdles were boneless "except for two light front stays for the fuller figures."[6]

WAAC skirts had to be a regulation 16 inches above the ground so that when a company marched, the line of hems would be straight. This meant some variation of individual skirt lengths; an exceptionally tall woman would be issued a long skirt, whereas short women got shorter skirts. The WAAC hat came in for the greatest amount of criticism of any part of the uniform. Throughout the war, there were those who claimed its unfortunate appearance— "like an ordinary kitchen pot turned upside down"[7]— was a deterrence to recruitment. WACs in New Guinea were said to have regularly used their hats as valuable barter with natives who had a different fashion consciousness.

The Navy, once again, learned from the Army. WAVES were granted a "clothing allowance" rather than given their uniforms as "government issue." The Navy, of course, still designed the uniform and dictated how it was to be worn while the new WAVE had only slight discretion in how many items she bought with her allowance, but this was a subtlety that seemed important to the press. The fact that private enterprise was involved in the sale somehow made the WAVES uniform more acceptable. Marshall Fields, for instance, transported employees from Chicago to the University of Wisconsin to outfit WAVES who would be studying there. They turned the gym into a store and brought the women in by groups to purchase their uniforms. Spending as much of their $200 clothing allowance as they chose, the WAVES "removed civilian outer garments at a check rack and proceeded along the uniform line . . . First stop . . . was the blouse table. Each girl wore away one blouse, carried several others . . . For final alterations, clothes went to Chicago by truck and were scheduled for return . . . by the end of the week."[8]

Even as late as 1943, when the Marines, as the last military branch, began to enlist women for the war, interest in the uniform had not abated. *Newsweek* found it necessary to run a half-dozen paragraphs to adequately describe the Marine apparel. In the view of these fashion experts, the Marines "gave war-minded women a chance to don the most colorful uniform so far," one whose "visored hat, incidentally, is the first women's service headgear which takes the feminine hair-do into consideration."[9]

Though it is doubtful that many women chose a military branch on the basis of the clothing offered, the uniform was truly an important part of the military experience. For men and women alike, it was essential to the definition of who they were and what role they played in the war. To be without one was indeed to be without identity.

The Army Air Force, timorous as it was regarding female pilots, at first issued no uniforms to WAFS. More than symbolic of their lack of recognition, the absence of a uniform led to real, practical problems as airport employees refused to heed the orders of women in civilian clothes. One WAFS pilot recalled that she "had to stand by at a hinterland airport while a group of Argentinian pilots, training at a U.S. field, ate all the Red Cross sandwiches, because neither they nor the sweet old ladies doling them out to members of the armed forces could be convinced that I was in the Army Air Forces . . . So I went hungry."[10]

Not only were uniforms necessary, but also they were a source of pride, and women were eager to wear them at every opportunity. "When we go into town in uniform, even after all this time," said one WAAC, "we are always stared at or find ourselves talking animately with perfect strangers. But last night when we were in civies, no one . . . gave us 'the eye.' It made us feel like orphans not to be the center of attention."[11] The ability of a uniform to bring welcome attention was thoroughly recognized; millions of women who did not join the military nonetheless found a way to get themselves into a uniform. They volunteered for the Red Cross or the USO or any number of other organizations and wore those uniforms proudly. Even at parties, weddings, and other totally civilian events, women wore uniforms (and their friends were disappointed if they did not).

It was something that had not been expected. Many observers believed that women, more than men, cherished their individuality and would resent uniforms that denied any personal expression. They were surprised to find that, despite a great quantity of expressed fears about loss of femininity and a fashion industry that continued uncurtailed throughout the war, uniforms became accepted by the public as an important part of fashion.

Women felt empowered by their uniforms. Jane Pollock wrote that while she was still at home she had been afraid to be out after dark, but in the Army, she was surprised to find that she enjoyed strolling alone in the evening. "The whole difference," she insightfully concluded, "is in my uniform! I feel perfectly safe when I have it on."[12]

For the military, the uniform was symbolic of many things. It stated pride in one's organization; it ensured equality among the members thereof; it provided instant recognition of who one was and what she was doing in the war. Other practical aspects of the uniform were that it eliminated decisions on what to wear and avoided competition between women over dress. The whole idea behind uniforms was to *be* uniform. It meant no longer being an outsider but, instead, being part of something larger than one's self; it meant belonging.

Once in uniform, a recruit first became a student. For men and women alike, the classroom was the first assignment. The military wanted things done its way, and its first need was to teach recruits the complexities of its ways. Totalitarian governments could (and did) send their troops into battle without serious educational effort, but American recruits would ask "why." Rather than risk disruptions during front-line danger, soldiers needed to have their questions answered in a safe classroom back home. Thus during World War II, the U.S. military emerged as the world's largest educational system.

More than the accumulation of knowledge, the military aimed to create changes in attitude. Through unyielding discipline, it intended to mold men and women who would obey quickly and unquestioningly; it sought to negate individual personalities and any form of ego and to replace that with personnel dedicated to team effort, proud to have committed their all to the group.

Whether truly educational or (as the military itself called it) indoctrination, boot camp was no easy life. Women, like men, faced grueling schedules and were under constant surveillance. WAACs in training worked a six-day week of 52 hours, excluding homework. A typical daily schedule, as described by one, was:

6 A.M. - *Cannon shot to wake you*
6:17 - *Lights glare on in barracks*
6:30 - *After a masterful struggle you are dressed and at attention*
7 - *March to mess*
7:30 - *Make beds, wash latrines, dust, police grounds*
8-12 - *Classes and close-order drill*
12 - *More chow*
1- 4:30 - *Classes and physical education*
5-5:30 - *Mess*
9 - *Lights out in barracks*
11 - *Bed check (and you had better be there)*[13]

The very first WAACs were sent for initial training to Fort Des Moines, Iowa. Here their presence personified historical change, for Fort Des Moines was a cavalry post that was no longer needed in modern warfare, albeit some regular Army men were reluctant to give up the polo grounds there.* Though the post needed adjustment and some of the very first classes were held outdoors while construction was completed, Fort Des Moines was a lovely place with a huge parade ground and stately elm trees.

That first WAAC class—the 440 officer candidates chosen from those 13,000+ applicants on the first day of recruiting—was truly an exceptional group. The average age was 30, for it took a while to accumulate the outstanding credentials they had. A male colonel said that "M.A.'s are as common as corporal's stripes on this post . . . I don't think anybody, anywhere, ever got

---

* As late as 1941, the Army's cavalry chief testified to a Congressional committee of his belief that "four mounted cavalrymen, spaced one hundred yards apart, could charge half a mile across an open field and destroy an enemy machine gun nest without injury to themselves." See David Brinkley, *Washington at War* (New York: Alfred A. Knopf, 1988), p. 59.

together any such bunch of women for any purpose whatsoever."[14] One WAAC lamented that 94% was too low for an A in her "Transportation and Records" class; "our class is so smart that it was a B. A was ninety-six."[15] Colonel Don Faith, commandant of Fort Des Moines, had "only one trouble . . . they work too hard." The women studied overtime, "risking demerits for reading under the red EXIT lights in the barracks after taps."[16]

The physical regimen was a bit hard for women of the age average of the first class and "many lost weight in spite of hearty eating—but the physical exams had been rigid and they held up."[17] Nor did WACs object to these demands, as many had expected. Enthusiasm for making a good show at parade continued unabated, and when the second WAAC training camp was opened at Daytona Beach, Florida, "an order had to be issued prohibiting WAACs from drilling by flashlight."[18]

As WAAC creativity was shown in the selection of a cavalry post as the first training camp, so was the second location an inspired choice. Daytona Beach was dying in the 1940s, because wartime rationing of tires and gas brought an abrupt halt to tourism. It was a perfect match between the military, which needed vacant space and a cooperative attitude, and a town desperate for people bringing dollars. "You can find the Fifth Avenue Gown Shop," wrote a reporter, "but you won't find any gowns inside. Instead, you'll find a crowded classroom, a WAAC teacher and a couple of hundred WAAC students."[19]

Classrooms and barracks had no distinction in the total-training atmosphere of boot camp. Shined shoes and latrine inspection were just as vital as good grades in class. However, despite the advantages of Fort Des Moines as a setting, there soon developed a critical shortage of barrack space. "The result was that even before the first day of the training, the Army had arranged to take over three hotels in the city of Des Moines and three buildings on the beautiful campus of Drake University."[20] Daytona Beach had worse housing problems; women lived the first few days in a tent city and returned there again at the end of training for out-processing. After induction, the four-week basic training course held 7,000 women in a cantonment area. Then (as at Fort Des Moines), they were considered trustworthy enough to live without total supervision while attending their specialist schools and were moved to hotels and apartment houses. Military discipline was nonetheless maintained as rigidly as possible in these locations. Beds might not be regulation size, but they were religiously checked; there were closets instead of footlockers, but WAACs arranged their possessions in them to appear as much as possible as though they were on post. Whether in quarters or in class, WAACs were under constant military discipline.

Military regulation was not exactly the standard, however, when it came to the inclusion of sex education in GI Jane's curriculum. The course outline prepared by the Surgeon General "after a rewriting by Director Hobby's office, sounded more like a moral than a medical discourse . . . Venereal disease was 'a national menace'; illegitimate pregnancy 'a personal tragedy'; . . . and as for abortion, 'no woman should resort to this.' There was absolutely no reference to prophylaxis except to say that . . . [it] was 'neither effective or practicable.'"21

It was Hobby's deliberate policy to maintain traditional double standards for her women, rejecting arguments for a "single standard" offered by some male officials, but even without such indoctrination these first WAACs were very aware that much of the public and even the military was skeptical about their worth and about whether women could be trained as soldiers. A strong desire to prove these doubters wrong was the fundamental drive behind their drilling by flashlight and studying under EXIT lights. Reporters trailed them about in the early days, and when the stories were favorable—as when *Life*, the mass magazine with the largest readership in America at the time, concluded that "you'll find no inattention, hear no grumbling . . . you'll find instead an enthusiasm which is contagious, and great pride"22—then they felt their efforts justified.

By the time the Daytona Beach facility opened, there was distinctly less media attention, and when the third WAAC training center began at Fort Oglethorpe, Georgia, in the spring of 1943 (and all officer schooling was transferred there), it was clearly non-news, and almost nothing was written. More than 60,000 women had graduated from boot camp, gone through a variety of specialist schools, and, with a thorough grounding in all aspects of their jobs, were hard at work. Military curriculum for women had proven itself.

The Navy set out on a rather different course in training WAVES. With Naval bases filled to capacity by men, and given WAAC experience with overcrowding, it was natural that WAVES Commander Mildred McAfee, an academic by background, looked to colleges from the beginning. Campuses were increasingly empty, as male students were drafted and female students found wartime wages more attractive than study. The first WAVES officers were trained at prestigious Smith College in Massachusetts, while enlisted women were sent to the somewhat more plebian state universities of Indiana and Wisconsin. The trend continued; soon WAVES were training at Mount Holyoke in Massachusetts, New York's Hunter College, Oklahoma A&M, Georgia State College for Women, Iowa State Teachers College, and others. The technical schools that WAVES attended after basic were spread all over the map and generally were not college-based. WAVES got training at Naval institutions from the Great Lakes to Pensacola and from Lakehurst, New Jersey, to San Pedro, California. The giant Naval hospitals at Bethesda, Maryland, and San Diego, California, also trained WAVES as technicians. Some lucky ones were chosen for advanced courses at Harvard Business School; others went to MIT and UCLA for aeronautical engineering. About 100 learned Japanese at the University of Colorado. Though WAVES drilled and marched like WACs, in many ways their college-based experience was quite different from that of Army women.

The other Naval branches did not follow McAfee's policy in this area. After a few months of experimentation in training with WAVES, the Marines announced an independent course: Their women would have a "tougher training course"[23] at the well-known Marine boot camp of Camp LeJeune, North Carolina. Classes of 525, with a new one starting every two weeks, would undergo six weeks of basic training in which "they will receive instruction and exercises similar to that given men. In addition, they will be shown all phases of Marine combat training to give them a better understanding of their tasks."[24] Less cerebral than the Navy's McAfee, director Major Ruth Cheney Streeter saw her Marines fire antiaircraft guns and drop from parachute towers.

It was the Coast Guard, however, that truly made history in training women. "Tradition took a trimming today," the New York Times reported on December 29, 1942, "as thirteen women sailed into the portals of the United States Coast Guard Academy. For the first time in American martial history a government military institution swung open its doors to women students."[25] Twelve of the 13 were WAVES who resigned their commissions for this better opportunity in the Coast Guard.

Although there were still some limitations, Coast Guard training gave women far more of a coed experience than that of any other service. While WAVES officer candidates were cloistered in semicivilian educational settings at women's colleges, their counterparts in the Coast Guard went to school with men.

Officer candidates for the SPARS train along with Coast Guard cadets at the U.S. Coast Guard Academy, New London, Connecticut . . . Cadet barracks have been bisected . . . separating SPAR quarters from those of cadets . . . The SPARS have their own lectures and their own drills, but their life is cadet life . . . SPARS go down to the sea in ships, but it's mainly for morale purposes and to teach them . . . Coast Guard cutters take them on occasional training runs, but never very far out. They learn to handle lifeboats, too.[26]

Enlisted SPARS, of course, did not go to the academy. Their boot camp at Palm Beach, Florida, and their specialist schools held to the traditional model of single-sex training. They would be led, however, by officers who had set an important precedent.

WAFS trained themselves—and paid dearly for the privilege. They learned to fly at their own expense, and once they passed the rigorous requirements for entry, went only to a four-week course in Army methods. WASPs, though they had to make a considerable financial investment to achieve enough flying hours to qualify, did then receive further training.

In "a regimented 22½ weeks" at Avenger Field, Texas, WASP trainees were "on the go from 6:15 in the morning till 10:00 at night."[27] They drilled and did calisthenics; they went to classes and flew (including night-flying assignments). Their course was "a stepped-up version of the nine-month course developed for male aviation cadets." Except for formation flying and gunnery, they learned "everything that regular Army pilots master."[28]

Training conditions were difficult and dangerous. To begin with, because of restrictions on civilian flying, many women had not actually been in the air for over a year and were understandably nervous about doing well. As civilians, they had seldom flown except in good weather and under good conditions, and some found actual military flying a shock—especially in the Texas skies over air bases crowded with trainees. "The air was full of ships," said one. "Not only our own planes were flying at all altitudes, . . . but also planes from Ellington Field. It was fairly certain that when you emerged from some violent maneuver and saw a lot of dark specks, those weren't spots before your eyes—those were airplanes!"[29]

WASP trainees "went through the usual stalls, loops, spins, lazy-eights, snap rolls, pylon-eights, and chandelles, and they had to be able to recover from any position."[30] They also learned instrument flying and radio use. The latter was new to most, for radios were not commonly used in civilian flying prior to the war. Radio failure occurred often enough that substitute coding had been worked out: "If the tower calls and you don't answer, then he comes back with this . . . 'If you can read me, rock your wings.'" One trainee whose radio was out saw that air traffic was piling up behind her; "she was growing frantic . . . She yelled into the transmitter, 'Houston tower from Army 335. If you can read me, rock the tower.'"[31]

Occasional boners aside, WASP trainees did well—or they washed out. WASP trainee failure rate was comparable to that of male cadets. In 1943, 26% of WASPS and 25% of male cadets were eliminated from their programs; in 1944, because only students with lower qualifications were available, the washout rate rose to 47% for WASPs and 55% for men.[32]

Though ostensibly civilians, WASP trainees were held to high standards and military discipline as strict as any, for their leadership was even more wary of the potential for damage if one of their women messed up.

With variations from the simplistic course in paperwork for WAFS to SPAR officer candidates who trained at the Coast Guard Academy itself, the military found ways of effectively educating female personnel. It is to the credit of Oveta Culp Hobby that this was so, for there were many who would have put the WAAC directly to work at menial jobs, traditional women's jobs. These people did not understand, as Hobby did, what a travesty it would have been to put women with such high credentials and abilities to work in kitchens and laundries—they did not quite realize that such bright, ambitious women existed. A debt is owed to Director Hobby and the first male instructors who had faith in women and taught those women to teach others.* They opened an important educational opportunity that for all of history had been a totally male reserve.

---

* Particular praise should go to the first commandant at Fort Des Moines, whose name, appropriately, was Colonel Don Faith.

Most educators and psychologists believed that one area in which women would encounter more difficulty than men in adjusting to military life would be the loss of privacy. Girls were more likely than boys to have had their own rooms at home and to have enjoyed the self-expression of decorating them. Girls were less often involved in team sports; they were more likely to have a few close friends, while boys were expected to be more an anonymous part of a gang. In many subtle ways, girls were prepared from birth to accustom themselves to the solitude of housework. Without delving into all of these reasons, it was a given among the public that women would have a hard time with the loss of individuality that barrack life required.*

Some did. One WAAC, on her first weekend liberty from Fort Des Moines, rented a hotel room and sat alone in it all weekend, enjoying her privacy. When Jane Pollock was transferred from boot camp barracks to a specialist school hotel, she enthused, "I simply cannot describe the joy of having a bathroom and being able to go in and close the door!"[33] Even worse than the loss of personal space, she thought, was the loss of one's very personal being: "It's bad enough having your bed and everything you own scrutinized, but you can feel impersonal about that compared to the way you feel when it's *you* that's being peered at."[34]

But she and thousands of other women adjusted well to the loss of privacy and the regimentation. "Barracks life," said one Marine, "taught me one big lesson—cooperation. I can be tossed in with any group of women anywhere now—and live pleasantly with them."[35] There was virtually none of the fighting or malicious behavior that critics had predicted.

An important part of the adjustment was learning to mock the military's ways while yet scrupulously complying; learning the value of an ironic smile. Women adopted the mentality of girls at Scout camp—a cheerful, getting-on-with-the-job compliance that still left room for shared griping and occasional mischief. One typified the attitude when she reported that Army beds "can be made three ways":

the white way, the brown way, the pie-bed way. Brown is for weekdays—square corners, a 6-inch space from top of bed to blanket—the blanket covers the pillow.

---

* Famous psychologist William Menninger was a Brigadier General during the war. He pointed out that the WAC had a genuine problem with a public that did not know what it viewed as proper behavior for women. "The approved feminine role," he pointed out, was "a passive and dependent one," while "at the same time the modern girl child in America is not taught to be passive [and] dependent." Treadwell, *The Women's Army Corps*, p. 623.

White is for Saturday inspection—square corners, a 6-inch space, meticulously measured with the GI toothbrush (exactly 6 inches), and a great deal of hocus-pocus with the pillow and the top sheet. Pie bed is the bed your companions playfully make for you. It's a mess.[36]

When allowed some individuality, as for the paramilitary WASPs, women expressed themselves, but their quarters still retained evidence of their work and the commitment that they had made to the war. Barracks became a mix that accurately mirrored the mixed status of WASPs. Though officially civilians, WASPs lived as junior officers when at their assigned bases, paying for their meals and rooms. There, "over each GI cot is a silken coverlet. There are lacy pillows. Window curtains run to the distinctly distaff side. Almost every room, however, shows the traces of serious work. There are maps and charts—no pin-up boys—on the walls. There are a few modern novels . . . but there are more text books on weather, flying, and artillery."[37]

Navy housing went its own way in a different direction. Commander McAfee, with her elitist Seven Sisters college background, was accustomed to dealing with young women's residences and had developed definite views. Holding out for at least compartmentalization of bunks, she insisted that some privacy was essential to female mental health. "There are certain niceties it would be lovely for men to have, too," she said, "but if women don't have them their efficiency is jeopardized."[38]

She made life as comfortable as possible for her WAVES. Officers at Atlanta Naval Air Station, for instance, had maid service; enlisted women kept their own rooms, but "Negro cleaning women . . . attend to the recreation rooms and for a small fee provide 24-hour laundry service."[39] WAVES were also allowed to entertain men in barrack recreation rooms, with McAfee saying, "It usually takes two to achieve recreation."[40]

Weekend dates that were at least semiofficially arranged by the military were common. The Daytona Beach WAC camp on Saturday nights attracted male soldiers from posts as far as 150 miles away. Despite early fears, such mixing brought no riotous behavior, but simply "thousands of young men and women who quite naturally enjoyed one another's company."[41] Many civilians whose children had gone to war went out of their way to welcome the troops assigned to their hometowns. The first WAACs back at Fort Des Moines found immediately that "girls on the street are treated respectfully and hospitably."[42] Everywhere they went, military women found that local women organized teas and dances for them; invited them into their homes for relief from the tedium of barrack life; proudly conducted them on tours of local sights.

One young woman wrote of an elderly Tennessee couple who shared their gas ration, taking a WAC group out for a Sunday drive. Since neither "would ever see eighty again and the man's head and hands were none too steady," she, as a Motor Corps member, offered to drive. "Politely, I was put in my place.

Lookout Mountain was no place for a woman driver. The mountain," she said, "is beautiful, I've been told. Someday I shall see it . . . After we were safely back, one of the girls remarked that we would have been better off with a drunken sailor; she was darned right! One of us might have conked the sailor and taken the wheel."[43]

While Sunday dinner invitations were always appreciated, women had relatively few complaints about military chow. The loudest complaint was at the beginning, when WAACs made clear their unhappiness with the lady-luncheon type of food the Army had arranged especially for them. Their calorie count was soon adjusted upwards to match their active lives.

There were no shortages at chow, for the military got more and better food than civilians, who were forced to ration. At one Naval installation, a reporter wrote that in the mess hall, "where Wave officers eat all of their meals with men officers, meals are definitely prewar for us civilians—succulent friend chicken, hot biscuits, and as many pats of butter as we butter-starved reporters could spread."[44]

Jane Pollock's WAAC diary every 10 pages or so made reference to an especially good meal in the mess hall, nice boxes from home, going out in the evening to restaurants, or enjoying a treat in the day room. A typical entry: "Barbara . . . invited me after this party to another one in her squad-room, and we had a regular . . . feast from S.S. Pierce, flavored with other good things from Oregon that another girl in the same room had. The meals are so good and I eat so much at them that I wasn't very hungry, but it was fun."[45] Margaret Flint, another WAAC who wrote of her experience, had been unemployed before enlisting and was so economically depressed and underweight that she stayed in bed to gain the 105-pound minimum the Army required. After a few months in the military, however, she had to worry about overweight. That some of her colleagues followed a similar course was clear by 1944, when the WAC adopted new exercise regimens and low-calorie diets to aid weight reduction.

The food was good and plentiful, a circumstance perhaps not unrelated to the fact that, at least in the WAC, it was usually cooked by other women. To cope with early demands that women take over all Army mess duties, War Department policy "limited WAC food-service assignments to the maintenance of WAC messes."[46] The official reasoning was that thus women's units would be self-sustaining, with all essential functions capable of being carried out. Since providing food was one of those essentials, WACs ate food cooked by other WACs—the cooks that male officers had requested in vain.

There was more good news in regard to chow; despite attractive food and hearty appetites, the military announced it saved money in serving women. An amazingly detailed investigation towards the end of the war claimed that a WAC's "daintier appetite" would "save the Army $2,700,000 on its yearly food bill . . . The average WAC can be adequately fed on 650 calories per day less than her brother soldier." (Even so, WACs ate 600 calories per day more than was needed by "moderately active women.") Other dietary differences between the sexes were noted: Army women preferred salad oil, whereas men chose mayonnaise; WACs took just one egg at breakfast and ate only half as much sausage; the average WAC ate 50% less cereal and preferred fruit to pastry for dessert. She even drank 25% less coffee.[47]

If there were relatively few complaints about the quantity and quality of the food, the atmosphere in which it was served usually did leave something to be desired. While officer messes could be quite pleasant, the majority of women ate three meals a day from the newly designed aluminum trays, "conveniently divided into compartments." They usually sat on hard benches at long tables and were never free from supervision and regimentation. "After mess," wrote one diner, "I elbowed my way to the door, where three oversized garbage cans stood. Carefully, I dumped liquids into one can, the solids into another, and stray papers into a third . . . and was happily exiting when one of the KP . . . detail called me back. I had thrown some of the solids into the liquids. Penalty: I had to dish it out by hand."[48]

There was the bad and the good, the significant and the trivial. That was simply life in the camps—and a new life-style for women.

SOURCE NOTES

1. Pollock, *Yes, Ma'am!*, p. 46.
2. Vera Clay, "Newsweek Synthetic Waac Samples Six-Day Slice of Training Routine," *Newsweek* (July 5, 1943): p. 47.
3. "Major Hobby's WAACs," *Time* (May 25, 1942): p. 72.
4. Blake Clark, "Ladies of the Army," *Reader's Digest* (May 1943): p. 86.
5. "Army's Most Unusual Rookies Processed into WAACs," *The Nation* (July 7, 1942): p. 29.
6. John David Kingsley, "Battle of Manpower," *Current History* (September 1942): p. 30. See also "Wacks War Bonnets," *Newsweek* (June 1, 1942): p. 31; P. Frankau, "Women in Uniform," *New York Times Magazine* (March 21, 1943): p. 61; "Our Girls in Uniform," *Ladies Home Journal* (January 1943), p. 63.
7. Peters, *American Mercury*, p. 296.
8. "Decking a Wave," *Business Week* (October 3, 1942): p. 90.
9. "Devil Dames," p. 37.
10. Marjorie Kumler, "They've Done It Again!" *Ladies Home Journal* (March 1944): p. 29.
11. Pollock, *Yes, Ma'am!*, p. 109.
12. Ibid., p. 77.

13. Clay, "Newsweek Synthetic Waac," p. 47; see also "WAACs Get Underway," *New York Times Magazine* (July 26, 1942): p. 8.
14. "Meet Officer Candidate Mary Johnston," p. 65.
15. Pollock, *Yes, Ma'am!*, p. 119.
16. "They Work Too Hard," *Time* (August 24, 1942): p. 59.
17. "Meet Officer Candidate Mary Johnston," p. 65.
18. Clark, "Ladies of the Army," p. 86.
19. Octavus Roy Cohen, "Municipal Love Affair; Daytona Beach Takes the WAACs to Its Heart," *Collier's* (May 29, 1943): p. 14.
20. ———, "She's in the Army Now," *Collier's* (September 5, 1942): p. 16.
21. Treadwell, *Women's Army Corps*, p. 617.
22. Cohen, "She's in the Army Now," p. 16.
23. "Toughening Up the Women Marines," *New York Times Magazine* (June 20, 1943): p. 12.
24. Ibid.
25. "Coast Guard Halls Fall to the SPARS" *New York Times* (December 29, 1942): p. 16; see also "SPARS: Women's Reserve of the U.S. Coast Guard Reserve," *Education for Victory* vol. 1 (January 15, 1943): p. 27.
26. Bradley, "Women in Uniform," p. 445.
27. "Girl Pilots," *Life* (July 19, 1943): p. 73; see also J. Arthur, "Wings for the Working Girl," *Flying* (December 1942): p. 41.
28. Ibid.
29. Kumler, "They've Done It Again!," p. 167.
30. Boom, "Women in the AAF," p. 531.
31. Kumler, "They've Done It Again!," p. 168.
32. Boom, "Women in the AAF," p. 531.
33. Pollock, *Yes, Ma'am!*, p. 124.
34. Ibid., p. 23.
35. Eleanor Lake, "A Smarter GI Jane Comes Home," *Reader's Digest* (Condensed from *Glamour*) (September 1946): p. 35.
36. Clay, "Newsweek Synthetic Waac," p. 47
37. John Stuart, "The WASP," *Flying* (January 1944): p. 163.
38. "Miss Mac," *Time* (March 12, 1945): p. 23.
39. Vera Clay, "Bounding Waves," *Newsweek* (November 1, 1943): p. 48.
40. "Miss Mac," p. 23. See also Joan Angel, *Angel of the Navy* (New York: Hastings House, 1943).
41. Cohen, "Municipal Love Affair," p. 14.
42. "Lady's a Soldier," *Collier's* (October 10, 1942): p. 34.
43. Margaret Flint, *Dress Right, Dress: The Autobiography of a WAC* (New York: Dodd, Mead & Co., 1943), p. 113.
44. Clay, "Bounding Waves," p. 46.
45. Pollock, *Yes, Ma'am!*, p. 46–47.

46. Boom, "Women in the AAF," p. 511.
47. "WAC's Daintier Appetite to Save Army $2,700,000," *Science News Letter* (January 20, 1945): p. 41.
48. Clay, "Newsweek Synthetic Waac," p. 47.

5

WHAT GI JANE LEARNED

WAAC diarist Jane Pollock was surprised to find that, far from lamenting her loss of individuality, she was instead rather relieved to be in a position in which all decisions and responsibilities could be shifted to superiors. She viewed her time in the Army as a kind of mental vacation, one that she thought all civilians could benefit from at times during their lives. "For the duration," she wrote in a neat philosophical summary, "we don't have to struggle with our destinies, because everything reposes in the lap of G.Hq."[1]

It was an interesting ambivalence; military women were both more responsible and less so, in different senses. On the one hand, they did give up individual decision making in everything from what shoes to wear and what time to go to bed to what work they did and whether they did it in Africa or Atlanta—but despite this seeming abdication, many women cited responsibility as the very first thing they had learned from their military experience.

Outsiders cited that, too, for often the first thing they noticed about a young woman who had joined the military was that the experience had made her more mature, more self-sufficient, more responsible. A *Ladies Home Journal* article exemplified this, saying:

> *When Mary came home, it was the Johnston's faithful maid who got the first impact of what had happened to the daughter of the household . . . "I went in to straighten Miss Mary's room . . . and unpack her suitcase and see what needed washing and mending . . . You could have knocked me over with a feather—her bed was made . . . and her suitcase was unpacked and . . . everything was in the right drawer."*[2]

The change in Mary and other women came from a military system that stressed over and over again that little things meant a lot; that every cog was necessary to the wheel; that every person had a part to play and must play it responsibly for the whole to succeed. It was a system of thought that did not end when classes did; it went on every day as women learned to take responsibility in totally new jobs, in work that came in infinite variety.

Though at first the WAAC had been discussed in terms of just a few jobs, by the time it was only a bit more than a year old women were serving in or being prepared for 401 of the Army's 625 occupational categories.[3] They were working all over the world at more than 225 Army posts.[4]

As they would go into many types of work, so they came from many. WAAC Margaret Flint wrote that she couldn't "imagine circumstances under which one would meet and know at close range a more varied assortment of women."

One is a colored dental surgeon of many years' experience. I have mentioned the judge with whom I played KP. I've come in contact with several lawyers, many more teachers and nurses, and newspaper women, one of whom has also been a scenario writer in Hollywood. There are scores of librarians, secretaries, clerks and waitresses . . . There are debutantes . . . I know two girls who were employed breaking eggs in a dehydrating plant.[5]

In the Army, these egg breakers might do anything from raising carrier pigeons for the Signal Corps to packing parachutes or printing pictures. The majority of women, of course, would work in that clerical area that was uppermost in Congressional minds when they thought of jobs that women did better than men—even in the progressive Army Air Force, about half of all Air WACs were in office jobs. Traditional though the field was, however, this new setting made the work new and interesting. Though one might still be typing or talking on the phone, it was entirely different from work back in the old hometown. There were colleagues with backgrounds vastly different from one's own, and most of all, the subject matter was entirely new to women.

They may have been stereotypical phone operators, for example, but WACs assigned to the War Department Signal Center in Washington had every reason to feel that they were a significant part of the war:

Working around the clock in eight hour shifts, the Wacs share responsibility for the operation of circuits to all parts of the globe. This station, the world's most important communication center, handles more than 10,000,000 words daily. Through the Wacs' hands pass messages destined to change the course of battles, to bring reinforcements to tired GI's in the front lines, to send supplies to places where they are desperately needed . . .

They carry a heavy burden of responsibility, for a message garbled or incorrectly transmitted might cost thousands of lives . . .

Security of military communications is of first importance. The Wacs must be alert at all times to prevent valuable information from falling into the hands of the enemy. They must recognize messages which require censorship and must see that the messages are censored.[6]

While their clerical skills might be old, the work they did was new in every way. There were new procedures to learn, a hugely complex organization and even a new language. For WAVES, especially, Naval nomenclature required relearning language fundamentals, as life ashore emulated life on ship. The office walls were now "bulkheads"; things were "fore" and "aft" instead of front and back; left and right were "port" and "starboard."

Office assignments, too, put even enlisted women into positions of authority and influence over men simply in following their job functions. Women, for example, kept personnel records and ran supply depots in charge of thousands of pieces of equipment. From the time a man entered the military to his out-processing, he was likely to find a woman behind the desk. WAVES, for instance, were involved in every phase of training Naval aviation cadets: "Waves will schedule his flight and log in his flight hours, direct his take-offs and landings, pack, check, and issue his parachute . . . refuel and make minor repairs on his plane, give his pay and make out his allotments . . . and instruct him in mathematics, celestial navigation, instrument flying, and free gunnery."[7]

Mundane though the paperwork often became with its endless rainbow of carbon copies produced from manual typewriters, record-keeping skills were vital to a fighting force that by the end of the war was more than 15,000,000 strong. If these millions of men were to be treated as individuals, then someone simply had to keep the facts straight—billions of facts, recorded individually.

As the Army historically was said to have moved on its stomach, now it moved on paper. Without orders, and the vital information behind the orders; without supplies, and the thousands of purchase orders behind the supplies, an Army simply could not move. All of the typewriter pounding was truly important. Women understood this and were in fact extremely adept at handling multiplicities of detail. Their numbers at headquarters increasingly showed that the brass also understood and appreciated their presence; near the end of the war, more than half of the uniformed personnel in the Washington Navy Department was female. So completely were they accepted that "a small boy, seeing a male ensign on a streetcar, cried, 'Look, mummy, a boy Wave!'"[8]

The WAVES at headquarters personified the vision of Mildred McAfee in creating an elite service of educated women. Their work classifications often called for intelligence testing and security clearances; once qualified, they could be in on the ground floor of exciting changes. In this desperate war, the government was financing research in a number of areas that would lead to a postwar explosion of knowledge. "Some day this war will end," said the head of the War Department's Office of Scientific Research and Development.

Then the electronic devices used so effectively to help end it, will be available for commercial purposes. I wish that I might tell you of the possible uses of these devices. They are marvelous beyond the comprehension of the average person, but I assure you that there will be a need for a large number of skilled men and women to install and operate them for use in every-day life.[9]

Computers that would revolutionize the world of white-collar women were one of those "electronic devices," and the mother of computers was a WAVE,

Grace Hopper. So new was the world of electronics that the very terminology had not yet developed; an article aimed at recruiting SPARS listed among its job classifications "International Business Machine operator." Nor had sex segregation developed in many jobs of the new technological explosion, for they were new to men as well as women. *Time*, for example, thought it necessary to explain to their readers what an air-traffic controller was before going on to say that WAVES had begun doing this work. The work itself was rudimentary compared with what it would become, as illustrated by the WAVE who, "on duty during a thunderstorm, discovered that static was jamming her radio. Quickly she grabbed a pair of code signal lights [and] blinked directions to the planes . . ."[10]

Like this air-traffic controller, thousands of women did work other than clerical—hundreds of types of work in the military's elaborate MOS* system. WACs worked as "chemists, cartographers, geodetic computers, typographers, sanitary inspectors, and even dog trainers."[11] They were mechanics, sheet-metal workers, weather forecasters, electricians, parachute packers, bombsight-maintenance specialists. They operated teletypes, sent up weather balloons, sorted mail, spotted planes, ran motor pools, played in bands. They literally did hundreds of things.

Sometimes they virtually took over a previously male area, as in photography. By October 1943, 400 Air WACs had graduated at Lowry Field near Denver, where they learned "how to develop negatives and print pictures, how to mix their own solutions and repair cameras."[12] At a major North Carolina Marine post, the photography department became "exclusively a woman's domain."[13]

The Signal Corps gave many occupational opportunities to women beyond that of phone operator. At communication schools, "women soldiers worked side by side with men, . . . learning to wind coils, take voltage readings, splice wires, analyze circuits, etc. The instructors were amazed at the ease with which women became accustomed to the intricacies of building and repairing radio sets."[14]

WAVES were even more likely than WACs to be in the occupational specialties of the new technology because of the college backgrounds required of the WAVES. Education didn't necessarily mean a desk job, though. "WAVES report aboard as aviation machinist mates, metalsmiths, instrument workers, gunnery specialists, Link trainer instructors, parachute riggers, control tower operators, aerographer's mates, and 'pigeonmen,'"[15] who worked with birds trained to carry silent messages from ship to shore.

Beyond new technologies, women learned to do older types of work in fields that were new to them. Women were sawyers, carpenters, plumbers, mainte-

---

* Military Occupational Specialty

nance engineers. Typical was an all-woman crew at the Marine's huge camp at New River, North Carolina.

> *Corporal Billie Holcomb, who has . . . an Army sergeant husband in the Aleutians, is boss. In her crew are Electricians Myra Iorg and Thelma Watson . . . Carpenter Ruth Wallick, who . . . says she used to do all the carpentry around home; . . . Plumber Laura Derrickson, who once attended the Fort Wayne Bible Institute, now zealously preaches the doctrine of not throwing anything in the 'heads'—because if one gets stopped up "we'll have to take out that whole doggone bulkhead."* [16]

Though Director Hobby had done an excellent job of making sure that the WAC did not become a service for Army laundries and kitchens, there were, of course, women who worked there. Many cooks and bakers who were unhappy with their lot became much more content, however, when by 1943 it was clear that they generally had a better chance of getting overseas than a woman with a more glamorous MOS. Others saw this work as highly practical experience for after the war, when one might open a bakery or run a restaurant.

And every enlisted WAC at some point made her acquaintance with the kitchen via KP. Little was written about KP; it didn't make an attractive topic for the media, nor was it something the military wished to publicize. But neither does it loom large in memoirs, perhaps because for most women, KP rotation didn't come around often. Jane Pollock had been in the WAAC for several months before her turn came. Then she found it not at all a joke, but an exhausting, dreadful experience. In addition to the time-honored potato peeling, she did other chores, including the washing of 1,200 plates. "The water was literally boiling, and my fingers and knuckles are so sore that I can hardly hold my pen . . . My mind is still clouded with steam."[17]

Though for Pollock this was a rare experience, there were those women whose work took them into kitchen or laundry steam every day. Proportionally, they were far more likely to be black than white. Army officials, after repeated complaints from black organizations that "Negroes were being sent only to cooks and bakers school," agreed that black job assignments were "highly embarrassing";[18] nonetheless, officials continued to believe that any discrimination was more apparent than real and was based solely on the lower test scores of black WACs.

Even as the Army insisted that WAC recruits were desperately needed, "Negro recruiters were not returned to duty," at least in part because their activity was "prejudicial to white recruiting." Indeed, California "intelligence operatives" complained of "a serious situation caused by Negro WAC recruiters who 'appeared in public places giving public speeches.'"[19]

Those black women who did manage to enter the WAC often found themselves faced with attitudes such as that expressed by the Surgeon General's

Office in 1944. While casualties mounted and the media cried for medical aides, that office refused to accept these women "even as ward orderlies," saying that "no suitable assignments exist for such personnel upon completion of training and further accumulation of surplus colored WAC enlisted women . . . would constitute an increasing embarrassment."[20]

Refused an MOS in the military's more skilled areas, most black WACs were assigned to the Army Service Forces, which was the service that provided the rest of the Army with the essentials of life in terms of food to eat and clean clothing to wear. The second-largest employer of black WACs was the Army Air Force, which, as the largest requisitioner of WACs, got their quota of black Air WACs along with the white. There, because "comparatively few Negro women were skilled in clerical and related fields,"[21] they again could expect largely menial work.

Although the major media paid little attention to black women or KP or similar subjects they deemed unnewsworthy, they gave plenty of press to the small percentage of women who were involved in the romantic new field of flying. Since the Army was reluctant to publicize the WASPs, however, attention focused instead on the women behind the men in aviation. Typical was this report of Whiting Field near Pensacola, where

> . . . 40 WAVE "mechs" are charged with the entire responsibility of one flight of 20 planes. Whiting is big. The air is hot and gritty, and scores of bulldozers roll up the dust. But for all that, WAVE "mechs" are on duty there 12 hours a day and seven days a week (with an eighth day off). Almost all of them are plane captains. Assigned to a certain plane, a WAVE develops pride and devotion for it. So confident are the pilots . . . that many . . . [say], "We'd rather take up a plane that has been serviced by a WAVE."[22]

Most "Air WACs" never saw the inside of an airplane. They were simply WACs assigned to the Army Air Force, and they worked with typewriters, not turbines. The AAF's reasoning was that "since men in these skills usually could be found, and since the need for women's clerical skills continued unabated, no significant attempt was made to train women."[23] Even so, the AAF "as an experiment" did staff one entire flight line with WAC mechanics. Eventually there were over 600 women in AAF Airplane Mechanics and another 650 who were classified as Aviation Specialists. Women largely took over the parachute rigging and maintenance on which men's lives depended. Many more worked on planes as sheet-metal workers, welders, woodworkers, etc. Occasionally, WACs went on flights as radio operators, but this was rare; "for every woman flying an army plane, there are about 750 doing a ground job in aviation . . . to 'keep 'em flying.'"[24]

To be a female pilot, therefore, was to be an extremely rare bird. Those 1,074 women who graduated from WASP training had proven themselves repeatedly, and they continued to do so every day they worked. At first, the work of the WAFS* was one simple assignment—ferrying. They were essentially an airborne delivery service, taking planes from the factories where they were built to the air bases where they were needed. "When a ship is delivered, ferry pilots get back to their bases by the fastest means possible. Their transportation priority ranks next to the President's,"[25] wrote *National Geographic*. Sometimes called the homeless WAFS, they flew all over the country, sleeping where they could find hotel space on the way to base and the next job. "After several months of puddle-jumping and haystack-hopping, they have made a log of what towns not to get stuck in."[26]

Though most ferrying trips were for light planes, WASP pilots flew a total of 77 types of aircraft throughout the war. Moreover, the fact that a plane was small was not necessarily a positive for the pilot, for small planes sometimes had no radios for emergency communication and their open cockpits "frequently" meant that WASPs flew in "sub-zero conditions."[27] Nor were they safer; single-engine pursuit planes, for example, crashed about five times as frequently as heavy bombers. WASPs, like male pilots, were faced with "sometimes guarding their own planes at understaffed airfields, sometimes having to improvise refueling facilities."[28] Real life was certainly not the glamor of adventure movies; it was fog and pouring rain, painful sinuses and dizzying ears, frost-bitten fingers, and urinating into a bottle.

The worst difficulty WASPs faced, however, was not with planes, but with people. Their abilities were so unusual that many refused to believe women were capable of doing what WASPs in fact did. The male pilot speaking here reports incredulity that was entirely too typical:

This day the overcast was so deep Orlando had practically knocked off flying. It was the day my Thunderbolt was due . . . The apron sort of filled up with guys who wouldn't admit they were worried, of course. But they did want to see what was coming in through this stuff. Sure enough, a Thunderbolt broke out at about 500 feet, made a smooth turn to the end of the runway and rolled to as pretty a stop . . . as I ever saw . . .

I ran up to the wing and out stepped the teeny-weeniest little girl . . .

"Your plane, captain?" she asked me, and I nodded. She went on, "Needs a little right aileron but I don't think it's serious enough to put in a shim."

Just then the tower man ran up. "Look here, you, why didn't you tell me you were a girl?"

---

* See Chapter 3 for explanations of WAFS/WASP terminology.

"You cleared me in, didn't you, soldier?" and it was a tough voice from a kid like that.
"But if I'd known you were a girl," the tower man started, but she cut him short.
"Listen," she said, . . . Where's that Skytrain" for back up north you told me to hurry up and catch?"29

Despite prejudice and other hardships, women proved so adept at ferrying that, with the availability of more WASP graduates, duties were soon expanded. While WASP head Jackie Cochran referred to many of the dull chores her pilots were assigned as "aerial dishwashing," some of the expanded duties were not only new but also distinctly dangerous.

WASPs piloted planes that towed targets for male gunnery students to shoot at. These antiaircraft artillery units practiced during day and dark, and many of them never knew that the plane at which they fired was flown by a woman. Other WASPs towed gliders that male cadets were learning to fly. Most of these flights occurred over and through ravines in Texas and were dangerously low—WASPs were told not to fly above the height of a windmill. Gliders, of course, had no radios, and again many of these male students were unaware that they were being towed by women. WASPs did "tracking" in which "you fly a prescribed pattern, while batteries sight and follow your moving plane. It's a tedious job at all times, and at night, in the blinding glare of searchlights, a mean one as well. It is also the kind of aerial undertaking at which women shine."30

And there were WASPs who were known as test pilots. They were assigned to the mechanical departments of air bases and tested repaired planes before turning them over to students to fly. They also synchronized the speeds of twin-engine planes, getting the two engines at exactly the same setting so that students would not be confused by engines pulling at different rates. Another of their assignments was to slow-fly any plane that had a new engine to break it in; that meant flying the aircraft for a tedious hour-and-a-half as slowly as it would possibly go without falling out of the sky. These WASPs also checked out planes that students reported as malfunctioning; they deliberately put themselves into spins and other perilous maneuvers to see if the malfunctions might reappear.

WASP test pilots appeared to be military but actually were civilians; beyond them, there were a few civilian women test pilots who worked directly for aircraft manufacturers, testing new planes. Ten of the very best were employed by Grumman Aircraft, each making five or six flights a day. "Men come in here for these jobs who have been flying ten hours a day, six days a week, and they find they can't take so much of this," said a Grumman official. "It's up and down and in and out all day, and that tells. And then there's the element of nervous strain—for after all, these are new ships and anything can happen."31

It did happen to one woman whose controls jammed while she was in the air:

Over her radio telephone she told the tower at the field what had happened and in a minute all of Grumman was gripped by suspense. The chief test pilot . . . got on the telephone and stayed there, suggesting that she try this and try that to free the controls. Nothing worked. Another pilot was sent up to fly alongside her.

"I knew he couldn't do any good, but it was sort of comforting just to have him there," she said.

Teddy had to decide whether to take her parachute and let ninety thousand dollars' worth of navy airplane go to smash, or try for a lopsided landing, at the risk of crashing and burning up with her plane on the field.

She decided to try for the landing, made it and climbed out of the cockpit intact . . .[32]

Those American women who flew with the British ATA* faced all these dangers and more. Enemy aircraft could and did appear over British skies, but women flew unarmed. If they spotted an enemy plane, they were simply expected to get out of sight as soon as possible. Many also flew without radios, and thus were without weather updates in the island's dangerous fog. And if American skies were sometimes crowded, those over southern England were absolutely jammed. Barrage balloons, sailed up by their military sisters below, were designed to ensnare low-flying German planes, but they were equally deadly to mistaken Allies. "Schools of trainees are dotted all over the place. The path may be crossed by an artillery range. Wide detours must be made to avoid . . . convoy routes protected by ack-ack. So, even the shortest journey must be made in a series of zig-zag hops."[33]

About half of all WASPs were assigned to the AAF's Training Command, where some worked in target-towing, glider-towing, and searchlight-tracking of objects while male students practiced their skills unaware of the roles of women. Others, however, were up front and visible as teachers. WASPs assigned to the Training Command taught bombing, strafing, and smoke screening.

Teaching seemed such a natural occupation for women that other services also put women to work teaching men various aspects of flying. WAVES, college-educated and often experienced teachers, learned the rudiments of instrument flying in a 10-week course and then became instructors of men. The Navy wanted women for this who had "a personality that will enable them to teach a class composed entirely of men." They were assured that "such WAVE officers are not resented by male cadets provided they know their field thoroughly and are able to hold the interest of the classes."[34] One young male student summed up the attitude the Navy sought in saying, "A woman taught me to walk. Why shouldn't a woman teach me to fly?"[35]

WAVES taught gunnery as well, finding that "young pilots at first reluctant to learn from women instructors have now changed their minds."[36] Besides

---

* See Chapter Three.

70

pistols, a gunnery teacher had to be "able to fire a shotgun, belt and fire a machine gun, assemble and dismantle arms, and operate and repair synthetic tracers."

Out on the turret range she is the teacher who shows the student how to fire at a moving target on a high-speed range.

This takes courage, too. One station is not likely to forget the time when a student gunner in sudden confusion turned his turret away from the target toward instructors and students . . . The WAVE instructor, with battlefront coolness, ordered him to hold fire and then rushed to the turret to swing his gun . . .[37]

In addition to the uniformed women who taught men military procedures, there were also civilian women in this role. Many were employed as "Link Ladies," who operated the Link trainers used to simulate flying. These women would "sit at a central desk and instruct the pilot by phone, giving instructions for various maneuvers. The pilot's performance is recorded by automatic stylus."[38]

These Link-trainer instructors were not unusual, for the military recognized early on that there were women whose abilities and skills were essential to their success, but who would never volunteer. Lacking a draft, they hired women by the hundreds of thousands as civilian employees. Their numbers grew to be much larger than the number of women in the WACs or WAVES; by June 1943, the Army Air Force alone employed over 150,000 civilian women. They "took care of fur-lined flying suits, repainted radium dials, riveted, and welded";[39] they replaced spark plugs, camouflaged planes, refueled tanks and cleaned up after pilots.

The Corps of Engineers hired over 80,000 civilian women, among them map makers, architects, and engineers; the Chemical Warfare Division employed women to make gas masks, while the Quartermaster Corps used them in more traditional areas as dieticians and seamstresses. The Army desperately sought women among the nation's mere 3,000 psychologists to do "mental testing for local draft boards, . . . planning for re-education of wounded soldiers, particularly the brain-injured; solving special problems connected with mentally deficient women and girls near Army camps . . ."[40]

These civilians often had very good reasons for their failure to enlist. Most, of course, had family obligations that made it impossible to surrender their entire lives to the service; they simply could do no more than be available for the working day at a permanent location. The result, however, inherently made for conflict.

It meant that the WAC corporal who worked all day at a desk next to that of a civilian woman would have her seemingly second-class status endlessly reinforced. The military woman could be assigned to work late or on weekends, but the civilian could not. The military woman could be pulled off the job for

KP, drill, or any number of other tasks, while the civilian woman could control her work assignments (and still reasonably resent her colleague's leaving the job). The civilian woman could attract male interest with fashionable, feminine clothes that the uniformed woman was not permitted to wear. A civilian could date any man she chose, while military women were limited by the officer/enlisted chasm. One general was mystified to lose an excellent WAC secretary as soon as she was eligible for discharge. It turned out that she had been irrevocably angered when arrested for eating out with her officer husband.

The service woman had to submit herself to any number of military stupidities that the civilian did not have to suffer; for instance, during most of the war, "WAC field units operated under the ASF requirement of four hours' weekly repetition of basic courses."[41] This meant that after a long day of work, WACs had to sit in boring classes at night, tiredly restudying what they already knew, while the civilian had her leisure hours free.

Sometimes civilian women were assigned interesting work that many WACs would have much preferred to do. The Corps of Engineers, for example, used few WACs, but sent civilian women to the field for measuring water depths and wave action, charting levee seepage and soil erosion. WACs in the Medical Corps particularly seemed to be discriminated against; while WACs were assigned the most menial work, civilian nurse's aides not only were paid three times as much for half as many hours, but also had officers' privileges. The ultimate insult to WAC devotion came when these civilians were allowed to wear the WAC uniform.

The military woman could have her entire MOS changed and be assigned to a field of work she disliked; she could be transferred anywhere on earth, regardless of her desire to go there. Working among a group of uniformed women whose fate was the same made military capriciousness easier to bear, but being in daily contrast to civilians surely caused many a woman to doubt her sanity when she volunteered.

One of the primary reasons why women volunteered, though, was to have an all-important shot at something that the civilian woman would not get—the chance to go overseas at government expense. Throughout the war, the majority of women in every service expressed a desire for overseas duty, while many in Congress busied themselves with banning such assignments to protect women who did not want protection.

Indeed, the very first officers who arrived in North Africa at Christmas, 1942, had a disastrous trip. Torpedoed one day out of London, a British destroyer rescued some from the burning ship, while others survived in a lifeboat manned by one violently seasick crewman. "The women fished five or six men, one badly injured, from the water," and eventually, filthy and covered with vomit, they arrived in Africa, to be greeted by touchingly worried generals who offered oranges, toothbrushes, and a half-used jar of hand cream. General Marshall, who was leaving on a trip stateside, took a list of their needs and when he found that there was no legal means of replacement, personally bought new clothing.

Had the public known about these perils, it is possible that overseas duty for women might have come to a halt even before it began, but the torpedoing was a military secret and so there was no publicity. Military experts wanted no mention of danger and instead would have pointed out that overseas duty, after all, had been uppermost in the minds of of those WAAC creators who remembered World War I. They understood the need of our forces to have available English-speaking workers with standard U.S. skills and procedural habits.

The first enlisted women, arriving in January 1943, demonstrated immediately the importance of this common background. They sat down to work at North African headquarters on the very afternoon of arrival, "and the next day were still on the job, without let-up, despite the fact that they took less than an hour to rest."[42]

Phone service after WAACs arrived in early 1943 improved "100%." Major General W.B. Smith, "Eisenhower's right-hand man" at headquarters said, "We had to have them. We feel that we cannot get along without them; they work like the devil . . . They don't complain or fuss."[43] Their jobs called for more than just hard work and a good attitude; these switchboard operators had to be multilingual, personally intelligent, and capable of the greatest trust. They handled highly confidential information every day and "proved they can keep their mouths shut."[44]

Nor had their trip across been any restorative pleasure cruise. One, with typical WAAC cheerfulness, described her voyage to Africa:

The first day out we were afraid a submarine would sink us. The second day we were afraid it wouldn't.

With waves breaking over the ship, the skipper told us to be careful, "as water is scarce!" It developed he was referring to fresh water. We could only get two canteenfuls every twenty-four hours, and whatever bathing we did was in cold salt water.

We were never without our Mae Wests . . . We felt dirty, bedraggled, and exhausted the whole way over . . .[45]

WAC units in North Africa learned to live with falling bombs, "going through 40 air raids." Some lived in tents; others in old hotels, while some "shivered in a deserted convent, washing hair, clothes, and persons in helmets of water carried up several flights of stairs."[46] They moved with the troops through North Africa and, in November, on to the invasion of Italy.

Operating from 12–35 miles behind the lines, WACs lived chiefly in tents amid the bombed-out rubble of towns that had, ironically enough, been destroyed by orders that may have passed through their own hands a few months earlier. Rousted out of bed at 6:00 A.M. for calisthenics and allowed a shower once a week, WACs also were required to keep an 8:00 P.M. curfew at night. They got a half-day per week off-duty—but no one ever requested a transfer home.

By May, WAACs were being sent to England in preparation for the D-Day that would come a year later. They, of course, like the millions of male soldiers, knew neither what the grand plan was nor very much about what their personal role was going to be. They simply followed orders and kept quiet. Embarkment areas in the United States impressed on them the seriousness of secrecy; restroom mirrors were imprinted with the words, "If you talk, this woman may die."[47] At a staging area for those bound for England:

> *Personal movements are heavily restricted. Telephoning, even by officers, is out without special permission. So far as his family is concerned the soldier has already left America . . . One girl learned that her mother had died. A lieutenant received a letter from her soldier fiance whom she had not seen in a year and a half. He was on leave in a near-by city and wanted her to call him. She couldn't. Another WAC heard that her brother-in-law had run amuck, had critically wounded her sister and killed their baby. Her company commander soothed her as best she could—but there was no break in the embarkation blackout.[48]*

With German submarines hunting down U.S. convoys for deadly attacks, as few ships as possible were sent. They were packed to "a point that no self-respecting sardine would tolerate. Each voyage is such a tremendous enterprise, so expensive to arrange, that it must pay off in manpower. Eighteen WACs slept in one cabin" that would have been a single-room when the ship was used for pleasure travel. Men aboard were even worse off—they were out on the decks in "incredibly narrow bunks" for "all their sleeping and living."[49]

Like their counterparts in North Africa, the WACs in Britain went straight to work. "Plain secretaries and file clerks" were soon "doing a thousand and one different jobs."

> *Wacs . . . interpret combat films to determine the success of our bombing missions, they make maps, struggle with codes and ciphers and do prisoner-of-war work. Wacs are photographers, radio mechanics, mess sergeants and cooks . . . Wacs plot the missions of Allied as well as hostile aircraft in the secret plotting rooms at Air Force bases.*
>
> *Recently, they've had to plot the precise course of incoming flying bombs, and it is a weird spectacle to see a Wac corporal stand calmly by the plotting table, pushing the small gadget which represents a bomb. When the siren has sounded, the bomb itself is droning overhead and every nonessential G.I. has scrambled for cover. Incidentally, four Wacs were recently awarded the Purple Heart for injuries received in a robot-bomb explosion.[50]*

Often riding a bicycle to and from work, WACs found that their English living quarters could vary greatly. Those in London were generally assigned flats. Others were housed in quickly built "huts heated by a single stove,"[51] and some were assigned to private housing requisitioned by the British government for the emergency. Though life in an old manor house may have sounded luxurious to folks back home, in fact most WACs found their rooms terribly cold and drafty by U.S. standards. Being awakened by screaming sirens and exploding bombs was always a possibility.

Their mission in England complete, WAC units again followed the troops into the Continent after D-Day. "It was in the European theater, where Wacs are now referred to as 'Eisenhower's secret weapon,'" announced the *Saturday Evening Post*, "that our women's army graduated from the experimental stage. Their versatility and their competence have earned them the privilege of crossing the Channel into France . . ."[52]

Halfway around the world, other WACs working in steaming jungles had a different set of problems from those shivering in Europe. Those assigned to the headquarters of the Far East Forces lived in tents and dealt with snakes, fungus and endless heat and rain. Some had to scatter lime around mess tents to control the stench from shallowly buried bodies of enemy dead.

Their commanders feared their capture by Japanese, so women slept in guarded compounds with their personal movement rigidly restricted between quarters and work station. Off-duty entertainment was limited to mass events to which women were escorted by armed guard; the names of any dates had to be given to a WAC officer 24 hours in advance.

Yet women volunteered knowing all this. The general in command of WACs moving into New Guinea, for example, told them that they "would be subject to bombing, it would be the roughest of living conditions, they would probably stand in mud up to their ankles in the mess line, the atabrine line, and to get to the shower."[53]

Even more than in the States, most overseas WACs were assigned to those all-important clerical duties and did their jobs under serious handicaps. Nevertheless, "Wacs in the Far East Forces, sometimes with only a tent for an office, managed to type clean, accurate copy while picking strange insects out of the typewriter and sweltering in the steaming jungles of New Guinea."[54] When finally the Philippines were retaken and American women could move back to where they had been driven from three years earlier, "it was a busy, crowded time," said a male reporter.

There were a million things to pack and take care of and to think about . . . and it was one of those times of moving everything when the male element is utterly at a loss, walking around and kicking at things, taking a drink of water, sighing, plainly hoping that somehow or other things will start packing themselves . . . Leave it to the Junglewacs.[55]

By the end of the war, WACs were serving in every major theater of operation. Commanders who had hesitated to request them because of fears of disciplinary problems soon found their misgivings groundless. Although it was true that some male soldiers hadn't seen American women in years, it was also true that if the leadership saw that the women were treated with the respect and dignity that was due their essential work, then male soldiers behaved themselves and the presence of women became an asset to morale, not a liability.

Housing, which again had been anticipated as a particular problem regarding women, also worked itself out. While in many cases it was less than comfortable, sometimes the opposite was true. Air WACs in India, for example, lived very pleasantly with native labor available to replace them at all menial tasks. Similarly, after Paris, Berlin and other cities were captured, WACs were treated to "luxurious"[56] housing that was an ironic contrast to both the bombed areas around them and to their previous conditions.

But it was her work station and not her barracks that was the focus of a WAC. Being close to the action made that work all the more relevant and imperative. Teletyping a weather report became much more meaningful when a WAC could see that the men who followed it had come back alive; doing geodetic computations of artillery fire made much more sense when she could see, after the battle, that targets had been hit and victories won.

WACs often worked during their off-duty hours, usually heading for the hospital to help out the overburdened women of the Army Nurse Corps. They wrote letters home for soldiers who could not write; they held hands and lit cigarettes and did all of the little things that meant so much to the men and that the nurses did not have time to do. "All over the world," wrote *Reader's Digest*, "front-line Wacs . . . spent much of their free time doing volunteer work in Army hospitals, saw death and disease at close quarters. Yet when they were interrogated, only one percent wanted to go home . . ."[57]

Pauline Abell was one of the WACs who saw the world during the war, and she profiled well how it could change the life of a woman. She lived in Spokane before the war and met her husband there. A regular Army man, he was transferred to Hawaii, and she followed, arriving in time for Pearl Harbor.

This experience as well as the death of her husband . . . led her to volunteer for the WAC . . .

Pauline came to England as an officer in the first separate WAC battalion landing at Glasgow in July, 1943 . . . [She] was taken into the then highly secret organization of the United States Group Control Council for Germany . . .

Now in Berlin, she shares a small private house with two other WAC officers . . . and is usually too tired at night to do more than go home. Pauline is one of the minority of Wacs who want to remain in the Army . . . She knows that winter is going to be grim . . . so she has enrolled for language classes . . . to learn Russian. She wants to get to know more Russian girls and men as she has got to know British and French girls, for she sincerely believes . . . [in] getting to know one another and understand one another.[58]

Pauline found a big world outside Spokane. In seeing it via the WAC, she not only learned new skills and types of work, but also came to understand new places and people. She gained the most valuable sort of knowledge of all—an awareness of the need for better communication and deeper understanding to prevent the millions of cruel deaths that ignorance can cause. This was more than knowledge; it was wisdom.

SOURCE NOTES

1. Pollock, *Yes, Ma'am!*, p. 33.
2. "Meet Officer Candidate Mary Johnston," p. 73.
3. Bradley, "Women in Uniform," p. 451.
4. "WAC Members Serve in 225 Army Posts," *New York Times* (July 21, 1943): p. 18.
5. Flint, *Dress Right, Dress*, pp. 104–5.
6. Edgar F.G. Swasey, "WACS at Work," *Radio News* (February 1945): pp. 35 and 116.
7. "The WAVES," *Flying* (October 1944): p. 158. See also O.M. Plunkett, "The WAVES: Women of the Navy Release Men to Fight at Sea," *Scholastic* (April 19, 1943): p. 60; "Salute to the Women of the Navy," *Travel* (September 1943): p. 20; "WAVES Unbound," *Time* (September 25, 1944): p. 74.
8. Lake, "Smarter GI Jane," p. 34.
9. "Twenty-Five Thousand Women Will be Employed by Armed Forces," *Science News Letter* (March 28, 1942): p. 196; see also Lt. Gen. B. Somervell, "Women at War," *Independent Woman* (November 1942): p. 344.
10. "Rulers of the Air," *Time* (June 21, 1943): p. 68.
11. Boom, "Women in the AAF," p. 517.
12. "Signal Corps WAC," *Radio News* (February 1944): p. 247.
13. "Birthday: The Marine Corps Women's Reserve," *Time* (February 14, 1944): p. 65.
14. "Signal Corps WAC," p. 247.
15. "The WAVES," p. 158.
16. "Birthday," p. 65.
17. Pollock, *Yes, Ma'am!*, p. 140.
18. Treadwell, *Women's Army Corps*, pp. 593–94.
19. Ibid., p. 594.

20. Ibid., p. 595.
21. Boom, "Women in the AAF," p. 519.
22. "The WAVES," p. 159. See also C.N. James, "Womanpower in Airline Maintenance Shops," *Aviation*, (December 1942), p. 126; "Sisters of the Silk," *Independent Woman* (March 1945): p. 70; G. Slack, "Tennessee's Airwomen," *Flying* (May 1943): p. 46; "Women are Welcome in Aviation," *Education for Victory*, vol. 1, no. 31 (June 1, 1943): p. 22.
23. Boom, "Women in the AAF," p. 519.
24. Barbara Selby, "Fifinellas," *Flying* (July 1943): p. 76.
25. Bradley, "Women in Uniform," p. 458.
26. Ibid., p. 457.
27. Boom, "Women in the AAF," p. 532.
28. Ibid.
29. Stuart, "The WASP," p. 73.
30. Margot Roberts, "You Can't Keep Them Down," *Woman's Home Companion* (June 1944): p. 91.
31. Ibid., p. 19.
32. Ibid., p. 91; see also "Hellcat Teasers: America's First Feminine Testers of Combat Fighters," *American Magazine* (March 1944): p. 123.
33. Gower, "ATA Girls," p. 32.
34. Jay Allison, "The Air WAVES," *Flying* (June 1944): p. 57.
35. "Women with Wings," *Scholastic* (April 19–24, 1943): p. 23.
36. "The WAVES," p. 159.
37. Ibid.; see also "Women Instructors Graduated," *Aviation* (April 1943): p. 239.
38. "Link Ladies," *Flying* (August 1943): p. 54.
39. Boom, "Women in the AAF," p. 539.
40. "Twenty-Five Thousand Women," p. 196; see also "Forecast: Fair," *Newsweek* (November 9, 1942): p. 38, on women who worked for the Weather Bureau.
41. Boom, "Women in the AAF," p. 517.
42. "Signal Corps Wac," p. 406.
43. "WACs in North Africa," *New York Times Magazine* (January 23, 1944): p. 17; see also "WACs in Africa," *Collier's* (October 30, 1943): p. 16.
44. Ibid.
45. Harry Irving Phillips, *All-Out Arlene, A Story of the Girls Behind the Boys Behind the Guns* (New York: Doubleday, Doran, & Co., 1943), p. 174.
46. Lake, "Smarter GI Jane," p.35.
47. Doris Fleeson, "650 WACs Defy the Subs," *Woman's Home Companion* (October 1943): p. 21.
48. Ibid.
49. Ibid., p. 62.

50. Ernest O. Hauser, "Those Wonderful G.I. Janes," *Saturday Evening Post* (September 9, 1944): p. 27.
51. "Hobby's Army," *Time* (January 17, 1944): p. 57; see also Frank S. Stuart, "Invasion by Angels," *The Rotarian* (August 1944): p. 14.
52. Hauser, "Those Wonderful G.I. Janes," p. 27.
53. Boom, "Women in the AAF," p. 525, citing George C. Kenney, *General Kenney Reports* (New York: Duell, Sloan and Pearse, 1949), pp. 423–24.
54. Boom, "Women in the AAF," p. 525.
55. Donald Hough, "The Junglewacs," *Saturday Evening Post* (June 2, 1945): p. 51.
56. Treadwell, *Women's Army Corps*, p. 390.
57. Lake, "Smarter GI Jane," p. 68. Women's morale in the Pacific was not as high as that in Europe, partly because of difficult jungle conditions and the ferocity of the Japanese, but also (and probably largely) because General MacArthur was not supportive of WACs in the way that General Eisenhower was. See Treadwell, *The Women's Army Corps*, especially p. 456 ff.
58. "Women of Three Armies," *New York Times Magazine* (September 9, 1945): p. 19.

6

THE PROBLEMS SHE FACED

While Army women were going to Europe and the Far East, those in the other military branches could only look on with envy, for they faced a Congressional ban on service overseas. Some Congressmen had tried to keep WAACs from going there, too. "It is a shocking thing to me," said one back in 1942, that we "who have treated our women with the greatest solicitude" would consider such a thing. "Heaven forbid we should . . . say to them that they shall go any place men go, in view of all the cruelty of war they may face, from the Japs, for example."[1]

Representative Edith N. Rogers replied that women wanted to go; gave a powerful review of women's contributions to past wars and calmed the gentlemen's fears with reasoned responses. It wasn't just the Japanese that they feared, but also our own troops; their questions on female quarters clearly reflected masculine knowledge of potential male behavior. Rogers, a soothing maternal woman, reminded them that "the fact the men are in the Army in uniform is a very great protection."[2]

But sentiment was strong, and when the WAVES formation bill came up a few months later, a ban on overseas duty was included. The Navy, though it led the way with women in World War I, did not fight to include them so fully in this war. Similar restrictions were made on SPARS and Marines. Not until late September 1944—less than a year before the war ended—did the Navy put enough pressure on Congress (and especially chief opponent, Senator David Ignatius Walsh of Massachusetts, who almost single-handedly held up House action) to get a limited modification of the ban.

Naval women were at last allowed to serve outside of the United States, but only in the Western Hemisphere. In practical terms, it meant that some of them might finally see duty in the peaceful Caribbean, Alaska and Hawaii. It was little and it was late; SPARs, for example, had their "overseas" ban lifted about the same time it was announced that no more officer candidates would be accepted and that general recruitment also was at an end. Instead of newspaper headlines about Naval women headed for distant shores, the stories were of demobilization plans. What recruiting continued was concentrated on finding women with medical qualifications to work in hospitals for returning soldiers.

It was a major disappointment to many, for recruiters had continually held out hope that Naval women might also see the world. Mildred McAfee herself, as early as August of 1942 when the WAVES were still in the formation stage, lent credence to the possibility that "women will be sent overseas"[3] in a front-page news story. The fact that most WAVES would never have this dream come true typified to many their experience as underutilized and overprotected units.

Although certainly the military gave thousands of women opportunities they otherwise would never have had, it was nevertheless true that sometimes women's abilities were not used wisely. Underutilization was also a problem for men, but it seemed to reach exaggerated proportions with women. Army investigators found, for example, WACs in California who were being used as babysitters and personal servants. The Corps of Engineers and the Medical Service were especially bad about making "mop commandos" of highly qualified women.

Egregious examples of misuse appear repeatedly in news reports that were intended to flatter and portray women well; the assumption that readers would not object shows that lower status for women was generally accepted. An article on overseas WACs, for example, described them as mostly "business and professional women" who were "handpicked from among thousands of volunteers." Also featured, however, without comment on the waste of ability, was a former journalist who covered the invasion of China and who now was working as "chief cook."[4]

Similarly, Mary McMillin was a WAC stationed at Fort Benning, Georgia; she held the women's world altitude record in parachuting, having jumped from 24,800 feet. Prior to the war, she worked in a daredevil flying circus and specialized in jumps from one plane to another at 2,000 feet. Now, "grounded by the war," a female author wrote complacently, "she is happy to let the men do the jumping these days while she serves as a section leader in the parachute riggers' division."[5]

In January 1945, at nearly the end of the war, this remarkably qualified woman was still packing parachutes for male trainees who had never jumped in their lives. She held the rank of private. Likewise, a WAC with an MA in bacteriology and 12 years of public health experience who did research on wound infections, was a Private First Class. Another with that rank was a former director of a medical laboratory at Yale. Though the female writer notes that "enlisted women were eventually given work of real responsibility," there is no comment on these comparatively low ranks.[6]

Assigning women lower rank than that of men with similar abilities was an old but unacknowledged tradition, dating from the days when the only women in the military were nurses. In this war, Army chief nurses in the Philippines, who held monumental responsibility under horrible conditions, were only lieutenants. In comparison, Army Air Corps member Ronald Reagan spent the war making movies as a captain.

Military leadership acknowledged with their praise of women's work and their repeated requests for more that they appreciated women's abilities, yet reevaluation of rank was not discussed. "The other day," a male reporter wrote of WACs in England, "a headquarters post offered to trade in three male sergeants for two Wac corporals, but found no takers."[7] That two women could out-work three men is not the only point here; it is also that the men were sergeants while the women were corporals and that no one questioned such practices. Injustice was instead viewed as somehow cute. Similarly, the first female physician to enlist in the Marines made headlines when she was also the first enlistee to be promoted—all the way to sergeant. While the *New York Times* did not point out that male doctors and even nurses ordinarily were automatically officers, it did mention that this physician had been working, immediately prior to enlistment, as a secretary in the War Department.[8]

Perhaps one reason why inappropriate ranks were not reviewed was that the leadership of the women's military units found it a personally embarrassing subject. They, too, were under-ranked in comparison with their responsibilities. Oveta Culp Hobby was given no rank at all when the WAAC was first formed; her title was "Director" and she was addressed as "Mrs." When the auxiliary status was dropped and WAAC became WAC, Hobby was sworn in as a colonel. She had by then formed an organization from scratch, solved a multiplicity of complex problems, and taken responsibility for 60,000 women—and was rewarded with a rank equal to men who sometimes commanded no more than 500. Shortly before she resigned in July of 1945, there was talk of promoting Hobby to Brigadier General (with members of both the military and Congress blaming each other for the failure to take this routine move) but she never rose above the rank of colonel.

Hobby did not speak of this, and her modesty set the tone for other women. Mildred McAfee was sworn in as a lieutenant commander, the Navy's equivalent of an Army major, and an even lower rank than Hobby's. When she left the WAVES at the war's end, she was a captain, the Navy's equivalent of an Army colonel, or the same as Hobby.

Both were seriously under-ranked compared with the heads of the SPARS and the women Marines. Dorothy Stratton began her career with the SPARS by transferring from the WAVES. Awarded the rank of commander then and later promoted to captain, she held the same ranks as her old boss, McAfee, who directed almost 10 times as many troops. Ruth Cheney Streeter, who had about twice as many Marines as Stratton had SPARS, began as a major and ended as a colonel, and was still another evidence of the failure of the male brass to think carefully about women's roles and responsibilities.

———

Jackie Cochran and Nancy Love, as heads of the WASP and WAFS, never held military rank at all. Cochran used her maiden name and was addressed as "Miss"; Love used her married name and was "Mrs." Even though they and the women they commanded had both work and living quarters at Army air bases, and even after they were granted uniforms,* WASPs remained in their troublesome paramilitary position.

WASP problems were far greater than simple under-rank or under-use. No other organization faced difficulties like theirs; nowhere else did all the discriminatory attitudes towards women compact themselves comparably. Discrimination ranged from invasions of privacy (with attempts to ground menstruating women) to the public repudiation implied in the lack of a uniform. The very existence of their organization was always tenuous, even though they proved themselves repeatedly.

WASPs were extremely proud of their work and had every right to be, for, especially in the early days, it was an elite corps of the very best. WASPs assigned to the training command at Camp Davis, North Carolina, for example, did not crash their planes at nearly the rate men did; their record was "more than five times safer than that of the home Air Forces as a whole."9 But there was a sad note of defensiveness in their pride, for they understood that others would debate, not congratulate, them. One WASP pilot wrote at bitter length:

> If you don't think we proved our worth, let me purr the following anecdote: On an "L" (liaison) trip, my flight had the same destination as 12 men flying the same type airplane. My flight delivered okay. The men delivered two! Ten little airplanes, in various stages of disintegration, lay along the way. Each little airplane cost you, and me too, somewhere in the neighborhood of $3,000 apiece. And that wasn't an isolated instance.
>
> . . . Before leaving the subject of cost, however, let me remind you that a single pursuit aircraft costs about $100,000. During the past 18 months, until the present writing, the girls ferrying pursuit have had two fatal washouts. On the other hand, during two-thirds of that time (one year), the male squadron on the base where I was stationed had 62 fatal washouts—more than one a week. Even considering the larger number of men ferrying pursuit, computation on the accurate basis of miles flown gives the girls a lower percentage . . . One of the few statistics emanating directly from AAF Headquarters enumerated pilot error percentages a few months ago: .007 per cent for the male pilots, and .001 percent for the WASP . . .10

It was the lack of recognition and the constantly argumentative attitude they were forced to assume that bothered WASPs the most, but their unclear status created practical problems as well. Probably the most serious was their inability to insure themselves in this dangerous work. Because they were not part of the military, they received no hospitalization or life insurance; yet because the work they did was so perilous, private insurance companies refused to accept them.

---

* Few people recognized the uniform, however, because of the lack of publicity on WASPs, and so it did little to clarify their status.

Although the problems that WAACs faced during their paramilitary period were not nearly so serious as those of the WASPs, they too were based on the military's initial unwillingness to clearly and proudly include women. WAACs also were experimental enough that the Army originally wanted them merely as an auxiliary. It was only after the bureaucratic difficulties of dealing with their vaguely defined status proved too complex that they were acknowledged as a real and valued part of the Army. Neat organizational charts and smooth paper-flow made women's case more effectively than any sense of justice.

Several Congressmen had pointed out the logical contradictions of the War Department's auxiliary request in debate on the formation of the WAAC.* The military's *raison d'être* for the new organization was to be able to command women to go anywhere and do any kind of work, yet they were unwilling to grant WAACs benefits equal those given men. WAAC ranks were not standardized with those of the rest of the Army; their pay and pensions were inferior; they did not have free mailing privileges as men did. In many little ways, the Army assumed the inferiority of female troops.

When the WAVE formation bill was introduced, Congress took note of the Army's failure to write enacting regulations that provided the protections for women Congress had been assured would be forthcoming when it passed a knowingly vague WAAC bill. The Naval women's units were therefore given full military status by Congress. The result was that WAVES, SPARS, and Marines received higher pay and better benefits than WAACs.

WAACs by then were well-experienced troops, some of whom were already serving overseas in dangerous areas. It was an outrage that they should receive inferior pay and benefits. More important to the Army, recruitment was damaged by this obvious unfairness. The Army finally asked Congress to rewrite the legislation that created the WAAC. On July 2, 1943, when President Roosevelt signed the bill, women were no longer "auxiliary."

The Army had created a problem for itself as it turned out, for now things did not go as smoothly as planned. Women in the WAAC were expected to routinely reenlist in the WAC, and most did (along with banquets, ceremonies and first anniversary celebrations). A disconcertingly large number, however, did not go along with the Army's plans. Almost 15,000 women, given this opportunity to honorably leave the service, chose to do that. Disappointment and disillusion was apparently a greater problem than public relations people ever indicated to the press. It took the WAC six months after the transformation to regain its former size.

There were lessons to be learned in looking at who reenlisted and who left. Most officers stayed, but women in the ranks were far less likely to do so, presumably feeling that their skills could be put to better use in the civilian

---

* See Chapter Three.

world. The War Department discouraged this thinking by announcing that WAACs who failed to reenlist would be barred from military employment. This ban would seem to indicate both an awareness that WAACs felt unfairly treated compared with civilians doing the same work, as well as a military petulance that was willing to waste valuable skills rather than accept an implication that personnel policies may have been wrong.

Where women felt they were respected and their abilities wisely used (as was the case with Eisenhower's WAACs in North Africa), they reenlisted in droves. Air WACs, who had been well-treated by the Army Air Corps, reenlisted at a rate of 80%.[11] The clear conclusion is that when women were utilized in accordance with their abilities, they continued to be happy to serve (as the new phrase put it) *in* the Army, instead of *with* the Army.

Although few WAACs enlisted for the money, it did bother them that WAVES were paid $50 a month as compared with the base pay of $21 that WAACs earned. The whole area of pay and allotments was a crazy quilt of constantly changing rules that nevertheless maintained a fundamental inequality. While some women were rewarded better than other women, none were treated comparably with men.

From the very time of enlistment, a woman faced problems. She had to be older and better educated than a man, but she would not get all the benefits automatically given to him. Though many women had obligations to financially assist elderly parents and others, women could not make out allotments and have the military, in effect, subsidize their enlistment as men could. In theory Naval women had full status with men and were never considered auxiliaries, and yet the WAVES Commander wrote in 1943 that women in the Navy were "not entitled to receive . . . death gratuity, retirement pay, or pensions . . . The Army and Navy Nurse Corps do have servicemen's benefits . . ."[12]

Like many other areas, the inequity was so buried in complexities and rationalizations that it was best if a woman simply did not think too much about it. Her psychological health was better protected by internally reinforcing the belief that she had volunteered to win a war.

In time the military did address many of these troublesome issues, such as the rules on dating and marriage. At first there were many restrictions in this area, which even some feminists found appropriate. *Independent Woman* wrote, "Imagine what it would do to . . . discipline, to have husband or wife outranking each other!"[13] Only nine months later, however, *Collier's* (surely no leader in women's rights) reported that the Navy had recently "repealed the pointless regulation which forbade the 'social mingling of Wave enlisted personnel and naval officers' . . . It also removed the ban against a Wave marrying a man in the Navy."[14] WACs found that different rules applied in different theaters of war, with practices that directly contradicted War Department policy. The European theater was especially harsh on marriage, even after General Eisenhower discovered the dating problem via complaining letters to *Stars and Stripes* and, after inquiring "what is all this?," said that he wanted "good sense to govern such things."[15]

Black WAC officers, as a minority within a minority, faced an especially bleak social life; since many male black units were commanded by whites, eligible men were seldom to be found in the places where these women were stationed. For most white WACs, however, the situation resolved itself with time. Yet such solutions as were eventually reached were based on sexual distinctions, for class divisions between male officers and enlistees never changed. Liberalizations regarding women were not so much a democratization as a necessity for recruitment; they did not mean philosophical change, but expedience.

Like dating and marriage, questions of military courtesy became overblown issues at the beginning of women's service, but these problems also soon worked themselves out. Etiquette was important in the 1940s, and much ink was devoted to debate on enigmas such as should a female enlisted woman stand at the approach of a male officer and should she give up her seat on the bus to him? There was also that troublesome dilemma of who should open the door.

Form of address was another favorite topic of discussion, which was resolved by two of the organizations in opposite ways: WAC officers were addressed as "Ma'am," but SPARS used "Sir" even when the officer was female. The conclusion finally drawn by most was that all of these questions really did not matter much, and that they remained problems only to those whose objections to military women were actually much more fundamental.

The problem of supplies also had its peculiar applications to women. Quartermasters responsible for feeding, clothing and housing troops understood the historical importance of supplies and that inadequacy could quickly turn victory into defeat. While in this war supplies generally flowed freely, a new organization with a wholly new type of member was bound to encounter unique problems.

Over a year after the WAAC had been organized, *Time*, while reporting the failure of women to fill the 150,000 quota, acknowledged: "But the Army was not ready for even a 58,000 enrollment. There are WAACs, duly sworn in, who still wear civilian clothes because they have no uniforms."[16] Jane Pollock, who was assigned to hotel quarters at Fort Des Moines, wrote of the late arrival of winter uniforms: "Today we were all called in and presented with one pair of leather gloves apiece . . . The heat is on at last, so we are not so desperate . . . The girls from the Fort say it is terribly cold out there and they don't have sweaters yet either. But they do have winter bathrobes—all size 18!"[17]

The Quartermaster Corps did indeed seem to have an initial stubbornness about thinking through the differences between supplying these troops and those of the past. There were wool-in-the-tropics fiascos that happened with men also, but women's problems with the Corps were more than that. Showing totally illogical reasoning, women's uniforms were designed to emphasize femininity, while disregarding how women would function in them. Size 18 bathrobes were only one example of the irony of stressing *vive la difference* while simultaneously ignoring it.

Margaret Flint, who was a WAAC photographer, wrote of the difficulties posed for her by supply. She rode "an Army bicycle, not designed for a lady, and starting off thereon involves a series of contortions. There's the short, narrow skirt . . . there's a bag of bulbs, film, etc., and the white bag with the camera gun and extension. I have no basket yet."[18] The first air-traffic controllers in the WAVES were annoyed to find that not only did their skirt design prevent them from climbing the tower to their jobs, but also provided amusement for males below.

WACs in the South Pacific experienced even more serious problems because of supply. It was the only place in the whole world where "the medical evacuation rate [was] higher for Wacs than for noncombat men; several surveys concluded that . . . deficiencies in uniforms and supplies had a major bearing on the high rate of loss."[19] Despite mud more than a foot deep during the rainy season, "there were no overshoes for women," and their feet developed "jungle rot" because of shoes that "never dried out."[20] Malarial danger required the wearing of pants, but the first WACs to arrive had been issued only one pair—made of wool that caused dermatitis.

Finding the Army unable to supply their needs in the routine way that was done for men, women discovered that they could not even purchase them; "post exchange supplies of any sort for women were extremely scarce. Several large groups had never . . . been able to purchase any sanitary napkins—these also being considered 'nonessential' items."[21] WACs resorted to writing home and asking their families to send needed items, but mail delivery too was undependable.

A woman with the recurring effects of malaria for the rest of her life due to a uniform that was no match for jungle mosquitoes probably also would find that she was treated with skepticism and indifference when she tried to use the veterans' benefits routinely granted to men. Her problems, like those of WASPs, were profoundly serious. Most women, however, never faced such difficulties. Problems of supply became jokes about size 18 bathrobes, and the issues of who dates whom and who salutes first dissolved into the trivialities that they really were when compared to the task of winning a war. Mental health was best preserved by laughing such problems away.

───────────

Mental health (morale in the military lexicon) ranked high on any officer's checklist of problems that troops might face. Demoralization was viewed very seriously; a case can be made that historically it is the ultimate factor in bringing about surrender.

To feel mentally good, one must feel physically good. The military, therefore, viewed health as the first fundamental of morale. Entrance physicals ensured that only the strong were admitted. Enlistees then followed the military's regimented diet and exercise plan. Occasional preventative techniques (such as the mandatory prescription of salt tablets to those stationed in warm climates) were wrong by modern standards, but always they indicated that the military cared about maintaining health.

The results showed that women were at least as strong as men in comparable circumstances. The "annual noneffective rate" for Air WACs at 2.7% was better than that of noncombat men, for the noneffective rate of "all personnel exclusive of battle injuries" was 3.6%.[22] Like the strength shown by the Army Nurse Corps, WACs overseas "proved to be no special problems despite frequent moves necessitated by combat . . ., rain, snow, fog, cold, heat, mud, and humidity, and deprivation of citrus fruit, milk, and other items of normal diet."[23] At home, too, women were at least as healthy as men. A Naval doctor reported that "Waves don't get sick as much as the men . . . The per capita ratio is one sick Wave to four sick men."[24]

As their health record was better, so was women's discipline record—far better, in fact. The military saw discipline as another fundamental of morale, for "good conduct" was absolutely essential to the order, efficiency and camaraderie that made up good morale. Discipline was another problem that had assumed huge dimensions in the minds of many before the WAAC became reality. They envisioned potential WAACs as loose women who would bring endless male brawls, drunken parties and lurid sexuality. Considerable debate during formation of the WAAC centered on questions such as whether discharges for illegitimate pregnancy would be honorable or dishonorable, whether women in their auxiliary status would be subject to court martial and other topics that turned out to be virtually moot.

Instead of the anticipated problems, reporters were soon saying things like, "For every WAAC we saw at a hotel or in a bar . . . we saw 50 who were spending Saturday evening in their barracks busily engaged ironing their shirts."[25] On women's first anniversary in the Marines, Colonel John M. Arthur, their training commander, stated that he "could recall only four serious cases of wrongdoing . . . Two girls went A.W.O.L.; one turned out to be a drunk; one was a thief."[26]

The same was true overseas; "from three whole battalions" in England, marveled *Time*, "only three Janes had gone A.W.O.L."[27] Air WACs in Europe had an offense record "from ten to a hundred and fifty times" better than men, depending on the type of offense. Those that women committed were mostly "minor infractions which could be attributed 'chiefly to tension, exhaustion, or loss of respect for authority.'"[28] Early plans for a women's military police unit never developed, for lack of need.

Indeed, the inclusion of women in the ranks proved a definite boon to morale in all sorts of ways the military thought significant. Women, "with an uncanny ability to scrounge or create cleaning and pressing facilities,"[29] soon were reputed to have the most military appearance. More than one reporter expressed amazement that WACs overseas set water-filled helmets in the sun so that they could bathe with warm water—an idea that seemed never to have occurred to others. The anticipated arrival of WACs in the South Pacific sent dozens of men to line up for haircuts; the barber, whose chair normally sat empty, worked until midnight. "The WACs were like tonic," said a European commander. "They gave men competition on the job and a new interest in social life on the base. The Wac Detachment was the finest morale booster that the base ever had."[30]

Particularly in these overseas locations, WACs did indeed give a new dimension to "social life." Men not only organized entertainments that would not have happened otherwise, they went to great lengths to ensure that women would come and would enjoy themselves. At one jungle outpost where women were prohibited from wearing skirts because of malarial danger, the men even went so far as to build the "only authentic Poudre Room in 10,000 square miles"[31] so that women could change from slacks to skirts for dances. Then, because the hall lacked a restroom, they added a covered passageway to the latrine. Some men were so anxious for female guests at their parties that they hijacked women who actually had intended to go elsewhere.

That 180 WACs received Good Conduct medals in this literal and figurative jungle becomes even more admirable. This sort of social pressure perhaps was some justification for military insistence that female troops be older than male ones; mature behavior and self-discipline on the part of women was even more necessary than the usual double-standard required.

Women, however, were not necessarily dependent on men for good morale; they found their own recreation as well. WACs in England did "more sight-seeing than any other variety of G.I."

Those stationed outside the capital are issued bicycles, on which they cover huge distances whenever they can wrangle a pass, visiting . . . historic places . . . Wacs frequently ask permission to visit a family in their seersucker fatigue dresses and work in the garden . . . Wacs are showered with free tickets to concerts and plays . . . Wacs have lectured to British audiences on a great variety of subjects . . . They mingle with their British hosts at tennis and golf.[32]

Back in their barracks, the behavior of these women was that of the "average young female. They put wet towels in each other's beds, tied knots in pajama legs." Gripes were typical ones about red tape and uniforms "not as cute as the Marines." Their chief complaint was that they didn't immediately get to follow the troops to the Continent. Their "chief wonderment was over the tales from home that WAC recruiting had fallen down. They favored conscription for women. They asked: 'What's the matter with them? Don't they want to live?'"[33]

But not everyone could do what these WACs were doing; not all women could afford to volunteer and of those who did, the vast majority would not be assigned to Europe. If the morale of those women was lower, it was almost always directly related to their inability to stretch themselves as far as they could go.

The public, however, did not generally think of health or discipline as aspects of morale. "Keeping up morale" was traditionally associated in their minds with quite another role for women in cheering men. Indeed, one of the first difficulties the WAAC faced was overcoming public misperceptions that WAACs would be used as "hostesses" and would entertain in "soldier shows." Both terms were commonly used in speculative news articles and lent credence to a widely held historical view of women's role in war being largely that of "camp followers."

Emphasis on models and showgirls in recruiting drives did nothing to discourage this grossly erroneous image, and the Army took far too long to fire the ad agency responsible. By early 1943 when WAACs were arriving in North Africa, leadership acknowledged the harm being done by this false image; among the actions taken was to close down an Algiers show entitled "Swing, Sister Wac, Swing."

Thus from the time a woman made the decision to enlist, she was faced with suspicion and hostility from a significant portion of the public. Some religious leadership, especially Catholic, was quick to speak out in objection when the WAAC was formed. The Bishop of Fall River, Massachusetts, told his flock that "he hoped no Catholic woman would join the WAACs, as it was opposed by 'teachings and principles of the Roman Catholic Church.'" In Rochester, the word went out that the entrance of women into war work constituted "a serious menace to the home and foundation of a true Christian and democratic country." *Commonweal*, a widely read Catholic weekly, wrote that "the amount of war work which she might do no longer signifies, for the soul of our society will already be lost." A Brooklyn church publication was most rabid, stating that the WAAC was "no more than an opening wedge, intended to break down the traditional American and Christian opposition to removing women from the home and to degrade her by bringing back the pagan female goddess of de-sexed, lustful sterility."[34*]

---

* Actually, WAC life was in many ironic ways similar to that of nuns. Both required irreproachable behavior, separation from men, menial work in comparison with skills, an oath of commitment and extraordinary dedication to a cause.

As women entered the military anyway, such virulent opposition faded. By 1945, a special patron medal was struck for Catholic members of the WAC, while SPARS were honored with a mass and breakfast at St. Patrick's Cathedral in New York City. Forgotten was the courage it took earlier for a Catholic woman to ignore her leadership and follow her own conscience.

Many women similarly had to go against the wishes of family and friends to take the crucial step of enlistment. Even families that theoretically were supportive often showed considerable ambivalence. The father of one WAVE said he was proud of his daughter, yet his comments indicate the opposite. "Embarrassed" by the "revolution" in his daughter's life, his confusion seemed to center on his own role, especially in terms of saluting etiquette. An old salt himself, he never attempted to give his daughter the nautical knowledge he passed on to his sons. After she had acquired it on her own, he was still capable of saying—in an article intended to portray her and the WAVES well—that "it annoyed me to have man's domain so ruthlessly invaded by these young snips."[35] Like many others, he clearly thought of women in the military as more cute than essential, a wartime concession whose end would be a relief.

Families often came to these views because a thoughtless press encouraged them, especially in the early days of the war. No matter what the text might say in contradiction, titles alone demonstrated a nonbelief in the seriousness of women's roles. "WAC's Wiles are Womanly" (*Recreation*), "Wacks and Warns in Prospect for Petticoat Army and Navy" (*Newsweek*), "Decking a Wave" (*Business Week*) and "Down to the Sea in Slips" (*Collier's*) were titles scarcely capable of creating positive opinion.

But to be treated as trivial was still preferable to the outright slander that built through 1942 and came to a head in June 1943. From the beginning, the WAAC was faced with a vicious whispering campaign fostered by those who were firm in the apparent belief that if a military woman wasn't a lesbian, she must be a nymphomaniac.

The undercurrent of gossip intensified when WAACs went overseas early in 1943. Its defenders decided to speak out, hoping that washing the dirty linen in public would cleanse it. Representative Edith Nourse Rogers "noted that rumors of Waac immorality had sprung up all over the country and were apparently 'Nazi-inspired.'"

> The worst . . . was the story that one group of Waacs had been guilty of misconduct down to the last member and that several had been sent home pregnant. She investigated and found that of 500 Waacs shipped to North Africa only two had returned. One was indeed pregnant—but she was married.[36]

When New York *Daily News* columnist John O'Donnell wrote that contraceptives and prophylactic equipment were to become Government Issue for WAACs, military leadership and even his media colleagues came down on him like lead. Calling him "flashy" and "pomposterous," *Time* wrote indignantly that "many an honest U.S. newspaperman was outraged" and that O'Donnell's "hatred for Franklin Roosevelt and all his works sometimes leads him to flout the standards of his own profession."[37]

From the Roosevelts on down, officials jumped into the controversy to defend and praise Army women. War Secretary Stimson denied the O'Donnell rumor in the strongest terms as completely false, making it clear that such comments interfered with recruiting and as such constituted aid to the enemy. Colonel Hobby was invited to testify before Congress as to the actual rates of pregnancy and venereal disease, which were lower than that of the civilian population, and the Appropriations Committee report expressed its support of the WAC. Generals Marshall and Arnold added their voices, the latter writing to all commanders that "any lack of respect for the WAC would not be tolerated."[38]

In the end, O'Donnell probably did military women an unintentional favor, for after mid-1943 the tone of reporting on these women is generally much more serious. They, and especially their families, were reassured that Washington's leadership really did value the contributions they were making. Parental fears that daughters had gotten involved with the wrong kind of people were alleviated.

One problem that women usually did not face was slander within the group. "You'd be surprised," wrote Jane Pollock, "at how little malicious gossip there is here. Everybody tells everything about herself . . . but with all these opportunities, there's practically no catty talk. Movies and plays give the wrong impression of women, I think."[39] Other writers confirm her impression, some marveling that women got along together as well as men.

Malignment of the WAC had its greatest effect on recruitment, because those already in the military knew what the facts were, and their morale generally remained good despite public gossip. Much of the credit for their high morale belongs to the female officers. Margaret Flint, more cynical than most diarists, nonetheless wrote: "These lady looeys are good, most of them. They take their work seriously and seem apologetic over the frivolity of one afternoon every other week which they call their own. It strikes me they could do with much more leisure. As a non-com, I'm really much more comfortable."[40] Jane Pollock concisely agreed, saying, "I think our WAAC officers are extraordinary."[41]*

Extraordinary was an apt word. These were special women, admirably well qualified for their positions, who planned carefully and worked hard. They commanded troops of dedicated volunteers eager to show the world what a woman could do. There was no way that such a woman could fail to find solutions to the problems she faced.

---

* The experience of Mary Lee Settle, an American in the British WAAF, was far different. See the last endnote of this chapter for detail.

SOURCE NOTES

1. Representative Joseph P. O'Hara, speaking in debate on WAAC formation. *Congressional Record—House*, 77th Cong., 2nd sess., March 17,
   1942, vol. 88, pt. 2, p. 2604.
2. Ibid., p. 2605. See also "Mrs. Hobby Reports 90% of Members Prefer
   Overseas Duty," *New York Times* (September 9, 1942): p. 18.
3. "Lt. Commander McAfee Sees Possibility Women Will Be Sent Overseas," *New York Times* (August 30, 1942): p. 1.
4. "As Soldiers of Uncle Sam They Ply Their Professional Skills," *Independent Woman* (December 1943): p. 364.
5. Mary Chute, "They Wear the Wings of Paratroopers," *Christian Science
   Monitor* (January 20, 1945): p. 8.
6. Treadwell, *Women's Army Corps*, p. 325.
7. Hauser, "Those Wonderful G.I. Janes," p. 61.
8. "Woman Marine Sergeant" *New York Times* (March 16, 1943): p. 16.
9. Stuart, "The WASP," p. 74.
10. Barbara E. Poole, "Requiem for the WASP," *Flying* (December 1944): p. 55.
11. Boom, "Women in the AAF," p. 514. Many of the remaining 20% were
    rejected by the AAF instead of vice versa, as they failed to repass physical
    exams or were refused reenlistment by commanding officers because of
    records as "troublemakers" or psychological problems.
       See also "WAAC to WAC," *Time* (July 12, 1943): p. 65 and "Waac to
    Wac," *Newsweek* (July 12, 1943): p. 42.
12. Mildred McAfee, "Women's Reserves," *Annals of The American Acad-
    emy of Political Science* (May 1943): p. 153. See also in the same issue of
    this publication, "Benefits to Women's Army Auxiliary Corps," p. 156;
    "Pay of Members of Army and Navy Women's Corps," *Monthly Labor
    Review*, vol. 57 (September 1943) p. 577, and in the same publication,
    "Women in Four Military Services," vol. 58 (June 1944) p. 1247.
13. Martha Strayer, "Washington Round-up," *Independent Woman* (Decem-
    ber 1942): p. 363.
14. Helena Huntington Smith, "Down to the Sea in Slips," *Collier's* (October
    16, 1943): p. 30.
15. Treadwell, *Women's Army Corps*, p. 403.
16. "Stepsister Corps," *Time* (May 10, 1943) p. 55.
17. Pollock, *Yes, Ma'am!* p. 57.
18. Flint, *Dress Right, Dress*, p. 107.
19. Boom, "Women in the AAF," p. 522.
20. Treadwell, *Women's Army Corps*, p. 430.

21. Ibid., p. 443.
22. Ibid., p. 372.
23. Boom, "Women in the AAF," p. 521.
24. Clay, "Bounding Waves," p. 46.
25. Clay, "Newsweek Synthetic Waac," p. 48.
26. "Birthday," p. 65.
27. "Hobby's Army," p. 57.
28. Boom, "Women in the AAF," p. 522. See Treadwell, *Women's Army Corps*, p. 399 for similar statistics.
29. Boom, "Women in the AAF," p. 522.
30. Ibid., citing "Wacs in the European Division, ATC, June 1944–Aug. 1945," in AFSHO files.
31. Hough, "Junglewacs," p. 51.
32. Hauser, "Those Wonderful G.I. Janes," p. 63; see also "WAC's Wiles Are Womanly," *Recreation* (May 1945): p. 108.
33. "Hobby's Army," p. 57.
34. "Catholics vs. WAACs," *Time* (June 13, 1942): p. 39; see also "Women and War," *Commonweal* (March 27, 1942): p. 549.
35. George F. Worts, "My Daughter's Gone to War," *American Magazine* (January 1944): p. 92.
36. "Waac Whispers," *Newsweek* (June 14, 1943): p. 46; see also in the same publication, "Waac Rumors," (June 21, 1943): p. 46. Damage to recruitment was judged serious enough that military intelligence spent much time tracking down the sources of slander. The rumor cited by Rogers was indeed broadcast by Axis radio, but the chief source consistently was found to be gossiping Americans. See Treadwell, *Women's Army Corps*, pp. 200–218.
37. "O'Donnell's Foul," *Time* (June 21, 1943): p. 90.
38. Boom, "Women in the AAF," p. 512.
39. Pollock, *Yes, Ma'am!* p. 57.
40. Flint, *Dress Right, Dress*, p. 45.
41. Pollock, *Yes, Ma'am!* p. 155.

Mary Lee Settle, in *All the Brave Promises: Memories of Aircraft Woman 2nd Class* (New York: Delacorte Press, 1966), found British officers to be much more authoritarian and often unreasonable in their discipline. In a memoir so pervasively sad it becomes painful to read, Settle felt the full effect of the British class system. She was rejected by lower-class enlisted women who viewed her American differences as evidence of snobbishness; once a group of drunken barracks mates attacked her and threw her in the mud. Officers not only did not prevent such morale problems, they created more of their own; a couple, jealous of the attention this American got from men, were especially unfair. They administered punishment so publicly humiliating that male witnesses turned away in embarrassment.

Settle was a volunteer, while many British women were draftees. The fact that they were in the military against their will created huge morale problems American organizations never faced. Settle wrote with particular pathos of a Cockney woman whose attempt to use the military experience to make something of herself was an absolute failure. Proud of a new hairdo, she went into hysterics when her head was shaved because nits were found. Worried about her sickly "Mum" and unable to eat the bad food, she finally hanged herself in the restroom one night. Another woman, a cultured musician, was so profoundly unhappy that she withdrew entirely and no longer spoke. Settle herself ultimately was traumatized when, in dark fog, a plane's whirling propellers decapitated a careless mechanic and sent his head flying at her.

7

THE SKEPTICS CONVERT

While it was true that the problems she faced could be overcome, it did take a while. Initial hostility from military men was real and strong. Inclusion of women was a decision made at the highest levels and imposed on the troops. WAAC advocates among military men were those who were either old enough and high-ranking enough to have observed women in World War I headquarters, or those professional enough to have studied British women during the first two years of the war before the United States entered. The average sergeant felt quite differently.

"We had a war to fight," was the initial view of one Regular Army man, "and war was man's business. Women would only clutter it up."[1] Some in the ranks held these opinions to the war's end. "To many soldiers," wrote the official historian of women in the Army Air Force, "the WAC was only a subject for crude jokes and injudicious remarks."[2] Such vicious "jokes" were well demonstrated by the comment of a colonel observing WASPS at target-towing; when the antiaircraft students sent her target blazing into the North Carolina sea, he was overheard to mumble, "Hell, they missed the girl!"[3]

Despite publicity efforts to counteract hostility, polls showed that negative views continued to be widely held. Six months after the WAAC formation, headquarters judged "the unfavorable nature of soldier opinion" to be so serious that Director Hobby asked for a survey of troop opinion. The results "were more unfavorable than even the worse expectations." Only 25% of men responded affirmatively when asked whether they would like to see a sister join the WAAC; the percentage was similar for girlfriends. A firm "no" was given by 40%, with 35% undecided.[4]

Yet the reasons behind these responses showed that most men were not acting out of hostility towards women; instead, they were trying to protect those that they loved from an experience that they themselves detested. Many also quite reasonably thought that their women could better contribute to the war effort by working in war industries or as civilian government employees unfettered by military regulation. Finally, it should be pointed out that the vast majority of these respondents never actually had seen a WAAC and had only the vaguest idea of the roles intended for these women. Given that, by the end of the war, 15 million men served in the Armed Forces compared with only a few hundred thousand women (most of whom remained in the confines of the United States), it was entirely possible for a man to go through the entire war without ever personally getting to know a military woman.

It was the experience of working closely with women that made all the difference; once that happened, men almost always quickly came around to favorable views. The Army man quoted above who feared the "cluttering" effect of women was asked twice to take command of the WAAC center at Fort Des Moines; he "got out of it both times."

Like most of my contemporaries, I wasn't much impressed by the thought of women in uniform . . .

Today, after watching some 40,000 or more women pass through . . . I've been completely converted . . . I will say that the WAC is a good deal more efficient than many all-male outfits that I could name. There are no better soldiers on earth.

. . . Partly because they are volunteers and mostly because they are women, they have an enormous personal pride and an acute sense of responsibility for the good name of the company . . . You won't find the name of a single WAC on the police blotter of the city of Des Moines. I defy you to duplicate that record in any other city adjacent to a camp where as many as 11,000 troops are stationed.

I was inspecting a barracks one afternoon when I noticed that three beds were made exceptionally well. I called out, "Who made this bed?" There was no answer. I repeated the question, sternly this time. A tight little voice said, "I did, sir." She was a half-pint private, about as big as a minute and scared silly.

I told her, "This is the best piece of bedmaking I ever saw. Is this your bed?" She said reluctantly, "No, sir. I just made it. I like to make beds." I demanded, "Did you make those others, too?" She said in her small voice, not sure whether it was a violation of the rules, "Yes, sir." She had made all three beds, and maybe others, partly because she liked to make beds, but mostly because she wanted the barracks as a whole to pass inspection. I'd like to see you find that spirit in a company of men.[5]

A veteran sergeant who also worked at the Fort Des Moines training center experienced a similar epiphany. "In all the years I've been in," he said, "I never saw a bunch of men rookies that caught on so quick . . . You can't make them complain."[6] One reason why women trainees did so well was their willingness to ask questions. A male instructor of WAVES reported that they took to mechanical studies "like ducks to water. If they are clumsy at first with tools, they are every bit as clumsy with a big needle on [airplane] fabric, and not a bit less adaptable . . . than city men I've seen. Besides, with all the questions they ask, they ought to know everything in half the time!"[7]

Having overcome skepticism in training, women encountered it again when they moved on to work assignments. Navy men were typical in having "their fingers crossed when WAVE tower operators were proposed. They doubted if they could master . . . charts, procedures, meteorological and radio skills . . . were suspicious of how women would bear up under control-tower pressures. But now the Navy is sold . . . [WAVES] will eventually replace 60% of men operators."[8]

Especially in the Washington Naval offices where they came to outnumber male uniformed personnel, WAVES soon made converts of doubters. A Navy Communications Center chief said, "Waves were the only employees I ever had that I didn't have to train on the job. They just reported one morning, sat down and went to work."[9] Admiral Ernest King, Chief of Naval Operations, said on the third anniversary of the WAVES, "they have become an inspiration to all in naval uniform." Though earlier there were Navy men who "bucked and roared at the idea," WAVES had "done so well that . . . efficiency increased in offices where they have replaced men for sea duty."[10]

Like the Washington WAVES, WAACs arriving in North Africa also just sat down and went to work. They found less skepticism and more immediate appreciation there, for the need for the special skills of American women overseas was one of the chief reasons for the WAACs formation. Eisenhower, as Supreme Commander of the Allied Forces, had learned from the British services what women were capable of contributing. "The simple headquarters of a Grant or Lee were gone forever," he said later. "It was scarcely less than criminal to recruit these from needed manpower when great numbers of highly qualified women were available. From the day they first reached us their reputation as an efficient, effective corps continued to grow."[11]

Other overseas brass joined the chorus of praise. Famous Fifth Army Commander Lieutenant General Mark Clark went out of his way to make sure that WACs were awarded medals, and he insisted on their inclusion in postwar occupation units. Allied Air Commander Lieutenant General Eaker declared that WACs "keep more calm than men in emergencies," and that they were "the best photo interpreters . . . keener, and more intelligent than men in this line of work."[12] Speaking of his WAACs in North Africa, a Signal Corps official averred:

They were fast and they were accurate . . . We could have used hundreds more. In fact, had we had enough of them, we could have used them to operate all our fixed communication installations—telephone and telegraph—throughout the rear areas. Every one of these girls released some man for Signal Corps duty up in the combat zones.

. . . Don't tell me a woman can't keep a secret. Why, their own company commander doesn't know where the [switch] board is located, and we've tested the girls again and again.[13]*

These women proved themselves so valuable that when the war was over, the theater held on to its WACs as long as the "military necessity" clause of demobilization policy would allow. In February 1943, less than a year after the WAAC was formed, the Army's big guns were so impressed by women's capabilities that supreme recognition was given "when 16 Waac officers began classes at the Command and General Staff School of the U.S. Army at Fort Leavenworth, the first time that women have been admitted." Leavenworth, of course, was "long reputed to be the toughest military school in the country."[14]

·   ═══════════

The ranks heard this praise with some ambivalence, for it often seemed to implicitly question their ability to measure up. Another convert by 1944, *Time*, wrote, "Old soldiers fear that the busy WACs are on the way to end forever the enlisted soldiers' time-honored practice of 'gold-bricking.'"[15] Though he might smile, the average GI Joe's internal response to such comments couldn't help but be ambivalent. It wasn't merely that women in the military were turning out well; it was also the implication that if her record was good, his must be less than good. Many of the evaluations of women's work seemed valid only if they were compared with men—in a way that reflected poorly on men. It was a role reversal that they found bewildering.

Teenage boys in preflight training at the Atlanta Naval Air Station marched to the "Sound-Off" tune, singing of their WAVE instructors: "The Waves are going to win the war—What the hell are *we* fighting for?"[16] Though their lyrics can be interpreted as admiration for their teachers, at the same time there is more than a hint of resentment. After all, even these youngsters realized that a WAVE was not going to the real war; her chances of dying in combat were extremely

---

* A male American writer early in the war made the same observation on secrecy of British women. "Experience in England," he wrote, "proved quite conclusively that women can keep secrets better than men and that women habitually do not talk about government business as much as their husbands and brothers. It may be because you are habitually secretive, because you are not interested enough in military or naval affairs, because you are not inclined to give enough attention to understand them, or because you have a greater sense of duty than men. I will not argue that out with you, but I will lay on the line that there is less careless talk among women employed on government jobs than among men." See Keith Ayling, *Calling All Women* (New York: Harper and Brothers, 1942), pp. 137-38.

remote, while her students could very possibly end their young lives falling from the sky in a burning plane.

Over and over again, the reason cited for the existence of women's services was "to replace men at desk duty" and "to release men for combat." These were glibly spoken phrases with fatal potential. While many men were eager to get into the action (or said they were), it is only understandable if a man gave a cool welcome to the woman who made his number come up. Considering the deadly implications for men that the women's services represented, it becomes almost surprising that there wasn't more male hostility.

The relationship that developed between men and women in the ranks was much like that of siblings. There was resentment, rivalry and conflict, but there was also support, understanding and pride. Enlisted women and men soon came to see each other as people. It was a relationship that was often new to both sexes. Old behaviors were no longer appropriate: "I defy anyone to feel like a 'femme fatale' in khaki panties,"[17] wrote WAAC Jane Pollock. "Coquette" was replaced by "hail fellow," as she commented perceptively:

> I like so much the comradely feeling one gets from being a part of the army. The men seem to like it, too, because . . . we talk together about our experiences and reactions in a way that wouldn't be possible in civilian life. I was delighted to see that the men don't resent WAACs, but really like and admire us. There's a good feeling between us . . . It's too bad that in ordinary life men and women can't share experience and work the way we do here. We'd be a lot more understanding if we could.[18]

Margaret Flint echoed Pollock's observations. She told of a WAC who on her first day of duty overheard a phone report on herself. "Boy," said the enlistee to his buddy, "youse ought to see de WAAC I got up here. Geez, is she good lookin'! Don't youse wisht youse was up here?" In subsequent calls, she "heard him boasting that his WAAC was a sergeant."[19]

Outside of the work station, these comradely attitudes continued. Romances and serious relationships did develop, of course, but much social time appeared to be devoted to the pursuit of pure fun. Perhaps courting patterns abated because in this highly mobile and deadly war, contact was likely to be fleeting; perhaps it was because military women were more career than marriage minded; perhaps also serious intentions were diminished by the fact that women were more likely to be older and better educated than most of the men they encountered. Again, it is Jane Pollock who most amusingly describes the light-hearted attitude of social life in the ranks. After months in North Africa, she wrote:

> I had an idea I must have terrific appeal . . . , the way I was rushed, I mean. But I jumped to conclusions. These jeeps are so hungry for girls who speak their own language that they will go for a witch if she rides a broom with "USA" on it. We have a couple of [older women who] . . . are both bricks, but rather a strain on

the eyes. Yet they have been in steady demand as dance partners. "Hell, they can walk, talk, and hear in one ear, can't they?" seems to be the attitude of the boys . . .

I got so exhausted I tried to fake a sprained ankle, but the boy who was dancing with me said, "Just support yourself on the one good leg, lady, and I'll take care of everything."

. . . More and more WAACs have been arriving all the time, and the novelty is wearing off, for which I am grateful. The sentiment which marked our early days here was rather embarrassing . . . I've been proposed to by eleven majors, six colonels, fourteen captains, twenty-two lieutenants, so many sergeants and privates that I lost count . . . but there's been a big decline lately.[20]

More than one woman also noted that being in the military sometimes revived the interest of males who had disappeared from her life. Letters arrived from men long forgotten, who seemed now to see these women in a new light. Married women, too, reported that husbands wrote more frequently and were more attentive now that they were aware that their wives were surrounded by other men. In being active and independent, women found new esteem. From the President down to the men in their personal lives, women gained new respect.

Even the WASP—that half-wanted waif, stepsister to the rest of the women's services—achieved some grudging respect. "The WASPs," *Time* wrote in April, 1944, "have shown how to be spectacularly useful. They have flown more than 30,000,000 miles, towing sleeve targets for A.A.F. gunners to shoot at, breaking in new planes, taxiing A.A.F. officials around the country. Their chief chore has been, and still is, delivering new planes . . . They sky-hop from coast to coast."[21]

But the bright springtime of 1943 was not to last; by the cold of winter 1944, the WASP would be dead. They were the first World War II veterans, pushed into this unwanted status even before the war ended.

"In a way," *Time* mused in an October 1944 article that moved back towards earlier ambivalence, "the WASP had asked for it."[22] Like the other women's services and supported by their AAF chief, General Hap Arnold, the WASP "had asked for it" by going to Congress in search of justice. A bill to end their paramilitary status was introduced about the same time that Congress struck the WAAC's auxiliary position; chances looked good for comparable action for the women pilots. The WASP bill failed by just 19 votes on September 30, 1943.

From then on, however, it was downhill for the WASP. As the war looked more winnable, these women's chances of participation in the action decreased. While men were willing to leave many areas of mundane work to the WAC and WAVES and had never objected to giving nursing to the ANC and NNC, the territory that the WASP had encroached on was coveted space. Men expected women to give back the skies.

101

"The Air Force ladies," *Time* continued, "fed up with their civilian status gave their ultimatum. Said Jackie Cochran: The WASPs should get military status or be washed out altogether. As Congress showed no disposition to change its mind, there was no choice . . ."[23] The WASP program would be scheduled for cancellation at the end of 1944. Women would be replaced by men—often men that other women had trained.

Cochran perhaps made a political mistake in not allowing her WASPs to write their representatives in Congress about the issue.[*] She was only following proper protocol in preserving the crucial separation of the military from politics, but she forgot that the WASP was not yet military except in its own mind. While legislators received no letters from their WASP constituents who were most critically affected, the mail did stack up from civilian men who now wanted their jobs. To the minds of many in Congress, the arguments of these male pilots (that they were older and more experienced—which was why they were draft-exempt in the first place) seemed reasonable.

Barbara Poole was one WASP who could have written an excellent letter to Congress. She bitterly spelled out her views as the WASP program wound down to its sad end:

We have spent large sums to train the WASP. Now we are throwing this money away at the demand of a few thousand male pilots who were employed, until recently, in a civilian capacity on Government flight programs. The curtailment of the programs has thrown these pilots out of work. And now they are to get the WASPs' jobs.

. . . This state of affairs is very sad for the pilots, but after all we're running a war, not an employment bureau for disgruntled flyers.

. . . To be blunt, at [our] inception . . . there was a shortage of pilots. Where were the over-age, experienced pilots then? They were instructing . . . or flying . . . making a far better salary . . . with far less work.

. . . When the women first starting flying . . . was there any protest from . . . [them]? Not at all. Flying for their country in a more arduous, lower-salaried capacity didn't interest them—then.[24]

---

[*] Another possible political misjudgment on Cochran's part was the lack of a female sponsor in Congress. Edith Nourse Rogers had mothered the WAAC; Margaret Chase Smith, after her election to the House, looked after the women in the Naval branches; the Nurse Corps had their champion in Frances Bolton. Men in Congress respected the views of women colleagues about women's issues, and the lack of female sponsorship may have been critical. Moreover, because its leadership had deliberately chosen not to publicize the WASP, there was no national support from women's organizations.

This go-it-alone attitude of Cochran's was understandable in a woman of such exceptional personal achievement, but probably was a terrible political mistake. Both Cochran and her chief AAF supporter, Hap Arnold, had celebrity images and received much publicity that individuals in Congress may have quietly resented.

Unhappy though they might have been about it, WASPs were home for Christmas in 1944. They drank their New Year's toasts to an uncertain future. Though they were the first war veterans, they would receive no veterans' benefits,* because, of course, officially they had never been in the military. For this, 37 of them had given their lives.**

"One . . . was known to be one of the most capable pilots, male or female, at her California base. She was . . . a professional pilot with 2,500 hours, the sole support of her family."[25] Long after the war was over, another WASP remembered a friend who was killed when copiloting for a man who had just returned from overseas. Showing off for students, he crashed into a mountain. WASPs had to take up a collection to ship her body home.

Unlike the WASPs, other service women were entitled to veterans' status and postwar benefits. Veterans became a tremendous political power after the war; Congress and a grateful public showered them with very meaningful benefits. But few women seemed to think of themselves as veterans. Men encouraged that view, excluding women from such organizations as the Veterans of Foreign Wars.*** The fact that these women had actually served in the war mattered not. They were relegated to membership in female auxiliaries, together with wives of male veterans.

The Veterans Administration itself found it easy to overlook the relatively few women among millions of men.† While men used the GI Bill of Rights to buy houses, start businesses and go to college, few women availed themselves of these opportunities. Discharge briefings were presumably intended to make women aware of their entitlements, but somehow the message was far from clear. VA counselors did not seek out women, male role models did not seem relevant and veterans organizations excluded them. Many women, accustomed throughout the war to an ambivalent, semiofficial status, became convinced that

---

* When the feminist movement strengthened in the late 1970s, WASPs finally received some belated benefits in an administrative ruling by the Air Force. This simple, but long-postponed, papershuffle probably was mainly a Pentagon response to the WASP's chief Congressional advocate, the powerful and ordinarily conservative Senator Barry Goldwater. He had flown with WASPs during the war and pronounced them "equal to or better than their male counterparts."

** A memorial to them is located at their old base in Sweetwater, Texas.

*** The Carter administration, in response to growing feminism in the late 1970s, tried to pressure the VFW into admitting women veterans on an equal basis, but administration officials were shouted down at the VFW convention.

† The VA did not even have an accurate idea of how many female veterans there were until 1980, when a question on military service was added to the Census.

they were not truly veterans. They did not apply for benefits that could have greatly improved their lives.* As of June 1946, the *New York Times Magazine* reported, "No women veterans' applications for GI house loans have been received in this region . . . None . . . has applied for a GI business loan."[26]

Women were, however, more likely to use the educational benefits. Some 3,000 in the New York area applied for use of the GI bill for college, "but like the men, not all of those who want to go will be able to get into the overcrowded colleges and universities."[27] Indeed, colleges were so packed the first year after the war that "the majority . . . are taking the simple way out, by excluding women entirely."[28] Although women's colleges did not have a postwar crush of applications comparable to other institutions, they did little to reach out to these potential students.

New Jersey College for Women (Rutgers) developed "a program especially designed for Jane's plans and pocketbook," but on the whole *Time* was right in its assessment that "there has been much ado about the postwar schooling of G.I. Joes, but very little about the prospects for . . . G.I. Janes."[29] Traditional women's schools seemed to find it more important to adhere to tradition rather than reap the financial bonanza the GI Bill could have meant to them. Despite the unique position of Mildred McAfee as a leader of both military women and female academia, virtually no bridges between the two were built. It is indeed possible that women's colleges viewed the advanced age and worldly experience of veterans as a liability rather than an asset.

A female veteran, though she had lived for the last several years in quarters with other women, was expected to "feel more at ease on larger co-ed campuses,"[30] where she had to compete with men for a space. A minority so small that the media took almost no note of them, one English professor found female veterans to be interesting students who adjusted to their new lives quickly. "Few women have come back to us from the service," he wrote, "but so far, they, too, seem to settle into college life . . . with plenty of vitality."

An ex-Spar came bounding into my office one day and gaily announced her coming marriage. Her war experience had set her up for life. A very plump Wac appeared in a class and sent the students into hysterics with tales about her basic training. A Wave officer who was provoked because she had to remain in Washington throughout the war nevertheless had plenty of interesting stories to tell . . .

---

* One woman, quoted in an article written 40 years after the war was over, was still unaware of her entitlements. "I wanted to go to college, and I saw GIs get those benefits," she said. A VA spokesperson in Florida, where millions of veterans retire, added her observation that women veterans use their hospitalization benefits only as a last resort in dire financial circumstances. "The men tend to feel like it is something they are owed," she said. "The women tend to be more humble and apologetic. They'll say, 'I came here because I couldn't afford to go anywhere else.'"

One Wac has remained something of a puzzle. She has found it hard to write anything for the class because, she said, she had seen so much raw stuff she just did not dare put it down on paper. After her first piece, it was plain that something . . . had happened. It will take time and help to work out these problems which bother her.[31]

Women veterans, like men, also had a theoretical right to their prewar jobs. The Selective Service system ruled that "servicewomen honorably discharged from the military forces are entitled to reemployment in their previous positions if they are able to meet the requirements . . . "[32] It was a right that meant little and was wanted by few. Estimates were that only 25% of servicemen wanted their old jobs back; women were even less likely to exercise reemployment rights, for fewer of them had held good jobs in the first place.

Women had grown in maturity tremendously in the military, and they knew now that they were capable of more than the jobs they clung to during prewar Depression years. SPARS officers, for example, had studied at the elite Coast Guard Academy before taking command of their troops; these women would make "ideal executives."[33] Their director, Captain Dorothy Stratton, and other military leadership worked with national women's organizations to assist in the reorientation of women veterans in official cooperation with the Selective Service System, the Veteran's Administration and the U.S. Employment Service.

Well-intentioned as they were, though, women's leaders did not necessarily see the war experience as a chance for women to expand into male-dominated fields. The limitations of their views are clear in this report of a national meeting on the subject:

All of the speakers stressed the fact that since by far the greater number of servicewomen are doing much the same type of work which they did before entering the service, therefore most of them will be wanting to go back to their old fields, but at better jobs. Relatively few will seek opportunities in the newer and less familiar types of work in which a minority of specially trained women have been engaged. It was also pointed out that since most of the servicewomen have simply continued with familiar types of work, but under the unfamiliar condition of military exigencies and discipline, the training and experience which they have received have served chiefly to polish up their already existing . . . skills.[34]

Their aim was a better place for women, but it would be essentially the same place. For women who had loved being mechanics, control-tower operators, carpenters, photographers and certainly pilots, they offered no hope or support. Such a woman would find mostly isolation, loneliness, and a feeling of freakishness should she continue to seek work in her new field.

But then most women couldn't find jobs that took account of their growth and experience even in traditional fields. A former secretary, who in the military became a disbursing officer responsible for $50 million a month, found no employers who seemed to view this as real money. She was not atypical:

> *In one voice, the girls of the Wac, Waves, Spars and Marines complain that prospective employers completely disregard their two or three years' experience in the services. Some employers even count it against them, the women veterans believe. One veteran reported that when she applied for a position as physiotherapist, at work she had done before and during service, the employing doctor was shocked to learn that she had been in the Army.*
>
> *Two thirds of a group of 150 women veterans who met recently at the New York Veterans Service Center felt that they had been discriminated against by employers. Most had found themselves barred from professional fields in which they had some training in the services.*
>
> *. . . Many of them complain that they cannot live on the wages that are offered. Most clerical jobs start at $25 or $30 a week, far less than service pay plus living expenses.*[35]

Those living expenses came as a shock to women who had become accustomed to the military providing their housing, food and clothing. One SPAR had to face reality within days of dismissal. "I wanted to spend my terminal leave pay on a trip," she said, "but it took all my money just to clothe me. The clothes I bought not only cost too much, but they are made of such shoddy materials they won't last long."[36] Another, a former WAVE, had looked forward longingly to the privacy she envisioned in postbarrack life. Instead, she searched in vain for a place she could afford, "staying with friends, sharing rooms with the baby or sleeping on living room couches. I've been promised one-third of a room in a girls' club for August,"[37] she concluded sadly.

Women veterans needed jobs at decent wages to continue the same standard of living they had in the war, and they knew they deserved those wages. But the business world often had no understanding. "GI Jane, the belle of the military world," *Reader's Digest* observed, "is often a wallflower in civilian life." One WAC, "a ten-cent store clerk before the war," was cited as an example:

> *The Army gave her aptitude tests, sent her to . . . school . . . then shipped her to the Pacific . . . Betsy learned to organize her work in improvised offices in the steaming jungles of New Guinea . . . When her colonel put her in charge of setting up the paper work for a special intelligence office, she did it well . . .*
>
> *Back home, she pinned her discharge emblem proudly on her purse and went to look for a job. She found that the Army's notes on her record meant nothing to civilian employers. She was offered jobs as a waitress, messenger-file clerk and, full circle, a ten-cent store girl.*[38]

There were many employers like the former World War I doughboy who told Betsy that "you can't tell *me* you learned anything in the Army."[39] Their imagination was limited to infantry and artillery; they had never held rank high enough to see the inside of a headquarters office and know the complexity of the work that women did there. Once again, women's best advocates were those men with personal experience. Men who worked with women in the war and who now were civilian employers "almost universally" were "eager to hire" ex-servicewomen. One former Naval chief, setting himself up in the oil business, planned to staff his entire office with ex-WAVES. "They are highly educated, and they have character. Anyone who went through what they did can take it."[40]

But those employers were few, for most male veterans either had not worked with women or were not yet in a hiring position in the civilian world. Few civilians saw that military skills were transferable to the commercial world. If racism was added to this lack of understanding, the odds against black women veterans became very high. Even the government itself took no care to use the skills it had taught at considerable expense; an all-black WAC unit "set a record for speed in mail handling in France,"[41] but it was unlikely that any of these women could go home and realistically expect to be employed at the local post office.

Quite understandably, some saw their personal future as best protected by staying in the military. Private First Class Thelma Giddings, a black, was "representative of this group." She intended never again to work as a maid. "They're just going to have to kick me out of this Army," she declared. "Ever since I was a little girl I wanted to be a soldier. The Wac was made to order for me."[42]

While most women had no childhood dreams of soldiering and were glad to return to more traditional life, other veterans wrote to friends who were still in the service about the shock of civilian life. "Stay where you are as long as you are not forcibly ejected,"[43] said one ex-Marine to her friends back at Camp LeJeune. Reality was more than the vision of freedom, privacy and nonkhaki underwear they had talked of back in the barracks.

The future was a common topic of barrack conversation. Thinking about it eased the difficulties of wartime life, and in an ironic way, thoughts of the future made the past more real and comforting. "What will we have to talk about when the peace finally comes?" mused Jane Pollock in a letter to her sister.

What will it be like when we can get in the car and drive . . . or even just go out to a party where no one is in uniform? It seems hard to believe that we ever were so carefree . . .

One of the girls . . . said the other day that she hoped everything would be different after the war. She is a very intelligent girl and had had a good job, but she suddenly realized that she had gone just as far as she could and was faced with either staying on forever or forgetting it all and getting married. She's not a bit of a feminist, but she says that it appalled her to realize that being a woman meant you could go just so far and no farther, and that you don't have much control over your own life . . . She thinks that . . . is making people change a lot of their ideas, and that the WAACS are the best symbol of it.[44]

Most wartime commentators adopted Pollock's hopefulness about new ideas and the importance of WACs and other women as symbols. They assumed that because real change had taken place in the military, it would also take place in the civilian world, and the future for women would be bright. Many writers were excessively optimistic in their predictions; nowhere was this more evident than in aviation.

Because it was a new field and women moved into it at much the same time as men, it was assumed that this relative equality would be retained. Not having studied the short history of the WASP sufficiently, such writers presumed that women who were control-tower operators, mechanics and pilots would continue in those jobs; they generally did not foresee that women with those skills and a love of airports would soon find themselves able to stay in the field only as stewardesses and reservation clerks.*

The WAC director for the Pacific seemingly had valid reason to believe that the truly important experience of these women would count in their future. "The ex-servicewoman," she predicted, "will probably return to civilian life . . . self-reliant and adaptable; eager to find her place in the postwar world."

She will be proud of women's war participation throughout the world . . . She will have an increased sense of civic responsibility and will actively support women who are taking part in public affairs. She will strive to translate to business, industry, and the professions the Army policy of regarding women as equal partners with men.

Working with women under women officers, respecting those officers and observing the good work which women are able to perform will make them acknowledge as a matter of course that women have the ability to hold public office . . .

They will . . . expect to be treated as partners in business and industry, with equal pay for equal work, and will expect equal rights under the law.[45]

Such broad predictions and optimistic comments were typical, but they sadly lacked specificity about how the skills women had acquired could be transferred to civilian employment. The military did little to provide out-processing education that would help women think creatively about what they had learned and how they could use this knowledge in the future. There were occasional excep-

---

* One prognosticator even assumed that everyone in the future would fly, just as everyone had learned to drive a generation earlier.

tions. For example, one yeoman in the Merchant Marine Hearing Unit hoped to use her experience by becoming a court reporter; another who did art work for the Coast Guard had aspirations of joining Disney; a third who was an expediter in the Coast Guard's shipbuilding program wanted to start her own small boat-building company.[46] There was indeed genuine applicability of military knowledge to the civilian world, but actual cases of this were rarely cited. Most did not understand the possible correlations that might have given women truly new futures.

Since military women soon found that the civilian perception was that knowledge acquired in the military was largely irrelevant, they—and especially their leadership—continued to emphasize the personality development that their experience fostered. Marine commander Ruth Cheney Streeter was typical when she said, "Our Marines have grown up fast. They learned to think for themselves."[47]

The troops agreed. A discharge questionnaire completed by 1,500 exiting WACs showed that "not one . . . thought she was coming out of the Army the same girl who went in two or three years ago. Two-thirds of them felt that their greatest gain had been tolerance. Others felt that they had learned self-assurance, responsibility, organization of time, neatness, tact. One girl, probably a meek mouse turned sergeant, answered that she had acquired 'the ability to tell people off.'"[48]

"The Army has taught me things about myself I never knew before," echoed another WAC. She had been asked to give radio interviews about her experience in North Africa for recruitment purposes. "Terrified," she "tried to get out of it," but the Army would not let her. After giving a few talks, she discovered that she loved radio and now planned "to scrub floors in a radio station for the chance to do some acting and announcing. I'm certainly not going back to teaching . . ."[49]

While self-confidence and ambition were indeed personal growth achievements essential to success, few employers in the 1940s viewed "the ability to tell people off" as a personality asset, especially for women. Instead of stressing new independence, advocates for female veterans placed their emphasis on more acceptable personality change. The ability to take orders was an aspect of military life with natural appeal to employers. Another favorite topic was the increased tolerance military women developed as a result of working closely with women different from themselves. The underlying message was that women, who were often regarded by employers as excessively individualistic, were capable of work-force amity.

Though employers might see increased tolerance merely as a happy omen of office tranquility, the change was far more important than that. "In the Army," said a WAC sergeant who won the Bronze Star overseas, "we lose eccentricities, prejudices, and pettiness . . . We lose intolerance built on ignorance, and, believe me, there is not one of us who is not a better woman because of it."[50]

The picture for minority women was still bleak, but the fact that two-thirds of WACs cited increased tolerance as the most important change of their war experience boded well for the future. Many white women got to know blacks and other minorities for the first time in the service; this personal contact usually worked to destroy negativism in the same way that men working with women changed their views. The personal experience (and the telling of it) was of incomparable value in eliminating myths.

Jane Pollock wrote of a woman "from the North" who "got up and said she just felt she had to comment . . . on how surprisingly intelligent and pleasant the colored WAACS were." Her patronizing attitude was greeted with indignation by a Virginian who averred that she would "have never gotten through mathematics in high school if [a] colored girl . . . hadn't helped me." Bostonian Pollock added that, to her surprise, "other southern girls said much the same thing . . . There's a girl from Tennessee here who has a devoted friend in the colored WAAC company . . . Betty says she would die of homesickness and depression without her."[51]

This WAAC classroom not only taught a military subject, but also a human one; preconceived notions about both blacks and white southerners were forced into re-examination. Mildred McAfee, in a summarization that conveniently ignored her lack of leadership in admitting blacks to the WAVES, nevertheless saw such experience as one of the most vital of the war. Women veterans, she wrote, "will have a tolerance for variation . . . which was forced upon them by exposure to difference from which they could not withdraw and with which they had to work. They will revert to most of their prejudices, but there will be left a somewhat enlarged area of enlightened tolerance."[52]

McAfee was sadly right in predicting the reversion to most of the old ways. While some individuals made profound and permanent change and all were certainly influenced to a degree, for most the military experience ultimately proved to be an aberration in their lives. Most returned to their hometowns, developed new relationships and lost old ones, went back to old jobs instead of new ones, or (even more probably) made a new job of marriage. They disappeared from each other and became isolated. As each felt more and more alone, different and alienated, they stopped talking about the experience that had briefly changed their world.

They received little or no support for change from those around them. "GI Jane will retool with ruffles," predicted an advertisement in *House Beautiful* even before the war was over. The rumors of lesbianism among servicewomen had their strong, if unacknowledged, influence; a woman was made to feel freakish if ruffles were not high in her future priorities. The female veteran's role was prescribed: "They'll want homes that express the feminine individuality they gave up for the duration and six months . . . You can expect her to demand privacy, the right to be her own boss, and as much satin, velvet or *frou frou* as she's a mind to . . . It will ease the frustrations of becoming a civilian again."[53]

110

For some, the frustrations were crushing, but they found that their friends and families had little understanding and virtually no sympathy. "Almost every anxious wife or mother of a GI," said one writer who did understand, "has read at least one article on the feeding and care of returned soldiers." None of this, though, was assumed to apply to a female ex-soldier: "she is supposed to take up with the dishes and dusting right where she left off." Said one veteran:

> *The home folks are usually overanxious to make allowance for returned male veterans, but there is more than a slight tendency to make light of the effects of military life on women. Barracks life influenced us as much . . . But I found on coming home that my friends and relatives regard the entire episode as just that—an episode, over now and best forgotten.*[54]

The memories were packed away with the uniform, seldom to be taken out and reexamined. Many women said in response to wartime questions that they had volunteered to be able to tell their children what Mommy, as well as Daddy, did in the war; when they realized, though, how different this made them from other mothers and how embarrassed children are by nonconformity, WAC or WAVE life was rarely mentioned.

The heads of the women's military organizations provided almost no leadership to them as veterans. Commander McAfee made clear her eagerness to return to academia, getting married and taking her husband's name in the process; Colonel Hobby went back to her children, retiring even before the war was over;[55] their troops soon went to PTA meetings instead of veterans meetings. While the military seldom can (and probably should not) be looked to for leadership in a democracy, these women had no professional military background that should have hindered them from continuing as leaders. Certainly, women like Cochran and Love learned a bitter feminist lesson in the war, but no feminist organization grew out of it.

Reunions were held, but they were largely limited to reminiscence, not action. Relationships that continued were personal, not political. The war itself was an aberration in American life, and women's role in it an even greater one. It was over now and best forgotten. Few flags flew when Janie came marching home.

And yet she had done something important. The record remained for those who cared to read it. Military leadership had accepted the principle of a place for women, and Congressional advocates remained, with even stronger arguments. Although during the immediate postwar demobilization the future of women in the military was uncertain and headlines proclaimed the end of this emergency aberration, slowly and without fanfare, the peacetime military began recruiting women again. Eventually they would be truly absorbed into the organization, without separate corps and with genuine opportunity. Individual women would face the same daily battles of proving themselves for decades, but the women of World War II had given them a significant beginning.

SOURCE NOTES

1. Colonel Frank McCoskrie, "I Learned About Women From Them," *American Magazine* (November 1943): p. 17.
2. Boom, "Women in the AAF," p. 507.
3. Stuart, "The WASP," p. 74.
4. Treadwell, *Women's Army Corps*, p. 171.
5. McCoskrie, "I Learned About Women," pp. 17 and 113.
6. "Lady's a Soldier," p. 32.
7. Bradley, "Women in Uniform," p. 454.
8. "Rulers of the Air," p. 117.
9. Lake, "Smarter GI Jane," p. 34.
10. "They Do a Sailor's Job," *New York Times Magazine* (July 29, 1945): p. 13.
11. Boom, "Women in the AAF," pp. 506–07, citing Dwight Eisenhower, *Crusade in Europe* (New York, Doubleday & Company, 1950), pp. 132–33.
12. Treadwell, *Women's Army Corps*, p. 383, citing Eaker in a speech on November 17, 1945, and in ETO Press Release 1601, 14 August 1943.
13. "Signal Corps Wac," p. 406.
14. Clark, "Ladies of the Army," p. 87.
15. "Hobby's Army," p. 120.
16. Clay, "Bounding Waves," p. 48.
17. Pollock, *Yes, Ma'am!*, p. 39.
18. Ibid., p. 67.
19. Flint, *Dress Right, Dress*, p. 163.
20. Pollock, *Yes, Ma'am!* pp. 180, 182, and 192.
21. "Saved From Official Fate," *Time* (April 3, 1944): p. 63; see also "Unnecessary and Undesirable?" *Time* (May 29, 1944): p. 66.
22. "Home by Christmas," *Time* (October 16, 1944): p. 68.
23. Ibid.
24. Poole, "Requiem for the WASP," pp. 55–56.
25. Ibid., p. 148.
26. Nancy McInerny, "The Woman Vet Has Her Headaches, Too," *New York Times Magazine* (June 30, 1946): p. 18. For additional information on the out-processing of women from the Army, see also "Des Moines: WAC to Vet," *Newsweek* (February 11, 1946): p. 52; "Distaff Dismissed!" *Time* (February 11, 1946): p. 23; F. Lord, "Wacs Sight New Objectives," *New York Times Magazine* (September 2, 1945): p. 12; A. Newman, "Separation for GI Jane is Practically Painless," *Newsweek* (October 29, 1945): p. 55.
27. Ibid., p. 20.

28. Margaret Hickey, "What Next for Women?" *Independent Woman* (August 1946): p. 255. Hickey chaired the Women's Advisory Committee of the War Manpower Commission.
29. "For G.I. Jane," *Time* (January 15, 1945): p. 72.
30. Ibid.
31. R. W. Babcock, "Youth Wins Out," *Survey* (July 1946): p. 185.
32. "Reemployment Rights of Servicewomen," *Monthly Labor Review* (September 1945): p. 465.
33. "Our Hand of Fellowship to Returning G.I. Janes," *Independent Woman* (July 1945): p. 204.
34. Ibid., p. 195.
35. McInerny, "Woman Vets," p. 39.
36. Ibid.
37. Ibid.
38. Lake, "Smarter GI Jane," p. 33.
39. Ibid.
40. Ibid., pp. 34–35.
41. Ibid., p. 34.
42. "When G.I. Girls Return," *New York Times Magazine* (April 22, 1945): p. 40.
43. McInerny, "Woman Vet," p. 18.
44. Pollock, *Yes, Ma'am!*, pp. 88–89.
45. Alma Lutz, "When Mary Comes Marching Home," *Christian Science Monitor* (October 13, 1945): p. 12.
46. "SPARS Look to the Future," *Independent Woman* (March 1945): p. 72.
47. "Our Hand of Fellowship," p. 204.
48. McInerny, "Woman Vet," p. 18.
49. "When GI Girls Return," p. 40.
50. Lutz, "Marching Home," p. 12.
51. Pollock, *Yes, Ma'am!*, pp. 45–46.
52. Mildred McAfee, "Women in the United States Navy," *American Journal of Sociology* (March 1946): p. 448.
53. See Lord & Taylor advertisement, *House Beautiful* (January 1945): p. 32.
54. McInerny, "Woman Vet," p. 18.
55. McAfee's married name was Horton. On Hobby, see "Hobby Out," *Time* (July 23, 1945): p. 26. Neither this article nor any other major media reported that in fact Hobby had been hospitalized several times in 1944, suffering from exhaustion. Especially during 1942 when the WAAC was forming and every detail became a policy decision, she and her top staff routinely worked 14 hours a day, 7 days a week; often she had just 2–3 hours of sleep a night. Reaction to her resignation, however, was quite negative because none of this was known, not even by her troops. See Treadwell, *Women's Army Corps*, pp. 51–52 and 719–23.

OVETA CULP HOBBY,
DIRECTOR OF THE FIRST AMERICAN
MILITARY ORGANIZATION OF WOMEN.
U.S. WAC CENTER, FT. McCLELLAN, ALABAMA.

A PHOTOGRAPH HONORING ITS
NAMESAKE IS ON DISPLAY AT THE
EDITH NOURSE ROGERS MUSEUM,
WHICH IS DEVOTED TO THE HISTORY OF
THE WOMEN'S ARMY CORPS.
ROY WEATHERFORD, AT U.S. WAC CENTER, FT.
McCLELLAN, ALABAMA.

CAPTAIN CHARITY ADAMS, ONE OF THE FIRST BLACK WAAC OFFICERS, LEADS HER
COMPANY IN DRILL AT FT. DES MOINES, IOWA, MAY 1943.
U.S. WAC CENTER, FT. McCELLAN, ALABAMA.

GENERAL EISENHOWER REVIEWS WACS
ASSIGNED TO SERVICE IN NORTH AFRICA.
U.S. WAC CENTER, FT. McCLELLAN, ALABAMA.

BARRACKS INSPECTION,
FT. HUACHUACA, ARIZONA. NOTE THE
OBVIOUSLY QUICKLY BUILT WALLS AND
THE WHITE COMMANDING OFFICER,
WITH THE BLACK SUBORDINATE
OFFICER AND SERGEANT TAKING NOTES.
U.S. WAC CENTER, FT. McCLELLAN, ALABAMA.

THE FIRST WOMEN MARINES REPORTING FOR DUTY AT WASHINGTON MARINE CORPS
HEADQUARTERS. THEY HAD JUST FINISHED TRAINING AT
HUNTER COLLEGE IN NEW YORK.
U.S. MARINE CORPS; LIBRARY OF CONGRESS.

WAVES MARCHING AT SMITH COLLEGE,
NORTHAMPTON, MASSACHUSETTS, DECEMBER 1942.
OFFICIAL NAVY PHOTO FROM THE OFFICE OF WAR INFORMATION. LIBRARY OF CONGRESS.

WAVES PISTOL TRAINING AT TREASURE ISLAND NAVAL BASE,
CALIFORNIA, FEBRUARY 1943.
NATIONAL ARCHIVES.

SPARS WORSHIPING WITH MALE NAVY COLLEAGUES ON THE HANGAR DECK OF
A SHIP DOCKED AT NORFOLK, VIRGINIA, DECEMBER 1944.
NATIONAL ARCHIVES.

AIR WAC RADIO OPERATORS AT THE
9TH AIR FORCE BOMBER COMMAND
IN ENGLAND, AUGUST 1944.
PHOTO BY U.S. ARMY AIR FORCES:
U.S. WAC CENTER.

AMERICAN AND BRITISH ATS MILITARY
UNITS WORKING FOR SHAEF, THE
SUPREME HEADQUARTERS ALLIED
EXPEDITIONARY FORCE, FRANCE, 1944.
NOTE THE SEVERELY CROWDED
CONDITIONS.
U.S. ARMY PHOTOGRAPH:
U.S. WAC CENTER.

MARINE BAND COMPOSED COMPLETELY OF WOMEN AT
CAMP LEJEUNE, NORTH CAROLINA.
OFFICIAL U.S. MARINE CORPS PHOTO: NATIONAL ARCHIVES.

THE FIRST BLACK WAC UNIT IN CONTINENTAL EUROPE TAKES PART IN A CEREMONY IN
ROUEN, FRANCE, CELEBRATING JOAN OF ARC DAY, MAY 27, 1945.
U.S. ARMY PHOTOGRAPH; U.S. WAC CENTER.

WACs WRINGING OUT THEIR CLOTHES AFTER THEIR TENT COLLAPSED IN A RAINSTORM;
ADVANCE WAC DETACHMENT AREA, TACLOBAN, LEYTE, DECEMBER 1944.
U.S. WAC CENTER.

A WAVE OPERATES AN AIR-TRAFFIC
CONTROL TOWER AT BENNETT FIELD,
NEW YORK, NOVEMBER 1943.
NATIONAL ARCHIVES.

A WAVE LAUNCHING A WEATHER
BALLOON TO CHECK WIND VELOCITY
AT THE NAVAL AIR STATION,
SANTA ANA, CALIFORNIA.
NATIONAL ARCHIVES.

AIR WAC INSTRUCTING A CADET PILOT ON A LINK
TRAINER THAT SIMULATED FLIGHT.
SMITHSONIAN INSTITUTION PHOTO NO. 27503AC.

A WASP GOES OVER A MAP WITH A GROUND CREW AIRMAN AT ROMULUS ARMY
AIR FIELD, ROMULUS, MICHIGAN, JULY 1944.
SMITHSONIAN INSTITUTION PHOTO NO. 29686AC; ORIGINAL PHOTO FROM THE AIRFIELD.

PARACHUTE-LADEN WASPS HEADED FOR THEIR PLANES.
SMITHSONIAN INSTITUTION PHOTO NO. 29685AC;
ORIGINAL PHOTO FROM ROMULUS ARMY AIR FIELD, JULY 1944.

MEMORIAL PLAQUE TO WASPS
KILLED ON DUTY.
SMITHSONIAN INSTITUTION PHOTO NO. 6277AC;
ORIGINAL PHOTO FROM GENERAL HAP
ARNOLD'S OFFICE, JULY 1945.

A MEMBER OF THE WAFS (WOMEN'S
AUXILIARY FERRYING SQUADRON) WHO
HAS JUST COMPLETED THE FERRYING
OF A PURSUIT PLANE.
SMITHSONIAN INSTITUTION PHOTO NO. 23856AC;
ORIGINAL PHOTO FROM ARMY AIR FORCE AIR
TRANSPORT COMMAND.

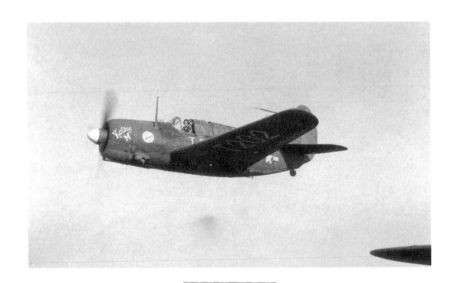

A WASP TOWING A TARGET AT CAMP STEWART, GEORGIA, JUNE 1944.
SMITHSONIAN INSTITUTION PHOTO NO. 11052AC;
ORIGINAL PHOTO FROM WASP HEADQUARTERS IN WASHINGTON, D.C.

PART III

THE NEW INDUSTRIAL WOMAN

8

RECRUITMENT OF A NEW LABOR FORCE

In September 1943, the editors of *Business Week* summarized tersely: "Now it can be seen. Our entire manpower problem is most acutely a problem in womanpower."[1] Ten million men had gone to war, and virtually all of those who remained at home were already employed; clearly the additional planes and tanks and ships that were needed would have to be built by women.

More than any other war in history, World War II was a battle of production. The Germans and Japanese had a 10-year head start on amassing weapons, and, moreover, the Allies had suffered critical materiel losses at Dunkirk and Pearl Harbor. It was clear that we were playing a game of catch-up, and it was equally clear that the side with the most bombs, aircraft and weaponry would be the side that won the war. Production was essential to victory, and women were essential to production.

Women accepted the challenge. When President Roosevelt asked in 1940 for 50,000 planes a year, his political opponents saw this impossible goal as clear evidence that he had gone mad, but by 1944 the United States was producing 120,000 planes annually. Many of these aircraft were built in plants where more than half of the employees were female.[2] Most of these women had never seen the interior of an airplane before; they did not know a fuselage from landing gear, but they left their kitchens for this and other industries, learned quickly and were wonderfully successful.

At the beginning of the war, of course, the United States was still plagued by Depression unemployment, and the first defense jobs naturally went to men. Then came the women who were truly unemployed and underemployed—those who had been denied decent jobs in the thirties and who wanted and needed them. By the end of 1942, these ranks had been absorbed, and the cry went up for a new type of worker—the housewife who didn't necessarily want or need to work.

Many things might have persuaded women to stay at home: Gas rationing made transportation difficult; wartime shortages made necessary shopping more time-consuming; household help disappeared as better job opportunities opened; and many male employees and unions were still hostile to women workers. Also, a married working woman might lose her "dependency" status and make her husband more vulnerable to the draft, and public disapproval of working wives still lingered. All of these factors and more had to be overcome if labor sufficient to win the war was to be found. Convincing women that public need should override their personal convenience became one of the biggest selling jobs of the war.

Over the radio came the call for women workers; the air waves informed, cajoled, persuaded and, most of all, appealed to one's patriotism. Women were reminded that men—their brothers, husbands, sons—were in danger of death for lack of the goods they could supply. Turning from emotional appeal to specific job information, the method was soon a success.

In Seattle, where a multitude of defense plants created an acute labor shortage, the first four weeks of radio effort was responsible for the placement of 2,200 women.[3] In coastal Virginia, the response of this housewife was typical: "Over and over for months I heard from the radio the call for women to enter war work. I had been delaying for one reason or another but I finally recognized these arguments in favor of my going to the shipyards."[4]

The print media played its part, too; magazine ads showed starving prisoners of war clinging to barbed wire under tropical sun, looking desperately for help from beyond the seas. "Womanpower Days" were declared with special stories and photographs of women at work. Posters proclaimed, "Victory is in Your Hands," "Shopgirl Attacks Nazis," and (trying to allay nagging doubts) "War Workers Stay Womanly."

Another method of labor recruitment was the registration drive. Several localities conducted such drives during the start-up year of 1942, with varying degrees of success. Oregon led the way in February, looking explicitly for women who would take jobs in civilian production, thus allowing men to go into war work. A strong majority of Oregon's women responded to the registration questionnaire, and although they indicated no great desire for factory work, one in three replied that she would be willing to help in crop-harvest emergencies.

Detroit, with its car factories converted to war production, was in desperate need of labor and so planned its recruitment campaign carefully. Every household in Wayne County received one of the over 500,000 registration forms distributed. The result was 142,000 women available for work, 62% of whom wanted factory jobs and many of whom had previous industrial experience.[5] The campaign was conducted in August, and the hiring patterns in September and October showed 80% of the new employees were women. Written in the margins of their registration cards were clues to their motivations. "My husband is in Australia," wrote one, "and I want to help make weapons for him and his buddies."[6]

New Britain, Connecticut, used an especially innovative method of recruitment to fill its shipyards. Instead of volunteer recruiters who were sometimes scorned as not practicing what they preached, 22 women workers from several local factories were selected, given two days of training, and sent out to talk one-on-one with "the five thousand women who had not replied to the recruiting letters. Each recruiter went in and sat down with the housewife and told her . . . about war work as only a worker could do. The result was an average of sixty housewives were recruited by each interviewer."[7]

From North Adams, Massachusetts, to Dayton to Seattle, cities conducted campaigns and found similar pockets of hidden talent that would help win the war. Organizations, too, acted in the recruitment effort. Such groups as the national Federation of Business and Professional Women (BPW) assembled master files of the special abilities of their members and their availability for work. Industrialists went to Washington for advice, too—so often that one War Manpower official said tiredly, "We have so many requests from nervous employers for special material on the training of women that I've asked my secretary to go out and buy a rubber stamp to use on every printed piece we send out, reading, 'This includes women, Negroes, handicapped, Chinamen and Spaniards.' The only difference between training men and women in industry is in the toilet facilities."[8]

Toilet facilities, as may be expected, came in for their share of attention. One female adviser to management said unequivocally, "Any employer who expects to be using women should start fighting early for priorities on plenty of restroom facilities."[9] Cleanliness-conscious housewives could not be expected to put up with the dirty restrooms that had been good enough for men. Really progressive managers would include showers and lockers so that women could put in a respectable appearance on the street after a grimy factory day.

Industry and education (with prodding from government) cooperated in opening up vocational-training programs to girls and women. In 1941, only 3% of such classes were female students; a year later they constituted 30%.[10] Thousands of women enrolled in machine-shop courses; they learned welding, drafting, sheet-metal work and other techniques necessary to industrial success. Apprehensive teachers thought that teaching methods would have to be radically different for mechanically inept women. Some even called training women impractical because they assumed that new schools would have to be built; they could not envision male and female students working side by side. More reasonable heads prevailed, though, and before long vocational teachers were saying that the very lack of familiarity with the mechanical world was an asset for female students, for they had no bad habits to unlearn.

Having discovered that "the hand that rocks the cradle can also run a drill press,"[11] Republic Tool & Die Company of Chicago was one of the industrial leaders in accommodating women. The plant layout was designed with women employees in mind; safety glass was installed between drill press operators and

118

their work to save faces from being scarred by hot metal snapping; machine oil was changed regularly so that it didn't stain hands. Even more innovative was the plan for different uniforms for trainees and experienced workers, so that supervisors could "spot a new girl instantly in case of trouble." Beginners also worked a shorter day so that their muscles could break in gradually, and all workers received frequent rest periods. The services of a doctor and nurse were available 24 hours a day, and quality production was rewarded by bonuses (a beauty kit was typical). So pleased was management with their new employees that they had "accepted the woman worker, not only for the duration but forever."[12]

This permanent acceptance of women into the labor force and the growth of enlightened management were only two of the many changes World War II brought. Another—directly related to the recruitment of labor—was the mass migration of people. Other historical periods had seen such mass movement (virtually all of the United States west of the Mississippi was settled in the 30 years after the Civil War, for example), but never before had so many people moved in so many different directions in so short a time. In Europe, of course, millions of people were uprooted from their ancient homes; throughout the world millions of men (and some women) joined military units that carried them halfway around the globe. But even in the relatively peaceful U.S. and even among civilians, a giant restlessness characterized the land. Though generations of families had lived unmoved in the hills of West Virginia and North Carolina since the Revolutionary War, people went from there to the Atlantic shipyards; from Missouri and Arkansas, they migrated to Los Angeles and Detroit; from small towns and farms everywhere, people traveled to new job sites.

While it was true that defense industries needed labor, nevertheless government policy had to discourage this migration. The nation simply could not afford the use of materiel involved. Not only were long journeys inadvisable because of gas and tire shortages, but also—and especially—the boom cities could not absorb any more people. Many localities saw their population double and triple seemingly overnight. Burbank, California, went from a sleepy 12,000 to 60,000 in the first two years of the war.[13] Elkton, Maryland, was a quiet farm town until a giant ammunition plant was built there, after which the population zoomed from 6,000 to 12,000, 80% of whom were young women.[14]

Many big cities grew bigger; the number of households in the Norfolk, Virginia, area, with its mammoth Naval shipyards, rose 61% during the war years. Several metropolitan centers, including Dallas, San Antonio, Los Angeles, San Francisco, Portland, Seattle and Washington, D.C., had a population increase of more than one-third.[15] Every available space was taken in these boom towns. Because precious steel and aluminum and time were needed for weaponry, they simply could not go into housing. Therefore, the industrial labor that was needed had to come from what was locally available—from housewives, from women who could but didn't work.

Census figures for December 1942 estimated that although 14 million women were employed, there were 27 million who listed themselves as homemakers, 17 million of whom had no children under 10.[16] The problem was that many of these women lived where there were no factories; women in rural Tennessee and Utah could live their lives pretty much as usual, but in Baltimore and Buffalo and Portland, they had to be shaken from their apathy and persuaded to go to work.

The need for locally available labor complicated the whole question of women's war work. Although many women in New Mexico or Vermont would have responded to the call for workers had there been work available to them, accusations appeared in the press that women were not responding to the call and that vital production was slipping for lack of workers. The cry went up that lazy bridge-playing ladies should be required to register for a draft.

Without definitely committing themselves to such legislation, administration officials warned that a National Service Act might soon become necessary, one that would give "the government power to direct any ablebodied citizen, man or woman, to work where needed."[17] Its advocates pointed to the example of our fighting sister, Britain, where compulsory registration of women for war work had already proven itself. Almost two-thirds of Britain's women were in factories, civilian defense or the military itself, many of them assigned to jobs that were not particularly their choice.[18]

Some Americans felt there was no reason why our women shouldn't be equally patriotic, and a lively public debate of compulsory war work for women began. Dramatic headlines appeared: "Draft for Women," proclaimed *Business Week*; "There Must Be No Idle Women," *Independent Woman* announced; "Shall we Draft Women?" proposed *The Nation*; even *Woman's Home Companion* frightened its audience with "Should Women Be Drafted?" In most of these gripping titles, "draft" actually meant only compulsory civilian work, but just the suggestion was enough to stir a good deal of controversy.[19]

In Congress, Representative Joseph C. Baldwin, a New York Republican, introduced a 1942 bill "providing for the registration of women between the ages of 18 and 65 under the Selective Training and Service Act."[20] After being assigned to the House Military Affairs Committee, H.R. 6806 died without hearings, but considerably more attention to the issue was paid in the Senate. Several bills were introduced in 1942–43, the chief of them being S.B. 666, which came to be known as the Austin-Wadsworth Bill or the National War Service Act.

Senator Warren Austin, Republican of Vermont, worked long and hard on his bill "to provide further for the successful prosecution of the war through a system of civilian selective war service."[21] It called for compulsory registration of women 18 to 50 (men 18 to 65 already being registered under Selective Service), but more importantly, it would have required both sexes to serve in whatever industrial or agricultural jobs they were assigned. It was true that pregnant women and those with children under 18 or with incapacitated dependents were exempt, and moreover, the War Manpower Commission was authorized to call for volunteers before drafting labor, but nevertheless the proposal was a very significant one.

For the first time in American history, it was being seriously proposed that women, like men, could be drafted for the service of their government. Senator Austin and his supporters believed the situation was sufficiently critical to put aside maxims about women's place and compel women—whether they liked it or not—to do war work. "It is dangerous," said Mr. Austin, "to postpone this legislation. Such postponement has the immediate effect of deficiency in production and transportation." He pointed out that at that very time, while S.B. 666 was being debated in committee, a "mission from General MacArthur was in Washington begging for planes. Five hundred planes to MacArthur in February probably would have saved the lives of many of our brave boys."[22]

A coalition of senators agreed with him. Six bills had been introduced on the subject, all sponsored by men who were Republicans or conservative Southern Democrats—Senators Reynolds of North Carolina, Hill of Alabama, Bilbo of Mississippi, McKellor of Tennessee, Taft ("Mr. Conservative") of Ohio, and Austin, a Republican from Vermont.[23] Perhaps because of their antipathy to Roosevelt in pre-Pearl Harbor days when he tried to warn them of war, they were anxious to outdo him in later effort. Perhaps their concept of compulsory labor was actually a subtle attempt at union busting. But for whatever reason, support for the notion of drafting women came, oddly enough, from conservatives. A Citizens Committee for a national War Service Act was formed, led by a man from Alabama and vice-chaired by Henry D. Cabot. The American Legion worked actively to support the legislation.[24]

Although it was unusual that it was conservatives who pushed for this radical change in the status of women, it is equally strange that there was very little debate in Congress on that factor. The argument instead centered on such issues as whether it was consistent with democratic principles to draft any civilian; whether this was best accomplished by legislation or executive order; what the proper method was of carrying out such a labor transfer; whether the legislation was an attack on organized labor; and most importantly, whether the legislation was needed at this time. Other than perfunctory assurances that the sanctity of the home was being protected, there was no particular attention paid to the issue of drafting *women*.

Though Secretary of War Stimson gave his support to the bill,[25] other administration officials continued to believe the need was not yet real; they warned that premature action could do more harm than good. Thelma McKelvery, women's representative on the War Production Board, declared that it would be "unwise to raise the enthusiasm of women and then see that enthusiasm turn to skepticism because a sufficient number of outlets for their productive energies have not yet developed."[26] The Director of the U.S. Employment Service was among many who agreed: "A compulsory registration of women at this time . . . would be a handicap to any future *necessary* registration." [27]

The Selective Service itself studied the question, issuing a report favorable to the British and Russian systems of compulsory allocation of female labor and concluding that the drafting of women would present no problem for them administratively, but questioning the value of a nationwide, compulsory system until our situation was as grave as that of our allies.[28] Paul McNutt, Director of the War Manpower Commission, continued throughout the war to warn in strong terms that if people did not volunteer "they bring closer the day when a national service act may be passed and an Employment Service agent may appear at their door, registration blank in hand."[29] Although he called the need critical, he too backed off from actually drafting such legislation.

These administration officials were certainly not opposed to the concept of registering and drafting women—they did not think women should automatically be exempt, and "home and family" seldom appear in their comments—but they simply saw the question as more complex than did Congressional proponents. It was a question of timing; a question of *local* need—New York City, after all, had unemployment figures in the hundreds of thousands. This was not a problem, FDR's people thought, that could best be solved by requiring every woman from Maine to Oregon to sign up for a potential draft.

The public consistently told poll takers that they were willing to be called for an industrial draft if the government so decided. Just a month after the war began, the Gallup organization inquired: "Would you be in favor of starting now to draft single women between the ages of 21 and 35 to train them for wartime jobs?" A firm 68% said "yes," with more women than men supporting the idea (73% to 63%).[30] Even more interestingly, when the question was asked of those who would be most likely to be drafted themselves, support was still higher, a remarkable 91% of potential draftees agreeing that "the government should draft persons to fill war jobs."[31] Throughout the war, the question was asked in various forms, and a majority continued to support the concept of an industrial draft that included women.

Perhaps it is indicative of the great aversion that people had in World War II to being called "slackers"; perhaps too, an industrial draft would have given them more pride in being civilians. For a woman who was reluctant to take the big step of enlisting in the military, an industrial draft provided a real opportunity to prove that she too was part of the war. Finally, it is interesting to note that when polls were broken down by region, it was the South, the home of the Southern belle, that was most strongly supportive of industrial conscription.[32]

Yet despite an apparently broad base of public support for industrial conscription of women, opposition remained. Far from supporting a draft, *Catholic World* believed that "we might ponder whether there should even be such a thing as women in industry," finding ideally there should not be. "Women have a special dignity . . . and a special duty—that of being the heart of the home," they concluded. "Let us realize that God made women to be mothers . . . "[33]

Magazines in general took a cautious approach on the idea of conscripting women for war work; although most of them enthusiastically ran articles designed to attract women to the factories, few were willing to advocate compulsion. They preferred, instead, to accent the positive.

This was also the approach taken by the White House. Roosevelt, who so often had been accused of regimentation by his Congressional opposition, preferred to avoid regimentation in this area while his rivals in the legislature advocated it. For reasons that probably have more to do with party politics and labor unions than with what various people deemed the "proper role" of women in a society, the National War Service Act never came to a vote. Public-opinion polls supporting a draft showed a comforting reservoir of good will, a possibility, a potential to meet future needs. But unless the war became worse, it was the natural inclination of true democrats that compulsion be avoided.

If women were to come voluntarily, the government recognized that certain changes in industry were essential. One of the surest ways to discourage women was to pay them less than men for the same work. The "equal pay for equal work" principle was far from accepted in the forties. A survey by the Women's Bureau of the Labor Department in 1942 found that of 18 major ammunition plants, only three paid the sexes equally.[34] Many unions that insisted on equal-pay clauses did so to keep industry from undercutting male wages by hiring women, and not out of any belief in justice for women workers. The Roosevelt administration tried to change this situation, to insist on fairness for the women workers they were trying to attract. The War Labor Board consistently ruled in favor of equality in wage disputes, but employers of course continued to evade the principle by setting up "women's jobs."

Again, there was public support for the principle of equality. Asked by Gallup early in the war, "If women replace men in industry should they be paid the same wages as men?," 78% of the public responded "yes." Women were supportive of their sex again, with only 7% responding negatively.[35] However, although the public and the administration endorsed the idea, there was no legislation; the Equal Pay Act would not be passed by Congress until 1963. Nor was the executive branch itself any model of equal opportunity. A tabulation of women in policy-making posts in 1942 showed 2 out of 401; in 1944, the women had risen to 8 of 537.[36] Given the outstanding record of Secretary of Labor Frances Perkins, it is indeed strange that Roosevelt did not make greater utilization of the abilities of additional women.

Of course, "war work" in the strict sense was not the only important work. People still had to eat, they still had to be clothed and housed and nursed and even, occasionally, entertained. "Essential civilian work" was the official term for it, and throughout the war it was in danger of being too greatly downgraded. Because of better pay in defense industries, because of the glamour of working in a job that was connected to the "real war," millions of women left their old jobs for new. Laundries, restaurants and stores were constantly shorthanded, and even schools began to be affected as teachers discovered they could earn more in an unskilled job. Within civilian business, women sometimes transferred to jobs that had previously been a male domain; for example, telephone operators became phone repairers during the war.

Though attention was focused on the new jobs and the war industries, it is important to remember that by far the majority of women continued to work throughout the war in traditional women's jobs, doing "essential civilian work," and sometimes feeling a bit left out. Waiting on more tables, teaching more students, ironing more laundry, these women in civilian employment worked doubly hard so that others could go into defense plants.

Voluntarily and without compulsion, the adjustment was made. Women poured from civilian work into war work, and more important, they came in a steady stream from nonemployment in the home. In 1940, 12,000,000 women were at work; five years later, there were 19,000,000.[37]

Donald Nelson, Chairman of the War Production Board, summarized their achievement dramatically:

This is the record: for nine years before Pearl Harbor, Germany, Italy and Japan prepared intensively for war, while as late as 1940 the war production of peaceful America was virtually nothing. Yet two years later the output of our war factories equaled that of the three Axis nations combined. In 1943 our war production was one and one half times, and in 1944, more than double Axis war production—a remarkable demonstration of power.[38]

Women played an important part in this production; they responded to the need, and voluntary recruitment was a success. Some of these women had always worked or wanted to; others went to work because of economic need when wartime living costs proved too great for a serviceman's allotment. But millions of them came largely because of a strong inner desire to do something meaningful to help win the war.

It was on this premise that recruitment came to be largely based. Women told interviewers again and again that this was their strongest motivation: "My brother went into the Army, and now I feel that I'm in the fight, too." "My husband is in Iceland . . . Here to do the best I can . . . Women are in this to the end." The War Manpower Commission decided that while they would not ignore "the money appeal," they would "concentrate on patriotism,"[39] for the kind of woman that was needed was likely to be moved by factors more mental than material.

Those who thought compulsion would be necessary were proved wrong. Perhaps their mistake was in thinking that women naturally enjoyed housework and their present roles and would have to be forced from them; they failed to understand that most women never really had any free career choice. Given the opportunity of earning their own paychecks and the satisfaction of contributing to the war effort, millions were glad to move from the kitchen to the factory, and their numbers made the margin of difference that won the war.

SOURCE NOTES

1. "Cherchez la Femme," *Business Week* (September 25, 1943): p. 108.
2. "Proportion of Women in Selected Industries" *Newsweek* (August 23, 1943): p. 54.
3. "Recruiting by Air; Seattle Tries Radio Appeal for Women Workers," *Business Week* (July 10, 1943): p. 115; see also "Women for War," *Business Week* (August 15, 1942): p. 24.
4. Virginia Snow Wilkinson, "From Housewife to Shipfitter," *Harper's* (September 1943): pp. 328–37.
5. "Enrollment Campaigns for Women Workers," *Monthly Labor Review* (March 1943): pp. 488–90.
6. "190,000 Workers; Registration Drive of Women in Detroit," *Business Week* (September 5, 1942): p. 33. See also "Detroit Hunts Help," *Business Week* (July 4, 1942): p. 72.
7. Anthony, *Out of the Kitchen*, pp. 61–62.
8. "Margin Now Is Womanpower," *Fortune* (February 1943): p. 98.
9. Ibid.
10. Earl L. Bedell, "Training Women for Wartime Industries," *Industrial Arts and Vocational Education* (January 1943): p. 3.
11. Marguerite F. LaBelle and Maria Heuer, "Beauty Kits for Bonuses," *Nation's Business* (January 1943): p. 36.
12. Ibid.

13. Elizabeth Field, "Boom Town Girls," *Independent Woman* (October 1942): p. 296.

14. Mary Heaton Vorse, "The Girls of Elkton, Maryland: Munitions Workers," *Harper's* (March 1943): p. 347.

15. U.S. Department of Commerce, Bureau of the Census, *Statistical Abstract of the United States—1949* (Washington: Government Printing Office, 1949), p. 54.

16. Minnie L. Maffett, "Mobilizing Womanpower," *Independent Woman* (December 1942): p. 380. See also "Labor Reserves Among Women," *Monthly Labor Review* (December 1943): p. 1098.

17. "Margin Now Is Womanpower," p. 90.

18. Ibid. See also "Second Report of the Director of Selective Service," *Selective Service in Wartime* (Washington: Government Printing Office, 1943), p. 399.

19. "Draft for Women," *Business Week* (July 11, 1942): p. 72; "There Must Be No Idle Women," *Independent Woman* (August 1943): p. 232; Maxwell S. Stewart, "Shall We Draft Women?" *The Nation* (April 25, 1942): p. 483; Anne Maxwell, "Should Women Be Drafted?" *Woman's Home Companion* (December 1942): p. 56; see also "Mrs. Roosevelt's Plan; Drafting U.S. Girls for a Year of Compulsory Service," *Time* (June 23, 1941): p. 18.

20. *Congressional Record—House*, 77th Cong., 2d sess., 1942, Vol. 88, pt. 2, p. 2691.

21. *Congressional Record—Senate*, "Proposed National War Service Act," 78th Cong., 1st sess., February 8, 1943, Vol. 89, pt. 1, p. 666.

22. Ibid., Part 3, May 10, 1943, p. 4122.

23. Ibid., Part 1, February 8, 1943, p. 668.

24. Ibid.

25. Ibid., March 1, 1943, p. 1375. See also *Appendix to Congressional Record*, 78th Cong., 2d sess., 1944, Vol. 90, pt. 8, pp. A437–38.

26. "On Registering Women: Voluntary or Compulsory?" *Independent Woman* (May 1942): p. 145.

27. Ibid.

28. *Selective Service in Wartime*, pp. 389–413.

29. Paul V. McNutt, "Why You Must Take a War Job," *American Magazine* (December 1943): p. 100. See also *Congressional Record—House*, 78th Cong., 1st sess., February 8, 1943, Vol. 89, pt. 1, p. 671.

30. Gallup, *The Gallup Poll*, p. 316. Interviews in January 1942.

31. Ibid., p. 404. Interviews in August 1942.

32. Ibid., pp. 327 and 487. Interviews in March 1942 and February 1945.

33. Joseph B. Schuyler, S.J., "Women at Work," *Catholic World* (April 1943): p. 26; see also O.G. Villard, "Shall We Conscript Women?" *Christian Century* (August 4, 1943): p. 888, for a similar view.

34. "Equal Pay for Women Workers," *Monthly Labor Review* (January 1943): p. 63; see also "Labor Dilution," *Business Week* (November 8, 1941), p. 22.

35. Gallup, *The Gallup Poll*, p. 322. Interviews in February 1942.

36. Minnie L. Maffett, "D-Day and H-Hour for Women," *Independent Woman* (August 1944): p. 240.

37. U.S. Department of Commerce, Bureau of the Census, *Statistical Abstract of the United States—1948* (Washington: Government Printing Office, 1948), p. 174.

38. Donald M. Nelson, "What Industry Did," *While You Were Gone: A Report on Wartime Life in the United States*, edited by Jack Goodman (New York: Simon & Schuster, 1946), reprinted by Da Capo Press, 1974, p. 213.

39. "The Margin Now is Womanpower," p. 102. See also Evelyn Steele, *Wartime Opportunities For Women* (New York: E.P. Dutton & Co., 1943), a compilation of wartime occupations available to young women. Other books intended to promote industrial recruitment included Laura Nelson Baker, *Wanted: Women in War Industry* (New York: E.P. Dutton & Company, 1943); Elizabeth Gurley Flynn, *Women in the War* (New York: Workers Library Publishers, 1942); and Eva Lapin, *Mothers in Overalls* (New York: Workers Library Publishers, 1943).

9

ROSIE THE RIVETER RALLIES
TO NEW JOBS

Margaret Flint, who was tremendously impressed with her WAC experience, nonetheless wrote, "I believe that some of the women who are really highly skilled technicians should have remained in the war industries."[1] Though the Army was a wonderful experience for many, it did not guarantee that one's skills would be used most effectively. In the civilian world, however, a woman was free to find the occupational slot that fit her best.

She could become instead a "production soldier," for, more than any other war in history, World War II was a contest where the side that had the most won. Nor was it false pride to refer to oneself as a "production soldier," for many of the millions of women in the defense industries worked harder than the average military woman. Ruth Millard, whose regular schedule called for 53 hours a week at work for month after dreary month, wrote of her belief that in comparison "KP looked like a vacation."[2]

The standard work week was 48 hours (six days of eight hours each) with only Sundays off, and many women routinely worked overtime. Vacations and most holidays were canceled for the duration. The endless work—most of it interminably repetitive and boring—stretched out on an infinite assembly line far into the dim and unknown future. What they were building was aimed for destruction, and no one could predict how much would have to be built and destroyed and replaced again before all the madness would finally be declared over.

"The first thing to do to win the war," said Dorothy Parker, "is to lose your amateur standing."[3] While the work that most women did was unskilled by industrial definitions, it was definitely not amateurish. Nor was there anything amateurish about the transformation that business itself made after the trauma of Pearl Harbor. As women went from housework, school teaching, and sales clerking to war work, so industry was reborn. Factories converted from "lingerie to camouflage netting; from baby carriages to field-hospital food carts; from lipstick cases to bomb fuses; . . . from ribbons and silk goods to parachutes; from beer cans to hand grenades; . . . from vacuum cleaners to gas-mask parts."[4]

Rosie did much more than rivet in these newly retooled factories. Women operated cranes, moving huge parts of heavy tanks and artillery—a 15-ton crane in an aircraft factory was run by a girl just out of high school. At proving grounds, women worked as ordnance testers, loading and firing machine guns, antiaircraft guns, and other weaponry to test the equipment and ammunition. All day, every day, they were surrounded by the cacophonous sound of battle. Women became guards at plants where lives depended on security against sabotage and spying. In metal foundries, middleclass American women shoveled sand and did the hot, heavy work of core making that had been performed by Slavic immigrant women a half-century earlier. Women operated huge hydraulic presses; they drove tractors up and down miles of assembly lines; they even gave their free time as volunteer fire fighters trained in the special techniques of industrial accidents.

Women in California worked as miners, sorting ore and operating equipment. "In one mine," *Business Week* wrote admiringly, "women wield an 8-pound sledge in the best of manlike tradition."[5] Not far away, in one of the many plane subassembly plants of southern California, contrasting women worked as instrument makers on navigation equipment "so delicate that all work must be done in washed-air, pressure controlled rooms."[6]

From the heavy to the light, from the banal to the exquisitely difficult, women did it all. There was scarcely any area of defense production that was not touched by women. In November of 1942, less than a year after the U.S. involvement in the war began, *Newsweek* reported that "depending on the industry, women today make up from 10 to 88 per cent of total personnel in most war plants."[7] They had poured in as soon after Pearl Harbor as industry could accommodate them; in Buffalo, for example, a survey on January 1, 1942, showed just 4,000 women in war work, but a year later, on January 1, 1943, a less extensive survey found 43,000.[8] In Minneapolis, Minnesota, the highest possible percentage of women (100%) was achieved at Strato Equipment, where a woman headed a small company employing only women, who, with consultants from the University of Minnesota and Mayo Clinic, researched and designed high-altitude pressure suits for pilots. The only male involved was a department store dummy.[9]

It was not surprising that this all-woman factory should be related to the aircraft industry, for it was there that women gravitated in the most dramatic way. Some of the first women to be employed by aircraft manufacturers were those banned from civilian flying and, in pre-WASP days, unable to do anything else in their field. Before long, however, these women were joined by hundreds of thousands who had never seen a plane close up before. Because the industry was new, it did not hold the prejudices of other, older manufacturers; because it valued lightness and grace over massive ponderousness, it seemed a natural for women.

Two years after Pearl Harbor, there were 475,000 women working in aircraft factories—almost five times as many as ever joined the WAC. At Douglas Aircraft, they made up 45% of the labor force and were adding to that percentage every day. At Boeing, during "the first 12 months that the output of B-17's was doubled, nearly half of the men . . . necessarily were replaced by completely inexperienced women."[10]

Although inexperienced by industrial standards, women soon found that many of the skills they had accumulated through lifetimes of varied activities were easily transferred to industry. Riveting, after all, was nothing more than "a kind of needle point in metals."[11] They found, to their own surprise and certainly that of others, that soon reporters could describe factory scenes where "a . . . frame starts down the powered conveyor . . . bare and skeleton-like. It emerges as a completed fuselage . . . and nowhere en route does a man touch it."[12]

Aircraft plants were so large that they resembled small towns, "only the streets are lined with machines. Electric trucks honk at you constantly and people on bicycles flip past as you wend your way from the locker room to your machine a mile or so distant."[13] Women were thrilled by the bigness and bustle of the scene, so different from the isolation of housework. One wrote that after many months,

> I still love to come in under the huge dome, to blink at all the thousands of lights . . . It isn't a bleak place. Rather it sparkles with shining steel surfaces, it sings a busy song of industry and action: and for some unknown reason the gods of harmony decided that nile green and blue made swell priming coats for airplanes.[14]

They soon made themselves at home. "Through acres of bombers and chopped-up parts of bombers," wrote one reporter,

> We made our way from one roaring assembly line to another. At one point we stopped to speak to a small taffy blonde . . . sitting in the midst of hammering machinery, her feet propped up on a bench, reading a book. It was her lunch hour and the manual, Pneudraulic Power Machine and Riveters. One of half a million housewives who had never been in a factory, she suddenly figured . . . that maybe the talents of her toolmaker father might be developed in her. They were.[15]

The initial adjustment period was rougher than such scenes might convey. One woman said of her first day, "By noon protesting nerves began to scream for relief. My head ached with the vibration and noise."[16] Another, who was both an athlete and an anthropologist, admitted to self-defeating nervousness:

the work "has to be just right or it may cost a pilot his life. I had to hurry to keep up with the line. I got clamps on backward; I felt all thumbs. And the other girls razzed me."[17] Her hands were swollen for three weeks.

Virtually every account of aircraft factories mentions that women initially were upset by the tremendous noise level, and even after long and successful experience on the job, there were days when the noise "got to them." One described working in the tight confines of a plane's nose: "Two riveters would be screaming through the skin of the plane to give each other instructions. Their gun would go off, screeching hollowly into my eardrums. There would be two men hammering on the outside just over my head . . ."[18]

Rumors circulated that the vibrations of riveting caused breast cancer, and the term "riveter's ovaries" soon developed for any gynecological problem. Back aches and muscle strains were predictable, the pain magnified by muscular tension—which in turn was in many cases caused by women's fear of failure and excessive determination to do well. It was hardly surprising that many cried themselves to sleep the first nights.

The pressure on a newcomer was intensified by the knowledge that not everyone wanted her to succeed. "All mistakes, for the first few weeks," said one, "were ascribed to me."[19] As the war lengthened, though, and male employees were lost to the draft, management did more to discourage hostility from male coworkers. If blue-collar men were not yet reconciled to women in the factory, white-collar men were soon happy to praise them.

Glenn Martin, "builder of famous fighting and patrol bombers," declared: "We have women helping design our planes in the Engineering Department, building them on the production line, operating almost every conceivable type of machinery, from rivet guns to giant stamp presses."[20] Martin Aircraft even had an "all-girl test crew" for final tests and adjustments of the finished plane. Women also checked bombers, with one operating the controls and another checking the release mechanisms, using interphones to yell "bombs away!"

It was Vultee, a maker of trainers and pursuit planes, that set the pace when it hired 25 women "early in 1941—months before OPM [Office of Production Management] asked aircraft plants to experiment with women workers . . . In three weeks the experiment proved a success: weekly production of some units had increased 25 percent, a few had zoomed 50 percent."[21]

The reasons for women's success, of course, were frequently attributed to those "natural causes" so easily believed. A bomber plant foreman, for example, said that:

Many young men came to work with notions about plane-building being a romantic business, but after working at a machine that trims tiny pieces of metal, half a mile from final assembly, they are disappointed and dissatisfied. Women are more realistic . . . After men have mastered a single operation they usually

131

want to move on to something new, but women are satisfied to stick to one job and learn how to do it better.[22]

The plant manager at Consolidated Aircraft in southern California similarly averred of women: "They're better than men for jobs calling for finger work. They will stick on a tedious assembly line long after the men quit . . . It's funny about women," he mused, "they are more conscientious than men on the testing machines . . . Nothing gets by them unless it's right."[23] The ultimate praise of another was, "They take orders easily, have the patience of Job and are more frank than men. When they make an error, they come tell me."[24]

Foremen who initially resisted women were now begging to supervise them. Those nimble fingers that gave women jobs in America's very first factories (the 18th century textile plants) proved themselves again. "Ages of sewing and knitting have conditioned women to monotony," wrote one reporter. "Their finger dexterity has been proved superior to that of men; they have more patience."[25] At Lockheed, two black women with just a year of experience set an all-time record for riveting speed.[26]

Sometimes the analogy to women's traditional work was very direct, as with forming the initial covering of a plane's frame.

Women cut and fashion this fabric more carefully than any Bond Street tailor. They draw the pieces taut over the aluminum ribs of the wing; then with dexterous fingers they sew them into place.

Their long, curved needles flash in and out with amazing rapidity . . . upon those slender stitches will be thrown a strain of 600 pounds to the square foot when a dive bomber pulls out of its shrieking power dive.[27]

A plane's electrical and communication mechanisms also called for a dexterous touch, and those departments began to hire great percentages of women when it was shown that they could set higher production records than men. Sometimes efficiency increased by 100%, as with the woman who pulled "a mass of wires through a long, tight tube—in 15 minutes against her male predecessor's half-hour."[28]

In addition to building planes, women worked for the airlines in maintaining them. Western Airlines began by training a few women to do the same jobs their husbands did—cleaning spark plugs and making minor repairs. In Kansas City, TWA experimented with 110 women; their program was soon emulated by airlines coast to coast. While some did mundane work in the upholstery and cleaning departments, the first woman hired was an artist who painted radium dials. Others repaired gauges, an "intricate" job, "since the tiny needle of the analyzer . . . on a small graph must be in exact alignment." A foreman enthused, "these jobs are just *made* for women."[29] Other WAMS (Women in Airline Maintenance) got a chance to do "a real man's job—engine overhaul." Women

132

worked on carburetors, pistons, and valves, and "some of the girls are even taking their places with the lead engine mechanics on the test stands."[30]

Because of crowded conditions in traditional industrial locales, many women employed in aircraft manufacture actually worked in rural and suburban areas at "feeder factories," where plane parts were crafted before being shipped to the giant assembly plants. Sleepy California farm towns saw the lives of their women transformed as factories moved in and hired huge numbers of women who had never before been employed. Convair Aircraft in 11 feeder factories around San Diego employed 90% women, whose motivation was so strong that soon they were out-producing the home plant. An all-woman shop at Coronado, California, showed the frugality of housewives as "rivets, swept up by the thousands from assembly line floors, are salvaged, separated into various sizes and sent back to San Diego."[31]

A few years earlier, during the Depression, most of these women never expected to work outside the home, let alone have an opportunity for a job that was well-paid. Because aircraft plants were new, they were more likely than other industries to adhere to Rooseveltian equal pay ideals. Women in general earned 60–90 cents an hour, compared with prewar jobs that averaged around 45 cents. With overtime, it seemed a fortune.

Single women with no family obligations worked as many as 70 hours a week. If she gave up a Sunday, one would earn $14—more than a third of an expected weekly wage. Such money was a big motivation to skip church; its appeal could change a woman's life in many ways.

In several states, protective labor legislation had to be amended to allow women to work at night and on weekends. It is arguable whether these laws originally were passed to protect women from the genuine evils of sweatshop labor earlier in the century, or whether they existed to preserve jobs for men during Depression unemployment—but it is indisputable that when the war demonstrated a genuine need for female labor at any hour of the week, the laws were quick to go.

Although there was little comment about the amendment of these laws, the change represented a significant shift in the ideals of feminism. From a 19th century view of benevolent protection for the weaker sex, feminists were almost unconsciously switching to a more egalitarian, directly competitive view. However, any discussion of this change (on the rare occasions when it occurred) was framed in terms of the needs of the war and not the needs of women. Changes that really meant increased opportunity for individuals were announced in terms of the needs of the nation, so that once again, women found themselves putting the group ahead of their personal needs.

The result was that, although there was always a core of women who worked because they needed the money, over and over again most women said that they were working, not for the relatively high pay, but to win the war. A young woman who dropped out of college for an aircraft plant is typical in her

133

ambivalent motivations: "I used to earn $15 month . . . baking biscuits. Then when I got my first pay check here—$32.60, all in one week—I tell you! But somehow, when you get working, it's more than the money. You learn about the war and you feel different about a lot of things."[32]

Those that the press quoted repeatedly told others that their motivations were patriotic. "Every time I finish a piece for a bomber," declared a woman who lost a son at Pearl Harbor, "I feel that we're that much closer to winning the war." Another, whose husband was missing in the Pacific, "I haven't heard from Russell, and I can't get word to him, but every night I write half a page of a letter to tell him what I did that day to help finish a plane. I'm saving the letters . . ."[33]

Shipbuilding, in contrast to aircraft manufacture, was an ancient craft. Long accustomed to an all-male work force, shipyards were slow to take on women, despite governmental encouragement to do so. The tremendous expansion necessary to replace ships sunk at Pearl Harbor and later Pacific disasters, however, soon made the need obvious. Overall numbers in shipbuilding jumped a phenomenal 15 times—from 100,000 in 1940 to 1,500,000 in early 1943.[34] Some of that million-and-a-half simply had to be women.

In contrast to the 36 women who had been employed by shipyards when the war in Europe broke out in 1939,[35] by March 1943 at least 23,000 women were working there, with predictions calling for 225,000 by the end of 1944. According to the personnel manager of the Kaiser yard in Portland, Oregon, "30 per cent of all shipbuilding tasks can be carried on by women. There is a British shipyard where two-thirds of the workers are on the distaff side."[36]

Other men in shipbuilding echoed the new-found conversion to the need for women. Norfolk Navy Yard announced that it would hire 7,500 women; Brooklyn yards lifted their 141-year ban on employing women; Mare Island Navy Yard in San Francisco had 6,000 women and expected more. Mobile, Alabama, wanted 1,000 women workers. Electric Boat Company in Groton, Connecticut, found an especially motivated group of women to work in the tight confines of submarines—the wives of Naval submarine men at sea.

Shipfitting classes at some vocational-training schools found that half of their new enrollees were female. Black women were especially eager to take this route as a way to get past the employment gate. Black publications cited particularly the training programs run by the National Youth Administration as significant in giving these women certification of their abilities. One black woman in fact made the highest grade among 6,000 taking the Civil Service exam for Navy yard jobs.[37]

Training programs, however, varied greatly, from a 270-hour course in welding to simple on-the-job experience. Some that had offered high-quality training before the war now drastically cut their curriculum, with the result that women were inevitably less well-trained than most men. The clear message was that the employment of women was to be temporary.

Again the analogies to the kitchen were clear. One housewife-turned-shipfitter summarized, "It's really simple to build a ship . . . You get your plan, cut out your pattern, prefabricate it, fit it together, and launch it. Men have always made such a job out of it!"[38] Yards that at the beginning hired only college women soon discovered that almost any woman had "an aptitude for pattern making."[39] Josephine Von Miklos, another shipyard ingenue, commented, "The other day a woman who had never seen a metal saw in her life . . . cut a complicated pattern on it in half the time it has ever taken an experienced man to do it. The foreman was delighted."[40]

In addition to the similarities to sewing, there were applications from cooking: "Making sand cores, or molds, for magnesium castings is 'easy as pie' for women used to kneading pastry dough at home. Fine, flourlike sand is painstakingly molded into precision forms, sprayed with oil, and baked."[41]

Welding—"sewing a fine seam"—was the most common shipbuilding job women did, but they also operated drill presses, grinders and lathes. They worked as expediters and truck drivers, and were found in electric and sheet-metal shops as well as warehouses. Women were praised for dexterity with wiring and pipe threading.

Their working conditions were far from pleasant, for shipbuilding often required exposure to wind, rain, snow and cold. Josephine von Miklos wrote:

The girl shipfitters are outside, right on the ships; and in the barges, right on the edge of the water front where winds always blow and the temperature is always fifteen degrees lower than anywhere else. They are out there those days of biting gales and icy planks . . . A hundred men walked out on one of those coldest days. The girls stuck.[42]

On hot summer days, welders bent over an electric arc that was 6,500 degrees of pure heat. Down in the bowels of a ship's hold, the noise of construction magnified and echoed. One woman described "chipping" as "a mild understatement" of the noise generated by "grinding through steel with a drill or electric chisel, which is as nerve-splintering as a dentist's drill multiplied by a hundred."[43]

It was also dangerous. Virginia Wilkinson on her first day of shipyard work climbed high onto scaffolding near red-hot rivets. Nervously she asked her mentor whether people often fell from the scaffold to the concrete far below. "Not often," he replied. "Just once."[44]

Later she described this highly inefficient shipyard as showing the greatest competence when it dealt with accidents. "A piece of steel would drop on someone's feet and sever them from his body, but there would be no outcry or fuss . . . The ambulance would come silently and quickly, and as silently and quickly remove all traces of the tragedy, with no work stopped, few words said, no fuss made."[45] Josephine Von Miklos also testified to the frequency of accidents: "Our fingers get forever cut and bruised and infected from the incredible filth around us. We wear small and large bandages and we go on with the work . . ."[46]

Despite the difficulty and danger, there was little attempt to pay women in this industry equal wages with men, even when the work men did also was unskilled. Reports of low pay were especially likely on the eastern and southern coasts, while labor shortages in the west kept wages higher. Despite the obvious inequality in pay between the sexes many women considered their wages to be good. Social Security and other benefits also were new for former housewives; these benefits were especially important to black women who did not receive them in their traditional domestic work.

More annoying than unequal pay was the attitude of many men who went about their work as though the war had changed nothing, as though the traditions of their craft were so precious that they should not be modified by anything. These women, eager to do anything at all for the war effort, found shipyard men ridiculously proprietorial about job categories. Welders, for instance, refused to do even a few minutes of "tacking" (a temporary weld), even when there was no tacker available and the work was held up for all as a result.

Women, long accustomed to diaper changing and toilet scrubbing, had an attitude of acceptance and found few tasks beneath them. They were ready to try any new work assigned. It wasn't long before shipyard management acknowledged that the addition of female labor was proving successful. Their experience was summarized in a government publication at the end of 1942:

> The yards were practically unanimous in reporting that on the whole the work done by women was considered equal to that of men . . . Foremen . . . often found that women were quicker to learn than the men available . . . Women exhibited a greater interest than did the men and were more anxious to know "why" and "how."[47]

While women's industrial success came as a surprise to shipbuilders, the munitions industry had long been aware that women were excellent employees. In this literally explosive work, female traditions of caution, precision and safety-consciousness were tremendously valuable. Already in 1941, before America became involved in the war, "at least 30,000 women were employed in shell loading, small arms ammunition, and fuse plants."[48] As the fighting in Europe worsened, women entered areas of munitions manufacture previously closed to them—and did so successfully without special training.

Two years ago [1939] the Frankford arsenal in Philadelphia employed 200 skilled men to make time fuses . . . they served long apprenticeships . . . When the defense drive began there were not nearly enough skilled men to meet the demand. Efforts to introduce hastily trained men from other fields brought a dismayingly large proportion of rejections of the completed fuses. Then someone had the bright idea of trying women who were expert embroiderers . . . The Army found it could train these women to do the job satisfactorily in thirty days.[49]

Protective labor laws were quickly adjusted so that, even before America entered the war, "Governor Hurley of Connecticut . . . lifted the ban against women working on night shifts of factories, at the urgent request of the Winchester Repeating Arms Company, which informed him that cartridge inspection was a 'natural woman's job' that could not be done nearly so well by men."[50]

Quality control was more important in this industry than almost any other. Both the amount of explosive material and the alignments of its container had to be *exact*, and women were very much aware that the lives of soldiers depended on how well they did their tasks. Josephine Von Miklos, who worked in an arms plant before getting her shipyard job, described the precision required:

Maybe the tool . . . is for the time-fuse rings. Then it is simply this: if your piece of steel is one-thousandth larger than it is designed to be, there will be too much powder—by a minute fraction—in the ring, and the fuse will go off too late. If your piece of steel is a thousandth too small, there will be a minute fraction of powder missing, and the fuse may go off too early. The shell will either not hit the enemy, or will hit your own lines. This is how important a couple of thousandths are. There is no tolerance in tools like these. There is no tolerance in death.[51]

Munitions jobs thus seemed a natural for women because the industry allowed no bravado, insisting instead on strict adherence to standards. From the time a woman arrived at work until she left, her every move was dictated by safety. At a shell-loading plant, women and men entered work each morning by different doors and took off their outer clothes. Wearing a dressing gown, they were examined for contraband such as silk undergarments, which could attract static electricity. Cigarettes and matches were obvious contraband, but in addition hair pins, watches, and most items of jewelry were forbidden, since metal and precious stones can spark. Once past the inspection area, each woman went to her locker where rubber-soled shoes and a flame-proof uniform, laundered every other day, were placed. Her hair was pushed under a fire-resistant cap. One "gunpowder girl" told about a man "who refused to wear a cap. Leaving the plant, he stopped to light a cigarette. His hair went up in flames."[52]

Munitions plants were typically built in remote areas where an explosion would do the least harm, with workers segregated as much as possible from each other for safety's sake. "In small steel booths," said one writer of the Bellevue Naval Magazine—which was "a healthy distance downriver" from any other site—women "would receive an element through a hole in the wall, put in the measured milligrams of powder and pass it quietly through an opposite hole to the next booth for another cautious twist, or tap, or turn."[53]

A newly built plant in southern Indiana employed 4,000 women working in small groups closed off from each other by yard-thick walls and heavy bronze doors. The rooms were kept at a steady temperature and humidity to prevent static electricity that might spark; each was equipped with a shower that could be "yanked on in a jiffy."[54] Buildings were separated from each other by hundreds of yards of lawn and contained just two stories, with the second story used only for hoppers that poured gunpowder into the lines below. Fire drills were held once a week and there were automatic sprinklers. Women also mopped their floors twice each shift, and walls and ceiling were hosed down at night to prevent dust accumulation.

Despite all this attention to safety, women found that the greatest hazard to their safety was the sheer monotony of the work—its repetitive nature simply made attention difficult after a while. Josephine Von Miklos wrote, "There isn't any glamour and excitement in making bombers and shells . . . [It is] a job to be done day after day . . . doing it exactly the same way, maybe a hundred times a day, or a thousand times or five thousand times . . . There is no glamour in pressing a lever five thousand times a day."[55]

Beyond the danger of boredom, fatigue was induced by the fact that some gunpowders were made with solvents that contained ether, and the remaining residue made workers sleepy. They sang to ease the monotony (favorites being "Smoke Gets in Your Eyes," "Star Dust" and "number one on our hit parade, 'Praise the Lord and Pass the Ammunition'"). Since gunpowder was packed in bags, they also sang "a home-grown ditty called 'Bag-Plant Blues.'"[56]

Not all plants were as safety-conscious as they should have been. The one where Von Miklos worked was in rural New England; it had been there through four wars and saw no particular urgency about this one. Management preferred to pay excess profit tax rather than improve conditions. Machines often broke down and few comforts were provided for employees.

Training was so poor in this plant that Von Miklos had been there for some time before she finally realized how dangerous were the little granules with which she worked. As the war's demands increased, more enlightened plants also began to cut back training; some formerly held "corn colleges" where new employees practiced with corn instead of actual explosives, but, under contract pressure, more and more sent women straight to the line without such training.

Accidents resulted, some of them terribly tragic. Fifteen production soldiers were killed at Elkton, Maryland, in May 1943, and 54 were wounded. A few months later, in September, another explosion brought more casualties. At the Pine Bluff, Arkansas, Chemical Warfare Arsenal there were also two explosions in one year. A black woman, Anne Marie Young, received the highest civilian award given by the War Department for her courage in rescuing others from those fires, with a brigadier general citing her "calm judgment and presence of mind."57

Probably because the work was so dangerous, munitions was the defense industry that was most likely to employ black women. A *National Geographic* reporter wrote:

> *We found women in steel-barricaded rooms measuring and loading pom-pom mix, lead azide, TNT, tetryl, and fulminate of mercury.*
>
> *Most of them were colored. They seemed delightfully blase as they passed the stuff along. Some would wink or give a big grin as we poked in their booths. But they treat powder with respect. They know that any snip of it could blow them to flinders.*
>
> *I asked the officer if their temperament—their lack of nerves, say—had anything to do with their being here in such numbers.*
>
> *"No," he said, "they like that extra six cents an hour hazard pay. This is one of the few jobs in industry which has a waiting list of applications."*58

Both the presence of numerous blacks in the industry and the fact that munitions plants were located in noncompetitive rural labor markets meant that relatively low wages were likely. Average pay rates were 45–60 cents an hour, or less than $30 a week. Although this industry clearly saw the advantages of women as workers, once again there was no attempt at enforcement of equal pay ideals. A government evaluation of gun plants reported tiredly, "Time and again the maximum rate paid to women on comparable operations was lower than the minimum rate paid to men working on the same machine and same part."59

In contrast to the light and careful touch of the "gunpowder girls," there were also women who did heavy, traditionally masculine work because of the war emergency. Conservative *Nation's Business* wrote enthusiastically of "Amazons in the Arsenal"—the extra large women sought out and hired by Boeing to staff its warehouse.

> *[They] tackle the job of unloading a freight car as if they were wading through a bargain counter. That's not all! When men were handling the job, they used carloading machines to stack big boxes nine high in the warehouse. Now there aren't enough carloaders and it's almost impossible to get more. So the women do without. They form bucket brigades and toss the boxes from hand to hand up as high as ten feet. They've not only replaced the men; they've replaced the machines.*60

Women also did heavy work in that industry basic to all others—steel. In the steel town of Gary, Indiana, for example, women were employed in more than 20 job categories of the industry. Feminist reporter-photographer Margaret Bourke-White wrote that "the length of this list is especially significant because before Pearl Harbor virtually the only women employed . . . were the sorters in the tin mills."61

These women were of the same motley ethnic mix as their men, who had worked in the steel mills for decades before war needs expanded to include their sisters. Black women were hired as well as white, and both did hot, heavy, dangerous tasks. Bourke-White concluded, "The women steel workers at Gary are not freaks or novelties . . . In time of peace they may return once more to home and family, but they have proved that in time of crisis no job is too tough for American women."62

Before the steel came the ore, and women worked at producing it, too. Mines in western states found that they had a problem with men who got draft deferments as being in essential employment, and then, as soon as the opportunity became available, skipped to the California coast for higher-paid construction jobs. Women in isolated mining towns had few occupational choices and so, by 1942, as the war looked increasingly serious, the mines reached out for women. *Business Week* concluded:

> *The hand that wields the powder puff also must be able to swing a heavy sledge, for much of the rock must be broken before it reaches the mill. It's hard, dirty work, even though not underground, but the former school principal, factory worker, and four housewives who comprise the vanguard of the movement receive regular beginner's wages of $6 or $7 a day with time-and-a-half after 40 hours.63*

Railroads were another industry tremendously affected by the war, for in the 1940s most of the nation's freight still moved by rail. With millions of additional tonnage in war materiel and millions of soldiers, too, trains were pushed to capacity throughout the war. They also reached out to women, although not nearly as much as they should have. Government agencies nagged, and by 1944, the railroads finally reached their goal of employing more women than they had in America's short involvement with World War I—106,000 women, a 68% increase over the previous year.64

Yet most of the increase was in the menial work of cleaning (69%) and baggage/station attendants (165%). The vast majority of women worked in clerical positions, and the hiring of college-educated women as ticket agents was hailed as an achievement. Out on the tracks doing real railroading were only 250 females. Just 18 of the 14,385 in top management were women, most of whom had been hired in World War I.65 In this war, however, "Mrs. Casey Jones" was not being used by the railroads to do nearly what she was capable of doing; at the war's end, women railroad employees were still less than 10% of the total.66

The situation reflected the one that existed for women throughout industry. The new occupational opportunities were indeed real, and hundreds of thousands of women proved themselves successful in them. However, throughout

140

the war, approximately five times as many women continued in "essential civilian employment" as worked in the newer war industries. This majority saw media attention given almost entirely to the minority, and they frequently felt excluded and defensive about their work. One former housewife was typical of millions; after her two sons went off to war, she took "a job as a cook in a restaurant downtown. The man they had there before went into the Navy. Aunt May says, 'Sure, I've got a real war job. Don't I feed the people that buy the War Bonds that build the ships that beat the Japs?'"67

Even in the essential civilian area, women found millions of new jobs open to them, some of them in fields dominated by men, some of them not previously offered to these women because of their race or age. "In restaurants," one thoughtful observer wrote, "waitresses are in their sixties and even seventies. It hurts you to see them carrying heavy trays—until you see the pride in their bright eyes. Grandsons, maybe, in Africa?"68

There was a 100% increase in women employed by food stores between 1941 and 1942; women replaced men as "window trimmers, buyers, shipping clerks, stock clerks, and porters in department stores; as clerks in . . . meat markets and shoe stores; as cleaners and ushers in movie houses; as cashiers, drug clerks, bakers, dishwashers, checkers . . . "69

Some of the jobs women took—such as movie usher, telegram deliverer, and elevator operator—were marginal positions that probably would not have existed at all but for the depressed labor conditions of the 1930s. These jobs would disappear in the 1950s, yet having held them was not a total loss, for they gave women an all-important entrance into the work force.

Rosie did much more than rivet airplanes and weld ships and test guns and pack ammo—she also planted trees and fought fires for the Forest Service, read meters for gas and electric companies, installed telephones, delivered mail, drove cabs and pumped gas. She was even the department store Santa.

SOURCE NOTES

1. Flint, *Dress Right, Dress*, p. 105.
2. Ruth Tracy Millard, "53 Hours a Week," *Saturday Evening Post* (June 12, 1943): p. 87.
3. Anthony, *Out of the Kitchen*, p. 5. See also Dorothy Parker, "Are We Women or Are We Mice?" *Reader's Digest* (condensed from *Mademoiselle*) (July 1943): p. 71.
4. Frances Perkins, "Women's Work in Wartime," *Monthly Labor Review* (April 1943): p. 663.
5. "Women—Now!," *Business Week* (January 9, 1943): p. 72. See also "Amazons of Aberdeen," *American Magazine* (January 1943): p. 98.

6. Ibid.
7. "Output: Ladies Welcome," *Newsweek* (November 30, 1942): p. 56.
8. Katherine Glover, "Women as Manpower," *Survey Graphic* (March 1943): p. 69. For more information on the numbers of women in war industry, see also "Employment of Women in Defense Industries," *Monthly Labor Review* (May 1941): p. 1147; "Jobs and Workers," *Survey Midmonthly* (November 1941): p. 330; Mary Hornaday, "From French Hells to Slacks," *Christian Science Monitor* (June 27, 1942): p. 4; "When Women Wear the Overalls," *Nation's Business* (June 1942): p. 70; "Women's Factory," *Business Week* (July 4, 1942): p. 20; "Employment of Women in Wartime," *Monthly Labor Review* (September 1942): p. 441; Steve King, "Danger! Women at Work," *American Magazine* (September 1942): p. 40; Frank McSherry, "Women Workers Wanted!" *Flying* (October 1942): p. 34; "About 3,000,000 Women Now in War Work," *Science News Letter* (January 16, 1943): p. 44; Paul McNutt, "Wake Up and Work," *Woman's Home Companion* (May 1943): p. 70; "Wartime Employment of Women in Manufacturing," *Monthly Labor Review* (October 1943): p. 723; "When Shopping for a War Industry Job," *Independent Woman* (October 1943): p. 291; C.E. Warne, "Cherchez la Femme," *Current History* (November 1943): p. 214; J.E. Walters, "Women in Industry," *Annals of the American Academy of Political and Social Science*, vol. 229 (1943): p. 56; "Females in Factories," *Time* (July 17, 1944): p. 60.
9. "Manless Industry," *Business Week* (March 10, 1945): p. 41.
10. LaVerne Bradley, "Women at Work," *National Geographic* (August 1944): p. 193.
11. Ibid., p. 198.
12. Don Wharton, "New Workers Speed Plane Production," *Reader's Digest* (condensed from *Aviation*) (June 1942): p. 103.
13. Elizabeth Hawes, "My Life on the Midnight Shift," *Woman's Home Companion* (August 1943): p. 25. See also Elizabeth Hawes, *Wenches with Wrenches, Or Why Women Cry* (New York: Reynal & Hitchcock, 1943).
14. A. Louise Fillebrown, "I Helped Build Fighter Planes," *Independent Woman* (November 1943): p. 348. See Marjorie M. Potter, "I Started on the Swing Shift," *Christian Science Monitor* (January 27, 1945): p. 8 for a similar comment.
15. Bradley, "Women at Work," p. 194.
16. Fillebrown, "I Helped Build Fighter Planes," p. 333.
17. Elizabeth Meyer, "Ma's Making Bombers!" *Reader's Digest* (condensed from *The Washington Post*) (November 1942): p. 49.
18. "A Woman on the Assembly Line," *American Mercury* (December 1942): p. 759. (Anonymous letter-to-the-editor in the publication's "Open Forum.")
19. Ibid.

20. Bradley, "Women at Work," p. 193.
21. Wharton, "New Workers Speed Plane Production," p. 102. See also "Women at Vultee," *Newsweek* (September 1, 1941): p. 2.
22. Ibid., p. 103.
23. Frank Taylor, "Meet the Girls Who Keep 'Em Flying," *Saturday Evening Post* (May 30, 1942): pp. 30 and 57.
24. Ruth Matthews and Betty Hannah, "This Changing World for Women," *Ladies Home Journal* (August 1942): p. 27.
25. Wharton, "New Workers Speed Plane Production," p. 103.
26. Kathryn Blood, "Maybe We Can't Carry Rifles," *Pulse* (August 1944), p. 27. See also by this author, "Women Warriors," *Pulse*, December 1943, p. 20.
27. Frank S. Adams, "Women in Democracy's Arsenal," *New York Times* (October 19, 1941): p. 10.
28. Wharton, "New Workers Speed Plane Production," p. 102.
29. Charlie James, "Women in Airline Maintenance Shops," *Aviation* (December 1942): p. 39.
30. Ibid., p. 168.
31. Harold Keen, "Feeder Factories," *Flying* (February 1944): p. 27.
32. Meyer, "Ma's Making Bombers!," p. 50; see also "Employment of Girls on Government Contracts," *Monthly Labor Review* (June 1942): p. 1328.
33. Taylor, "Meet the Girls," p. 31.
34. "Vocational Training Speeds Building of New Planes and Ships," *Education for Victory* (February 1, 1943): p. 3.
35. Bradley, "Women at Work," p. 194.
36. Beatrice Oppenheim, "Anchors Aweigh!," *Independent Woman* (March 1943): p. 70.
37. Mary Anderson: "Negro Women on the Production Front," *Opportunity: Journal of Negro Life*, April 1943, p. 37. (Anderson was head of the Women's Bureau of the Department of Labor.) See also in the same issue of this publication, Charles C. Berkley, "War Work—A Challenge to Negro Womanpower," p. 58; George E. De Mar, "Negro Women Are American Workers, Too," p. 41; and "Negro Women Employed for First Time by Washington Navy Yard," p. 79.
38. Bradley, "Women at Work," p. 199.
39. Ibid.
40. Josephine Von Miklos, *I Took a War Job,* (New York: Simon & Schuster, 1943), p. 195. A similar book is Ann Pendleton (Mary Beatty Trask) *Hit the Rivet, Sister* (New York: Howell, Soskin Publishers, 1943).
41. Ibid., p. 196.
42. Ibid., p. 195.
43. Wilkinson, "From Housewife to Shipfitter," p. 333.
44. Ibid., p. 329.

45. Ibid., p. 333.
46. Von Miklos, *I Took a War Job*, p. 195.
47. "Employment of Women in Shipyards," *Monthly Labor Review* (February 1943): p. 280. See also Susan B. Anthony II, "Working at the Navy Yard," *New Republic* (May 1, 1944): p. 597.
48. "Women at Work," *Newsweek* (January 1942): p. 36. See also Beulah Amidon, "Arms and the Women," *Survey Graphic* (May 1942): p. 244.
49. Adams, "Women in Democracy's Arsenal," p. 10.
50. Ibid.
51. Von Miklos, *I Took a War Job*, p. 98.
52. Dorothy Warner, "Gunpowder Girl," *American Magazine* (June 1943): p. 72.
53. Bradley, "Women at Work," p. 199.
54. Warner, "Gunpowder Girl," p. 72.
55. Von Miklos, *I Took a War Job*, p. 16.
56. Warner, "Gunpowder Girl," p. 73.
57. Blood, "Maybe We Can't Carry Rifles," p. 26.
58. Bradley, "Women at Work," p. 199.
59. "War Work of the U.S. Women's Bureau," *Monthly Labor Review* (December 1942): p. 1180.
60. "Amazons in the Arsenal," *Nation's Business* (July 1943): p. 65; see also Nona Baldwin, "Woman Mans the Machine," *New York Times Magazine* (August 23, 1942): p. 8.
61. Margaret Bourke-White, "Women In Steel," *Life* (August 9, 1943): p. 75.
62. Ibid.; see also Perkins, "Women's Work in Wartime," p. 663.
63. "Women in Mines," *Business Week* (September 12, 1942): p. 35.
64. "Employment of Women in Railroads," *Monthly Labor Review* (September 1944): p. 590.
65. Ibid. See also Marie Deems, "Full Speed Ahead," *Independent Woman* (December 1942): p. 360; "Mrs. Casey Jones," *Business Week* (November 28, 1942): p. 83.
66. "Women Employed by Class I Steam Railroads," *Monthly Labor Review* (September 1945): p. 506.
67. Josephine Ripley, "Woman . . . Armed With Power," *Christian Science Monitor* (September 4, 1943): p. 15.
68. "How You Are Helping," *Woman's Home Companion* (June 1943), p. 81.
69. "Replacement of Men by Women in New York Service Industries," *Monthly Labor Review* (March 1943): p. 487; see also "Women in Forestry," *New York Times Magazine* (October 4, 1942): p. 31, and "Women Without Uniforms," *Woman's Home Companion* (September 1943), p. 46.

10

WOMEN'S PROBLEMS ARE PRODUCTION'S PROBLEMS

A woman's first day at work might mean that, naked and shivering under a dressing gown, she submitted to a factory's routine physical examination. Such an exam may have been a rude beginning for a woman's work life, something dehumanizing and intimidating. It was a first indication of the total invasion of privacy that war work entailed.

Most factories dictated how a women must clothe herself. The objective was to ensure safety, but for women who had never before appeared in public wearing anything other than skirts, the adjustment to dressing like men was a profound change. A great deal of media attention was given to this revolution, and while most of it was written in the determinedly shallow style so popular with World War II editors, the public nonetheless seemed to grasp that this transformation in dress represented a serious and permanent change in women's roles. Wearing male clothing was indeed a genuine liberation for women— brought about, ironically, by a need to conform.

Even at plants that did not insist on uniforms, dress codes were enforced. Slacks and sturdy, low-heeled shoes were mandatory. Similar regulations were enforced on other aspects of feminine appearance. Only a decade or two earlier, bobbed hair was controversial, but now women found that long tresses were a definite factory taboo. If her hair were not as short as a man's, it had to be pushed under a turban. Management would assume no risk that she could be scalped by whirling machinery.

Particular factories had particular requirements; women working near airplane instruments, for example, could not wear sweaters or anything else made of wool because "even the tiniest piece of lint can destroy the accuracy of an instrument which might be on the dashboard of a bomber." [1] Jewelry often was forbidden, including even wedding rings that could be caught in machines. In one plant, when "it became apparent that devout Catholic girls would not easily be parted from wedding rings," management went so far as to "invoke the co-operation of the priests—who promised the girls that when the war was over they would again bless the rings."[2]

Consolidated Aircraft allowed the first 200 women they hired to vote on whether or not to wear uniforms, and the women's response was affirmative. Uniforms in many ways were easier for busy working women, for now there were no morning wardrobe decisions and few shopping needs. Moreover, as with the first WAACs, uniforms showed an *esprit de corps* and were a daily demonstration of one's participation in the war. For the company, of course, uniforms made supervision easier in many ways; one plant, for instance, designed lattice-work pockets to ease contraband inspection and cut down on daily frisking.

Sometimes, however, even after the decision for uniforms was made, providing the necessary items was still difficult. The harried personnel manager of Todd Shipyards wrote of the stupendous effort she made to obtain work shoes for the first women hired— and when they arrived, the women refused to wear them. Their reason:

> "The soles aren't heavy enough, oxford-cut low shoes aren't safe enough; we want them over the ankles too. And we want steel toes like the men."
>
> . . . We started searching the city for men's heavy, bulky safety shoes in the smallest sizes . . . But the women were right, only it never occurred to us who were planning that they would be willing to wear those unshapely, bulky, men's shoes. The thing we learned was that women really cared about doing the job safely.[3]

A trade publication on leather goods went so far as to criticize its industry for failure to understand women's apparel needs:

> It was pointed out editorially in this magazine not long ago that "women, married and single, have always worked and have often worked harder than men."
>
> . . . Refusal to accept the bald fact that women work has been for many years the underlying reason why most women are not properly dressed for their work . . . Last year the shoe industry made 32,249,177 pairs of work-type shoes for men, but it didn't make a single pair of shoes under a woman's work shoe classification.[4]

Two years before the war ended, glove manufacturers also had not yet realized that they were missing a market. "I do not know of a single manufacturer of women's gloves who has gone into the manufacture of women's work gloves," said one expert. "Yet at many plants steel-reinforced gloves are essential."[5]

The result was that women wore clothes designed for men, and this could be dangerous. Welders in shipyards wore leather pants, but as "it seems next to impossible to get a pair which leaves room for the hips and yet is not too big round the waist," women wore men's pants. Accidents were inevitable. One, "working clad in ill-fitting leathers which she held up by a belt," constantly reached down to pull up her pants. At last she tugged too hard, "the belt gave way, the pants fell down, the woman dropped her iron in an effort to grab up her pants and received a nasty burn."[6]

Newsmen found this accident to be a source of considerable hilarity. That, too, was typical of the nervousness men felt at working with women. Clothing codes were in fact often spelled out not so much for the protection of the woman being regulated, but rather for the man who worked with her.

Business Week argued for uniformed factory women by saying, "tight sweaters, snug slacks, and feminine artifices of color and style were distracting influences involving equal hazard to the men."[7] *Time* reported regretfully, "No problems like these bothered factory managers a year ago. But now perhaps, a very shapely sweater girl wanders in to take her place in the swing shift. Low whistles follow her as she ambles down the aisle between machines." Cost accountants even busied themselves by figuring the price of "the distraction caused by a woman walking through the plant." It was an expensive bit of strolling in their minds, valued at $250.[8]

Management's first response was a time-honored one in many prewar industries that employed women: Segregate them into jobs where they work apart from men. Sexual segregation was still so common when the war began that one of the more unreasoned habits in some locales was that "men apply [for jobs] in the morning, and women in the afternoon."[9] Such customs made it easier for business to categorize the sexes and pay them at different rates. Even some new war plants with modern cafeterias still held outmoded thinking on the sexes, for they separated men and women—husbands and wives could not eat together. Cadillac in Detroit, now producing war materiel instead of cars, exhibited a wariness that strained *Time*'s credulity, as it reported that management "keeps its first 25 women workers behind a *padlocked* door. Says an executive, 'You know how men are.'"[10]

Such solutions were obviously not realistic in a modern world, and as women proved their abilities as workers, these apprehensive restrictions faded. Instead of changing male behavior through education and appropriate discipline, however, management placed the burden on women. Typical solutions to sexual harassment, for example, were to design uniforms that made women indistinguishable from men and to hire "gray-haired factory chaperones" to "catch" distracting women "in the ladies room"[11] and advise them on disguising their appearance. Women, however, figured out on their own the best method of dealing with excessive male attention; several accounts report that women spontaneously held meetings and planned reversed-role response. When men were faced with catcalls, whistles, and sexual aggression by women, their own misbehavior stopped.[12]

But much male hostility was more direct than flirtatious. Older men in particular resented the introduction of women into fields in which they had, in their view, earned domination. They were less likely than younger men to have gone to coeducational schools and more likely to have lived lives in which work roles were rigidly determined by sex. Some exhibited their hostility even before women entered the factory gates, as the man so spitefully unchivalrous that "he'd drive 10 miles out of his way each morning to pick up a carload of all-male passengers, while the girl who lived just down the street had to walk 2 miles to take the bus."[13]

Such men simply didn't believe that women could do their work, even when women did. Shipbuilding especially, as an ancient craft, harbored men unwilling to work with women. Their attitude was that "she didn't, and even if she did, she couldn't have." This account by Josephine Von Miklos is far too typical:

> *"You're a pretty good mechanic," he said finally, and added, "for a woman."*
>
> *"Why for a woman?" I asked and wished I hadn't. I knew what was coming. I had heard it a dozen times before.*
>
> *"Well," he said, and spat a hunk of tobacco on the floor, "it ain't women's work."*[14]

It was not easy for women to dissolve into this male world. They attracted attention like lightening rods, and most of that attention was negative. "Diehard old foremen resent like blazes having females underfoot," said one. "We women look as obvious as sore thumbs if we aren't busy at something all the time. The old factory hands can fritter away time with ease, knowing how to look busy while cleaning their tools or tatting up some new gadget to entertain themselves."[15]

Indeed it seems that one of the fundamental—though unrecognized—conflicts between the sexes was a basically different attitude towards time. Women generally were in a hurry to get the job done and to get on with their lives. Blue-collar men sometimes took the attitude that there was nothing of an emergency nature, that both they and the work would be there a decade from now. In part, this difference derived from women knowing their industrial situation was temporary (whether or not they approved), and in part it may indicate that most women had more experience with personal time management than these men had. A woman didn't have a foreman at home and she did not need the discipline of a time card; she knew she could not fool anyone into thinking housework got done if she simply watched the clock until her "workday" was over.

Repeatedly, however, women who took defense-plant jobs from a war-effort motivation complained that men did not work hard and allowed them to work even less. There was in fact a regrettably large amount of enforced idleness that was actually the fault of company managements. Having the protection of cost-plus purchasing by the government, they overhired in fear of later labor shortages, planned supplies poorly and bungled contract signings. Out on the line, however, the result was that bored workers fought for something meaning-ful to do and created lasting hostility for each other.*

When management did intervene in work relationships between the sexes, most likely it was simply orders to men to follow the rules in working with women rather than any genuine attempt at changing negative attitudes. It was the women who by their example did what reeducation was done. Moreover, while management was generally more enlightened on the subject of women than most of the male workers, it did sometimes stoop to divide-and-conquer techniques. Believing that their long-term workers would be male, management took that side in most disputes and sometimes tried to reassure men of their inherent superiority, as this ad in a Buffalo paper:

Are you a tough guy? Have you got red fighting blood in your veins? Then here's your chance to do a vitally needed job in heavy war industry—a job that calls for a REAL TWO-FISTED HE-MAN! The pay is good. But more than that, you'll get the satisfaction of doing a job that's really important to winning this war! A JOB NO WOMAN CAN DO![16]

As with military women, the key to acceptance of the group was in each individual proving herself. One reporter told of a foreman who swore, "'When the first woman is sent to my shop, [they can] send my release with her.' Some months later, I mentioned a few of the usual objections to women in industry . . . and this same foreman defended them hotly. He specifically pointed out the girl who was turning out five assembly units to her male predecessor's two."[17] Many managers agreed that the presence of women had "very beneficial effect upon much of the dead wood found among men who were inclined to ride along upon no more secure grounds than the fact that they were men."[18]

It was the production records that over and over again proved indisputably women were capable. It may well be true that Rosie the Riveter's competent image is directly owed to the fact that cost accounting had been developed to a fine science, for without those production statistics the arguments could have raged endlessly.

---

* In shipyards afflicted by idleness while awaiting supplies, first-aid nurses were nonetheless terribly busy. It is probably typical of most planners to overestimate the number of industrial workers needed for a task, while underestimating the need for social services.

As it sometimes divided to conquer in the war between the sexes, management also was guilty of philosophical duplicity in dealing with labor legislation and women. When seeking amendment of protective legislation designed to limit the hours and improve the conditions of women's work, management argued for female equality to choose, as men chose, their work status. Yet when it came to equal pay regulations, management found principles of equity easy to ignore.

Business Week frankly acknowledged that "only a third of the companies . . . adhered to the policy of equal pay for equal work."[19] Neither government nor unions seriously pressured business on the subject, so it is not surprising that the principle was largely ignored. The National War Labor Board helped business with concealing artifices: "The board ruled that, no matter how efficient women may be, it is right for them to be paid less for the same work if the men are doing their work in another shop."[20]

Unions, of course, should have been there to uphold worker rights, but their leadership in the case of women was sadly lacking. By June 1944, when female employment was more than 18,000,000, the Department of Labor reported that women union members had increased from 800,00 in 1939 to 3,000,000[21]—but this still meant that less than 20% of women workers were union members. Yet even that low figure is inflated in reality, for it reflects dues collected in closed shops and indicates nothing of the limited involvement of women in union locals. Women were generally not encouraged to join unions and got even less encouragement to be active participants.

In other places where they paid their union dues, women's rights were nonetheless unprotected. As late as November 1944, there were "still a few shops where union contracts . . . actually provided that a man may 'bump' any woman in the plant off her job no matter how much longer that woman may have been working than he has."[22]

Even in industries where unions were powerful, there is little or no evidence that they reached out to welcome women as part of the labor force. In the car plants that were retooled for war, the United Auto Workers union was well established by the 1940s; yet, management took, and seemed to deserve, the credit for including women. When Ford, for instance, broke its 40-year precedent of never hiring women and employed 12,000 for its giant Willow Run plant, it was Ford, not UAW, that got media attention for enlightenment and patriotism. Labor's wartime contribution seemed merely acquiescence.

Similarly, many of the young women recruited and hired for eastern munitions plants were from the mining towns of West Virginia and western Pennsylvania. Presumably, they were the prounion daughters and sisters of United Mine Workers, yet there is no evidence that UMW or any other union tried to organize these women. Munitions remained the war industry most likely to have low and unequal wages.

Instead of creatively availing themselves of this tremendous opportunity to expand membership, union leaders instead sometimes busied themselves with fantasies that revealed how little they understood women workers. Female cab drivers in some cases found unions unwilling to believe that they did not wish to use the taxis as convenient fronts for prostitution. Oregon shipyards allegedly had the same troublesome women workers:

> The AFL unions in the Portland shipyards are trying to screen the prostitutes from their membership rolls. Fifty women lost their union work permits because they were discovered plying their trade in the holds of new Liberty ships; others because, with date books in hand, they spent their working hours in the shops soliciting patrons for their leisure hours.
>
> A collateral fear is that the prostitutes may consort with negroes, who then might try to take liberties with other white women—and this might lead to serious race complications.[23]

Even the leftist *New Republic* had to acknowledge that "many old line AFL unions still vigorously oppose admitting women to their organizations."[24]* While they argued that the newer CIO unions were working on behalf of women, evidence supporting this contention was notably absent from their pages as the war labor force continued to grow. Perhaps unions were intimidated by the right-wing press that did in fact accuse them of using strong-arm membership tactics in closed shops, but the reality was that a woman with prounion views sometimes found it difficult to figure out if there was a union in her factory and how she could join.

Perhaps, too, unions were so eager to demonstrate their patriotism that they overly generously expanded the wartime ban on strikes to include an effectual ban on any viable union activism, including the recruitment of women. The ultimate result, though unintended at the time, was that the exclusion of women and racial minorities strengthened conservatism in American unions.

---

* It is an interesting question why Labor Secretary Frances Perkins did relatively little to improve the status of women within unions. Perhaps, as the first woman on the Cabinet in U.S. history, she simply feared for her position. Male unions were politically powerful, and she may well have believed that President Roosevelt would not necessarily support her if she offended them. Beyond that, Perkins was a social worker by background and may still have held the typical Progressive Era view that women should be protected by labor legislation rather than by union activism. Women, in this view, were more an object of attention for benevolent organizations than militants capable of organizing themselves. Finally, there was the whole temporary nature of the war-labor situation; in the busy world of the war, it may have been simply a battle she didn't care to lead.

If women in general were only partially accepted into the labor force, older women in particular felt the sting of rejection. This account of a Bridgeport, Connecticut, woman relates the experience of thousands:

> *In an incredible short time after Pearl Harbor, it seemed one after another of my women friends . . . became absorbed . . . into volunteer services . . . But I wanted a full-time job . . .*
>
> *I soon discovered, however, that this wasn't so easy . . . The specter of age reared its ugly head whenever I struck out in the direction of an employment office . . . A little later, however, with everyone from the president of the local women's club to my own kitchen maid making for the assembly lines, it became evident that the supply of acceptable young workers would soon become exhausted . . .*
>
> *Sure enough, before long, the appeal "Women Wanted" jumped into large type in the "want columns." Thus encouraged, I girded myself for another try . . . My hunch was right. The age limit rose from forty to forty-five, forty-five to fifty; and then, in the more congested factory districts, it disappeared altogether . . .*
>
> *By that time, I'd ceased trying to impress the people who did the hiring with how much I knew.*[25]

Older women did feel that they had to hide their experience, lest it bring disconcerting questions as to their age. While it should have been obvious to industrial planners that work experience is advantageous and middle-aged women were a more likely labor source than younger ones with family obligations, once again prejudices had to be forced into examination. Just as the industrial truism that male was better than female had to be rethought, so management also had to learn that younger was not necessarily superior to older. Instead, at first, they sought a mythical 30-year old woman whose children were grown.

"Women over 40 are a nuisance and a liability. They slow up production," was the belief of many employers at the beginning of the war:

> *Older women are much slower on the uptake, in learning, thinking, moving, so production lags . . . older women are more of an insurance risk because they're more susceptible to disease and accidents, . . . [and] older women have no mechanical aptitudes; they dislike new ideas, are gossipy and are less adaptable to factory working conditions.*[26]

Soon, of course, there was evidence to the contrary. While in some cases it was true that older women were slower and more cautious when first employed, those characteristics were more than compensated for by the fact that they proved more reliable than younger workers. "They present no problems of discipline," said an aircraft plant manager. "Restroom loitering is at a minimum. They come to work on time, and their daily attendance is excellent, far superior

152

to younger women."[27] Shipbuilders came to prefer older women to the very young: "Some yards refuse to accept girls under twenty . . . The average age is twenty-five to forty-five; with surprising frequency one comes across women between fifty and sixty."[28]

Their carefulness and calm in emergencies was soon noted by munitions manufacturers, as with a supervisor who averred, "If I could choose the age group, I would not employ any woman under 40 on the [ammunition] loading lines."[29] Once again the actuaries came to the rescue of a maligned minority; insurers were soon saying that "injury frequency for workers of 60 or more turns out to be less than half that for ages 20 to 29."[30]

Nor were older women necessarily more mechanically inept, as shown by the accountant who could point to a Philadelphia woman who, after running a lathe for just three weeks, was earning $41 weekly on a piece-pay basis, whereas the previous top wage was just $22. Encouraged by this evidence, some employers even reached out to the physically handicapped. They found that many whose legs did not function had developed superior finger dexterity, and that even the blind were capable of doing excellent work in gauging machine parts.

Probably the most serious liability of older women was one that employers never noticed—their extreme lack of self-confidence. Most of these women were permanently psychologically scarred by the Great Depression, for never in the 1920s or 1930s would employers have encouraged them to take jobs. Their entire adult lives had been spent in self-abnegation. Thus, it is understandable that these women viewed themselves as valuable only in the abnormal condition of war and quietly retreated off the scene at its end.

The low self-esteem of one illustrates not only the condition of many older women, but also the importance of the new wartime female personnel managers in dealing with these potential workers. To a New Jersey war job headquarters came "an elderly woman who had never before worked."

> She had no children, no adequate means of income, nothing but a small bank reserve. She thought possibly a war job might solve her problem.
>
> It took her three visits before she was convinced that she had anything actually worthwhile to contribute . . . When we discovered that she was clever with her hands, I suggested a plant . . . for precision instruments . . . She applied for the job—but still wasn't ready to accept what was offered.
>
> I told her to try. "Don't be worried over your lack of speed," I said. "They don't expect speed from you at first."
>
> She decided to take the job. Now she likes it. She says a new world has opened up to her. New people have come into her life. And she makes enough to provide for her needs.[31]

One of the ways in which this woman and millions of other formerly isolated housewives changed their lives was the simple act of eating lunch in the company of others. It was a sociability much appreciated, although conditions for pleasant society at work were seldom as common as much of the business press would have preferred the public to believe. There was considerable publicity about modern cafeterias and break rooms that the new middle-class and feminine workers were forcing management to adopt, yet most worker accounts of their experience agreed that any leisure was short and harried.

Night shifts generally got two 10-minute rest breaks, while day shifts had only one. Twenty minutes for meals was not uncommon, and 30 was the general rule. It was a time constraint designed to give no alternative to the quick sandwich at the work bench. Josephine Von Miklos, whose awareness of European war reality seldom allowed her to complain, did complain "about lunch, for instance. About long wooden tables around which women workers sit and eat sandwiches . . . and go to the LADIES for a smoke— all in twenty minutes. And, of course, it wasn't LADIES but WOMEN, and it's an open latrine . . ."[32]Ruth Millard was a similarly highly motivated woman who greeted almost everything about her war job with cheer, but her lunch description makes it clear that the break was far from relaxing:

> Lunchtime offers a choice of two expedients. One is a sandwich out of a paper bag, eaten in our rest room, where about twenty girls crowd together in the space of my breakfast nook at home. The other is HARRY'S. Lunching at HARRY'S involves going down the four flights, getting waited on, eating, and going up the four flights, all within the thirty minutes allowed us by the time clock. Dolly and I do it about twice a week. We slip in through the smoke and the crash of crockery . . .[33]

There were exceptions to these rules. Nell Giles wrote about communal meals cooked by the women themselves when their work gave them access to a source of heat. "It was corn on the cob tonight . . . since there are so few on this second floor shift there is always a community supper, bought on the way to work by one girl and never costing more than 10 cents each."[34] And there were the new company cafeterias, a luxury undreamed of a decade earlier, but now adopted at some facilities eager to demonstrate modern-management ideals.

> Before the war few if any plants gave much thought to feeding their employees . . . Now the plant manager is beginning to wake up to the fact that a hot balanced meal is essential to keep production up. For some workers have not enough to eat at home, what with shopping difficulties, and the limitations of ration points. Sperry has a modern cafeteria seating fifteen hundred people . . . A dietician controls the menus . . . At Boeing a white tractor pulls a train of cafeteria trailers, each a self-contained unit. These stop every two hundred and fifty feet along the half-mile long aisles . . . One Ohio plant is feeding several thousand workers Vitamin A rations to improve their sight and protect them from eye fatigue.[35]

It was in a woman's off-work life, however, that the simple question of eating sometimes became an enormous problem. Few restaurants were open for swing-shift women when they got off work in the middle of the night, and most found it impossible to rent rooms where one could cook at that hour. War-industry boom towns never did successfully answer the question of how workers would eat. In the munitions town of Elkton, Maryland, for instance, "There is no one thing that has caused more complaint among the girls than food." Meals were hard to obtain, of poor quality, and so expensive that some literally found it too costly to eat. "Many girls go through the day on a cup of coffee and a piece of toast."[36]

The high prices were due not only to a huge demand, but also to an inadequate supply of food. In the shipbuilding town of Wilmington, North Carolina, "a war-swollen population endeavors futilely to get fed at five restaurants," where portions were small and the food poor because of rationing. The Chamber of Commerce "had not been able to persuade anyone to open new restaurants because of the 'impossibility of getting ration cards.'"[37] In other towns, restaurants actually closed, despite hungry crowds of customers, because they could not cope with the difficulties of getting food, equipment and workers.

Not only restaurants but also banks, stores, post offices and all services were strained to the breaking point with the excessive population attracted by defense plants. Cities the size of Sacramento, Seattle, San Diego, Buffalo, and Baltimore could not handle the growth that their defense plants brought, but the problems were magnified tremendously for rural areas officially defined as critically in need of labor—towns such as Aberdeen, Mississippi; Childersburg, Alabama; LaPorte-Michigan City, Indiana; Revenna-Warren, Ohio; Elmira, Sidney and Binghamton, New York; Cumberland and Elkton-Perryville, Maryland.* The federal government deliberately placed munitions plants in such remote locations, but by definition this meant that the ordinary needs of workers' lives could not easily be met.

Housing, of course, was the first and fundamental problem. Upwards of 25,000,000 people moved within the U.S. during World War II—10,000,000 more than the total Armed Forces—and many found themselves literally homeless. It was unlike Depression homelessness in that people had money for rent, but the housing supply was inadequate and would stay so because of the greater demand for war materiel. Though the causes differed, the result was the same as in the Depression—people slept in tents, in old railroad cars, and abandoned

---

* If these areas were gaining population in huge numbers, it is axiomatic that other locations were losing population. Among those cities were Omaha, Memphis, St. Paul, Boston, and New York, which still had almost a half million unemployed when the war was entering its last year. See J.C. Furnas, "Are Women Doing Their Share?" *Saturday Evening Post* (April 29, 1944): p. 12.

buildings. Women lucky enough to find rooms or apartments slept double in single beds, with night workers sharing these same beds by day.

Employers to some extent tried to assume responsibility for the homeless workers they attracted, as in this report:

> One rainy night the doorbell rang at Mrs. Betty Grubb's in Oxford, Pennsylvania. The bus driver of the Triumph Explosives Company of Elkton called out, "Mrs. Grubb, can't you take these two defense girls in?"
>
> . . . Nancy and Jo . . . had been riding all night in the crowded company bus. There had been interminable hours of waiting after they got to the explosives plant at Elkton, while they filled out papers, were photographed, fingerprinted, had their physical examinations, were blood-typed and finally were given . . . an identification number. After that there was another seventeen mile ride to Oxford. Now they were here, exhausted . . .[38]

Married women with families, of course, had even greater difficulty finding homes. One woman, whose husband and son were shipbuilders, could find no place except a garage. "I refused point-blank to stay home and keep house in a garage," she said. "So I came to work."[39] But the greatest problems of all were encountered by black women. If the whites of Elkton, Maryland, found their war situation untenable, imagine that of its tiny black community:

> Their houses are small, their families are large. There was no place to put the more than doubled colored population which flowed into town. Colored workers sat up all night in kitchens and sitting rooms, since their hosts had no beds for them; girls . . . slept cramped in their cars.
>
> Their pastor . . . is the only one to look out for their interests, and he meets almost as many emergencies as there are days. Over Thanksgiving he housed fifteen stranded people—men, women and children, migratory workers from Florida who had just finished digging potatoes in New Jersey. They had heard Elkton described in glowing terms . . .
>
> The company does not assume any responsibility for the Negro girls that come looking for work, nor for finding them places to live, as it does for the white girls. The theory is that the Negroes employed shall all commute, and if they come to Elkton, they come at their own risk.[40]

Property owners not only exhibited prejudice against blacks, but also, ironically, against their largest potential market, women. More than one writer commented on the "the anti-female tenor of many landladies, [whose] . . . good rooms were for 'gentlemen only.'"[41] When these gentlemen were accompanied by women, however, the suspiciousness of some owners returned; it was not uncommon for couples to have to provide their marriage licenses before they would be considered as tenants.

For the women who were property owners, of course, the war was a genuine and unexpected bonanza. Though certainly their lives were disrupted by the strangers in their homes, few provided kitchen privileges and even fewer served meals, so the extra work involved was minimal compared with the income potential. Landlady Betty Grubb, cited above, had seven tenants (one of whom had begged to have her "attic room") each paying $8 every week. The $56 Mrs. Grubb earned was about twice what the average industrial woman could expect. It was a tremendous amount of money for small-town women who never before had any expectation of personal income; the war was a real monetary bonus for them. One enterprising couple moved in with relatives and rented their home "to twenty-two girls at three dollars and fifty cents apiece. Four girls sleep in the living room, two in the kitchen. There is only one bathroom . . ."[42]

Ultimately housing problems became so critical that the government had to acknowledge that the private sector could not cope, and in some areas, dormitorylike housing was built for defense workers. *Architectural Record* summarized the rationale behind such facilities:

Many of our largest new plants are located well away from established communities; automobile tires are scarce; gasoline is rationed . . . In the face of shortages of materials, obvious advantages derive from concentrating plumbing facilities for use of many, rather than providing separate facilities for each individual or family unit. And since this shelter is urgently needed and in many cases only for the duration, it seems the height of folly . . . to build an entire house.[43]

Suggested blueprints showed rows of bed and bath rooms, as well as a porch, lobby, telephone, and space for a "pantry in case of occupancy by women; storage in case of occupancy by men."[44] Federal guidelines in such housing included rent control; no more than 20% of the worker's income could be charged. The Federal Housing Administration also undertook to build dormitories for blacks. Though they were fewer in number and segregated from whites, this was far more than local communities were willing to do.

War migrant families also sometimes were eventually able to move into quickly built planned communities. Vanport City, Oregon, was one such public/corporate venture. Spread out over 600 acres, it provided not only housing, but also other services of tremendous value to women:

[The project] takes care of forty thousand workers in the Kaiser shipyards at Portland . . . Wives are not admitted to the ten thousand war apartments unless they, too, are making ships or working in other war production . . . Working wives, instead of coming home from the day, swing or graveyard shift to start another eight hour job of marketing, cooking, and washing, eat at the cafeteria operated for them and their husbands, and for single workers.[45]

Professional planners and government administrators rejoiced at such innovations, undreamable a few years earlier. "Nearly two million people, not before able to occupy a new home on any basis," wrote one, "will live in a home built

157

by the government." War had done what the Depression could not do, and the government became the nation's largest homebuilder: "These things did not come about primarily through the efforts of the reformers. They were the result of the impelling exigencies of war."[46]

Such facilities, however, were available to relatively few of the millions of war workers. Many more crowded into bleak rooms, squalid trailer camps, and vermin-infested shanties for which they nevertheless had to pay high rents and commute many miles to work on dangerously thin tires. Even the new, planned housing was obviously temporary and furnished with spartan dreariness. Such housing also often assumed a parental attitude towards its female occupants, banning male visitors and restricting women's personal lives.

Moreover, the surrounding area often continued to be a drab and unwelcoming place, for these workers represented a serious disruption of small-town life. The young women received into Mrs. Grubb's lodging house that rainy night, for instance, were two of 1,000 workers absorbed into a little town whose normal population was 2,800. Though the company eased transportation difficulties by running buses to take them to work (for a fee), every other municipal service in such towns quickly became inadequate with the explosive population increases.

Old residents understandably resented the new when they opened their faucets to find no water or smelled the sewage from backed-up lines—nor could local governments reasonably be expected to cope with these problems, given material shortages and the probable temporary nature of the growth. Business, which should have been happy to have thousands of potential customers with money to spend, also was often unresponsive. Stores were slow to stock items that young women wanted to buy and did not increase their hours, despite crowds of shoppers.

Small-town traditions were disrupted on other levels, too: "Car prowlers from Wilmington swooped by, agog for a pick-up. It got so nice Elkton girls would not go uptown for a walk or to have a soda at Lyons' drug store. Sailors from the Naval Station jostled soldiers from Aberdeen."[47] Lacking often even a movie theater, these places offered nothing for young people to do in their precious leisure hours. The response of some city fathers was not to create wholesome activity, but rather to slap on curfews intended to dampen youthful spirits. Night workers found almost no recreational facilities, even in larger cities.[48]

While organizations such as the USO and Red Cross did sometimes establish clubhouses in these boom towns, their major emphasis was on male soldiers, not female defense workers. There was not, in that era, even the escape of going home to watch a little television, much less to rent a video of current entertainment. The result was that loneliness and boredom were real factors in creating fatigue and depression. Life could easily seem an endless cycle of dreary days to these women who worked as production soldiers at monotonous jobs six days a week, month after month, with no end in sight.

SOURCE NOTES

1. Nell Giles, *Punch In, Susie!* (New York: Harper's, 1943), p. 14.
2. A.G. Mezerik, "The Factory Manager Learns the Facts of Life," *Harper's* (September 1943): p. 289. See also "Girls in Overalls," *Popular Mechanics* (September 1942): p. 42; Louise Paine Benjamin, "Hats Off to the Girls in the Factories," *Ladies Home Journal* (October 1942): p. 98; "Girls in Uniform," *Life* (July 6, 1942): p. 41.
3. Elinore M. Herrick, "With Women at Work, the Factory Changes," *New York Times Magazine* (January 24, 1943): p. 4.
4. Augusta H. Clawson, "Safety Clothing for Women in War Production Industries," *Journal of Home Economics* (December 1942): p. 727, citing an editorial by Alfred Henderson, "What About Women's Work Shoes?," reprinted from *Hide and Leather and Shoes* (June 13, 1942).
5. Mezerik, "Factory Manager Learns," p. 291.
6. Ibid.
7. "New Headache; Infiltration of Women Workers into War Plants Turns Management's Eyes from Morale to Morals," *Business Week* (October 17, 1942): p. 48.
8. "Women and Machines," *Time* (May 11, 1942): p. 62.
9. Giles, *Punch In, Susie!* p. 5.
10. "Sex in the Factory," *Time* (September 14, 1942): p. 21.
11. Ibid.
12. For examples, see Taylor, "Meet the Girls," p. 57; Wharton, "New Workers Speed Plane Production," p. 104; and Von Miklos, *I Took a War Job,* p. 187.
13. Warner, "Gunpowder Girls," p. 73.
14. Von Miklos, *I Took a War Job,* p. 91.
15. "A Woman on the Assembly Line," *American Mercury* (December 1942): p. 759.
16. Glover, "Women as Manpower," p.70.
17. Bradley, "Women at Work," p. 194.
18. "Use of Womanpower in War Depends on State of Mind," *Science News Letter* (May 30, 1942): p. 345.
19. "Woman's Place," *Business Week* (May 1942): p. 22.
20. Elizabeth Hawes, "Do Women Workers Get an Even Break?" *New York Times Magazine* (November 19, 1944): p. 13.
21. "Women in Labor Unions," *Monthly Labor Review* (June 1945): p. 1269. (Data was as of June 1944.) See also Glover, *Survey Graphic,* p. 74; and Theresa Wolfson: "Aprons and Overalls in War," *Annals of the American Academy of Political and Social Science,* 1943, Volume 229, p. 54; and "Fade-out of the Women," *Time* (September 4, 1944): p. 78.

22. Hawes, "Do Women Workers Get an Even Break?," p. 13.
23. "New Headache," p. 46.
24. "Women in War Work," *New Republic* (May 4, 1942): p. 593.
25. Fillebrown, "I Helped Build Fighter Planes," p. 333.
26. Mona Gardner, "Only Grandmothers Need Apply," *Ladies Home Journal* (June 1943): p. 25.
27. Ibid.
28. Oppenheim, "Anchors Aweigh!," p. 70.
29. Gardner, "Only Grandmothers Need Apply," p. 25.
30. Ibid., p. 58.
31. Mary Kelly, "Calling All Women," *Christian Science Monitor* (May 27, 1944): p. 3.
32. Von Miklos, *I Took a War Job*, p. 28. See also "She Works in an Arms Plant," *New York Times Magazine* (April 12, 1942): p. 9; Dorothy C. Reid, "Pull Yourself Together!," *Independent Woman* (November 1942): p. 333.
33. Millard, "53 Hours A Week," p. 87.
34. Giles, *Punch In, Susie!*, p. 102.
35. Mezerik, "Factory Manager Learns," p. 294.
36. Vorse, "Girls of Elkton," p. 356.
37. Anthony, *Out of the Kitchen*, p. 175.
38. Mary Heaton Vorse, "Friendly Town," *Woman's Home Companion* (May 1943): p. 108.
39. Wilkinson, "From Housewife to Shipfitter," p. 333.
40. Vorse, "Girls of Elkton," p. 348.
41. Von Miklos, *I Took a War Job*, p. 22.
42. Vorse, "Girls of Elkton," p. 348.
43. "Duration Dormitories for Industrial War Workers," *Architectural Record* (July 1942): p. 44.
44. Ibid.
45. Anthony, *Out of the Kitchen*, p. 168.
46. Edmund N. Bacon, "Wartime Housing," *Annals of the American Academy of Political and Social Science*, vol. 229, p. 137.
47. Vorse, "Girls of Elkton," pp. 347–48.
48. Marjorie M. Potter, "I Started on the Swing Shift," *Christian Science Monitor* (January 27, 1945): p. 9.

11

BALANCING ACT: MANAGING JOB AND HOME

"All over the country," wrote one reporter, "mothers of young children seemed too exhausted to talk about their work. If they did talk to me I hadn't the heart to take much of their time or energy . . . The exhaustion of these women was heartbreaking to see."[1] By the end of 1943, one-third of women war workers were also mothers of children living at home. Though unexceptional today, then such a figure—dealing with middle-class women as it did—was revolutionary.

Moreover, the balancing act between job and home that may seem routine now was immensely more difficult then, for housework was far more laborious. It was an era of cooking from scratch and washing dishes by hand. It was before clothes dryers and permanent press; it was instead a time of wringer washing machines, tubs of rinse water, outdoor clotheslines, starch and ironing boards. Many Americans lacked even running water and an indoor bathroom. Many others had iceboxes rather than refrigerators. The work of running a home required a far greater commitment of time.

"The greatest deterrent" to finding the labor to fill the factories was this enormity of home obligations. *Independent Woman*, whose editors understood many things long before the rest of the public, stated the problem well: "There is a lack of understanding of the fact that upon these homemakers rests a double responsibility. Because a woman is unemployed does not mean that she is unoccupied."[2]

Her job at home was full-time and her job at work also often was longer than that of today. Not only was the six-day week standard, but also many days were actually nine hours rather than eight. Part-time work (though it proved successful in Britain where women split shifts into either morning/afternoon or three of the six-day week) was rarely implemented in the States. With commuting time, a week stretched far beyond the 40 hours fixed in media minds. Ruth Millard was not atypical in having a 66-hour week when an hour of commuting time in each direction was added to the six nine-hour days she put in on the job.

"People sometimes ask me," she said, "But nine hours on your feet? Don't you get terribly tired?"

> *Well, naturally. I make no bones about admitting that I do . . . Of course we don't take it without giving way, now and then. I understand that nervous breakdowns among women in factories have doubled. Of course they have . . . It's just eat, sleep, and no other life left. Sunday is no good when you sleep through half of it from sheer exhaustion . . .* [3]

Psychological pressures were intensified by the lack of any visible end to these exhausting schedules. Ruth Giles wrote of the shock initially felt when the promise of rest was revoked:

> *All vacations were cancelled today . . . Many of the girls have husbands in the service, and were planning to visit them before they leave for foreign duty . . . [We] have only Sunday for recreation, and not always that. If there is extra work to be done, the entire force works on Sunday, too. There are no holidays—not even the Fourth of July! But after the first blow—all vacations cancelled—THERE WAS NO GRUMBLING. Everybody understands WHY there is no time for vacations.* [4]

The two hours of commuting time that Ruth Millard had to add to her long factory day also was not uncommon. With gas and tires rationed, using public transportation and sharing rides became a necessity. "The chief discombobulation to my life," said one woman, "is rising in the dark at five, going twenty miles, picking up riders, and reporting ready for work at five minutes to seven." [5]

Given the semirural locations of many war plants and the consequent lack of nearby housing, trips to work were not only distant, but also were slowed by the necessity of stopping for others. As Ruth Giles wrote, "you seldom see an empty back seat." [6] Once the car was full of passengers, the driver still had to proceed slowly because of the need to preserve worn tires. Hitting a pothole on a dark road while rushing to work could become a major problem, for tires were not easily replaced. It is understandable that after some months, Giles would conclude that:

> *The distance you live from work is the most vital statistic in your life as a factory worker. It determines the number of hours you can sleep, the time you have to play, how often you can go to town to spend your money!*
> *. . . You can imagine, then, how "gas rationing," to a factory worker, is business pretty vital . . . If you have a "ride" you must fill out your name, address and the number of miles you go on a gasoline ration form . . .* [7]

Commuting problems and hectic schedules compounded for women who worked nights. Alma was a typical case who got home just before her children left for school. She worked all night and then went shopping so that she could get rationed meat for her husband before it sold out for the day. She sent the kids off, ate breakfast, cleaned the kitchen, and got to bed at about 10 A.M. At 11:30 the alarm rang to warn her that the kids were about to get home from school for lunch. She went back to bed when they left so that she could have a couple of hours of sleep before they arrived home again about 3:00. Then she cleaned house, did laundry and cooked dinner. They ate when her husband got home from work at 6:00. Afterwards, Alma took another nap before leaving for work at 10 P.M. Her sleep usually totaled five or six hours in three stretches of about two hours each.

The Almas who worked all night and most of the day abounded. These women were more likely to work because their families needed the money, while those who entered the labor force largely from patriotic motivation sought out the day shift, and yet that option was not always available. Union seniority rules often meant that day shifts automatically went to men while women, now exempted from protective labor legislation, worked at night. Black women believed that they were especially likely to be assigned to night shifts.

Even for single women with few home responsibilities, getting enough sleep was often a problem. One said, "you can always count on the phone ringing about three in the afternoon, because your friends think you've had enough sleep by that time. They visualize you as a 'lucky old thing, sleeping your life away all day!'"

But count it up by the hours. You leave the factory at 7. You get home by 8:30. It's 9 o-clock before you can possibly get into bed. If you go to sleep instantly and don't wake up until 3 in the afternoon, you've had just 6 hours sleep, and don't count on that. There are street noises and the neighbors and your family. At least twice you are awakened with a start and have to begin all over again: finding the place in the pillow which is softest, adjusting the cotton in your ears, retying the black cloth around your eyes. By that time the afternoon sun is beaming in the windows and you give up the whole thing.[8]

While the worker stumbled tiredly through the war years, the chief support she got from her family was emotional encouragement—something that, while not enough alone, was nevertheless important. Virginia Wilkinson, for example, said her main motivation for staying on when she wanted to quit her shipbuilding job was the "absurd pride" of her husband and sons, who bought her a special tool kit. Though overburdened mothers of the very young sometimes reported that their children felt neglected, mothers of teenagers discovered positive effects in their new self-image; one said that when she "got her welding job it took her youngsters just ten minutes to spread all over the neighborhood the news that, 'Ma's making bombers!'"[9]

But psychological support too often was all that was offered. Whether or not they wished to share in the reflected glory of a bomber-maker mother, there is little evidence that family members shared her housework—nor did the women seem to expect more than occasional help. Rosie the Riveter was almost always portrayed by wartime media as a solitary star who managed her balancing act between job and home with the greatest of ease. She asked her family for next to nothing in meeting the new obligations and received the same. Most husbands indeed seemed to feel that they had done all that was expected when they gave their wives permission to work. Women's magazines, with their deafening silence on the subject, supported that view.

In scores of magazine articles on Rosie's new life, the references to household help from her family can be counted on the fingers of one hand. The only article totally devoted to the subject was to be found not in a woman's magazine, but rather in that ancient advocate of radical ideas, *The Nation.* "America's Pampered Husbands," it warned, should be held accountable if "we aren't going to win this war," for it was their selfishness which kept their wives from defense work:

> *Husbandly pressure on housewives not to enlist for the war-production front takes much subtler terms than an overt "I object." Largely, it shapes up as men's time-hallowed, unspoken refusal to share in home responsibilities, an attitude that puts an intolerable double burden on the working wife.*
>
> *... Home-making minutiae are distracting and energy-draining. When household equipment needs replacement, when the children's shoe size changes, when the toothpaste runs out, it is Mother and not Father who scribbles memoranda on scraps of paper and squeezes in the necessary shopping sometime, somewhere ... If a woman can learn to run a drill press, why can't a man learn to run a washing machine?*[10]

But professed male ignorance of laundry procedures prevailed, with the inevitable result that sometimes a woman simply had no choice except to miss a day of work in order to provide her family with clean clothes, for the washing and ironing methods of the era mandated at least a full day of weekly work on this one household task. And when she was forced into thus skipping work at the factory for work at home, the media was quick to term her a "slacker," an apathetic, ignorant woman unknowingly aiding Hitler.

Because they received so little assistance with their double lives, women did quite naturally break down. No viable solutions were offered to ease their impossible burdens; it seemed that the only option was the either-or choice of quitting. The understandable result was that women did leave their jobs in large numbers. In some defense work, the turnover rate was incredibly high. *Newsweek* reported that one plant hired 4,000 women in a two-month period, of whom 3,000 quit; a shipyard hiring 800 in the same period lost 350.[11] Even *Independent Woman* acknowledged that "in many individual plants," the termination curve actually exceeds the hiring curve.[12] That their double lives were largely responsible for this turnover is clear from surveys showing that "the absence rate for women on the night shift was lower than that of women on the day shift."[13]

Ruth Millard, whose family was smaller and more supportive than most, admitted that even she was occasionally but understandably absent. In response to media criticism of absentee rates, she averred of her coworkers, "I can honestly say that not one of us has ever stayed away from work to go shopping or go to the movies.* Most of us have done it to sleep for about twenty hours ... I agree with [Labor] Secretary Perkins when she said that the greater portion of absenteeism was caused by overfatigue."[14]

Management usually seemed to prefer to pay war-imposed excess profits tax rather than spend money to research creative solutions for these personnel problems. Perhaps it was afraid of spoiling the labor force, which would continue to expect similar working conditions when the war emergency was over and the feared postwar depression returned. Perhaps also management realized that Millard was right when she said of absenteeism, "the burden does not fall on the company, but on the coworkers, who pitch in and get the job done just the same." What Millard resented far more than an absent coworker was time lost to poor planning, for there were "whole days when we had no work to do because we were held up for lack of materials ... You can't go home. You just have to wait."[15]

Industrial discipline had been drilled into prewar management attitudes in the same way that school masters believed in disciplining children. The idea that workers might be released when there was no work that could be done was too radical a notion for them. Social thinkers, however, began to propose just that sort of idea, as, for example, the *New Republic* writer who opined: "My own observation is that absenteeism for a day or two should be encouraged in a great many cases, in order to prevent a much longer period of absenteeism when the human mechanism at last breaks down and requires several weeks in bed to recover; a day or two out in the sun might have prevented that."[16]

It wasn't as though such relatively simple solutions were impossible, nor was the problem a failure to identify the reasons for absenteeism and turnover. Women knew what help they needed to get their jobs done and were glad to tell anyone willing to ask. United Auto Workers, for example, had given a questionnaire to female members that clearly identified five cures for absenteeism.

---

* While there was frequent critical note of the number of apparently idle women in theater audiences, one realistic explanation was ignored—probably, in an era before television, millions of women went to the movies regularly to keep up with the war via the newsreels.

Women needed: "(1) help in caring for children (2) better shopping hours (3) shorter working hours (4) better transportation (5) better planned production."[17]

When the business community did respond innovatively, they were apt to import ideas from England, where female labor had been in demand longer. *Nation's Business*, for example, reported in the spring of 1943:

> By the time the British war-working housewife gets around to the shops, most are closed or the limited quantities exhausted. To compete with the Woman at Home, the woman worker stayed away from work . . .
>
> British war production plants had to do something about the problem . . . Some closed down Saturday mornings. They found that production actually increased, because of the improved morale . . . The women discontinued their old habit of sneaking off in driblets through the week.
>
> Others . . . arranged for food shopping orders to be filled at their plants . . . A personnel department representative collected the workers' orders and relayed them to the grocer Monday or Tuesday. The grocer then had three to four days to handle them . . . Shortly before the scheduled delivery time, the personnel representative collected money and coupons for the "pointed" [rationed] foods.[18]

Though of course much better than nothing, these delivery plans nevertheless show male inexperience with shopping and underestimation of the task. Women were being asked not only to plan ahead to an almost impossible degree, but they also had to forgo comparison shopping for the best value. Moreover, in those presupermarket days of merchant specialization, there were many necessary household items that grocery stores did not sell. Shopping routinely involved separate trips to the butcher, baker and green grocer, as well as the "grocer"—and that only covered the food items. What of all the other family needs, to say nothing of trips to such places as the bank and the post office?

Banks, for example, operated only in the midday hours, and there were no credit cards or money machines. Few stores were open at night, and virtually none were open on Sundays. Customers had to accommodate themselves to business hours, for business showed no willingness to adjust to customer needs. Given that during the war demand greatly exceeded supply, there was no incentive to operate the hours that customers needed, and neither the government nor media pressured retailers to do so out of patriotism. The result, absurd as it seems, was that women literally could not go into war industry simply because their families needed them as errand-runners during working hours.

Beyond that, these *Nation's Business* proposals were suggested in 1943—two years before the war ended—and the United States was still looking to Britain for models because such programs had not been emulated to any great extent here. Nor could women who recognized the impact that the problems of other women had on war production interest business in their creative solutions. A program in San Francisco that was the brainchild of two women volunteers, for example, got no support until it was a success, when the San Francisco Junior

Chamber of Commerce belatedly agreed to sponsor it. By then, the women had a rent-free office and a staff of volunteers who operated what was essentially an employment service to do the specialized things women workers needed done. "The greatest demand the centers have," they reported, "is for cleaning on a weekly basis. Our second largest number of requests is for the care of . . . the aged by the hour. In child care, the centers receive the most calls for care of infants."[19]

By 1944, the needs and the possibilities of success were evident enough that more assistance programs finally came into place. Pratt-Whitney and Bell aircraft companies adopted shared-shifts for women who wanted to work part-time. Plants in New York and New Jersey improved on the weekly grocery order plan with "a representative of a certain store [who] comes to the plant every morning, takes food orders from women workers, and brings food back at the end of the shift."[20] Other of the larger manufacturers arranged for local department stores to open branches in their plants. Not surprisingly, the newly built Pentagon led the way to modern marketing with installation of a shopping center for the use of its thousands of employees.

On the West Coast, the innovative Henry Kaiser led the way at his shipyards with child-care centers that also featured carryout food:

> A mother can buy the main dish and dessert of her evening meal for her entire family, picking up these when she calls for her child after a day's work. The plan here is to prepare those foods which take a long cooking period.
>
> A menu suggesting other foods which can be prepared quickly to supplement the home service food is furnished to the mother one week in advance. Menus for all meals served to the children at school and suggestions for other meals to complete an adequate day's diet . . . are also sent to the mothers a week in advance.[21]

Baltimore County supported eight child service centers, run not only for preschoolers, but also for after-school care of older children. They offered a phenomenal range of services, including marketing; transportation to doctors, dentists, and barbers; handling laundry and dry cleaning pick-up and delivery; packing lunches for school children; taking shoes to the cobbler; shopping for scarce articles; and cooking the family's evening meal, which was packed in containers brought by the mother that morning. The latter, they said, was the most popular service, and "has been a real boon during the summer months, for many of the homes in Middle River have only coal cookstoves which when used makes . . . sleep impossible."[22]

Such programs, however, were little and late, developed only in areas of critical labor shortage and in response to massive need as demonstrated by deplorable absenteeism and turnover rates. It is another of those ironies of war and peace that it took the consumer age of the 1950s—so decried by feminists in the 1970s—to turn business around and give women the more convenient marketing opportunities that they greatly needed during the war. The shopping mall and evening/weekend hours are in fact little noted, but tremendously liberating, factors in the use of women's time.

———

No other issue relating to a woman's job/home dilemma came in for so much discussion as did the care of her children. While the media had virtually no suggestions on how to get the dishes washed, it was full of advice on child care. Much of the wisdom offered, however, was controversial and contradictory and reflected society's ambivalence on the subject of children. There was little to alleviate the anxieties of working mothers.

The controversy began even before a child was born. *Business Week*, discussing the "Touchy Problem" of maternity leave, clearly expressed male confusion, fear and guilt about pregnancy:

> *In many cases, the first reaction of the production boss who finds that one his workers is pregnant is, "get her out of here quick." Chief reason is fear of a damage suit if the work causes any injury (particularly a miscarriage). Some employers consider it "indelicate" for an obviously pregnant woman to stick to her workbench, and a few think it embarrasses men workers. Other companies discharge pregnant women because of a genuine conviction that continued work is harmful to mother and child . . .*
>
> *In a recent survey . . . the Dept. of Labor found that the majority of employers fired women as soon as pregnancy was discovered . . .*[23]

A pregnant woman simply had no right to work. Only six states had any regulations even addressing the subject of maternity leave, and "comparatively few union contracts take cognizance of the pregnancy problems, even in industries where there is a high percentage of women workers."[24] Despite the fact that Labor Department investigation could not turn up a single case of a woman having sued an employer for a pregnancy-related injury, business continued to ignore governmental suggestions for dealing with the problem more rationally and humanely. Although they complained of high turnover rates and the cost of training new employees, they were not willing to assure that investment by guaranteeing a woman the right to return to her job; only one of 73 factories surveyed had any maternity leave policy.

While *Business Week* was willing to state parenthetically that "one of the most common causes of abortion is a woman's fear of losing her job,"[25] *Harper's* took the issue even further, in a display of candor rarely seen in World War II media:

> *Perhaps the problem would be solved more easily if every pregnant woman wanted her baby, but more don't than do. Unmarried women obviously don't and many a married woman wants to continue at work without the burden of another child. Their way out of their predicament is dangerous . . .*

> *Some deliberately strain themselves by lifting heavy objects while on the job*
> *...More go to abortionists. The result is that abortion rings are doing a land-office*
> *business—less dangerously than of old now that the sulfa drugs have lowered the*
> *death rate ... In Rochester, New York, a group of doctors set up a private hospital*
> *and performed abortions legally, therapeutically ...*
>
> *Counselors cannot and do not want to exclude unmarried women from the*
> *benefits of child spacing, which is the accepted term for birth control ... The need*
> *for this information has finally brought the former Birth Control League into a*
> *position of prominence. Now called Planned Parenthood, it serves an increasingly*
> *important role in industry.*[26]

Women's magazines, meanwhile, had not a word to say on the subject. The idea that women perhaps should have a right to knowledge about their bodies, including information on how to prevent pregnancy, was instead tentatively proposed to a largely male audience, whose interest was primarily defined by their business and war production needs. Birth control "served an important role in industry"—not for women who wanted to live free from pregnancy.

The silence that surrounded problem pregnancies for Rosie the Riveter is in ironic contrast to the experience of women in the WAAC, for there this sexy subject was hotly debated during the formation. The energy spent on this discussion, however, turned out to be largely academic, for the question seldom arose. In contrast, pregnancy was a far more real possibility for the millions of women in defense industries, since they were much more likely to have male relationships, and yet the question of their pregnancies received virtually no attention.

Finally in the fall of 1944, when victory was in sight, the War Department got around to setting policy for its civilian employees. It "put into effect an official pregnancy policy governing the employment of women in its more than 1,000 plants . . . , where about 500,000 of the workers are women, more than 60 percent of them married."[27] While still cognizant of employers' interests, the new policy was generally aimed at protecting pregnant women from arbitrary bosses. It set post- and prenatal leave limits; disallowed night work, overtime and heavy assignments; and protected seniority.

Once a baby was born, institutional care for infants was virtually nonexistent, and that for older children was sadly lacking. The concept of profit-making child-care centers that are common today was only beginning to develop in the 1940s. Until this time, children's nurseries were likely to be of two sorts: preschools designed to provide enriching experiences for upper-class children or charitable institutions in existence to philanthropically serve the needs of women forced into the workplace because of poverty. Middle-class women were expected to care for their own children.

The result was that when they entered the factories by the millions, there was no place for their children. The need quickly became obvious, reaching a crisis state early in the war:

A mother of one family carries her baby with her as she goes to her job in a war factory. She meets her husband as he is going home from work and passes the baby to him. This is a solution of sorts.

A twelve-year old child is locked out of the house all day while her parents are at work.

A woman on the graveyard shift drives her car close to the windows of the place where she is employed, and her four children sleep in the automobile.

These are not isolated cases . . . You can multiply them and cases similar to them by the thousands. Next year, unless prompt action is taken, you can multiply them by the hundred thousand.

How do these things happen? First, let it be understood that this country has long had a serious child-care problem never adequately met.[28]

The Children's Bureau reported one Alabama site with 156 working mothers of 167 preschoolers in a community that had no day care; "in Illinois a survey of only a few blocks disclosed 178 children from one to six years of age in need of care."[29] In Los Angeles it was pointed out that "lack of 25 child-care centers can cost 10 bombers a month. Plane plants in the area now employ 101,000 women who have 19,000 children needing care."[30] Similar reports came in from all over the country:

In a small Pennsylvania town three hundred women have petitioned for 24-hour care for their youngsters . . . On the California coast a tragic group of mothers, widowed overnight by the disaster at Pearl Harbor, have already put their babies in nursery school and taken their places behind desks and in the assembly line. In Ohio day classes for two-to-five-year-olds have increased 125 per cent in three months.[31]

The WPA, a bureaucratic vestige of the Depression, redirected the nurseries it had run for the children of the very poor to this new need. There were 1,500 of these nurseries (at least one in every state) but that was not nearly enough to meet the demand. The WPA found "that every three previously unemployed women taking jobs means one child needing care while they work. So adding 5,000,000 women to the national labor force means at least 1,600,000 children for somebody to look after. That is an awful lot of children."[32]

Once again, the situation did not exist because of women's failure to identify the problem. Dr. Grace Langdon, WPA nursery director, not only understood the need but also had imaginative answers to questions not yet raised:

The need for night care for children is already upon us, and this problem will grow as all-out production makes it less and less possible to schedule women for work only during daylight hours. We must also make plans—though we hope they will never need to be carried out—to provide services in case of the necessity for evacuation. Communal feeding may well become an immediate reality . . . We have not even begun to care properly for the school-age children.[33]

The problem was not undefined questions, but a lack of public will on the answers. Ironically, even those who best understood difficulties and had the best chances at solving them were sometimes forced into defeat. The woman who headed the Magazine Bureau of the Office of War Information resigned late in 1943, citing a "definite neglect" that her job forced on her two children. Though she had "launched more than a score of nationwide campaigns urging women to take war jobs," she now felt compelled to say that Americans had not reciprocated by supporting the women who made patriotic efforts. "Women wouldn't need to neglect their children if the whole community felt it important to help them do war jobs," she said, "but the communities do *not* feel it important."[34]

The problem was inherent in employers' contradictory views of what they wanted, for they continued to search in vain for the young workers with grown children—a thirty-year-old with the freedom of a fifty-year-old. Paul McNutt and his War Manpower Commission reinforced this irrationality with ambivalent guidelines that discouraged hiring of women with children, even though they knew that this age group was what business sought and that many of these women needed jobs. The policy, announced in late 1942, stated:

I. The first responsibility of women with young children, in war as in peace, is to give suitable care in their own homes to their children.

II. In order that established family life may not be unnecessarily disrupted, special efforts to secure the employment in industry of women with young children should be deferred . . .

III. Barriers against the employment of women with young children should not be set up by employers . . .

IV. Whenever it is found that women with young children are gainfully employed in essential activities . . . it is essential that:

(a) Such women be employed at such hours and on such shifts as will cause the least disruption in their family life; and

(b) If any such women are unable to arrange for satisfactory care of their children . . . adequate facilities should be provided . . . Such facilities should be developed as community projects and not under the auspices of individual employers or employer groups.[35]

It was the last sentence that ultimately did the most damage in failing to place the responsibility for adequate child care where it belonged—with the industry that had created the need and was earning the profits. Instead, the burden was shifted from business to local governments and volunteer "community projects."

Some tried to cope. Vallejo, California, had a program where "a thousand children [are] being well cared for from 7 a.m. to 6 p.m. while their mothers are working in war industries . . . The Mare Island Navy Yard . . . contributed money, materials, and equipment."[36] Other communities extended kindergarten for

171

children younger than standard age, and a few added after-school care. The Los Angeles school system was probably the most advanced in the country, operating over 20 child-care centers by mid-1943, with "plans for 29 more, enough for 2,000 children."[37]

But 2,000 children placed was not nearly enough for a community the size of Los Angeles, and major groups of the young were omitted, for they did "not provide for children under two, who are 8.3% of the total, nor for the 5-to-16 group."[38] The report on the successful Vallejo project had no other outstanding models to include, and with careful understatement acknowledged that "not all school systems have accepted this service with enthusiasm."[39] Yet the lack of enthusiasm was sometimes understandable, because for many communities the task so blithely assigned by the War Manpower Commission was an obvious impossibility.

Childersburg, Alabama, for example, was a poverty-stricken town of 515 when Du Pont located an ordnance plant there and 21,000 people poured in overnight. Quite naturally, Childersburg's town government saw no reason to assume responsibility for the children of these migrants. Surely Du Pont's profits were such that they could have more easily dealt with the need by providing in-plant care, yet they were explicitly excused by the government from any obligation.

Presumably FDR's men simply were not affected by child-care problems enough to cancel out the political propaganda damage the right wing could potentially cause with this seemingly totalitarian and antibusiness move. The end result, however, was neglect, as official policy on children developed into a model of confusion, ambivalence and inadequacy. A year after the war began, Washington's policy was largely one of vague hope:

> A few war factories, such as the Douglas Aircraft plant in Santa Monica, California, have set up their own professionally managed day nurseries for women employees' children. Washington, however, is not sympathetic to such a program and hopes that, perhaps with WPA co-operation, local communities can do the job on a public basis. So far a mere $6,000,000—only enough to bring total children cared for to 110,000—is all the WPA has to work with.[40]

Douglas Aircraft, though the largest private employer of women in the United States, was now excused from doing anything more for their children. The real shame of this lay in that, while industrial projects were rare, when they were set up, they were excellent examples of what was possible. The Kaiser shipyards in Portland, Oregon, for example, accepted children as young as 18 months. Centers operated during both the day and swing shifts, with fees of 75 cents a day for the first child and 50 cents for additional ones. The new buildings consisted of 15 connecting units, each of which held 25 kids of similar age. There was a sick room with nurses and a doctor on call; a social worker and dietician were also employed, with meals and nutritious snacks served. "The Kaiser Child Service Centers," said *Architectural Record*, "are among the first places where working people, people of average means, have been able to afford good nursery education for their children."[41]

Kaiser, in this regard as in others, was a historic innovator, but its examples were more often praised than emulated. Private child care was not a wartime priority, and public programs saw far more talk than action. In the spring of 1943, the WPA—its Depression era *raison d'être* gone—was abolished, with few but educators noting the nurseries under its aegis. After the "WPA died a lingering death," a whole year elapsed with nothing done on child care: "Hard as it is to believe, Congress is still dickering and rival agencies still bickering over bills that would start things moving again."[42]

There was far more talk than action, and more bureaucracy concerned with "development" than delivery. The overlapping jurisdictions of various agencies made it easy to pass the buck; besides state and local groups, federal agencies included the Day Care Section of the U.S. Office of Defense Health and Welfare Services; the U.S. Office of Education; the Children's Bureau of The Department of Labor; and the Child Protection Program of the Works Projects Administration. Conferences held in mid-1943 (halfway through the war) were still basically of a planning nature. What finally filtered down to the actual child was little and late.

Though "Washington's responsibility for this lunatic gap is plain," it was not uncommon for the victim to receive the blame. "Principally because American women have done little but talk about the matter," *Saturday Evening Post* proclaimed, "there are few communities in which Rosie can find a good place for her kids."[43] Yet Rosie might well have found its tears to be of a crocodile nature, for, like too many others of its press colleagues, this magazine also seemed to prefer to emphasize the negative, implying that Rosie, lured by defense dollars, willingly left her babies in horrible situations. In another article, they wrote of Los Angeles—where the population exploded by a half-million in the first months of the war—and where a state investigating committee found

> . . . *commercial nurseries where children slept in damp cellars, were slapped, choked, and beaten . . . [A committee witness testified] that in one . . .* "the odor was so bad I couldn't stand it. I went into the back yard and found children in individual kennels; not play pens—they were more like kennels for cattle. The children looked at me though the bars and cried."[44]

It was typical of most of the media in stressing the need, while offering little but platitudes as solutions. Virtually every other popular source of potential influence showed the same ambivalence, the same confused lack of thoughtfulness on child care. *Good Housekeeping*, for example, ran in the same issue an article on the need for nurses and another article encouragingly titled "How to

Start a Nursery School,"[45] but which (amazingly) made absolutely no mention of the war. Its editors clearly expected their readers to see preschool as a beneficial experience for privileged children, and not a need for working mothers. They presumably never saw the connection between a need for nurses and a lack of child care.

If addressed at all, the most likely answer to Rosie's problems was an implication that she should quit her job—and yet accusations about apathetic American women aiding Hitler might well be found on the next page. It was a reflection of a public that simply didn't know what it wanted women to do.

SOURCE NOTES

1. Meyer, "Ma's Making Bombers," pp. 51–52.
2. "There Must Be No Idle Women," p. 232.
3. Millard, "53 Hours A Week," p. 22.
4. Giles, *Punch In, Susie!*, p. 45.
5. " A Woman on the Assembly Line," p. 759. A poll in June 1942 showed that 40% walked to work. Another 23% used public transportation. Gallup, *The Gallup Poll*, p. 338.
6. Giles, *Punch In, Susie!*, p. 47.
7. Ibid., pp. 110–11.
8. Ibid., p. 106.
9. Meyer, "Ma's Making Bombers," pp. 51–52.
10. Edith M. Stern, "America's Pampered Husbands," *The Nation* (July 10, 1943): p. 40. Other articles that devote at least a few paragraphs to the subject of family assistance are L.B. Hohman, M.D, "Can Women in War Industry Be Good Mothers?" *Ladies Home Journal* (October 1942): p. 100; Bernice Gray Cook, "Mother—1943 Model," *American Home* (March 1943): p. 29; "The War Needs Women," *Parents* (September 1943): p. 37.
11. "More Women Must Go to Work as 3,200,000 New Jobs Beckon" *Newsweek* (September 6, 1943): p. 74; See also "Why Women Quit," *Business Week* (October 16, 1943): p. 94.
12. "There Must Be No Idle Women," p. 253.
13. Glover, "Women as Manpower," p. 74.
14. Millard, "53 Hours A Week," p. 89.
15. Ibid.
16. "Housewife-War Worker," p. 519.
17. Elizabeth Hawes, "Woman War Worker: A Case History," *New York Times Magazine* (December 21, 1943): p. 21.
18. "'Shopping Leave' Boosts Output," *Nation's Business* (March 1943): p. 34.

19. Katherine Doyle, "Keeping Women on the Job," *Nation's Business* (July 1944): p. 73.

20. Mary Heaton Vorse, "Women Don't Quit, If—," *Independent Woman* (January 1944): p. 24.

21. Miriam E. Lowenberg, "Shipyard Nursery Schools," *Journal of Home Economics* (February 1944): p. 75.

22. Lora Swartz, "Child Service Centers," *Journal of Home Economics* (February 1945): p. 76.

23. "Touchy Problems," *Business Week* (September 25, 1943): p. 80.

24. Ibid.; see also "Leave for Mothers," *Business Week* (October 30, 1943): p. 100.

25. Ibid., p. 82.

26. Mezerik, "Factory Manager Learns," p. 296.

27. "Maternity Policy of the War Department," *Survey Midmonthly* (September 1944): p. 262.

28. "Eight-Hour Orphans," *Saturday Evening Post* (October 10, 1942): p. 20.

29. Amidon, "Arms and the Women," p. 271.

30. "Women Drop Out," *Business Week* (August 21, 1943): p. 89.

31. Baldwin, "America Enlists Its Women," p. 282.

32. J.C. Furnas, "Woman Power," *Ladies Home Journal* (November 1942): p. 148.

33. Grace Langdon, "Uncle Sam Takes Care of His Youngest," *Saturday Evening Post* (January 1943): p. 34. See also "Are Nursery Schools and Kindergartens Affected By the War?" *Education for Victory* (July 15, 1942): p. 24, and, in the same publication, "Are Nursery Schools and Kindergartens Serving the Children of Working Mothers?" (August 1, 1942): p. 3.

34. Vorse, "Women Don't Quit," p. 8.

35. "Employment in War Work of Women With Young Children," *Monthly Labor Review* (December 1942): p. 1184. See also "Policy of War Manpower Commission on Woman Workers," *Monthly Labor Review* (April 1943): p. 668.

36. "Extended School Services—An 'Accepted Part' of the School Program," *Education for Victory* (February 3, 1945): p. 3.

37. "Women Drop Out," p. 89.

38. Ibid.

39. "Extended School Services," p. 3.

40. Furnas, "Woman Power," p. 148. See also "Extended School Services for Young Children," *The Elementary School Journal* (April 1943): p. 439, and in the same publication, "Nation's Manpower Program and the Problems of Children" (February 1943): p. 319; and two articles by Catherine MacKenzie, "Round-the-Clock Supervision" and "Wartime Nursery

175

School," both in *New York Times Magazine* (October 15, 1944): p. 31, and January 31, 1943: p. 28, respectively.

41. "Designed for 24-House Child Care," *Architectural Record* (March 1944): p. 86. See also Lowenberg, "Shipyard Nursery Schools," p. 75.

42. J.C. Furnas, "Are Women Doing Their Share?" *Saturday Evening Post* (April 29, 1944): p. 12.

43. Ibid.

44. "Eight-Hour Orphans," p. 21.

45. Ruth Leigh, "How to Start a Nursery School," *Good Housekeeping* (December 1942): p. 27. On the need for nurses, see "We Are Trying to Find One Hundred Thousand Women," *Good Housekeeping* (December 1942): p. 14.

12

FROM BLUE COLLAR TO PINK: WOMEN AND INDUSTRY CHANGE EACH OTHER

"Women Lagging in War Effort," *Newsweek*'s headline screamed in January of 1943. Not mentioning that a few months earlier the magazine had run stories entitled "Women Find Troubles in Path of Connecting with War Jobs," "Women Want to Join for War but Run into Some Skepticism" and "Women Demand Greater Role in National Defense Program," it now trumpeted statistics to show how little women were doing compared with men.

"Apathy" became a common charge against women, as almost every mainstream magazine ran accusatory articles. *Saturday Evening Post*, for example, joined the chorus in saying, "The implication . . . that the ghost of Molly Pitcher would approve of her female descendants is dubious. Mistress Pitcher, a rough-and-ready type, would probably ask harsh questions about why, if women are doing themselves so proud, the Wacs have recruiting trouble [and] hospitals still clamor for nurses' aides."[1]

"Women," added a female author for *New York Times Magazine*, "generally are apt to take to themselves credit for the record of these few, to feel that all women, including themselves are praised, and deservedly."

> *The girl who goes to dances for servicemen and has been kissed by perhaps more than one second lieutenant feels herself, by the mere fact that she is a woman in wartime, on a level with the Wac kissed by the decorating general . . .*
>
> *"Womanpower shows" are put on and professional models demonstrate clothes for women at work, all the pressure of publicity and appeal to patriotism is constantly applied, yet proportionately there are eight times as many women in war jobs in Great Britain.[2]*

Unlikely sources took up the banner. *House Beautiful* attacked its audience with amazing candor, saying, "Our overall response . . . has been cause for deep and bitter shame . . . Ask yourself questions such as these: Do you start your day hours after . . . [other] women arrive behind their desks or machines? Do you smugly assert that your would not work for pay because you don't need the money? Do you claim your children need you full time and then spend the afternoon gossiping over a bridge table?"3

Even Republican Representative Clare Booth Luce (no friend of labor) stung her upper-class friends by admonishing, "Many a woman who squawks to her neighbors about the 'feather-bedding' in labor unions is herself living a feather-bed life." She, too, pointed to the example of our allies, saying, "There need perhaps be no . . . large-scale conscription of fathers if all the nieces of Uncle Sam would do their duty as well as all the women of Russia and China and Great Britain have done theirs."4

Yet if it was true, as *Life* alleged, that "there is scarcely a woman's club where the war is not discussed solely in terms of the servant problem—over the bridge table,"5 then it was also true that in these same elitist clubs, men discussed the war primarily in terms of profits and taxes. If there were apathetic and selfish women, there were also apathetic and selfish men.

There were many reasons why women appeared to be lagging in the war effort, including the fact that "women don't have wives."6 Perhaps more fundamental than the genuine obstacles imposed by home responsibilities, however, was the concept of idealized womanhood that had been developing for the past century, which was reinforced by the idleness imposed on women during the job-scarce Depression years. Female leisure had become a prime American status symbol. It was not surprising that more than a few years of war would be necessary to erase a view so thoroughly fostered by the movies and advertising. Taking the longer view, *Current History* pointed out:

> *We as a nation [must] change our basic attitude toward the work of women. If, in war-time, we continue to idealize the woman who possesses the romantic allure of the soap-ad and who, by her grooming and her manner, clearly indicates that she has never played a part . . . we shall not attract women [to the labor force] . . . We must dispel the atmosphere that pictures women as playing delicately with minor war duties in the moments that they can spare from cocktail parties.*7

Not only had women's magazines promoted an image of women in which success was crowned by leisure, but their most serious failure (and that of the media as a whole) was to fail to portray the war with the seriousness it deserved. Public relations and advertising—new fields during World War I—responded to that war with hyperbolism on the Huns that many Americans later looked on

RIVETING A B-17 AT DOUGLAS AIRCRAFT
IN LONG BEACH, CALIFORNIA.
COURTESY OF McDONNELL DOUGLAS
CORPORATION.

THE 2,000TH C-47 TO COME OFF THE
LINE AT DOUGLAS'S LONG BEACH
PLANT WAS AUTOGRAPHED BY
JUBILANT WORKERS.
COURTESY OF McDONNELL
DOUGLAS CORPORATION.

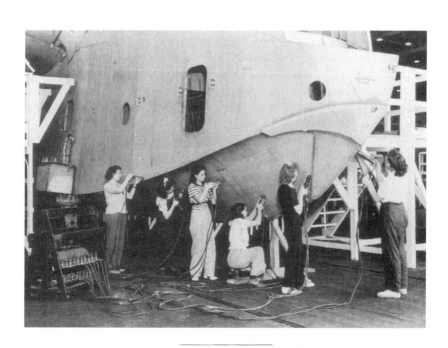

WOMEN AT THE GLENN L. MARTIN COMPANY RIVETING THE PBM-3 MARINER,
A FLYING BOAT USED IN ALL THEATERS OF THE WAR.
COURTESY OF MARTIN MARIETTA AERO & NAVAL SYSTEMS.

MAKING PATTERNS ON A DRILL
PRESS WAS VERY ANALOGOUS TO SEWING.
COURTESY OF MARTIN MARIETTA AERO & NAVAL SYSTEMS.

WORKERS IN AN AIRCRAFT ENGINEERING DEPARTMENT LAY OUT FULL-SCALE DRAWINGS.
COURTESY OF MARTIN MARIETTA AERO & NAVAL SYSTEMS.

WOMEN LEAVING THE SHIPYARDS IN
BEAUMONT, TEXAS,
AFTER A DAY'S WORK, MAY 1943.
U.S. OFFICE OF WAR INFORMATION. PHOTO BY
JOHN VACHON; LIBRARY OF CONGRESS.

CLEANING A TRAIN LOCOMOTIVE WITH
HIGH-PRESSURE SPRAY. THIS YOUNG
PENNSYLVANIA MOTHER, WHOSE
HUSBAND WAS IN THE ARMY, EARNED
BETTER-THAN-AVERAGE PAY AT 58
CENTS AN HOUR.
U.S. OFFICE OF WAR INFORMATION. PHOTO BY
MARJORY COLLINS; LIBRARY OF CONGRESS.

A WOMAN OPERATING AN OVERHEAD CRANE FOR TODD SHIPYARDS.
U.S. OFFICE OF WAR INFORMATION, PHOTO BY AL PALMER; LIBRARY OF CONGRESS.

SORTING BOLTS AND SCREWS THAT FELL TO THE FLOOR WAS PART OF SALVAGE
CAMPAIGNS IN MOST MANUFACTURING PLANTS.
COURTESY OF MARTIN MARIETTA AERO & NAVAL SYSTEMS.

THESE YOUNG WOMEN WERE TYPICAL OF MANY BLACKS
ASSIGNED TO MAINTENANCE CREWS.
COURTESY OF MARTIN MARIETTA AERO & NAVAL SYSTEMS.

MAKING SHELL CASINGS FOR 105
MILLIMETER ARTILLERY IN
DETROIT, MICHIGAN, JANUARY 1943.
U.S. OFFICE OF WAR INFORMATION, PHOTO BY
ARTHUR SIEGEL; LIBRARY OF CONGRESS.

AN OLDER WOMAN LOADING
CARTRIDGES TO BE FILLED WITH
GUNPOWDER.
NATIONAL ARCHIVES.

ASSEMBLING OXYGEN MASKS FOR HIGH-ALTITUDE AVIATORS. A NEW PRODUCT, THESE
WERE MADE AT AMERICAN ANODE COMPANY IN AKRON.
OFFICE FOR EMERGENCY MANAGEMENT; LIBRARY OF CONGRESS.

THESE EMPLOYEES OF THE OFFICE OF
LEND-LEASE ADMINISTRATION WORKED
IN TYPICALLY CROWDED CONDITIONS IN
A WASHINGTON, D.C. APARTMENT
HOUSE CONVERTED INTO OFFICE SPACE;
DECEMBER 1941. NOTE THE EARLY
KEYPUNCH EQUIPMENT, A FORERUNNER
OF COMPUTERIZATION.
U.S. DEPARTMENT OF AGRICULTURE, FARM
SECURITY ADMINISTRATION, PHOTO BY
JOHN COLLIER; LIBRARY OF CONGRESS.

THIS PHILADELPHIA CAB DRIVER IS
INDICATIVE OF THE WOMEN ENTERING
NEW EMPLOYMENT AREAS THAT
OPENED TO THEM DURING THE WAR.
PREVIOUS TO THIS JUNE 1943
PHOTO, SHE HAD BEEN AN OFFICE
WORKER.
U.S. OFFICE OF WAR INFORMATION, PHOTO BY
JACK DELANO; LIBRARY OF CONGRESS.

ONE OF SEVERAL WOMEN LOGROLLERS EMPLOYED AT A NEW HAMPSHIRE SAWMILL
RUN BY THE U.S. DEPARTMENT OF AGRICULTURE.
U.S. OFFICE OF WAR INFORMATION, PHOTO BY JOHN COLLIER; LIBRARY OF CONGRESS.

A "TOURIST COURT" THAT RENTED TO DEFENSE WORKERS IN SAN DIEGO. RENT
WAS USUALLY $8 WEEKLY FOR A SMALL ROOM WITH BATH AND KITCHENETTE.
NO VACANCY SIGNS WERE FREQUENT AT THIS SORT OF PLACE.
U.S. DEPARTMENT OF AGRICULTURE, FARM SECURITY ADMINISTRATION, PHOTO BY
RUSSELL LEE; LIBRARY OF CONGRESS.

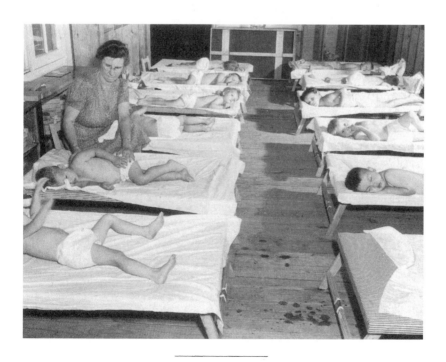

CHILDREN NAPPING AT A WPA NURSERY IN CHILDERSBURG, ALABAMA.
NOTE THE ABSENCE OF ANY BLACK CHILDREN.
U.S. DEPARTMENT OF AGRICULTURE, FARM SECURITY ADMINISTRATION, PHOTO BY
JOHN COLLIER; LIBRARY OF CONGRESS.

ONE OF MANY CIVILIAN WOMEN EMPLOYED BY THE ARMY'S QUARTERMASTER CORPS,
THIS WORKER IS SEWING INSIGNIA.
U.S. OFFICE OF WAR INFORMATION; PHOTO BY A. LIBERMAN; NATIONAL ARCHIVES.

HOUSING FOR BLACK WORKERS NEAR THE MUNITIONS TOWN OF
CHILDERSBURG, ALABAMA, MAY 1942.
U.S. DEPARTMENT OF AGRICULTURE, FARM SECURITY ADMINISTRATION, PHOTO BY
JOHN COLLIER; LIBRARY OF CONGRESS.

cynically. As a result, World War II propaganda was much more restrained—to the point of failing to tell the truth about the horrors that actually were happening.

While it was perhaps true that no one outside the intelligence community knew the extent of Nazi genocide, nevertheless there were millions of Jewish refugees in America who could have testified to genuine atrocities if they had been given access to public opinion. Publicity on Japanese inhumanity was more common, but it stressed breaches of military codes of conduct against our soldiers, not the outrages committed on civilians—on women and their children. Sloganeering about the abstract ideas of fascism and freedom substituted for personalized reports of brutality and fear. The government and media simply failed to bring home the war on a level that caused people to deeply care.

The experience of Josephine von Miklos aptly illustrates the point. A European herself, she understood the urgency of war production to liberate the death camps, but soon noted that her coworkers in a rural New England munitions plant felt no similar compulsion. They often shut off their machines before the shift ended and wasted time in other ways. After she obtained their friendship, she began the kind of education program that management should have promoted and found that they were very responsive to this dramatic, personal approach. To her surprise,

> A few days later the head tool setter got the idea that we might work on a few Sundays and give the money to the government.
> "But the girls won't do it," he said. "They . . . only work for the money, anyway."
> "I'll bet you are wrong," I told him.
> We didn't bet, but he was sure nobody would want to do a thing like that. I asked six girls that evening whether they would or not . . . They all said without a moment's hesitation that they would gladly do it.[8]

And so they worked on Sundays (which meant no days off for weeks) and "gave the money to the government" because they finally understood why this war was important. Instead of thus stressing the painful reality of the war, however, opinion makers spoke too often about "our boys" and about duty; while they naggingly compared American women with those of our Allies, they seldom spoke of real terror. American women debating factory jobs did not know about Slavic and Jewish women who were slave labor in German factories, who, starved and beaten, stayed at their machines only to cheat death for a few more months. They did not know about the millions of mothers who saw their children sent to gas chambers and ovens.

To *really* get an all-out effort on the war, the government should have shared with the public what its spies knew to be true about Nazi extermination factories. Though some racists would have used this as an excuse for noninvolvement, most Americans would have been angered enough to seriously buckle down to work. Instead, the business community aimed to preserve the status quo as much as possible, and they ultimately made the decisions on what was published, as well as how workers were motivated. They continued to believe that employees cared only about paychecks, failing to see that millions of women were fundamentally different and capable of much more than that.

In fact, while accusations of apathy flew, women's capabilities were constantly underutilized. Josephine von Miklos is again illustrative; she earned her prewar living in commercial design, developing a great deal of creative experience in lathe operation. Despite her qualifications, the only war job she could find was as a drill-press operator, something that required little training. She stuck it out for three months to prove she "could take it" before insisting on a transfer, but every upward step was accompanied by obstacles. Ancient machines in her factory often broke down, and boys who knew less mechanics than she were hired to repair them.

> *I was not allowed to use a screwdriver when I itched to repair my machine and saw no good reason to wait . . . until one of the boys was free to come. I used a screwdriver once, was caught and properly, if kindly admonished. I got mad. It made no sense to me. The next time something was wrong I used a dime. I was caught again, but this time they laughed. It was funny to have proved that a woman could do with a dime what the toolsetters were trained to do with much more elaborate instruments. I was asked not to do it again.*[9]

Women with mechanical talents almost always found themselves treated as freaks, as the woman shipyard worker who, according to her supervisor, "should have been a boy. Except that she's better than most of them." She operated a "big hydraulic shaper . . . and was trimming a bore for [an] . . . anti-aircraft gun to a tolerance of .001. She said she had always loved machines, but never had a chance to get her hands on anything like *this* before."[10]

There were thousands of women similar to her who had found no openings for their skills or education during the thirties. Now, with the pressure of war, such women were finally given a chance: "College graduates with degrees earned in naval architecture, engineering, or higher mathematics are finding the jobs they have always dreamed about but were unable to achieve in the past because of their sex."[11] Yet wartime opportunity still did not mean that they would have positions equal to their credentials, nor did it assure women that jobs offered would match their interests and background. Biologists and chemists were found working in airplane plants, presumably not because the nation had no need for these sciences but rather because women were commonly accepted in aircraft factories.

Nor was the failure to use available women limited to blue-collar work; women who were exceptions in other fields found that they continued to be exceptions despite alleged war needs. A 42-year-old lawyer wrote of her experience in trying to best utilize her background for the war:

I went to the local United States Employment Office to ask if women lawyers were needed anywhere. I was asked my age, and when I gave it I was told that if I were still in my twenties and a good stenographer I could be used, but that no employer wanted "old women past thirty."

... I took and passed the examinations for Treasury Enforcement Agent; Junior Investigator and Attorney; and Deputy U.S. Marshal. The information on ... these applications required several days work to complete ... When I called for this appointment I was told that the stenographer had made a mistake in sending out a notice to me as only men were wanted.[12]

Priscilla Crane was another woman who had succeeded in a man's world. She was in print sales and made over $5,000 annually at a time when most women workers could expect no more than $1,500. Despite this obvious ability, her WAC board turned her down "on the grounds that I have too much technical experience and not enough experience in handling people."

The regular Army captain who sat on the Board told me he wished I were a man, as his branch of the service badly needed the skills I possess.

... Lack of a college degree has barred me from [the] three [other] women's services, since on account of age I can only enter as an office candidate.

I might add also that I have ben refused work by thirty-two companies ... doing war work. Their ... [chief] reason, "we do not want women who are used to large salaries."[13]

She could not afford to lie about her qualifications and accept ordinary factory work because like men, she had financial obligations. Even the wages considered "good" in defense plants "will not pay my last year's income tax or the mortgage interest on my house."[14] Yet women's magazines were not above suggesting that women omit some of their credentials when applying for jobs, for many women were in fact overqualified for the work available to them. Rather than support women in searching for the best utilization of their abilities, leadership implied that women college graduates who looked for something other than menial factory jobs were guilty of an excess of snobbery and a lack of patriotism. Even the Labor Department's Mary Anderson, who had a long career of illustrious leadership in progressive causes, advised young women that "war is not a time to satisfy our career ambitions."[15]

Indeed the government, which endlessly nagged women to do more for the war, was itself an offender in failing to use women's abilities. Though Clare Booth Luce's motivations might well have been partisan, she was nonetheless right in pointing out FDR's failure to implement fairness in his own administration:

On the all-important War Production Board among one hundred and seventy officials there is not one woman. In the Office of Price Administration—one hundred and twenty top men, three women ... On the National War Labor Board, dealing with the problems of management and labor—thirty-eight officials, no

women. In the Office of Civilian Defense, thirty-five officials, no woman . . . On
the War Manpower Commission, which must recruit women workers for indus-
try—fifty top-ranking officials, two women.

. . . Could it be that the men have failed to solve the womanpower problem
because they have not understood the psychology of women?

. . . Equally provocative is the thought that among the hundreds of statesmen
. . . who have involved the world in one long diplomatic mess after another, who
in short brought World War II on us—there was not one woman.

I do not hesitate to say that if women had been as largely represented in
international statecraft as they are in population, this war might not have
happened.[16]

Business looked at what government did rather than what it said. In both
employment worlds, the reality was far more unenlightened than the propaganda
would lead one to believe. The forties were, after all, an extension of the thirties
when management didn't have to give a damn; nor were the sweatshop traditions
of the immigrant world entirely dead. Munitions plants who sent workers into
dangerous conditions without training, for example, were similar to the attitudes
that led to the notorious 1911 Triangle Fire.

The Women's Bureau of the Department of Labor found conditions in a
December 1942 investigation to be little better than earlier in the century. In
response to complaints, especially from women who had always worked but
found wartime circumstances more difficult, they interviewed 700 workers in
their homes and followed through at the factories, finding:

Older employees resent the fact that they worked without increases in pay for
years and now new employees earn as much as they do . . . Eating at machines,
in toilet rooms, or in automobiles . . . Employees would like to get hot coffee in
plant . . . The washroom is not available for half-hour before leaving . . . Since it
is frequently cold in workrooms, girls must either smuggle coats into the room or
go through a lot of red tape to get permission to get their coats.[17]

The key to improvements, however, would be not so much Labor Department
studies as the changed situation noted in the first complaint. There was a new
type of worker, and though the experienced women understandably resented her
equal wages, the fact was that these new women, whose labor had to be attracted
with a better offer, would eventually change things for everyone. As middle-
class women insisted on reasonable employment conditions, management discovered that a decrease in the industrial discipline attitudes of the past actually
increased production. The New York State Labor Department, for example,
reported "a substantial falling off in the number of requests for modification of
labor standards, and a growing belief on the part of employers that long hours

and the seven-day week, even as emergency measures, work to reduce output and to increase accidents."[18]

Changes became apparent from the very time women entered the application office. In Depression days, the door was festooned with a sign telling them not to bother; now the welcome mat was out. Raytheon in Massachusetts even served coffee and sandwiches to applicants who happened to be there between 11:00 and 2:00 and reimbursed their interview carfare within a 10-mile radius. More progressive than most, the company offered housewives the opportunity to "select any four- or five-hour shift they like between eight in the morning and five o'clock."[19]

One of the most significant changes was in the hiring of women to hire and supervise other women. Though there, too, they met with bias at first (as the executive who told *Time* that business would not hire women supervisors because they were "cats"),[20] when war production grew and more women were employed, these attitudes faded. "Prejudice against women supervisors is less pronounced," *Business Week* assured readers in the fall of 1942. "Any man is likely to feel that he knows all about his factory, but even the most self-sufficient male executive will admit that he doesn't know all about women."[21]

Indeed, plant managers soon learned that the disciplinary techniques commonly used for male employees not only were unnecessary for women, but were actively demoralizing. A boss who found defective work "was met with tears and he did not understand them any better than he does his wife's . . . In desperation, the manager began to employ women as counselors."[22] The importance of these women in aiding others of their sex was tremendous. They humanized the factory.

Theirs were new and vaguely defined job descriptions. They not only evolved methods of training and discipline that were essential for this new type of employee, but, with greater difficulty, had to teach old-time foremen how to cope with these changes. They "roamed the plant floor, straightening out snarls,"[23] solving little problems before they became big ones.

From the day an applicant walked through the hiring door, these new women personnel officers became a major influence on her life. "They are the ones who set the 'home talent' at ease, . . . the women leaders who see the value of a sociable attitude, a neighborly exchange of conversation about sons at the front, an informal knowledge of the rules of the business world and the best way of imparting these."[24] Using an approach that was creatively different from that of the male hiring officer of a few years before, these women personnel managers were truly in a key position to make war production goals real or to make them fail. The "humanizers of the production front" not only were a key to victory, but also tremendously expanded knowledge of personnel relations and created a new acceptance of women in that field.

These women ultimately benefited male employees as well as female, for they were willing to propose creative, humanizing ideas that would have been ridiculed earlier. The woman personnel director of Todd Shipyards, for example, pointed out the lax standards of the past when she said:

> *Often the company's first introduction to State sanitary codes may come through the employment of women . . . The idea of shower curtains for the women seemed a little startling, not to say unnecessary. Hand cream for the women was another innovation that seemed a trifle "fussy." I pointed to the practice of the experienced men . . . who always greased every inch of exposed skin heavily, . . . so the purchasing department investigated hand cream.*[25]

Dermatitis did in fact come to management's attention because women's softer skins were more seriously affected by industrial chemicals, but routine exposure to "ingredients containing lead, TNT, dinitro-benzene, sulphuric ether, mercury, [and] arsenic"[26] had not been good for men, either.

Changes appeared all over the industry. Probably the most sensible adjustment of all was also the easiest—seating for workers who didn't inherently have to stand. One plant found that merely providing seats for tired workers increased production 23%.[27] Other changes were more innovative. Public-address systems were installed for general announcements that gave a sense of involvement and provided relaxing music. Company newsletters were introduced. Employees were encouraged to form clubs and do off-work activities; some aircraft plants held get-acquainted dances on weekends. Annual picnics and parties became more common and more elaborate than they had been in earlier times. Raytheon tried to give its swing-shift workers a sense of Saturday night by showing a movie for an hour at midnight, albeit the film usually was a government release connected with the war.

While the media emphasized how factories changed to accommodate women, far less attention was given to how women changed factories with their common sense. Mentioned as an aside in a few other articles, the only one devoted wholly to the subject was by a man whose systematic study cited many cases:

> *Gray-haired Mrs. Cora Kepner helps make rubber life rafts at the Goodrich plant in Akron . . . Putting on the "abrasion strips" was a slow hand job. Mrs. Kepner observed it was something like handling pastry and she suggested using giant rolling pins . . . It works fine, as have forty-four other suggestions she has made which have won her $490.*
>
> *In the same plant, Mrs. Carrie Syler is one of thousands of women who make barrage balloons . . . The work made Mrs. Syler think of her home dressmaking experience. She always used pinking shears to scallop the raw edges of seams . . . Why not try them on the balloons? It is standard practice now.*
>
> *. . . Threading wires through flexible tubing . . . was a slow job with considerable spoilage of tubing. Mrs. Quincy Smith remarked, "If I had a thing like this to do at home, I'd use a tape needle." She proceeded to improvise one . . . It saved 4,992 man-hours of labor this year.*

At the Fort Worth plant of Consolidated-Vultee, they used adhesive tape to hold materials temporarily in place on . . . bombers until they could be riveted. Why not giant clothespins, asked Mrs. Mary C. Shelton . . . They save miles of expensive tape.

. . . Any woman who has made her own dresses knows that it saves time and material to place all parts of the pattern on the goods before starting to cut. Ida Basham . . . suggested this plain homebody technique would also save material in laying out patterns on sheet metal. Now wouldn't you think even a man would have thought of that? It has saved 4,320 man-hours a year in the one plant.

. . . In all, hundreds of women have made suggestions which have been adopted by their employers . . . Twenty-six . . . have been given national recognition . . .

Among the winners the archetype is Mrs. Mary Pritchard Vaughn, of Baltimore . . . She worked out a design for simplifying production by arranging the resistors and condensers in the radio compass. Mary Vaughn's idea saved 34,000 man-hours at the Bendix plant in the past year—enough hours to provide compasses for 3,400 planes. She was awarded the highest prize . . . a four-figure check. Then she went home to await the arrival of her baby.[28]

It is worth noting that all but one of the women cited was a "Mrs." They were the older, married women who in the past had to stand in the employment line behind the younger ones that management believed to be brighter. It is also interesting that these companies had cost accounting down to a fine art; they knew exactly how many "man-hours" any activity took, and yet these simple analogies had never occurred to them. Their management style had been that of the thirties, driving workers with a "speed-up" philosophy instead of looking for ways to cut labor costs by changing production methods. Finally, the long-term loss to the economy when the best and the brightest of these award-winning women went home to have a baby occurred to no one.

That having a baby meant an end to a creative woman's career was unquestioned. Similar silence prevailed in other areas involving the sexuality of these new employees. Despite attention to the point of hysteria when women were first hired, there was almost no public discussion of an underlying fear of male managers: menstruation. This physical difference between the sexes was not mentioned, whereas any number of arguable differences were magnified. While both business and women's magazines ignored this area of real concern to them, only *Harper's* was candid:

To many companies of course this is an old problem. The telephone companies and life-insurance companies have devoted years of study to it. But most plant managers didn't ask them what their experience had been . . . Managers who have learned . . . are offering physical-culture classes, teaching women remedial exercises, and giving them instruction in diet . . . In some cases, the answer has been to provide cots and give the worker an hour off to relax.[29]

Such acknowledgment of women's needs and a willingness to adapt the workplace to meet them showed a profound change in the thinking of managerial leadership. Unfortunately, this adaptability was less common among union leadership. Instead most unions, especially those of the craft-oriented AFL, continued to see women as a threat. There was considerable justification for their view, since the war-production miracle was possible only because of refinements of fundamental mass-assembly ideas. True machinists, for example, naturally resented the continued breakdowns of their trade, which happened because of the introduction of workers (male and female) trained to do only a small portion of the job.

What they failed to acknowledge, however, was that massive wartime production would have been impossible using the slow, methodical approach of union apprenticeship. The death knell of craftsmanship continued to sound, not because women entered the labor market, but because the war was a stage in our economic history between a manufacturing and a service economy. It was a clash between labor and management, between old ways and new ways—but women were caught in the middle of a fight they neither understood nor could affect.

It was clear that for valid reasons many women were eager to quit and stayed in industry only as long as they felt it was their patriotic duty. Though by 1944 it could be said that "about a third of America's manpower today is womanpower, . . . one- half are estimated to be there only because of the war."[30] For many women, war work was not so much an opportunity as a sacrifice—one that they were glad to see end.

When a Navy-operated plant at Elmira, New York, cut back production of bombsights, for example, about 500 women were temporarily laid off. Though the war continued, the general feeling in 1944 was that victory was in sight, and "of the 500, only 160 reported for work when recalled."[31] The pattern was repeated in other communities. In amazingly large numbers, women's industrial experience ended once they could see the probability of peace. When the Ordnance Works at Eau Claire, Wisconsin, shut down to retool for tiremaking, 3,475 of its 5,525 employees were women. "Of the 2,000 workers who found new jobs, 1,750 were men, representing 85 percent of the men laid off; 250 were women, only 7 percent of female layoffs."[32] Comparable reports came in from Minneapolis, Los Angeles, and Des Moines.

One key as to why these women chose not to work can be seen in Evansville, Indiana, where of 10,000 laid off, 90% of those collecting unemployment compensation were women. "A representative of the U.S. Employment Service offered employment to a number of those not working, but many refused. In most cases these workers contended that wage rates on the jobs offered were too low."[33] Los Angeles employment counselors reported that women laid off in the aircraft industry "had difficulty in finding employment nearer home at wages comparable to those which they had formerly earned."[34] It was the beginning of the phenomenon of women who could not afford to work, and who would take an actual loss if they did work. The government ultimately could have saved itself billions of dollars in welfare costs if it had undertaken then to see that women's wages were raised to a reasonable level.

Beyond the low wages offered, the other major reason women cited for bowing out of the labor force was "the strain and difficulty of combining wage earning with homemaking duties."[35] For the next two decades, women debated this subject and tried to come up with reasonable solutions (one of which was to make a true vocation of homemaking and consumerism). When they did start reentering the labor market in large numbers 20 years later, the chief difference was that they began to insist on wages high enough to make work profitable and on household help from other family members. Among the commonalities between the two eras is that inflation made women's work essential to family budgets, and husbands were forced to recognize that they needed their wives' incomes. Neither of these meant economic freedom or chosen careers for most women.

If the majority was eager to lay down the burden of war work, there was still a very large minority that had discovered a new world and had no intention of giving it up without a fight. They saw that there were solutions to dual career problems; some, like "First Lady Welder at Richmond Shipyard No. 2 . . . Louise Cox," were farsighted enough to contemplate role reversal. She was "looking for a husband . . . who can darn socks and fix interesting lunch sandwiches!"[36] Others learned from experience that they belonged in traditionally male fields instead of the jobs they had held, as the aircraft worker who said:

I was an average teacher, an average social worker, an average office worker, an average hairdresser; but foremen from other departments come to my machine to ask me to do some work for them if I have time because they say I'm the best countersinker in the vast building! At forty-nine I've at last become not better than average, but the best![37]

Changed awareness developed in other areas. Women reevaluating sex roles also discovered the limitations of class and race prejudice, for the factory had given them their first opportunity to work with people different from themselves. A Connecticut suburbanite described the epiphany of seeing her world with new eyes:

In common with most of you who read this, my working day used to begin somewhere in the neighborhood of nine o'clock—or even ten . . . The first morning on my new job I stumbled out of bed at six.

187

It was in early January . . . It had snowed . . . as I passed each house on our country road, a dark circle of cars . . . headed towards the city. Joining them, I felt like a new club member—as though I belonged, sort of . . .

I had never thought Bridgeport could be beautiful, but . . . I suddenly discerned in it a beauty that was strange and yet warmly human. Patient people tramping blocks in the wind and cold, all intent on the work that lay ahead! I've changed many of my opinions about our laboring classes.[38]

While some upper-class women gained new knowledge of the lower, by far the greater change was in the opposite direction. For millions who were economically deprived in the thirties, the war represented an unprecedented opportunity to move up the social ladder. One of many girls from West Virginia recruited into munitions plants typifies the pattern; when she got off the bus headed for the hiring hall,

She was a solitary girl . . . lonely and forsaken-looking. Her skirt flapped around her ankles, her hair fell lank about her ears. Everything about her spoke of some remote Southern hill town . . . She hadn't a penny in her pocket . . . She was going to let no "foreigner" see her disturbance, but you could feel her all aquiver like a taut violin string.

Two months later she had on a . . . pretty shirtwaist and some costume jewelry . . . Her dark hair was swept back . . . There was a discreet touch of rouge on her thin face . . . She was rich. She made more money than she had ever thought possible. The clothes were something she had not even dreamed of. Here all at once was companionship, adventure, a different status.[39]

Not everyone liked the changes the war wrought in Rosie's life, but even conservative women were forced to acknowledge that things had changed. Realizing perhaps that the days of arguing for inherent privilege were over, their new contribution in the arena of ideas was an interesting blend of leftist civil libertarianism and old-fashioned "women's place" conservatism. In discussion of a potential draft of female industrial workers, the National Committee to Oppose Conscription declared:

Our committee believes that there is no reason for objecting to the conscription of women on the basis of special privilege of sex . . . While in principle the conscription of women is no more objectionable than that of men, the movement of women on such a scale into war industries has far more serious social consequences in juvenile delinquency . . . and the foundations of the home.[40]

The testimony of a representative of Women's League for Political Education on a potential draft was far more emotional, but even she based her arguments not so much on privilege for the weaker sex, but an extremely libertarian point of view. "We regard this bill," she said "as utterly un-American and destructive of everything we cherish."

Not content with taking their sons to the extent of ripping even the youths of high-school age from their homes, a grateful Nation now proposes to take the mothers as well . . . If we willingly go into this complete regimentation we have betrayed the boys who left to defend us from this kind of life. I think the thought of meeting the little wife in a uniform down at the community kitchen for dinner and then getting a pass to see their child over at the Federal nursery would make our boys feel that they might better have stayed in Africa, or China, or wherever it was that they served.[41]

Ultimately, though, mainstream women made their decisions not on the basis of abstract philosophy, but on personal need and opportunity—whether or not they worked depended on what sort of job they could get, what it paid and what the family and community support services were. If they left the work force after the war, it was less in response to arguments about their proper place than because the promises made to them proved false.

Especially during the early stages of the war when women were being cajoled into industrial jobs, promises were made that, while honestly intended, could have been predicted to be unkept by a careful observer of history. Brigadier General Frank McSherry, for example, assured women that "many of the jobs on which women are now working are being done better by them than by men, and it's not hard to figure that there'll be plenty of work for women as well as men in the aircraft plants . . . after the war is over."[42] Yet a mindful reader might note the contradiction inherent in another statement in the same article: "At the close of World War I, 23 per cent of the employees in 40 airplane factories were women . . . Up to July 1941, practically no women were employed . . . except as sewers and upholsterers."[43] Another writer similarly said more than she intended to in praising the "only woman flash welder . . . master of a difficult trade and proud of her skill . . . In the last war she was a machine operator in a knitting mill; then she did housework for 20 years. Now she is back . . ."[44]

The message for the wary lay between the lines: Women were wanted for the duration only. Those who continued after the war could expect a lesser place, but this message also was so well hidden that it was hard to discern. A shipyard manager praised his new employees, saying,

These women who are willing to go through hard weeks of intensive training, then expose themselves to the arduous duties . . . to lend a hand with the war will be the . . . office personnel of . . . the future. Those who go to secretarial school now might well be the travel agents, cruise directors and hostesses of the peacetime merchant marine.[45]

War opportunity, while often meaningful for the duration, was oversold in regard to the future, and women's leaders did not provide the warnings and the support that they should have. The advice that experts offered was of the same vague nature that had been given to military women. A leading sociological journal, for example, summarized:

> "Women will have made further progress . . . in breaking down the prejudices and discriminations . . . It will be up to women to maintain these gains . . ."
> And when the women of America leave the machines, . . . take off their work clothes, and go back to their homes, they will have the satisfaction . . . of knowing . . . that they did not fail.[46]

How women were supposed to "maintain these gains" at the same time that they would "go back to their homes" was not spelled out. People continued to ask questions on sex roles, however, and hungered for leadership. There was strong response to an unusual editorial on the topic by *Life* near the war's end:

> Let us face the fact that the status of women in America, which was changing fast enough before the war, is changing with lightning speed during it . . . Women hold increasingly important committee jobs in Congress. Mrs. Roosevelt is a more active politician than any other First Lady in our history. More women than men voted in the last election. Both party platforms endorsed a constitutional amendment giving 'Equal Rights' to women; and while nothing will be done about this amendment because it is largely nonsense, it would have been foolhardy of either party to say so.
> . . . Forty-five women in uniform have been killed or wounded on duty; more than 250 have been decorated. Women are veterans of Bataan, of Anzio, of Normandy.
> . . . Of all the social revolutions now abroad in the world, that of the women is the least dynamic, the least predictable, the most aimless and divided—in short, the most feminine.
> . . . They are today themselves the greatest obstacle to their own further advancement. How brave, brainy, and competent some of them are! But how slack, unfocused, helpless and hopeless are others![47]

The lively debate that ensued divided almost completely on sex lines, with women defending themselves and men zeroing in on the critical points. One exception was written by an Ohio man, who well summarized the editorial's logical inconsistencies, saying, "These faults of which you find the girls guilty are faults we all share because we're human."[48]

Labor Secretary Frances Perkins, speaking of the changes that the war made in the labor force, concluded:

190

The most spectacular . . . is the great influx of women into fields normally considered masculine domains . . . We find there is a gradual replacement of men by women in laboratories, banks, businesses, ticket offices; . . . as tax collectors, radio announcers . . . A definitely encouraging trend has been a break-down in many quarters of prejudices against certain types of woman workers. Married women . . . older women . . . [and] Negro women in unprecedented fashion are gaining footholds.[49]

Miss Perkins, who had been personally involved in labor and feminist history for decades, understood that there was nothing new about working women in America—women had worked since the first New England textile mills. What was new in World War II was the upgrading of available jobs and the entrance of middle-class women into the labor force. It was the beginning of women who worked outside the home because they wanted to as much as because financial need drove them. The era also saw the advent of America's switch from a manufacturing to a service economy—a system in which physical strength became generally irrelevant.

In the forties, however, the switch for the woman who had always worked was primarily from outmoded service jobs to war manufacturing. Domestic servants, a feature of middle-class American homes for decades, largely disappeared during the war. Approximately a half-million women left domestic service during the war,[50]* many of them black women who finally found better opportunities open to them. Like their white counterparts, black women also replaced black men in traditionally assigned jobs— one black magazine hailed as newsworthy the replacement of black waiters in railroad dining cars with waitresses.[51]

Service jobs in hotels, restaurants, and laundries declined along with domestic service. Some, such as elevator operators, movie ushers, and messengers began to disappear. The reasons were clear in this statement from a New England munitions maker: "I used to work in a hospital—ten hours a day for $1.95, buy your own uniforms and keep them laundered, and take everybody's bad temper."[52] There was both more freedom and better pay in manufacturing than in service.

Even some nurses and other professional women left their public-service-oriented jobs for the better pay of defense plants. Although fewer than 10% of teachers left the classroom,[53] shortages soon arose, especially in critical labor areas that had an influx of new residents. "All former teachers" were "politely but forcefully requested" by the War Manpower Commission "to take refresher courses and get back into harness."[54]

Though it should have been obvious why teachers and nurses left their fields, all too often the reasons were missed. Just as volunteer nurses' aides were proposed as a means of dealing with hospital shortages, some suggested volun-

---

* The number might well have been higher, for record-keeping on household servants is unreliable.

191

teer substitutes for teachers, particularly at the primary level. While no one ever suggested asking aircraft manufacturers to donate planes, even *Independent Woman* was not above devaluating female labor by urging women to staff day-care centers on a volunteer basis.[55]

While nursing and teaching, which were seen as female endeavors, lost numbers during the war, professional areas that were traditionally male dominated saw women squeeze in past the barriers. One of the most visible to the public was journalism. Margaret Bourke-White, with her immensely popular photography and reporting for *Life*, epitomized this brave new woman. She was with nurses and WACs when their troopship was torpedoed on its way to Africa; she wrote about how they spent a frightening night bailing water from their lifeboats, listening to the cries of the wounded and dying whom they could not reach. Her pictures and words made women's war roles real for those at home.[56] Nor did she confine herself to simply reporting on women; she asserted her right to cover the "real war" and, over and over again, covered stories and took photos that no male news hound could equal.

Newsweek told readers that "war has added mightily" to the number of women reporters. "In 1933, only twenty women were admitted to the Senate and House press galleries . . . Now there are 74 women among accredited Capitol correspondents."[57] *Time* echoed the observation, saying that editors, "at the bottom of the manpower barrel, are recruiting more and more women. The United Press bureau, which had only one woman reporter before the war, now has eleven on beats . . . The newshens cover almost everything. . . . The editors' consensus is that they do remarkably well."[58]*

In professional fields that were new, women found it easier to be accepted from the beginning. Psychology and personnel were both growth areas that seemed naturals for women's presumed nurturing abilities. Moreover, large numbers of psychologists and rehabilitation workers would be needed to deal with the millions of returning soldiers. As early as 1942, "the entire graduating class in psychiatric social work at Smith College . . . had jobs many months before they had finished school."[59]

Even women lawyers eventually could find work outside of the steno pool, but most still were hired in family law or related areas. "Governmental services, particularly Federal offices, are . . . providing openings for them in consumer and social service fields." While it was reported that "some headway is also being made by woman lawyers in State and local government units,"[60] all but one of the half-dozen precedent-setting hirings cited were either clerkships or related to public service/legal aid.

---

* Yet, disappointingly, the only annual dinner that FDR attended during wartime was that of the White House Correspondents' Association—and it was stag. According to *Time*, the "pert" president of the Women's National Press Club lodged "a formal protest," but nothing changed.

Some of these lawyers chose the government over private employers explicitly because civil service offered them protection from postwar firings. They "had the impression that those taking private positions will surely lose them when the men come back at the end of the war,"[61] and saw the government as a surer friend for the career-oriented worker. They were not alone in this analysis, for while Rosie turned blue collar, there were hundreds of thousands of her sisters who adopted pink and became "government girls."

Although it was little noted at the time, the largest and most lasting change in women's employment during the war was having Uncle Sam as her boss. On June 30, 1940, there were 186,210 women working for the federal government's executive branch. A year later (even before Pearl Harbor) there were 266,407, or a 43% increase in one year. In the War and Navy Departments, more than 60,000 women were hired in this one-year period—before the WAAC was even formed.[62]

Washington's cherry trees, a gift from Japan, bloomed ironically in the spring of 1941, for though they would be winter-dead when the bombs fell on Hawaii's palms, the menace of war was already clear. Almost two thousand young women were arriving in Washington every month in response to advertising throughout the country for clerks and typists; after war was declared, the female newcomers would average 3,000 a month.

"On the whole, they are a pretty unsophisticated lot," commented the *New York Times Magazine*. "Many of them are away from home for the first time . . . They came to get a job. They came to get between $105 and $120 a month."[63] Recruited by the Army Services Forces, high school seniors, with all their fresh naivety and enthusiasm, got on the train after graduation and headed for D.C.

The government had good reasons for reaching out into the rural areas for these "unsophisticated" women who would work harder and expect less. Moreover, each one of them was known by her community, and that helped to connect people to Washington and the war. Rubes though they might have been, these young women changed the city even as it changed them: "Federal Triangle at 5 o'clock in the afternoon looks more like a college campus than the center of the nation's capital. These youngsters are turning the fashions of this city upside down . . . Washington women are learning to go hatless and like it."[64]

Perhaps the primary reason, however, why young inexperienced women were preferred was that Uncle Sam as an employer knew that his work was usually monotonous and not particularly rewarding. Often it was tedious beyond human (or at least male) patience. It was not unusual to type reports on forms with 20 copies—in a day before any method of correcting an error other than by erasing every single copy. Machines were not electric, necessitating strong hands. Nor were there any copy machines other than messy mimeographs.

The steno pool was "a kind of clerical factory" and the reaction of a woman who had been a private secretary back home was akin to that of a skilled machinist put on a numbing assembly line. Nonetheless, as *Independent Woman* wearily pointed out, "Stenography is still a woman's greatest opening wedge. Of the 200 women who held the highest positions held by women under Civil Service, the greatest number began as secretarial assistants." Moreover, the promise of a genuine career in government was more viable than in private business: "To enter Washington is like entering a great university. Even a typist can feel like a freshman . . . Most departments have in-service schools . . . Most of the schools and colleges in Washington have courses especially designed for government workers. Everybody from the highest to the lowest in Washington studies."[65]

Though her job might be dull, a woman's off-work life in Washington presented challenge enough to make a boring job a relief. Even more than the young women imported to work in munitions plants, these pink collar girls found Washington to be a crowded and expensive place to live:

There is no use enlarging on the impossible living conditions in our capital city. It has had plenty of publicity. Everybody is desperately trying to do something about it, but . . .

No girl should be insane enough to go to the city first and expect to get a job afterwards. She can probably get the job all right, but until she does, she is likely to be out on a long limb in the cold so far as sleeping and eating are concerned. If she takes her [civil service] examination locally and receives her appointment, she will be told to whom to report when she arrives, and something will be done for her.[66]

Government agencies did indeed do their best to arrange housing for new employees and even offered interest-free loans until the first paychecks. Nonetheless, women found themselves crowded into a small room with three or four others, with inadequate bathroom and kitchen facilities and expenses that were twice as great as at home. Salaries, while better, were not double. Restaurants were crowded to the point that diners ate standing up, and transportation services were similarly jammed. The result was that as many as half of the women quit and went home in disgust six months after Pearl Harbor. Better informed women would not consider employment there: "50 percent of the eligible stenographers are refusing appointment to Washington."[67]

President Roosevelt, who liked to fancy himself an architect, fiddled with plans for dormitories that were eventually built, but not to his specifications. Similar to the ones constructed for munitions-plant workers, they called for "31 residence halls with 12,291 rooms . . . within walking distance of likely places of employment."[68] Those at "the new War Department Building at Arlington Farms" (later known as the Pentagon) included a cafeteria and canteen, as well as administration and assembly buildings, a central laundry, infirmary and a combined garage, storage and maintenance building. Though convenient, this housing was depressingly temporary in style, only slightly better than slumlike.

It did reflect Washington's willingness to innovate, however, as did the flexible quitting times around town that staggered traffic by allowing some to leave their jobs as early as 3:30 (a wonderful opportunity for women with school children). Difficult though life might have been for single women, for women with families Washington was an even worse place to live.

A closed Southern town in the attitudes of many long-time residents, the Arlington elementary schools even refused to accept any more children, leaving newcomers at a loss. Nor were other suburban services up to the task; people were evicted from new housing in Arlington after having lived for months without any sewer hookups. One Congressman declared that military officers had come to tell him that they were more concerned with losing their wives and children to disease than they were about losing their own lives in battle. Washington's long-time native black population faced a housing crisis greater than whites as they were displaced by new government buildings and whites-only housing in their former communities of Georgetown and Foggy Bottom.

Black women, however, like white women, found new job openings in Washington as the war proceeded. They began to trade their maids' uniforms for office attire as at last doors that had always been closed were forced open by war needs. Though the pay was still low, expenses high and the work often unrewarding, women in Washington symbolized the advent of equal opportunity throughout the country.

These "government girls" were breaking a long tradition that federal jobs were reserved for males only. Less than a century earlier, the U.S. government employed no women. When finally the hand-copying required in the Patent Office proved so tedious that they could not persuade men to do it, the first women were hired—but only to work at home. These women delivered their work by mail and were strictly banned from entering the office. Their paychecks were sent in their husbands' names. By remembering this, women understood how far they had come.

SOURCE NOTES

1. Furnas, "Are Women Doing Their Share?," p. 12.
2. Margaret Barnard Pickel, "A Challenge to the College Woman," *New York Times Magazine* (March 5, 1944): p. 7. See also "Women Lagging in War Effort," *Newsweek* (January 25, 1943): p. 24; "Few Women Training," *Science News Letter* (April 17, 1943): p. 253.

3. Patricia Davidson Guinnan, "A Long War Is Paved with Good Intentions," *House Beautiful* (September 1943): p. 30.

4. Clare Booth Luce, "Victory Is a Woman," *Woman's Home Companion* (November 1943): p. 34.

5. "American Women," *Life* (February 19, 1945): p. 28.

6. Furnas, "Are Women Doing Their Share?," p. 12.

7. Warne, "Cherchez la Femme," p. 219.

8. Von Miklos, *I Took a War Job*, p. 86.

9. Ibid., p. 49.

10. Bradley, "Women at Work," p. 197.

11. Oppenheim, "Anchors Aweigh!," p. 90.

12. "Comments on 'Womanpower 4F,'" *Independent Woman* (November 1943): p. 334.

13. "Why Won't They Let ME Help?," *Independent Woman* (October 1943): p. 294.

14. Ibid.

15. Pickel, "Challenge to the College Woman," p. 35.

16. Luce, "Victory Is a Woman," p. 121; see also "Under-use of Womanpower," *Independent Woman* (August 1943): p. 230.

17. "War Work of the U.S. Women's Bureau," p. 1170.

18. Amidon, "Arms and the Women," p. 248.

19. Josephine Ripley, "It's Woman's Day Right Now," *Christian Science Monitor* (October 23, 1943): p. 6.

20. "Women and Machines," p. 62.

21. "Women's Bosses," *Business Week* (October 17, 1942): p. 44.

22. Mezerik, "Factory Manager Learns," p. 289.

23. Ibid.

24. Kelly, "Calling All Women," p. 3.

25. Herrick, "With Women at Work," p. 4.

26. Mezerik, "Factory Manager Learns," p. 291.

27. Ibid.

28. Laurence Hammond, "Kitchen Lore Speeds War Production," *Independent Woman* (December 1943): p. 362.

29. Mezerik, "Factory Manager Learns," p. 293.

30. Bradley, "Women at Work," p. 193.

31. "Women's Tendency to Leave the Labor Market," *Monthly Labor Review* (November 1944): p. 1031.

32. Ibid., p. 1032.

33. Ibid., p. 1031.

34. Ibid., p. 1032.

35. "Jobs and Workers," *Survey Midmonthly* (September 1944): p. 262.

36. Field, "Boom Town Girls," p. 298.

37. "Comments on 'Womanpower 4F,'" p. 347.

38. Fillebrown, "I Helped Build Fighter Planes," p. 348.
39. Vorse, "Girls of Elkton," p. 353.
40. "Women Against Conscription," *The Christian Century* (May 19, 1943): p. 612.
41. "Opposition to the Austin-Wadsworth Bill, by the Women's League for Political Education," *Congressional Digest*, Vol. 23 (April 1944): p. 125.
42. Frank J. McSherry, "Women Workers Wanted!," *Flying* (October 1942): p. 34.
43. Ibid., p. 89.
44. Bradley, "Women at Work," p. 194.
45. Oppenheim, "Anchors Aweigh!," p. 91.
46. Glover, "Women as Manpower," p. 75.
47. "American Women," p. 28.
48. "Letter to the Editor," *Life* (February 19, 1945): p. 2.
49. Perkins, "Women's Work in Wartime," p. 661–62; see also S.F. Porter, "Bright Girls Wanted," *Woman's Home Companion* (October 1942): p. 68, about other jobs available in formerly male fields.
50. "Changes in Women's Employment During the War," *Monthly Labor Review* (November 1944): p. 1029.
51. "Hands Across the Table," *Brown American* (Summer 1943) p. 6.
52. Amidon, "Arms and the Women," p. 248.
53. "Professional Women and the War," *School and Society* (January 12, 1946): p. 35; see also "The Nation's Manpower Program and the Problems of Children," *Elementary School Journal* (February 1943): p. 319.
54. Baldwin, "America Enlists Its Women," p. 282.
55. Ibid. See also "Definitely Women's Work," *Independent Woman* (April 1942): p. 107.
56. Margaret Bourke-White, "Women in Lifeboats," *Life* (February 22, 1943): p. 48.
57. "Ladies of Washington's Working Press," *Newsweek* (March 1, 1943): p. 64.
58. "Skirted," *Time* (March 13, 1944): p. 83.
59. Lucille Nelson McMahon, "Women and the War of Nerves," *Independent Woman* (October 1942): p. 300.
60. "Effect of War on Employment of Woman Lawyers," *Monthly Labor Review* (September 1943): p. 502.
61. Ibid.
62. "Women in Federal Defense Activities," *Monthly Labor Review* (March 1942): p. 640.
63. "Girl's Town—Washington," *New York Times Magazine* (November 23, 1941): p. 8; see also David Brinkley, *Washington Goes to War* (New York: Alfred A. Knopf, 1988), especially Chapter V, "Boom Town."
64. Ibid.

65. Marjorie Barstow Greerbie, "Women Work With Uncle Sam," *Independent Woman* (March 1942): p. 74.
66. Ibid.
67. Ibid. See also "Girl in a Mob," *American Magazine* (October 1942) p. 33; "Washington Packs 'Em In," *New York Times Magazine* (May 3, 1942): p. 8.
68. "Residence Halls For Women," *Architectural Record* (July 1942): p. 43. See also "Uncle Sam's Girls," *Good Housekeeping* (January 1942): p. 44.

PART IV

THE HOME FRONT

13

THE NORMAL HOUSEWIFE IN ABNORMAL TIMES

Although millions of women joined the labor force during the war, there were millions more who did not. The reasons why they did not were as varied as their lives, but one vital factor loomed large in any decision of whether to work outside the home: the fact that housework, 1940s style, was often a genuinely full-time job. The war emergency made this truth even more real. Women were warned at the beginning of the war:

> *For the coming year, at least half our productive effort must be spent making things that civilians cannot eat, wear, or live in—making things for military use. And goods are also scarce because some commodities like silk, rubber, and tin aren't produced here and must be brought across hazardous oceans on crowded ship bottoms.*[1]

Suddenly a housewife's job became much more difficult, for the tools of her trade were taken from her. She could not get sugar at her store because the cane fields in the Philippines were gone, nor could she drive from place to place in search of it because gasoline also was cut off. Recipes had to be modified because everything from Hawaii's pineapples to Indonesia's spices disappeared. In dozens of little ways, daily life changed for the worse.

New mothers could not buy rubber pants for their babies, nor could one expect to find fruit juice for her toddler, for tin also was an import interrupted, and canned goods of all sorts became precious. There might be no coffee or tea or even cocoa as refreshment after her futile shopping trip, for these too came from overseas.

A new silk blouse was out of the question, for India's silk supply had ceased; any silk that happened to be available was needed instead for parachutes and gunpowder bags. Its substitutes, newly invented nylon and rayon, were needed for aircraft and military clothing. The same was true even of humble cotton, a staple now requisitioned for tents and other heavy military uses. Wool, normally imported from Australia or elsewhere, became "very, very tight."[2]

The list would grow to include dairy products and meat and leather, and the resultant shoes. The chemicals needed for war production had an important trickle-down effect on the availability of products for civilians. Fuel-oil shortages meant chilly houses, and all things made of metal—from safety pins to refrigerators—became scarce.

In the panic after Pearl Harbor, millions of Americans, remembering World War I shortages, stripped their local stores of supplies. Prices naturally zoomed for those goods that remained. "The cost of living is racing up at two percent a month," *New Republic* reported soon after war was declared. "Prices are being driven up by shortages, and only a system that combines price control with rationing of available supplies can be effective."[3]

Rationing was not merely the eccentric whim of a left-wing publication, for a Gallup poll showed that two-thirds of the public supported the general concept.[4] There were two fundamental purposes of rationing: (1) to distribute scarce goods fairly so that the poor as well as the rich had a defined share, and (2) to keep prices reasonable, thereby preventing inflation and its consequent diminishment of the value of the dollar.

Once again the United States had the benefit of European experience. Rationing, which had been seen as a sign of weakness in World War I, instead became viewed as a necessity by both our Allies and our enemies in this war. Germany and Japan imposed rationing from the beginning of their militarization, and Britain's reluctance to emulate them dissolved when her food costs rose 14% in the first four months of war.[5]

Americans likewise placed pragmatism above ideology. The fact that totalitarian governments used rationing first was not seen as a sign of fascism, oddly enough, but rather of economic democracy. *Business Week* wrote early in the war that the fascists had "recognized that in total warfare, supplies can never come up to demand . . . Rich and poor alike shared in abstention."[6]

The level of abstention in America, of course, never reached anything like that of other countries. Midway through the war, *Ladies Home Journal* reminded housewives who found rationing difficult: "We still get ten times as much beef a week as people in England, twenty times as much as they get in Russia, and fifty times as much a week as the lucky ones get in China."[7] Still, for Americans accustomed to an unlimited bread basket, shortages were a great change. Even more significant was the daily governmental interference in small, personal decisions.

Despite this, public acceptance of the need for rationing was tremendous, for the short experience of empty shelves and high prices after Pearl Harbor quickly taught almost everyone the fundamentals of supply-and-demand economics. Pollsters soon found that an overwhelming 89% of Americans preferred rationing to "taking the chance of being able to obtain" a product. Women set about learning the new language of "certificate rationing," "coupon rationing," and "value points," with 76% of them (compared with 53% of men) responding that they understood how point rationing worked.[8] Like English women before them, American women made "rationing a topic of daily conversation, thereby educating themselves rapidly."[9]

It was soon so much a part of life—and of such fundamental importance—that even children understood. The tale was told of a Sunday school teacher who presented the story of Noah, and then asked her kindergarten children to illustrate it with Noah taking only his most valuable possessions in his crowded boat. "When the pictures were finished, every single child had drawn Noah holding a ration book in his hand!"[10]

On Monday morning after Sunday's bombing in Hawaii, apparently the first war action that many women took was going to the store for sugar. Eager purchasers knew from the first World War that there would be a shortage, not only because sugar had to be shipped over now-perilous seas, but also because industry would soon compete with housewives for the precious sweet stuff. Those too young to remember were reminded that "sugar cane makes molasses; molasses makes ethyl alcohol; and alcohol makes the powder which fires the guns . . . [and] not only gunpowder but torpedo fuel, dynamite, nitrocotton, and thousands of militarily important chemicals."[11]

After a "wild wave of buying," January's sugar prices were 35% higher than a year earlier.[12]* Rationing (which began on May 5) imposed a quota of one pound of sugar per week, with a quarter of that held back to be used as special supplements for holidays, home canning, and restaurants. The ration worked out to 12 ounces per person per week, instead of the 24 that people had used before.

Adjustments were quickly made. Restaurants removed sugar containers from tables and imposed a "lady who presides at the mammoth sugar bowl."[13] Radio cooking shows and women's magazines were full of advice on ways to cut consumption. *Good Housekeeping* readers, for example, were told to simply use less than a recipe called for—"you might find you like it just as well and it's better for you."[14] Readers were also told to stir sweetened beverages frequently so that sugar wouldn't stay on the bottom; to serve fruit instead of traditional desserts; and to use honey, molasses, corn syrup, maple syrup and sweetened condensed milk as replacements.

---

* At that time, each person's annual intake of sugar averaged 74 pounds, compared with about 60 pounds today. Any decrease in the average intake of sugar may be misleading, however, for home baking and canning were far more common then. Modern consumers buy endless items with sugar included that were not then on the market. With the development of many kinds of sweeteners based on products other than sugar cane, each American eats about 130 pounds of sweeteners annually.

When the Navy began to retake the Atlantic in 1943 by eliminating German submarines, Caribbean sugar shipments replaced a portion of those from the Pacific and the ration was slightly increased. In 1944, however, "prospects for continued relaxation . . . faded" because merchant ships were needed to supply the giant D-Day preparations and because "large quantities . . . were diverted to the manufacture of industrial alcohol."[15] More than a year later, the situation was unhappily the same. Even though the war was over, Secretary of Agriculture Anderson could foresee no immediate end of rationing, for cane fields had been bombed and refineries demolished. "Sugar rationing," he said, "may be needed for another year."[16]

Sugar was the rationed item that Americans told each other they missed most. Gallup invited respondents to fantasize near the war's end, asking which of four rationed commodities they would prefer if given a windfall. In a choice between 15 gallons of gas, 25 pounds of sugar, 5 pounds of butter or 5 pounds of beefsteak, 47% (almost half) opted for the sugar.[17]*

The scenario soon was replayed with coffee consumption. Caffeine addicts likewise stripped grocery shelves, assuming that the same importation factors that affected sugar would also cause a coffee shortage. Annual consumption figures rose from 13 to 16 pounds during 1942,[18] obviously a result of hoarding rather than dramatically increased drinking of coffee.

Such hoarding, of course, made it difficult for the poor to compete with the rich in buying their fair share of coffee, so rationing was imposed on November 29, 1942. The spartan amount allotted was a severe blow to coffee lovers. People over 15 were limited to one pound every five weeks: "This quantity will provide a cup of coffee per day per person—and a few drops over."[19] Restaurants announced that coffee could be served at only one or perhaps two meals a day. Ads appeared for chicory tablets which, added to a cup, gave a weak brew a stronger taste.** The first rationed pound purchased had to last through the Christmas holidays to January 2. Doubtless many found cold comfort in the thought that there would be no sugar cookies to accompany the coffee anyway.

The next Christmas, however, was far better. Unlike any other basic commodity shortage, the coffee situation improved so dramatically that the government was able to end rationing for it long before the war ended. As the Atlantic was retaken, Latin American shipping became safe, and coffee quantities improved to the point that rationing was dropped on July 29, 1943. Hoarders

---

* An April 1943 list of rationed goods that people found "hardest to cut down on" was headed by meat and coffee with gasoline and sugar next. Cheese was in the last place of nine items. A September poll on nonfood items showed tires and their inner tubes first with stockings second, followed by various appliances. Last was safety pins.

** Instant coffee had not yet been invented; there were no genuine substitutes for brewed coffee.

doubtless accounted for more of the problems in 1942 than genuine shortages.

Hoarding was less of a problem with the meat supply, for people did not commonly have freezers and thus could not buy ahead—but there were other, more complex problems involving meat. Unlike sugar and coffee, meat was seldom imported into the U.S.; instead, the problem was one of creating sufficient supplies for export, especially for military use.

There was no shortage of meat at the source, for farmers were hard at work producing a wartime meat supply much larger than in the past, but "military demands for meat will take 7,500,000,000 pounds, or almost exactly the total of the increase."[20] "Military demand" illustrates the most important factor in the wartime meat supply—that of increased demand. Obviously, the military was composed of people who had been part of the peacetime population—they simply had not eaten as much meat when they were civilians. The Army's standards were higher. Steaks and roasts that never graced family tables in the prewar Depression years were now common mess-hall fare.

At the same time, millions of civilians who had wages unknown to them a few years earlier wanted items in the butcher's case that they had not bought in the past. Rationing in this area thus became a problem quite different from that of coffee or sugar. Meat rationing was primarily a problem of how to fairly distribute a reasonably large supply, and its objective was to hold down prices.

After warnings throughout 1942 that rising prices would necessitate rationing, the Office of Price Administration reluctantly took on this huge bureaucratic task and began rationing meat in March 1943. The ration was a relatively generous amount, allotting about two-and-a-half pounds of meat per person per week. This was the equivalent of consumption during the 1930s, but it was a reduction from current standards. More than that, it forced housewives to plan meals in new and not necessarily welcome ways. Most of all, it turned a shopping trip into a major assignment in financial planning.

Sugar and coffee rationing were implemented by a simple coupon plan—a stamp equaled a pound, and one pound of sugar was the same as another. Meat, however, was more complex because a pound of beef steak is not equal to a pound of pork ribs. Thus the concept of "point rationing" had to be introduced. Ration stamps were allotted value so that one had to spend more points (as well as dollars) to buy good cuts of meat than to buy inferior ones.

Conditions improved during 1944, and Canada ended meat rationing. A year later, however, business and media leaders were calling the optimism of 1944 a mistake, for even with the end of the war, the need for meat rationing continued. Drought in Australia and Argentina (other large meat-producing countries) added to the problem of attempting to resupply both Allies and former enemies in Europe. When political considerations brought rationing to an end, there soon were calls by church and labor leaders for its reinstatement as prices rose and poor people quickly lost their former purchasing power.

The end of rationing was undoubtedly influenced by the public's belief that meat was the least effectively enforced of all rationed items. Estimates were that as much as 40% of meat mysteriously ended up in black markets; even major meat packers agreed that their product was not controlled. Armour's president was not alone when he said, "A substantial part of our meat is going into the black market."[21]

Cheese dishes could not substitute as entrees, for it was rationed at the same time as meat. Cheese was the dairy product most easily shipped abroad, and it became more scarce as the war neared an end because it is a staple of European diets. Additional millions of pounds of milk were shipped to U.S. troops in the new dried milk form. Butter, however, was the rationed dairy product most profoundly missed by civilians.

Once again, there probably was sufficient butter at the source, but rationing was necessary because otherwise "butter distribution would be so spotty that many sections of the country . . . would have to do without."[22] European distribution systems for civilian goods had so totally collapsed that butter became an almost unheard of luxury. "One of the most wistful stories of the war" told of a displaced English boy, who at his first meal in America, "tried to pass the pat of butter on his bread plate around the table. He thought the little square was meant for the whole party of six."[23]

Butter was fundamental to diets at the time, for margarine was not commonly used in the 1940s. Housewives depended on butter not only as a spread but also as an essential for baking and cooking. Even as butter was rationed, the need for it became greater due to the loss of various imported cooking oils. Olive oil, coconut oil, palm oil—all of which were imports—disappeared. As late as October 1945, the Agriculture Secretary warned, "the world will be short of requirements for fats and oils for many months, and rationing will have to be continued until . . . supplies are available . . . from the Pacific."[24]

Predictions of milk rationing never came to be, though fluid milk was price-and-distribution controlled at the source. Canned milk, on the other hand, was widely used in this era (because many people did not have dependable refrigeration) and it was rationed. This, though, was not due to dairy shortages but rather to that of metal.

Civilians were allotted a mere 15% of the nation's steel production in 1943—an extremely small piece of an essential pie. The result was rationing of "nearly all canned, bottled, dried, and frozen vegetables, fruits, juices, and soups."[25] This area of rationing probably imposed more difficulties on house-wives than any other. Women were expected to shop for fresh items that simply were not to be found in many locations during the nonsummer months; if by chance they were successful in finding fresh vegetables, then they had to find the extra cooking and preparation time. One feminist writer explained:

> *Shortages of meats and vegetables, and even of the lowly potato, mean that instead of the quick dash to the grocery for food, you have to wander around to two or three or even more stores before you can find what you need or want for properly balanced meals. One week there is no hamburger, the next week no tomatoes. You scurry around, wasting time and rationed shoe-leather . . .*
>
> *The shortage and rationing of canned goods affects workers more than any other group . . . Cuts of meat which are cheaper both in money and ration points mean more hours cooking. A steak can broil in a few minutes. Pot roast takes hours.*[26]

The women who were most able to cope with canned-goods rationing, of course, were those who lived on farms and in small towns who had the land and supplies—and foresight—to garden and preserve their own supply. America was still small-town during World War II, however, and a solid 75% said "yes" when Gallup asked in January of 1943, "Did you or your family put up (home can) any cans or jars of food this year?"[27]

City women were encouraged to experiment with new types of food. Dehydration was the big innovation of the war, as canning companies sought other methods of preservation. Dried soup mixes were probably most popular, but other forms of dried food were also introduced. Some, such as "pumpkin pie flakes," did not outlast the war.[28]

Entire cookbooks appeared aimed at facing wartime difficulties. *How to Cook a Wolf*, for example, offered ingenious methods of keeping the wolf from the door, such as recycling the water from cooked pasta or rice for use as a soup base and conserving fuel by cramming every inch of oven space with something, whether relevant or not to the current meal—baked apples, gingerbread, "war cake," and other things that could be used cold. A genuine gourmet, the author nevertheless managed to offer recipes suited to war needs, preferably with tantalizingly exotic names.[29]

The priority of military over civilian food needs was recognized by food-industry advertisers, who switched from selling their products to explaining why they couldn't be sold. Much of this advertising trivialized the housewife's problems, but some were thoughtful. Libby's, for example, ran this two-page ad:

> *. . . We've got to feed our fighting forces. We've got to help feed our allies . . .*
>
> *. . . Getting our crops harvested hasn't been easy. In many places help has been scarce, as on the Pacific Coast where alien field and orchard workers were moved away.*
>
> *. . . Before the war 86% of America's tin came from Malaya and the Dutch East Indies.*

...For the Armed Forces and lend-lease, we pack millions of cases of food ...Uncle Sam gets 40% of our fruit cocktail ... [and] practically all of our 1942 salmon catch. That tells you one big reason why you can't always find in stores just the Libby item you want.

...Many experiments in food preservation and in packaging methods are being made ... In our experimental kitchen, Mary Hale Martin and her staff of home economists are creating new dishes, new menus to aid you.[30]

Advertising mentioned the war at every opportunity, whether or not it was relevant, and new products were promoted for their wartime correlation. Vitamin tablets, a recent research achievement, found recognition as a way to be sure the rationed diet was adequate. Old products discovered new advertising possibilities, as with California date growers who promoted dates as a sugar substitute. Indeed, the attitude of some advertising agencies seems to suggest that they considered the war to be a terrific new-account bonanza. While some ads took the war seriously, more seemed to view it as a convenient anomaly for creative exercise. Wartime sacrifices were generally minimized and a light-hearted approach preferred.

But if advertising took the war less than seriously, magazine editorial policies were generally even greater offenders. Though of course every women's magazine ran some war-related stories, many issues contained no mention of the war and the vast majority of articles continued to be of the "home-as-usual" variety. *Good Housekeeping* even delineated this as a deliberate policy in the first post-Pearl Harbor issue that would reach their readers. In February 1942, they acknowledged that "every item of our apparatus . . . is now at our Government's command," but added significantly:

There is another obligation that we will recognize: that of being anti-hysterical ... We will try to remember that entertainment and instruction and homely advice must continue . . . While we are fighting to win, we shall try to know that love will stay in our world; . . . that life in American homes must go on and will go on.[31]

Gourmet magazine had the bad fortune to begin publication in the fatal year of 1941, but its response to the war's outbreak was simply a breathing indifference. Never in the four years of the war was even one article published that was directly connected to wartime shortages. Features on the cuisine of France, Italy and China made no acknowledgment of the fact that one could not travel there, much less find these foods. In response to a letter to the editor from a man requesting "ration recipes," the editors defensively replied that their recipes were adaptable to wartime: "Why ask for 'ration recipes'—and destroy forthwith in your mind the taste of what are still very savory dishes? The recipes that we give are not for rations; they are for good food."[32]

Mending stockings was a reality for most women during the war, for they quickly became so scarce as to be too expensive for women of ordinary means. "Women suffered a humiliating run in their national stocking," wrote *Independent Woman* after Pearl Harbor, "when the government embargoed silk."[33] As with coffee, the millions of women who thought they were prudently buying ahead instead actually pushed up prices and created their own crisis. In November of 1942, the Office of Price Administration issued ceiling prices, saying that "nylons were selling at inflated levels 'in almost every store in the country.'"[34]*

Still, one New York department-store executive averred that "The stocking situation . . . was nothing compared to . . . wool. I don't know what women think they are going to do with all the suits and coats they are buying!" Shoe rationing, according to the head of OPA, was imposed partly because of the military's needs for millions of new pairs, but also because of hoarding—some people bought "a dozen pairs or more."[35] A *Vogue* editor echoed her scorn for such hoarders in saying, "Think how demode they're going to feel going around in their old beige legs when black cotton stockings are all the rage!"[36]

But neither black nor any other color of cotton stockings ever became fashionable, and silk continued to be a status symbol throughout the war. Many a woman measured her status by such symbols, and many a man bought sexual favors with presents of silk stockings and other scarce goods.

Adult clothing made its wartime adjustment primarily in the promotion of fashions that used less fabric, heedless of the implication that new fashion guidelines implied new clothes. For example, the cuffs on men's pants were eliminated to save fabric, but then many men let their old pants hang in the closet to buy the new, "patriotic" style. Fabric saving was the rule:

Hats have shrunk . . . and many men and women go about bareheaded . . . Women who used to regard long skirts as an evening necessity have taken to shorter and less formal clothes for the duration. In Washington, D.C., . . . a Brotherhood of Sensible Men has adopted slacks with open-collar, short-sleeve shirts as an office uniform.[37]

Yet such "uniforms" did not become standard, and most middle-class women and men continued to think of a hat as essential to proper appearance. Any serious accommodation to war needs was slight. Newspapers and magazines ran hundreds of pages of advertisements for women's clothing, with very little notice of the war. Instead, a woman was more apt to be seriously affected by the rationing of clothing and shoes for her children. Her own wardrobe she could

---

* Even after price control, stockings were still expensive by today's standards—the maximum allowed for the best quality was $2.50 a pair.

redo and update, but growing children simply must have replacement shoes and clothing.

"More than anything else," wrote a mother of young children, "I'll miss zipper coveralls . . . The last pair I found cost $1 instead of the former 69 cents."[38] She recommended sewing children's clothes from seersucker fabric, since it did not have to be ironed, and told of making play clothes out of her old kitchen curtains. Another writer offered such tips as cutting apart old handbags to reuse the leather for elbow and knee patches on children's clothes. A dry cleaner also was to be chosen with care: "Normally it's unfortunate if garments are ruined in cleaning. Today it's tragic."[39]

Sheets were probably the biggest complaint in the household fabric area; the shortage was sufficiently severe that a decade later many women responded to the Korean War by buying sheets. A Cannon ad in *Ladies Home Journal* offered patronizingly detailed instructions for women on how to rinse, bleach, hang and iron sheets to cause the least fabric stress; there were admonitions not to use pillowcases as laundry bags; finally, Cannon warned, "You may be tempted by the slightly lower price of shorter-than-average sheets. But . . . they . . . wear out sooner."[40]

An additional fabric need at some times and places was blackout curtains. Once up, the heavy, dark curtains had a mournful effect, but (as with other problems), the media offered advice. One writer suggested that "funereal blackout curtains . . . will take on life with the addition of greenery. You might . . . do something giddy like big chintz roses cut out and mounted on them."[41]

Kitchens might be made uncomfortably hot by blackout curtains during summer, but in winter their warmth would be appreciated. "Fuel oil," wrote *Business Week* in early September 1942, "is the most complicated rationing problem yet tackled." The needs of each user had to be separately considered, with quotas imposed that varied "by regions and by periods of the winter, with constant adjustments based on 'degree days' of temperature."[42]

Sixty-five degrees was considered the maximum allowable daytime temperature, with nights to be even chillier. Women found themselves constricting their households to one or two heated rooms, with no more attic or basement play areas for children and quick dashes to icy beds at night. Again, the advice-givers came through; one writer had even this odd bit of lore on fireplace heating with finesse:

> *Get one package of fireclay from a fuel-man, and mix it into a stiff paste with water. Make it into balls about the size of oranges . . . Dry them in the oven: you are having baked potatoes and a pot roast anyway at night. Leave them overnight in the cooling oven if you can, and when they seem dry put them into the fire.*
>
> *That is all. They get red-hot, and give off a lot of heat, and if you treat them gently . . . they will last "for ages."*[43]

Not nearly all Americans, however, were such conscientious conservationists. In January 1943, *Life* criticized Midwestern indifference to fuel shortages, an attitude its editors believed was due to the influence of anti-Roosevelt newspapers, especially the Chicago *Tribune*:

> *When Government warnings were issued early last autumn that there would be a fuel oil shortage, the Tribune scoffed. Result was that throughout cool November Chicagoans made no effort to conserve fuel. Now, in the midst of the coldest December in 65 years, the shortage has actually hit them.*
>
> *But instead of trying to repair . . . [their] error, . . . [the Tribune] has exploited the cold spell to make an all-out attack against rationing. "How does it aid the war effort to make people uncomfortable . . . ?" . . . The effect . . . has been to create a mistrust of Washington so profound that it is becoming almost impossible for the Administration to govern in that area.*[44]

Midwestern indifference was based in part on their relative proximity to oil production. Easterners felt the fuel crisis much sooner, as gasoline rationing was imposed there with abrupt seriousness early in the war. Women quickly felt the impact on their lives, because much of their driving was rapidly defined as discretionary. Nursery schools, for example, closed because mothers no longer had the gas to drive their children to school. Gas rationing brought many changes to family life; vacations were canceled, and outings of all sorts had to be carefully considered. Tourism ended and resort towns closed; women working in these areas soon lost their jobs.

Though there was certainly need for increased gasoline exports during the war (especially from the East Coast at the time of the North African invasion), the primary reason for gasoline rationing was the forced conservation of even more scarce tires. Raw rubber simply would not be available until the Pacific was reconquered; synthetic rubber was not yet out of experimental laboratories; and the government, like a prescient parent, insisted on limiting the amount of driving people did in order to make their tires last for years into the unknowable future.

Hence, gas and tire rationing were tied together. While gasoline was bought with three types of coupons that varied by occupational needs, tires could not be purchased at all without a ration certificate specially issued by one's rationing board. When the first gas ration books were obtained, citizens had to "declare (under threat of penalties) that they had in their possession no more than five tires per car."[45]

Of greater concern to most housebound women, however, was the certificate rationing of metal items. Already in February 1942, "the production of refrigerators, vacuum cleaners, home radios, washing-machines, . . . and domestic sewing machines was stopped and that of . . . many other standard consumer goods sharply curtailed."[46] Replacement stoves or sinks could not be purchased, nor could women obtain such simple items as pots and pans. These shortages were especially severe for brides and women trying to set up housekeeping in new locations near defense industries.

210

A woman—especially one whose man had gone to war—found herself doing new tasks to conserve household goods. Old roller skates needed the rust removed, and worn bicycles had to be repainted, because these items could not be bought. Garden tools had to be oiled to prevent winter rust; leaking faucets had to be fixed to prevent the loss of water heated with precious fuel. Even the fuse box had to be monitored "now that no repairs on electric currents are allowed if there are usable ones in the house."[47] The same writer also recommended keeping dust off light bulbs, for dust, she asserted, could cut light by 20%. Doubtless there were women who dutifully dusted their light bulbs, believing—though the connection seemed somehow sadly vague—that they were helping to win the war.

A decade before the war began, America ended its great moral experiment with the prohibition of legal alcohol. Roosevelt's election represented not only action on the deep problems of the Depression, but also deliberate inaction on reform of citizens' drinking habits. The failure of Prohibition was a strong factor in the minds of ration planners, for they knew from recent experience how readily Americans will ignore laws that they do not personally support.*

Even though people philosophically agreed with rationing (as polls showed they did), millions were nonetheless willing to ignore governmental mandates when their personal interests were strong enough. In June 1942, when gasoline

---

* The role of liquor during World War II was very unlike that in World War I, when the Women's Christian Temperance Union and other organizations placed it at the center of wartime issues. The passage of Prohibition, as well as women's right to vote, were direct outcomes of World War I.

Though the WCTU tried to make similar use of this war, its leadership was elderly and its numbers greatly reduced, and World War II saw no serious revival of Prohibitionism. Instead, the tremendous frequency of liquor advertising during the 1940s shows that this was an area not even subject to conservation policy, let alone rationing. A shortage did exist, of course, of imports such as Scotch and European wines, but American producers clearly saw the war as an opportunity to promote their own brands and introduce new uses. The California Wine Advisory Board, for instance, promised, "Wine has a way with the foods of wartime," and ran recipes for nonrationed foods such as kidneys with red wine; calves brains with sauterne; and baked fish vin blanc.

Tobacco, another target of WCTU censure, also remained not only freely available, but automatically included by Uncle Sam as a part of soldiers' rations. Thousands of workers were diverted to growing tobacco and manufacturing cigarettes; there were Washington women who did nothing but type tobacco allocation cards. While men were often critical of women for wartime frivolity and waste, these two largely male vices were seldom mentioned.

rationing had just begun, 43% of respondents to a Gallup poll answered "yes" when asked whether "you have heard of any cases of where service stations or garages sell gasoline to customers without punching the full amount on ration cards?"[48]

Hoarding, of course, was the reason the first rationing was imposed—and again, millions of Americans ignored the national interest in favor of what they saw as personal prudence. The grocer who exclaimed, "You'd be surprised how many people come in here and *brag* they have 300 pounds [of sugar] stored away!"[49] was not, sadly, atypical. Similar reports came in from all over the country, as *Life* wrote in early 1943:

> *In San Francisco . . . a small run on vinegar developed when a man in a restaurant was overheard saying there would be a vinegar shortage. Denver had its first fire last week from an explosion caused by hoarded gasoline. Just before coffee rationing began, some people in Atlanta, Ga. discovered that there was a lot of coffee on the shelves of Monroe, Walton County, 40 miles away. They descended on the little town (burning up precious rubber to get there), swept it clean, left the local people coffeeless for days.*[50]

One of the Roosevelt appointees in charge of rationing wearily pointed out how little good such hoarders ultimately were doing for themselves, let alone the damage they did to the national interest. "What are we going to do about those extra cans of groceries on your pantry shelves?" he asked.

> *If you declared them as you should have, you have nothing to worry about. Your ration book was "tailored" to fit them; in plain words, coupons are torn out to put your rations on a par with everyone else's. But suppose you did not declare them. Suppose you're trying to cheat. Can you get away with it? I think not.*
>
> *We don't intend to march into your pantry and count the cans. We won't have to . . . Neighbors will whisper. Delivery boys will see them. The children will tell other children. If the housewife is lucky enough to have hired help, the servants will gossip. Someone, as surely as you live, will tell your neighbors or the rationing board. More important, you won't feel very proud of yourself.*[51]

Indeed, the fact that a fairly complex system worked so well was ironically related to the fact that life was simpler then. The small-town nature of much of America in the 1940s went a long way towards creating public support, which made the law self-enforcing. A second important factor was the nature of shopping in that presupermarket era, when grocers "waited on" customers, "put up" their orders, and often delivered them as well. They were keenly aware of what was bought by whom, and this also functioned as a real enforcement tool.

In more anonymous shopping situations, however, dishonest sellers were certainly to be found, and the evidence of black markets grew as the war continued. *Woman's Home Companion* sent a reporter on an 11,000-mile shopping trip early in 1944 without a ration book; she found that, with some effort, she could buy almost anything anywhere. On Chicago's South Side, a dozen butchers turned her down when she asked for frankfurters without coupons, but she "noticed other customers purchasing meat without red coupons and guessed that the butchers had suspected I didn't belong in that neighborhood."[52] Sure enough, in the Loop and in suburban Evanston and Oak Park she was more anonymous and bought her hot dogs without ration points at 10 cents a pound over ceiling.

Almost everywhere I had the same experience. In Kansas City a butcher sold me a perfectly good ten-pound ham because it was "in immediate danger of spoilage." Under OPA regulations such meat may be sold without points, but the price must be reduced accordingly. Instead, I paid 16 cents a pound above the legal ceiling.

. . . In every major city I visited I found that stockings were bought most easily in expensive restaurants, bars . . . [etc.] Nylons seem to have almost disappeared in the South, but I found a pair for $5 at a liquor store in Houston. In another Southern city I met a most distinguished . . . bank president whose desk drawer was full of nylons at $5 a pair to his best depositors.[53]*

Hoarding and black marketing were not the only areas for public admonitions; the subject of wastefulness was also frequently addressed. *Ladies Home Journal*, for instance, chastised its audience by saying "Hitler would laugh his fool head off if he were collecting garbage in this country . . . We throw away four billion dollars worth of edible food a year, . . . four times as much as the value of the food we sent abroad last year on Lend-Lease."[54] *Life* offered similar views, asking, "How can we get this country . . . to act and think like the Marines on Guadalcanal?," and answered the question by saying: "The ones on whom this responsibility chiefly falls are the women . . . If the women of America will take on this war as their own; if *they* will think war . . . then this country would begin to look like a real war machine." To achieve this "real war machine" status, women were to conserve fats and tin; they were to "just remember that everything your family consumes retards the war effort."[55]

---

* Neither this reporter nor others specifically mentioned any case of a woman retail clerk who cheated. While this is anecdotal evidence, it is true that virtually every article on black marketeers featured men as both sellers and customers, not women.

A statistical survey on the subject showed that slightly more women than men objected to illegal purchases. In response to a question asking whether "buying at black market prices is sometimes justified," 77% of women said "no," versus 71% of men. (Gallup, *The Gallup Poll*, p. 506. Poll date was May 1945.)

Like *Life*, government officials over and over again stressed the importance of the housewife's role in making the system work. Prentiss Brown of the Office of Price Administration was typical when he said in June 1943 that "the future of price control rests with American women."[56] But while the burden fell on women, rationing boards included very few of them. In part, this was due to the first rationing being that of tires and gasoline (an accepted male venue), but mostly it was simply old political habit. Rationing boards, like draft boards, were made up of community leaders, and it was usually the case that these were white businessmen.

Once rationing programs were in place, and "the functions of the boards became largely clerical,"[57] more women were included among the volunteers. By the end of 1943, there were 76,321 board members, with 91,000 more unpaid assistants.[58] They worked under the jurisdiction of almost 100 OPA regional offices, where volunteers worked alongside paid workers. They dealt with the range of human problems, patiently explaining the system to the ignorant and the irate. They had to weigh the evidence on special needs and on allegedly lost or stolen cards, and they had to deal with local emergencies.

These volunteers already began to think of the end of their duty in the spring of 1944, when administration spokesmen risked premature estimates on when various rationing programs might end. By fall, though, even *Business Week* was worried about too hasty a return to uncontrolled capitalism and resultant inflation; the next spring—even as the war in Europe ended—it announced:

> *Officials have now given up the hope (freely expressed a few months ago) that ration book No. 4 would be the last . . . Gloomy reports of food shortages, plus European needs, mean no relaxation . . . Food shortages will be with us for some months yet, and . . . may get worse before they get better . . . Rice probably will go off the market with heavy Army purchases for native irregular troops and relief feeding in the Far East.*[59]

Indeed, winning the war meant responsibility for feeding not only the semi-starved allies in Britain and Russia, but also dependent peoples in the formerly occupied territories of France, Scandinavia, the Baltic, the Mediterranean, India and the far Pacific—as well as former enemies. *Christian Century* spoke out strongly on behalf of the hungry:

> *For the sake of the half-billion in Europe and Asia threatened with starvation, the United States should restore food rationing . . . It has taken a tragically long time to arouse the American government and most of the American press to what is happening . . . [but we] now know that food supplies in the British and American zones in Germany . . . have recently been reduced again until they are now within a couple of hundred calories of the rations in the terrible Belsen concentration*

camp . . . Conditions in France and Italy [are] far worse than after the First World War . . . India is entering what is likely to be the worst famine in its history; in great sections of China the population is already living on grass and clay . . .[60]

They called Americans "selfish" people "concerned with how soon they can have . . . automobiles, clothes, houses, nylons, and electric refrigerators," who were ignoring the "great reservoir of ill will, resentment, and envy"[61] that was building in the rest of the world—but polls showed that Americans had a different self-image. They thought of themselves as a generous people, with 70% stating their willingness to return to rationing "in order to send food to people in other nations."[62]*

The government, however, did not call upon them for this sacrifice; through the Marshall Plan and other economic programs, Europe and Japan were nonetheless rebuilt. Some church and labor leaders, though, saw rationing and—especially—price controls as essential for the country's benefit, as well as that of the rest of the world. Fear that the end of rationing would signal the beginning of inflation was very real. Polls showed almost three of four respondents expressing a desire for continued price ceilings.[63]

The economy, however, made its transition to peacetime without either price ceilings or ruinous inflation. Women played a part in that transformation; despite stereotypes as compulsive shoppers, ultimately it must be said that women did a very good job in controlling wartime inflation and in understanding and supporting the government's economic plans. They managed under a complex system that largely excluded them from decision making. Women were not only seldom represented on ration boards, but they also went unconsulted in other areas directly applicable to them. A committee to advise the War Food Administration on nutritional needs, for instance, was composed entirely of male physicians—there was not one home economist or dietician, who presumably would know more about this field than MDs.[64]

It is therefore not surprising that nowhere were the special needs of pregnant and lactating women mentioned, nor was breast feeding encouraged as a way of coping with rationed canned milk and baby foods. These oversights become even more glaring since most pregnant and nursing women would fall into the category of "small families" that the public believed was discriminated against in the rationing system. There is a sad irony in that the people who probably were most badly provided for by rationing were the wives and young children of soldiers asked to lay down their lives.[65]

---

* A poll a month later showed somewhat less support (65%). Women were appreciably more generous than men, with 72% of them willing to return to rationing "to send food to people in other nations," compared with 58% of the men. (See Gallup, *The Gallup Poll*, p, 582.)

Similarly, *U.S. News*, in seeking opinion on the problem of overseas famine and rationing, interviewed leaders in churches, business, government and labor during a two-month period—but no women were interviewed.[66] Women had no real input into the plans they were expected to implement, and they did not demand leadership roles commensurate with the responsibilities they assumed. Instead they became excellent troops of followers, for ultimately the fact that the system worked well is largely due to their efforts. Women were repeatedly reminded that the burden of rationing was theirs, and so they deserve the credit for its success.

SOURCE NOTES

1. Mildred A. Edie, "Rationing for Civilian Strength," *Survey Graphic* (March 1942): p. 143.
2. Ibid.
3. "Rationing: Democracy's Test," *New Republic* (February 9, 1942): p. 192. See also "More and Better Rationing," *New Republic* (June 15, 1942): p. 817; "Ration Food!" *The Nation* (November 28, 1942): p. 155.
4. Gallup, *The Gallup Poll*, p. 328
5. "Rationing," p. 192; see also Ralph Robey, "The Problem of Rationing," *Newsweek* (May 25, 1942): p. 52.
6. "Rationing—The Lesser Evil," *Business Week* (February 21, 1942): p. 76.
7. "Let's Face Facts About the Food Shortage," *Ladies Home Journal* (October 1943): p. 24.
8. Gallup, *The Gallup Poll*, pp. 364 and 371.
9. "Pointed Rationing," *Business Week* (December 1942): p. 15. See also, in the same publication, "Rationing Is Not So Simple" (October 17. 1942): p. 104 and "America's Food Problem Recast" (October 31, 1942): p. 15; and Kurt Solmssen, "Ration Book vs. Pocketbook," *Harper's* (January 1943): p. 143.
10. Constance J. Foster, "Rationing Shows Folks Up," *Ladies Home Journal* (December 1944): p. 4.
11. Ann Starrett, "Rationing Is a Woman's Job," *Independent Woman* (May 1942): p. 138. See also Alice Fraser, "Be Thankful for a Ration Book," *Parents* (February 1943): p. 22; "Rationed Sugar and Gas," *Commonweal* (May 22, 1943): p. 99.
12. "Rationing," p. 192; see also "Rationing Just Around the Corner," *Scholastic* (February 9, 1942): p. 9.
13. "Adieu to Sugar," *Business Week* (March 7, 1942): p. 18.

14. "Easy Ways to Save Sugar," *Good Housekeeping* (April 1942): p. 98.
15. Chester Bowles, "When Will Rationing End?," *Collier's* (May 6, 1944): p. 59. Bowles was head of the Office of Price Administration.
16. Clinton Anderson, "The Food Outlook Today," *Hygeia* (October 1945): p. 765.
17. Gallup, *The Gallup Poll*, p. 520. Steak was chosen by 29% while only 14% preferred the gas and 10% the butter.
18. "Rationing for Victory" *Scholastic* (November 30, 1942): p. 10.
19. "Rations and Prices," *Newsweek* (November 2, 1942): p. 36.
20. "Rationing for Victory," p. 11. See also in the same publication, "Design for Buying—1943" (January 11, 1943): p. 5; and "Point Rationing," *Education for Victory* (April 1, 1943): p. 1; and "Let's Face Facts," p. 24.
21. "Is Food Rationing in the United States Necessary to Meet Famine Conditions Overseas?," *United States News* (May 31 and June 7, 1946): pp. 42 and 32. See also Anderson, "Food Outlook," p. 763; Paul O'Leary, "Wartime Rationing and Governmental Organization," *American Political Science Review* (December 1945): p. 1089; "Oil, Meat Rations," *Business Week* (September 5, 1942): p. 14.
22. Bowles, "When Will Rationing End?," p. 14.
23. Ethel Gorham, *So Your Husband's Gone to War* (New York: Doubleday, Doran and Company, 1942) p. 164.
24. Anderson, "When Will Rationing End?," p. 765.
25. "War Needs Hit the Home Front," *Scholastic* (January 11, 1943): p. 3.
26. Anthony, *Out of the Kitchen*, pp. 152–53.
27. Gallup, *The Gallup Poll*, p. 426.
28. See Clementine Paddleford, "What War Has Done to Life in the Kitchen," *House Beautiful* (September 1942): p. 63; S.S. Pfeiffer, "Grandmother Did It and So Can We!," *American Home* (March 1943): p. 10; Dorothy Marsh, "What We Have Found Out You Can Do About Butter," *Good Housekeeping* (April 1943): p. 86; J. Hindman, "Kitchen's Drafted, Too," *American Home* (December 1941): p. 46.
29. M.F.K. Fisher, *How to Cook a Wolf* (San Francisco: North Point Press, 1988), p. 183. Originally published in 1942; revised in 1954. I am indebted to my good friend Lee DeCesare for bringing this item to my attention.
30. The ad ran in the November 1942 issue of *Good Housekeeping*.
31. "Good Housekeeping and the War," *Good Housekeeping* (February 1942): p. 19.
32. Letter to the editor and reply, *Gourmet* (March 1943): p. 3.
33. Starrett, "Rationing Is a Woman's Job," p. 137.
34. "Rations and Prices," p. 36.
35. Prentiss M. Brown, "My New Plans for Rationing and Prices," *American Magazine* (May 1943): p. 21.

36. Starrett, "Rationing Is a Woman's Job," p. 137.
37. Faith M. Williams, "The Standard of Living in Wartime," *Annals of the American Academy of Political and Social Science*, Vol. 229 (1943): p. 117.
38. Mary Cunningham Baur, "The Farm Homemaker Faces War," *Journal of Home Economics* (October 1942): p. 518.
39. Margaret Davidson, "Ways and Means for War Days," *Ladies Home Journal* (September 1943): p. 96; see also in the same publication and by the same author, "Thrifty Ways for War Days," (July 1943): p. 96.
40. Cannon advertisement, *Ladies Home Journal* (April 1943): p. 41.
41. Gorham, *So Your Husband's Gone to War,* p. 56.
42. "Oil, Meat Rations," p. 14; see also "Point Rationing Overtakes Coupon System," *Business Week* (January 2, 1943): p. 7.
43. Fisher, "How to Cook a Wolf," p. 139.
44. "Me First Americans Fight the War in the Grocery Stores," *Life* (January 4, 1943): p. 16.
45. "Rationing for Victory," p. 10.
46. "America on Short Rations," *Current History* (February 1943): p. 486.
47. Davidson, "Ways and Means," p. 96.
48. Gallup, *The Gallup Poll*, p. 340.
49. Starrett, "Rationing Is a Woman's Job," p. 138.
50. "Me First Americans," p. 16.
51. Brown, "My New Plans," p. 21.
52. Patricia Lochridge, "I Shopped the Black Market," *Woman's Home Companion* (February 1944): p. 20 (condensed by *Reader's Digest*) (April 1944) : p. 69.
53. Ibid., p. 70; see also Pete Martin, "Solid Citizen," *Saturday Evening Post* (May 6, 1944): p. 102, for a similar story of black-market buying techniques.
54. "Let's Face Facts," p. 24.
55. "What Women Can Do," *Life* (September 28, 1942): p. 32.
56. Prentiss Brown, "What I Tell My Wife About Rationing," *Woman's Home Companion* (June 1943): p. 24.
57. David Demarest Lloyd, "Has Rationing Worked?," *Survey Graphic* (November 1943): p. 432.
58. Chester Bowles, "Rationing and Price Control," *Life* (December 13, 1943): p. 60.
59. "Ration Book No. 5 Coming," *Business Week* (May 12, 1945): pp. 19 and 20. See also Bowles, "When Will Rationing End?," p. 14; "Postwar Controls," *Business Week* (September 16, 1944): p. 17.
60. "Restore Rationing!" *Christian Century* (April 10, 1946): p. 454.
61. Ibid.
62. Gallup, *The Gallup Poll*, p. 576. Poll date was April 1946.

63. Ibid., pp. 535 and 561. Poll dates were October 1945 and January 1946. Opinion rates were 72% and 73% respectively.
64. "Point System of Rationing," *Science* (October 29, 1943) p. 379; see also Mary Brown Shimer, "Rationing for the Baby," *Hygeia* (January 1944): p. 64.
65. Anne Maxwell, "Rationing Has Its Points," *Woman's Home Companion* (August 1943): p. 8; and "Do Price Ceilings Work?," *Woman's Home Companion* (February 1944): p. 8.
66. "Is Food Rationing . . . Necessary?" *United States News* (May 31 and June 7, 1946): pp. 42 and 32, respectively.

14

VOLUNTEERS AND MORE

Once again, the United States learned from England. As Americans borrowed their model for rationing food, so they also took lessons in creating a new role for women in the production of it. Outside of the London and Liverpool vicinities, England is an agricultural country, and during World War II these islanders depended on British farmers for their very lives. Food production was so imperative that city women were assigned to work on farms, and the Women's Land Army was born.

American farmers were resistant to the idea, not so much out of a desire to protect the delicacy of womanhood, but rather because they did not think that city-bred, untrained women—who probably wouldn't know a corn seedling from a weed and were sometimes afraid of chickens—could be more help than hindrance. Their own wives and daughters shared farm work and expanded those roles when war production demanded it, but farmers were reluctant to allow expensive animals and irreplaceable machinery to be handled by giddy town girls.

Yet help was needed, for many traditional agricultural workers were no longer available. On the West Coast, thousands of Japanese who had labored in the fields were, against their will and all wisdom, interred in prison camps. The migrant "Okies" of the thirties settled down in the booming wartime cities and went to work in defense plants. Southern black sharecroppers found other opportunities. In midwestern agricultural centers, traditional "hired men" now joined the military or found better-paying jobs.

Women, once again, became the last available resource. By the first summer of the war, female farmworkers had risen from 1% to 14%. "Florida reported 24 per cent of its farm workers were women," whereas in four other states, at least one of every five agricultural workers was female[1]—and these were the official statistics, which always undercount housewives, part-timers, and other women who "help out."

During this first chaotic wartime summer, the movement of women into the fields was an unplanned, random process. "In this country we have no national Land Army, as have England and Canada," wrote one reporter, "although some states have organized land armies of women."

*Oregon inaugurated the first statewide, house to house mobilization . . . More
than 60 percent of last year's farm workers were women and children; 39,150
women enlisted to work on farms. This year with an even greater shortage of farm
help anticipated, Oregon is starting earlier and going at the problem more
systematically.*[2]

Further down the Coast, California's branch of the American Women's
Voluntary Services was also hard at work on this need.

*It took the A.W.V.S. five months to persuade the farmers that women should be
used. Now there are 1,000 women in five camps . . . The A.W.V.S. provides a cook
and stocks the commissary. Women pay $1 a day board and get the regular
migratory workers' wages. It's not an easy life; the thermometer may reach 105
in the day and descend to the depths at night. Warm water is rare; cold showers
are the rule.*[3]

By the summer of 1943, Washington bureaucrats had organized these local,
voluntary efforts into formal networks. Congress appropriated money to establish the United States Crop Corps under the aegis of the Department of
Agriculture, and the Women's Land Army was created as a subdivision of the
Corps. It was headed by a woman, Florence Hall, and like every other World
War II body, it created a uniform to be bought at the option of the woman. In
addition to the Women's Land Army, the Crop Corps had a subdivision called
the Victory Farm Volunteers, which, in cooperation with the U.S. Office of
Education and its various state agencies, recruited high school girls for local
labor.

Immediate success was reported. In New York City, 400 women, "instead of
dancing with armed forces on furlough . . . signed up with the farm section of
the US Employment Service."[4] Taking a ferry up the Hudson, they headed for
a former CCC camp and worked on upstate farms. Their average age was 22,
and most were college students; although there were also working women using
their vacation, servicemen's wives, and debutantes. None said they were going
for the money. Many were interested in the experience of being on a farm; some
wanted the exercise and suntans. Most cited a desire to help in a meaningful
way to win the war; they planned to earn the certificate issued by the Women's
Land Army for a month or more of work. All over the country similar groups
repeated the plan:

*A Connecticut camp of one hundred and forty girls and women picked the
strawberry crop. South of Baltimore . . . one hundred women and girls pick beans
. . . From the Ohio State University fifty YWCA girls are spending ten weeks on
farms . . . They are billeted in an old school building . . . About one hundred college
girls are working on Maine farms.*[5]

Some state agricultural schools saw women as potentially more than summer supplements and set up short courses training them to be year-round farmworkers. The University of Maryland, for example, taught women to shear sheep and dock their tails. Midwestern farm machinery dealerships taught tractor driving and equipment operation in classes set up for women.

By the summer of 1944, the idea of women in agriculture and the Women's Land Army itself were so well-established that recruitment articles were distinctly fewer, and those that did run had a comfortable "old-hat" tone. *Independent Woman*, for example, stressed the positives for the workers more than the war needs, implying that the experience was akin to a paid camp for office workers who needed summer sun:

> *You will hasten to offer your services, not only because you know how urgently they are needed, but because you will be remembering what a good time you had last time, and how, despite sunburn, lame muscles, poison ivy, and various other discomforts, you came out of the experience feeling like a million . . . You will be remembering the new friends you made, and the fun you had.*
>
> *. . . This year the attitude of farmers toward women as hired help . . . is far more hospitable . . . The farmers, for the most part, had to be persuaded to give women even a trial . . .*[6]

Farmers who were once skeptical became eager to echo the praise of women as farmworkers. Even conservative *House and Garden* joined their chorus, saying somewhat defensively: "Any woman who works on a farm, full-time or part-time, is a *bona fide* member of the Women's Land Army. And the Women's Land Army is every bit as official and every bit as important a part of the war effort as are the other official women's service units." Their case was summarized by a Vermont apple grower who said "any one of them is worth two . . . boys."[7]

By 1944, Agriculture officials planned to place 800,000 adult women farmworkers via their 6,150 field offices.[8] In addition, the high school-oriented Victory Farm Volunteers intended to have 1,200,000 workers in 1944—half of them girls.[9] Added together, this meant over a million female farmworkers, a number four times as large as ever joined the women's military units. Women as a Land Army was no myth!

They returned summer after summer to do back-breaking work in torturous heat. They calloused their hands, breathed pesticides, and did work that had been beneath most Americans even in Depression days. They came from every walk of life. In "one northeastern state alone," said Director Florence Hall,

> *WLA workers . . . were listed as: "accountants, actresses, artists, bank clerks and tellers, beauticians, . . . buyers, . . . dietitians, designers, editors, . . . musicians, masseuses, models . . . , stenographers . . . , singers, social workers . . . and women from many other vocations."*[10]

They did not come for big money. They could expect to get between $14 and $18 a week, appreciably less than industrial women earned, for agricultural pay still reflected the marginal living of traditional migrants. And, like migrants, these women also paid most of their wages back to the farmer or the farmers' organizations.

The average worker paid $10 a week for her lodging and meals, either to the farm family with whom she lived, or (more likely) to the camp where she stayed. Even *Independent Woman*, which ran at least one article every wartime spring encouraging women to use their vacations to work on farms, did not expect that this work would be profitable; most workers in the past, they wrote in 1944, were "able to earn enough to pay for their board . . . and have something left over for pin money."[11]

Before the Crop Corps was organized, in the first confusion of the summer of 1942, farmers—not realizing that 6,000,000 workers had disappeared from agriculture since 1940[12]—found themselves in emergency situations with crops that needed attention at once. Farm communities sent out appeals on the radio and in the newspapers for local, immediate help. Chambers of Commerce and other organizations (many of them women's volunteer groups) set up telephone networks to find willing hands. Most often, those who were available and willing were women.

In the small city of Kokomo, Indiana, 500 men, women, and children saved the important [tomato] crop . . . Fifteen town women and two men . . . working double shifts saved an apple crop near Hastings, Minnesota . . . Nine members of the Bethel Ladies Aid Society . . . husked 400 bushels of corn on a farm near Hooper, Nebraska. The Portland Oregon League of Women Voters served the community and cashed in on the crop emergency by enlisting members to pick beans and turn their earnings over to the league . . . A group of Sumas, Washington, women went out to save the [filbert] nuts. They stuck at the hard back-breaking job for over a month. Their boss said he'd never had a better crew.[13]

Women who worked all day at another job worked again in the long-lit evenings and on weekends. The same was true the next summer, as a government report verified that "Sunday, part-time, and vacation workers played a significant role." These "farmerettes" did everything from cotton chopping and asparagus cutting to hay pitching and peanut shaking. "Vegetable harvesting," the report continued, "is a major farm problem because it demands so much hand labor. Women, however, are deft at this kind of work."[14]

Regardless of whether women were deft, the work was still hard. It left them sunburned and itching; their hands were a mass of scratches, knees were scraped

223

raw and backs were bent to the point of breaking. The only women willing to do this labor were migrants unable to work their way out of agriculture into wartime industry due to language and cultural barriers, and those who worked for love, not money. They were the women of the Crop Corps and the female members of farming families.

"Farmwife" is indeed an apt term, for these women historically were married to the farm, with all the devotion and sacrifice implied. War only magnified the work to be done and the difficulties of doing it. "For centuries," wrote a black editor, "the rich soil of America's southland has been cultivated . . . by Negro men and women . . . With the basic manpower of the Nation's farmlands already in war plants or the armed services, women have found themselves hard against the task of carrying on."[15]

Even in more prosperous Iowa, a young mother of four wrote of how war multiplied problems in her life:

> It means being an obstetrician in the stock barns and a dietitian in the feed lots. It means working later and earlier in the fields . . .
> . . . We treat our machinery like priceless jewels . . . Today finding a large tractor for sale is like discovering Captain Kidd's treasure . . . When breakdowns occur, getting the repair parts and getting started again . . . may mean saving the crop.
> . . . I hope to gather eggs three times a day instead of two. If I save two eggs a day from chilling and breaking, in a year's time that would mean approximately 61 dozen more eggs to smash at Hitler.[16]

That women could be seen working in the fields showed the direness of the emergency. While their peasant grandmothers commonly did outdoor work in Europe, as immigrants they realized this practice was seen by Americans as a sign of poverty and Old World ways and, therefore, the farmwives kept increasingly to their homes. By the outbreak of World War II, it was rare to see farmwives working in fields, but once again, labor shortages changed things. "During the spring rush in the Corn Belt," reported *Saturday Evening Post*, "it wasn't uncommon for the men to drive tractors at night, with lights, while their wives kept the same equipment running during daylight hours."[17]

Even some girls took up farming, despite its repulsive and laborious aspects. *Life* featured, for example, a 17-year-old high school senior who undertook the entire care of her family's farm when her father and brother were displaced by the war. She milked over 30 cows by hand twice a day, cleaned their manure from the barn through the cold of winter and handled rambunctious pigs.[18] There were also, of course, women who were neither farmwives nor farmers' daughters, but were themselves the farmers. Many widows continued to farm after their husbands' deaths, including some in the South who had to manage their work with mules and without electricity. The war also saw women who ran farms and ranches alone after their husbands enlisted.

Such independence brought an assertiveness to farm women that was not often seen in women's groups, as shown by the platform developed early in the war by representatives of farm women; a document that these women produced contained fewer platitudes and more bold suggestions than that of any similar organization. They sensibly decided to work within current organizations and form no new war volunteer groups, and they pledged themselves to higher crop production and more home gardening and canning—but they didn't stop there. Not hesitant to jump into areas outside of those traditionally assigned to women, they offered a great deal of specific advice to government authorities at all levels.

Their platform called "upon draft officials to draft physicians for the armed services largely from cities . . . and not from rural communities which are already seriously underserviced." They recommended "that school schedules be adjusted to free children for farm work during seasonal periods," and urged the WPA "to terminate non-essential projects to release labor for farms." They not only recommended that farmworkers be draft exempt, but went further to say that "voluntary enlistment should stop." Recruitment of defense factory workers from farm areas should also cease, for "food production is as essential," they said, "as the production of munitions."[19]

Clearly, these were women who believed so strongly in their work that they demanded others do the same. Without any apology, they insisted that farming and food production be given the priority it was due and themselves a firm voice in their own fate. Though usually officially unpaid and often uncounted in employment statistics, these women were far from volunteers in the traditional sense. They were, and judged themselves to be, workers in the best sense of the word.

It was government policy to turn everyone into a minifarmer during the war. Through newspapers, magazines, radio, news reels and club speeches, people were given the message over and over again: Grow a victory garden. If patriotism hadn't motivated one to become a gardener, then the rationing of canned goods often did. From city rooftops, vacant lots and public parks to the vast prairies, almost everyone with access to a bit of land put in a garden.

In the farming Midwest, "the ten or twelve families" in a county who did not have a garden now planted one.[20] These gardens were larger than in the past, and some were prescient enough to grow more "keeper" crops that needed no canning—potatoes, carrots, onions, turnips and winter squash. Women even organized telephone networks to keep each other advised of garden surpluses and deficits and to share scarce tools. Rural gardens averaged a half acre; in small towns, the average size was 3,800 square feet; in cities, they were about 500 square feet. By region, gardeners were far more likely to live in the Midwest and the South. A March 1943 Gallup poll showed that 21,000,000 families planned to grow victory gardens—3,000,000 more than the government's goal. By May, an impressive 7,000,000 acres were under cultivation, an area about 10 times the size of Rhode Island.[21]

Moreover, most gardens were properly tended once planted, for the actual produce raised was enough to garner the praise of gardening experts. The chairman of the Victory Garden Committee of the U.S. Agriculture Department congratulated America:

You did well last year—superlatively well. Green as you were (many of you), often forced to work with soil so raw and poor that it looked hopeless to experienced gardeners, despite cold Spring weather, floods, droughts, bugs, and diseases you produced nearly 8 million tons of vegetables. That was more than the total commercial production for fresh sale for civilian and non-civilian use.[22]

In fact, the amateurs grew only about 4,000,000 tons less than those whose business it was. The next year, it was presumed that they would do even better, for they would learn from initial mistakes. *House and Garden* listed the most common errors of the zealous but inexperienced: They planted too much of one thing; they couldn't stand to throw away seedlings, so mature plants were too crowded; they, proud of large vegetables, let them grow until the flavor was gone; and, with an excess of hope, they sowed varieties wrong for the climate.

While men were likely to work in gardens, the preservation of the produce fell almost exclusively on women. Home canning required precise knowledge of technique, for a wrong move could result in glass and tomatoes exploding through one's kitchen, or in silent bacterial growth that could kill a family later on. The process was still fairly new in the forties, and home economists were kept busy teaching these skills. In the poorer parts of the country, especially in the South, communal canneries operated for families who lacked the necessary equipment or even electricity and running water.

Understanding that many women felt intimidated by the dangerous-looking gauges of the pressure cooker, *American Home* tried to minimize the task and to suggest alternative (but perhaps dubious) preservation methods:

You don't need to spend long summer and fall afternoons over a hot stove . . . Last month we gave you directions for the various methods of canning . . . This month we're continuing with instructions for drying and storing of fruits and vegetables (if you've never eaten dried string beans you've something in store for you).[23]

Besides being the target of publicity campaigns on gardening and food preservation, women were also continually urged to participate in salvage campaigns. The first step was to do a thorough housecleaning, giving away anything that could be spared. Even an old envelope, for example, would make a cartridge wad. Waste paper of all sorts could be "turned to war utility at 50 percent of the cost of paper milled from primary materials,"[24] and more important, it could be done faster.

"We are still lagging behind in our salvage contribution," *Independent Woman* admonished late in 1942. "Look about your home."

> *Examine the attic, basement, and closets. Old tools, Grandfather's clock, that iron statue . . . you're not using them and the government needs them. Do you know an old flat iron will yield enough steel for two helmets; . . . an old set of golf clubs will furnish enough metal for a .30 caliber machine gun; eighteen tin cans will make a portable flame thrower; fifteen feet of garden hose will make one life raft for the Navy; there is enough tin in seventy toothpaste tubes for the radiator of an army truck . . .*[25]

Once the overall housecleaning was done, daily salvage habits had to be developed. Ideally, every kitchen or back porch would have containers for tins, rags, bottles, paper and even bones, for "bones are precious . . . The Germans forgot what a bone looked like years ago, so vital are they for wartime industry . . . Bones make glue; glue makes glycerin; glycerin makes explosives . . . A single block of houses can supply several tons of bones a year."[26]

Unused pans were to be given up—their aluminum was precious. Tin cans were to be washed and flattened for collection. Tinfoil was equally important. Bottle caps, toothpaste tubes and chewing-gum wrappers were to be saved. Flashlight batteries were especially important, for they contained zinc, carbon, brass, copper and other ingredients.

Accumulated materials were given to any of numerous organizations (Scouts, Salvation Army and others) that were involved in salvage efforts. Women were likely to play major roles, too, in organizing these drives, lining up participants, donating precious gas on Saturday mornings to do the pickups, and being there again on Mondays for distribution.

Women also volunteered their time and skills at various workshops, such as those run by Bundles for Britain (and later, Bundles for America), where worn donations and scraps from textile mills were whipped into something usable. "The miracles performed by salvage sewers," enthused *Life*, "were exhibited last week at a national salvage fashion fair." They showed "17 pairs of children's drawers from one torn sheet, . . . bedroom slippers from men's felt hats; [and a] bathing suit from old tablecloth."[27]

Despite expressions of zeal, however, salvage may have been another area where talk exceeded action. While more than four of every five questioned by Gallup tossed sentiment to the winds and agreed that "metal statues, old guns . . . and other metal in parks and cemeteries . . . should be donated to the scrap metal drive," when questioned about personal possessions rather than public historical mementos, only a bare majority acknowledged that there was scrap metal around their homes which could be given.[28] *Saturday Evening Post* noted with chagrin:

> *Fat collections were disappointing last autumn until giving extra ration points for fat salvage was decided on. The first month it was tried, fat salvage in New Jersey, for a sample state, jumped 42 per cent. The nation's general need for fats, well publicized ever since Pearl Harbor, was no such stimulus as personal extra butter in the icebox.*[29]

Saving fats and planting a victory garden were fine gestures, but these things occupied only a portion of the time available for those who truly cared. It was not nearly enough to assuage the feeling of "I want to *do* something!" that pervaded millions even before the war broke out. "No woman of sense and sensibility," wrote *Harper's* in July 1941, "can be oblivious to the fact that humanity in many parts of the world is being tortured . . ."[30] The next 11 pages of text, however, served mostly to demonstrate that volunteerism was in a confused state with eager participants who had few real assignments. Literally dozens of organizations sprang up all over the country, getting in each other's way and doing little:

> *There is an epidemic of registering for possible war service. Such organizations as the National Women's Republican Club, the American Legion Auxiliary, and the American Association of University Women are collecting members cards, hopeful that as crises arise these cards may be consulted and the right women assigned . . . Some fifty cities so far have organized volunteer defense bureaus under the auspices of the welfare agencies and local defense council.*[31]

These organizations ranged alphabetically from the American Relief Society to the Women's Overseas Service League; an abbreviated list of what lay in between includes the Association of Army and Navy Wives, Citizens Committee for the Army and Navy, the Daughters of the Defenders of the Republic, Friends of Democracy, Junior American Nurses, National Security Women's Corps, Navy Mothers Club of America, Navy Wives Club of America, Women's Hospital Reserve Corps, and even Dogs for Defense.[32]* According to New York Mayor LaGuardia, who was doubling as civilian-defense director for the nation, "There are now in existence enough councils and committees and boards and agencies dealing with defense to cause confusion without the aid of an enemy."[33]

Obviously, there were endless amounts of wasted motion and duplicated effort. Once again, as with child care, the key words of these organizations

---

* Dogs for Defense was actually more sensible than it sounds, being a program for donation of guard dogs to the military.

seemed to be "development, planning and training," with little actually *done*. Part of the problem was a lack of guidance from the government (LaGuardia included) on what women could do, especially before war was declared.

> *On April 18th [1941], for instance, President Roosevelt called for five-hundred thousand volunteer roof-spotters prepared to detect approaching bombing planes, and suggested that many women could serve in this capacity; on the very same day Mrs. Roosevelt went out of her way to say . . . "Mass nutrition education is the most important defense work for women, far more important than learning how to drive an ambulance which may never be driven."*[34]

Newsweek, in August of 1941, echoed these complaints about governmental confusion and indifference to women's role:

> *In most of this patriotic activity, women have been on the outside looking in. A few have found outlets for their patriotism in Red Cross work and the entertainment of soldiers, but thousands of others have been unable to find constructive ways of aiding national defense. When women's organizations have asked what their members could do, they have usually been put off with vague talk about the necessity for women doing their everyday tasks more efficiently.*
>
> *Indicative of the national defense program's lack of interest . . . is the fact that in the whole defense setup there are only seven women with policymaking jobs.*
>
> *. . . The inevitable blowoff came last week when . . . the president of the powerful General Federation of Women's Clubs declared that women were being discriminated against "intolerably." . . . She complained about the lack of a women's division in the Office of Civilian Defense and . . . the exclusion of girls from . . . pilot-training programs.*[35]

One of the causes of the lack of official direction, of course, was that not even government officials could foresee exactly what efforts might be important in the future. After the panic of Pearl Harbor, millions of volunteer hours were spent by entirely sensible people on emergency preparedness programs that ultimately were unnecessary, but this could not be foreseen with any certainty. The possibility of sneak attack seemed very real; how seriously it was taken can be seen by the advice *Independent Woman* offered to its sophisticated audience of business women. As late as October of 1942, they asked, "Is Your Home Ready for War?"

> *Can you recognize the enemy—no matter what his disguise? He may be off our coast in a submarine; he may be in a long-distance bomber with charts of our target areas; he may be among us as a saboteur and rumor-monger . . .*
>
> *Is your home light proof? You know, light from a candle can be seen miles away from an airplane. Have you a safety room in your house with the proper items in it? Do you know how to fight fire bombs? Do you actually know what to do when you hear the air raid warning?*[36]

Other women went off on even more dubious organizational tangents. All over the country, paramilitary units of uniformed women drilled, marched and (in a questionable use of ammunition) shot at targets. Usually under the direction of retired male military officers, women formed the Green Guards of Washington; the Powder Puff Platoon of Joplin, Missouri; the Home Guard of Kalamazoo, Michigan; the Air Rifle Corps of Tulsa, Oklahoma; and the Prescott, Arizona, Rifle Corps. The 500 "girl cadets" of the New York Women's Defense Corps, pathetically eager to participate in these pre-WAAC days, "were hoping . . . to be voted an official status by the Legislature."[37]

There were other variants of preparedness. Before their weekly target practice, the National Security Women's Corps took an oath that included both an antifascist and an anticommunist clause (with the communists coming first), promising that they did not belong to any "organization which is not all American."[38] In an interesting blend of traditional domesticity and new militarism, the Women's Defense School of Boston developed a course in field cooking, "in which women are taught to cook 'the Army way.'"[39] A similar updating of traditional nursing duties brought 25,000 women volunteers into the Women's Ambulance and Defense Corps of America. With the daring slogan of "The Hell We Can't!," it had more than 50 chapters, mostly in California, training women to act as "air-raid wardens, guards for public buildings, and couriers for the armed forces."[40]

Since the chances of an armed woman actually meeting up with an invading enemy were remote, these paramilitary units generally invited scorn. A woman eager to "do something" was far more likely to find public approbation by offering her time to one of the on-going volunteer organizations. The most popular, both with officialdom and the 3,500,000 women who joined it, was the Red Cross. With its 10,000 paid employees, established reputation for disaster handling and quasigovernmental status, the Red Cross offered serious training and clearly defined assignments.

Among its divisions were the Home Service, which dealt with the problems of servicemen and their families; Production, which already had made 20,000,000 surgical dressings before Pearl Harbor;[41*] the Nurses Aides and Gray Ladies, who worked in overcrowded hospitals; First Aid with its

---

* The question of why surgical dressings were handmade rather than factory produced is an interesting one. Presumably because this was truly a vital role for women during the Civil War when the Red Cross had its beginnings, the tradition was continued in World Wars I and II. The military's Surgeon General doubtless was pleased to have these supplies donated, and so the practice persisted. In terms of both the value of women's labor and of sterility and quality control, probably it would have been better handled by medical manufacturers.

prestigious courses;* the Motor Corps, which ran errands and was available for disaster transport; and the new Blood Bank volunteers, who were just beginning their important war work.

Though the Red Cross called itself "Big Sister to the Army," its canteens were rivaled by those of the newer United Services Organizations, more commonly known as the USO. Food service, however, was perhaps the only area where there may have been serious duplication of effort, for the Red Cross's emphasis was on health, while the USO's was on recreation. Although the USO became known for its recruitment of star entertainment for the troops, most volunteers spent their time on the more routine activities of organizing local events and making the lonely feel at home.

There was in fact real prejudice against the outsiders who appeared in wartime boom towns and especially against the men at the hundreds of new military posts around the country:

> *Minister[s] ... warn the parents ... of the danger to the morals of their daughters by the presence of the troops, and in so many words warned them to keep their girls at home.*
>
> *If it occurred to any of those good townspeople not only that these very soldiers were civilians in uniform but that their own sons were probably having the same experience in other towns, none of them dared to say so; neither did they do anything about it.*[42]

The USO, with a donated budget of $32 million in 1942, not only built clubhouses and hired social directors, but also made an exceptional effort to include black soldiers. A few units were integrated (some because whites were drawn there by famous black entertainers), and there were almost three hundred clubs for blacks. In addition, USO and Travelers Aid stationed workers in the segregated quarters of bus and train stations to help blacks with their needs. Recruiting black women as volunteers was one of the few problems that professionals working in this area did not encounter; black women, like their men, had little recreational opportunity and were glad to participate.

Like the Red Cross, the USO had close connections with the military and a quasi-governmental status. In addition, one could volunteer directly for governmental bodies; the thousands of women who worked at rationing offices are but one example. The Office of Civilian Defense, largely run by volunteers, was an umbrella agency that through its myriad local councils dealt not only in emergency preparedness, but also operated the Civil Air Patrol, salvage projects, publicity campaigns for victory gardens and blood donations, and did whatever else needed doing under the broad term of "civilian defense." Though criticized

---

* See Chapter 2.

above for its failure to form a women's division, the OCD quickly organized itself by job function and included both women and blacks in its ranks.

One black publication, referring to the OCD as the "Civilian Army of the Nation," said, "integrated in this vast net-work of Civilian Defense, we find the Afro-American . . . they are serving as air-raid wardens, . . . ambulance workers, nurses aides . . . Black O.C.D. workers are pushing conservation programs, salvage drives, rationing cooperation, . . . war bond sales . . . and similar activities."[43]

The OCD seemed a natural for women; indeed a few days after Pearl Harbor, Eleanor Roosevelt formally wrote to the Business and Professional Women's Clubs, asking them to "man" these offices in the evenings.[44] "The first thing that impressed me," a male visitor wrote about one office, "was that the majority of workers there were women. The next was the extraordinary efficiency with which the volunteers went about their duties."[45] Without uniforms, without parading, they quietly went about their tasks—answering the phone, typing and teaching. They provided the leadership that made the difference in whether a town saved its toothpaste tubes and rendered its fats unto the government.

Besides the OCD, other governmental agencies also looked for volunteers. The Office of Price Administration, for example, used 50,000 women in five states to do a "three-day educational canvass" in July 1942. They were to "call on 450,000 retailers to acquaint them with the provisions of the general maximum price regulations." The project was so successful that a Senator suggested "the formation of a permanent volunteer force of women to assist in the enforcement of price control."[46] Such authority over business in the hands of volunteers was bound to be both controversial and intimidating to the woman in her role as a future customer, but nonetheless participation was urged:

> Even women with full . . . responsibilities can usually manage the war job of price-panel assistant—two or three volunteer hours a week checking price-ceiling compliance among local food stores. Not snooping—the girls wear badges and introduce themselves aboveboard.
>
> OPA . . . hopes for at least 100,000. The top figure so far is 30,000, of whom 7,000 are in the notably enterprising Atlanta area alone. The South . . . does best . . . New Orleans women . . . knocked the local cost-of-living index down 5 per cent practically overnight.[47]

Whether it was their own lack of supportiveness or women's reluctance to take on this threateningly new role, the OPA never came close to their stated volunteer goal for price enforcers. Similarly, turnover among other volunteers in government offices ran high. Much work was admittedly dull; there was "no glamour, no uniform . . . just a job that needs doing." Officials acknowledged that "many women, especially schoolteachers, have done invaluable work for local ration boards," but "clumsy handling"[48] and a lack of appreciation caused many volunteers to take their skills elsewhere.

232

One of the most popular—and controversial—volunteer options was the American Women's Voluntary Services. Founded in January 1940 by a wealthy woman with close ties to Britain and modeled after that country's Women's Voluntary Services, AWVS was a subject of debate from its start. Its intention was to train women to drive ambulances and render emergency aid when the bombing of U.S. cities began. What early members saw as prudent preparation, however, was to many isolationist Americans' empty-headed excitement, and "the first women to appear on the street in the blue-gray uniform of the A.W.V.S. were usually hailed either as warmongers or as British stooges."[49]

Nonetheless, AWVS women (many of them socialites with personal ties to the founder) went about their required 50 hours of training and were rewarded with some status by the authorities. Two days after Pearl Harbor, when New York was threatened by what turned out to be a false air-raid alarm, the police ordered the AWVS to sent out "its Civilian Protection unit to warn civilians off the street," but most of the volunteers found that they "were jeered at as silly busybodies."[50]

Though the major news media continued to be scornful,[51] the AWVS kept growing. Showing admirable organizational skill, in its first six months of existence AWVS formed 73 branches in 20 states. A year later, there were 350,000 members in 350 units, including Alaska and the Canal Zone. Another 20,000 nonmembers had taken their courses in air-raid work, fire fighting, motor mechanics, map reading, canteen feeding and signal coding.

The problem was that then these well-trained AWVS volunteers had little to do except wait for the war to start—and even after American involvement, to wait for an American bombing blitz comparable to Britain's. When this never happened, it became easy to mock these women's excessive zeal rather than to admire their prescience had things turned out differently.

Probably one of the fundamental causes of public derision of AWVS was the moneyed nature of its founders, for doubtless many not only were jealous of these privileged women but also felt threatened by their nontraditional activism. Aware of this hostility, AWVS went well beyond the bounds of most organizations at the time to make its membership inclusive. They organized several units in Harlem, some of which were Spanish-speaking, as well as a Chinese unit and one of women members of the Taos tribe. Defying conventions in the Deep South, its New Orleans chapter included blacks. Membership required only service time; there were no dues.

Lacking the blitz for which they were prepared, volunteers set out to find other worthwhile things to do. Already by 1942, AWVS units in New York had sold more than $5 million worth of War Bonds. California units delivered midnight "chuck wagons" to Coast Guard stations and other isolated servicemen; in San Francisco, they taught Braille to seamen blinded in Pacific warfare; they organized emergency agriculture work in California and Colorado and paid for workers' camps. A Montana unit raised funds by "rigging up a shooting gallery and selling pot shots at Hitler."[52] In suburban New York, they assisted in the health-care crisis, first taking the Red Cross's Advanced First Aid courses and serving a probationary period under a physician, and then staffed ambulances around the clock—"doing a man's job . . . strictly on her own."[53] AWVS earned the respect of the unbiased investigator:

> *I have seen millionaires' wives and working girls chatting and working together, colored folk, women of enemy alien descent, women in shabby clothes; and in working hours there is . . . [no] distinction unless it is that the wealthy women are at pains to make the other people comfortable . . . The word contemptible is too dignified to apply to people who commit this verbal sabotage at the expense of others who are shouldering the task of doing something for nothing . . .*[54]

In truly American individualistic style, all of these organizations were replicated by other groups going off in their own slightly different direction. In addition to the Ambulance Attendants of the AWVS, for example, there was the Women's Ambulance and Defense Corps of America; Relief Wings, Inc., which specialized in "air ambulances and disaster relief by air"[55]; and the Aerial Nurse Corps of America, which was made up of "air-minded registered nurses [who] stand by ready with medical aid to scenes of disaster anywhere in the United States."[56] Besides the Red Cross's various hospital programs, there was also American Women's Hospitals Reserve Corps, an organization primarily for business women too busy to fulfill Red Cross requirements, but who had time for military drill.

Still other organizations offered job-related volunteerism for full-time workers, such as the WIRES, made up of Women in Radio and Electric Service. The WAMS, or Women Aircraft Mechanics, was the corporate invention of Transcontinental, Western and other airlines. The WOWS, or Women Ordnance Workers, had a membership of 33,000 in May 1943 in "dozens" of war plants. "Three months of perfect attendance on the job and at chapter meetings earn any WOW the rank of private first class, with the privilege of wearing appropriate insignia and her WOW uniform . . ."[57]

The need for identification with a group seemed strong enough that *Ladies Home Journal* even "organized" its readers, calling them WINS, or Women in National Service. They were "the housewives of America, the largest army in the nation fighting on the home front."[58]

> *You are in charge at home for the duration: twenty million of you, with no uniforms or titles; on twenty-four hour duty, with no days off, and no furloughs till it's over. There won't be any citations—and you won't expect one. Medals aren't awarded for taking care of the two and a half million babies born last year, for washing*

behind the ears of ten million children under five and getting another twenty-five
million off to school every morning . . .[59]

Thirty-two governors' wives undertook state chairmanships of WINS, including blueblooded Republican Mrs. Leverett Saltonstall of Massachusetts,
who enthused: "I like the name 'WINS' . . . We are the mothers, grandmothers,
wives, aunts, and sisters who cannot take full-time war jobs."[60] She asked
women to volunteer in replacing canceled WPA school-lunch programs and to
organize war-related youth activities. Citing the "boys and girls of Norwell High
School [who] turned out for wood-chopping bees" to provide boxes for munitions shipments, she offered other project suggestions: Boys "can help on
playgrounds, serve as lifeguards, . . . repair household equipment and serve as
airplane spotters. Girls can take care of little children, pick fruit and can it for
welfare agencies, [and] wash dishes . . . in hospitals."[61]

Few women, however, could be persuaded to give up their leisure time for
dishwashing and child care. Though there were constant calls for the latter,*
women did not often choose to do as a volunteer the same work that they did
full time. Similarly, volunteer work in government offices, consisting as it did
of routine typing and filing that was the full-time employment of many women,
also saw great turnover rates. The secret of the AWVS's success should not have
been a surprise to any who thought creatively about volunteerism: Workers
wanted jobs that offered something new to learn, something different to do and
clear identification with a self-created group, ideally demonstrated by a uniform.

Eleanor Roosevelt, in a prewar speech, summarized well why a uniform was
important to success in volunteerism: "It saves time, explanation and the trouble
of identification . . . It is a passport and a protection."[62] A uniform made one
official; it rendered authority. If the OPA, for example, had been serious about
wanting women volunteers to work as price enforcers, they would have done
well to have taken the First Lady's advice and uniformed their volunteers.
Without that, a worker might well feel alone, without identification and nakedly
exposed to public hostility or scorn.

Being part of a group gave strength, and women, like men, were eager to
demonstrate their power with parades. In April 1942 (as soon after Pearl Harbor
as weather would allow a parade), 10,000 volunteers from various uniformed
organizations marched down New York's Fifth Avenue to show their support
for and role in the war. They were, in *Life*'s words, "10,000 determined women
patriots who give their time and toil without pay and ask as recompense only
the glory of uniform insignia."[63] The marchers wore so great a multiplicity of
uniforms that no reviewer could identify them all.

---

* See Chapter 11.

But instead of being seen as illustrative of the many varied activities of women, to some this multiplicity pointed out the duplication and excessiveness and thereby invited mockery. *Time*, for example, chortled about the "eight official uniforms" of the AWVS, including one "ski-troop suit for workers in the far North."[64] The *New Yorker* added, "Englishwomen on duty in New York are sometimes shocked by American women's frivolousness about wearing a uniform."[65]

Indeed, uniforms were *the* fashion statement of the early forties, so much so that fashion shows made up exclusively of uniforms were held. As with many new things, a high price tag seemed only to increase the fashion appeal. The uniforms of most organizations cost between $20 and $30—an average week's wages for most women, or the equivalent of several hundred dollars today. Clearly the costs involved should not have required a price this high. But when Eleanor Roosevelt (who strongly advocated the practical functions of uniforms) suggested at a fashion fair that since all volunteers ought to buy one, uniforms should cost no more than $3, the designers present "all but lost the curl in their careful coiffures."[66]

The uniform was only one expense, however, for volunteerism cost money as well as time. Women not only absorbed the price of transportation and child care in order to free their volunteer time, they also paid dues and donated everything from the gasoline used in a Red Cross motor pool to the cookies baked for the USO. Yet often their generosity was still far too little to tackle the genuine problems that should have been addressed. The war years saw tremendous needs in child care, housing and health care, for example, but such difficult economic problems were far too complex to be solved by voluntary action alone.

The Surgeon General, for instance, called it "a national disgrace" that as many as "40 per cent of men otherwise available for military service are being deferred by reason of physical defects," with many of those defects due to malnutrition and other poverty-based causes.[67] While women could and did run nutrition-education programs and even school-lunch operations, they could not be expected to do anything about the fact that during the decade previous to the war, much of the nation was ill-fed.

Volunteerism, by its very nature, could easily be seen as a bandaid on a wound that needed surgery, with the result that women who were doing all that they could do were viewed by critics as having only a part-time commitment to a full-time problem. Worse, often the effort that they made was just enough to allow the public to assuage its conscience with the belief that something was being done, and thus, ironically, to make the problem worse.

The volunteers who assisted overburdened wartime nurses, for instance, were viewed by thoughtful nursing professionals with understandable ambivalence.

"While it is true," wrote one, "that the use of these voluntary workers has relieved the immediate situation somewhat, it must be recognized that this method offers no real or permanent solution. In fact, if it were not for the urgency of the present situation, nurses might justly resent this importation of unpaid workers."[68] Women's donation of their time indisputably lowered the value of the labor of paid employees. It became easy for the public to believe, at least unconsciously, that labor given away could not be worth much.

Then, too, because organizations varied so widely, critics could easily overlook the serious work being done by one volunteer group while ridiculing the ambitions of another. When the war was only weeks old, for instance, *Time* enjoyed a laugh at "Women's Christian Temperature Union's Soldiers and Sailors Department . . . [which] rushed forward with a cookie-jar crusade," giving away 35,000 cookies at the gates of Fort Dix. "The Liberty Belles of San Antonio, Texas . . . [who] danced for their country at soldiers' balls"[69] provided another source of amusement.

Indeed, the emulators of USO-type entertainment probably were the organizations most worthy of criticism. Though assurances of chaperones and supervision were routine, some of the dances and parties arranged for servicemen bear real resemblance to the procurement of girls for less honorable activity. A staged social event between strangers was inherently a structure that encouraged men to pick women off the rack for a temporary relationship. The sexual objectification of women, however, was not the only problem, for many lonely boys fell for the alluring girls who frequented these dances, doubtless exaggerating their memories when shipped overseas. The girls meanwhile would have gone on to dozens of other boys, whom the girls also were forced to view in an objectlike way in order to protect themselves from the knowledge of the boys' possible deaths. It was a situation that asked for broken hearts, that promoted a certain callousness and an ephemeral attitude dangerously similar to prostitution.

Nevertheless, these entertainments found general public favor and happy portrayals by Hollywood, with the result that this was one of the few areas where there were always enough volunteers. "New York agencies seeking girls to dance with servicemen," said one reporter, "have waiting lists of more than 2,000 names."[70] To those who truly cared about the defeat of fascism, it seemed a shameful situation. A seasick WAAC on her way to North Africa wrote of her response to this sort of vapid volunteer on the silver screen:

The heroine was having one of the most luxurious hot baths in film history . . . I hadn't had anything but cold salt water to wash in since leaving port, and I felt especially dirty, drab, and dejected. But I stood it until the Hollywood glamour girl . . . said, "Tell Marsden I won't want the car, after all. I'm too tired to go to the canteen today."
That did it!

The operator avoided a mutiny at sea by putting on a Mickey Mouse film.[71]

By 1944, the media joined in complaining about women's apathy and lack of commitment to the war.* Critics charged, moreover, that much of what was done had the wrong motivation and the wrong attitude. A popular wartime book admonished:

> *All who want to play Lady Bountiful please stay out ... Handing out rosy-red apples and gingersnap cookies when the boys want beer and cigarettes is just so much social bazaar sweet stuff.*
>
> *... Too many reports have come through of those who have gone into the various motor-corps units in order to keep their cars in gas and their tires in rubber.*
>
> *... If you volunteer you should go in under the same kind of discipline and with the same point of view as the women who go into the WAACs.*[72]

While in 1942 they had been ridiculed for excessive zeal, two years later women were accused of doing nothing. Even in organizations with large memberships, careful observers saw relatively little actual work being done. "Of volunteers registered for various services in the American Women's Volunteer Services in the District of Columbia," for example, "hardly more than a quarter were active in a sample three months."[73] Clearly, many women talked of their bandage-rolling much more than they did it.

The lack of proper channeling of skills and serious direction from the government should have been seen as the main cause for this apparent indifference, but what was emphasized instead was the unequal sharing of volunteer obligations among women. "With great consistency," wrote one investigator, "the most ardent and longest lasting civilian volunteers are women who have already put in eight hours that day ... 'Busy women,' said a veteran volunteer handler with emphasis, 'can always work in one more thing.'"[74]

Advertising encouraged the negative by exaggerating the positive, allowing many a lackadaisical volunteer to believe that she was as committed to the war as a front-line soldier. "She's doing grim, exhausting work these days," ran the newspaper copy of one ad, "whether it's hurrying to the hospital every morning or learning all over again how to cook ... And she needs to be pampered this Christmas. Mink, of course, is the ... gift ... priced from $3500."[75]

While most women would see this ad as laughable, they also might well have an underlying nagging feeling that this was indeed the sort of symbol of achievement for which they were supposed to strive. Everything about her upbringing—the basic assumptions of her parents and teachers—taught her that she was not destined to be part of a khaki group of lock-step marchers, but rather that she was to be queen of her own dollhouse. "After all," as one writer cogently

---

* See Chapter 12 for a discussion of charges of apathy.

said, "women weren't brought up to connect what they do themselves with what happens generally."[76]

Often it took the very specific to awaken such a woman to the general point, to make her see the war personally and to allow her to see how her involvement could make a difference. Such was the experience of a woman with a Naval husband in the Pacific "who came in to donate blood. She came back again and again—five times in all. As she arrived home from the fifth time, there was news of her husband. Very seriously wounded; life saved by five successive transfusions of Red Cross blood."[77]

Then perhaps she would see that obtaining the necessary millions of pints of blood called for more than just a pass at volunteerism, and that these organizations—with huge budgets and complex responsibilities—needed workers who were serious about more than the chance to wear a uniform and march in a parade.

But even if both their volunteers and their media critics trivialized their efforts, the fact is that the Red Cross and other similar organizations did manage to accomplish tremendous things—with most of the work performed by donated labor. Very often it was simply all that a woman, given the limits of her life, could do. She perhaps understood that her volunteerism was vicarious, but it was as close as many women could get to the real thing. "A middle-aged Western farm woman volunteering her services to the A.W.V.S.," probably spoke for many when she said, "I have that honest yearning of an American. I wish I'd of been born a man. I'd of been out in front long ago."[78]

SOURCE NOTES

1. "War Time Harvest," *Independent Woman* (September 1942): p. 270; see also "Our Land Army Is Different," *Saturday Evening Post* (July 25, 1942): p. 25.
2. Glover, "Women as Manpower," p. 75.
3. "War Time Harvest," p. 271. See also "Women in the War Plan Land Army," *Pulse* (June 1943), p. 18.
4. Lucy Greenbaum, "At the Front With Our Land Army," *New York Times Magazine* (July 4, 1943): p. 12.
5. "They Are Getting In the Crops," *Independent Woman* (July 1943): p. 195; see also *Ladies Home Journal* (June 1944) for a letter to the editor from a woman who was a full-time, year-round worker on a dairy farm.
6. "To the Rescue of the Crops" *Independent Woman* (May 1944): p. 130.
7. "To the Land-Ladies," *House and Garden* (April 1944): p. 66.
8. "Women's Land Army," *Nation's Business* (May 1944): p. 48.

9. "Need for Women in Agriculture," *Monthly Labor Review* (June 1944): p. 1248.

10. Florence Hall, "The Nation's Crops Need You," *Independent Woman* (July 1945): p. 187; see also "Woman With a Hoe," *Christian Science Monitor* (June 9, 1945): p. 5.

11. "To the Rescue of the Crops," p. 130.

12. "Our Land Army Is Different," *Saturday Evening Post* (July 25, 1942): p. 25.

13. "They Give the Farmer a Hand," *Woman's Home Companion* (April 1943), p. 22. See also "They Are Getting In the Crops," *Independent Woman* (July 1943): p. 195.

14. "Need for Women in Agriculture," p. 1248.

15. "They Also Serve . . .," *Brown American* (Summer 1943): p. 12.

16. Baur, "Farm Homemaker Faces War," p. 518.

17. "Our Land Army Is Different," p. 25.

18. "One-Girl Farm," *Life* (November 23, 1942): p. 56.

19. "Without Fuss or Feathers," *Time* (January 12, 1942): p. 16.

20. Baur, "Farm Homemaker Faces War," p. 520.

21. Gallup, *The Gallup Poll*, pp. 378–9 and 389. That this was real growth can be seen in that garden plans dropped by 2.5 million as soon as the war was over, according to a March 1946 poll (p. 570).

22. H.W. Hochbaum, "Still Keep 'Em Growing," *House and Garden* (January 1944): p. 13.

23. "All for Victory," *American Home* (August 1942): p. 14.

24. Ayling, *Calling All Women*, p. 182.

25. "Is Your Home Ready for War?" *Independent Woman* (October 1942): p. 312.

26. Ayling, *Calling All Women*, p. 183.

27. "Fashion Fair" *Life* (June 29, 1942): p. 94. See also Josephine Robertson: "How Stay-at-Home Mothers Can Help," *Parents* (June 1943): p. 23.

28. Gallup, *The Gallup Poll*, p. 350 and 353. Interviews were in June and October of 1942; percentages were 82% and 53%.

29. Furnas, "Are Women Doing Their Share?," p. 42.

30. Dorothy Dunbar Bromley, "Women on the Home Front," *Harper's* (July 1941): p. 188.

31. Ibid., pp. 189 and 196.

32. For a complete description of all of these organizations, see Mary Steele Ross, *American Women in Uniform* (Garden City, NY: Garden City Publishing Co., 1943). (Ross, a former Washington WPA official, became director of the American Women's Voluntary Services early in 1941.) A similar book is Margaret Culkin Banning, *Women for Defense* (New York: Duell, Sloan and Pearce, 1942).

33. Bromley, "Women on the Home Front," p. 199.

34. Ibid., p. 189. For her views on volunteerism when the war was well underway, see also Eleanor Roosevelt, "American Women in the War," *Reader's Digest* (January 1944): p. 42.
35. "Women Demand Greater Role in National Defense Program," *Newsweek* (August 11, 1941): p. 33.
36. "Is Your Home Ready For War?," p. 312.
37. Bromley, "Women on the Home Front," pp. 188 and 190. See also "Dallas's Career Girls," *Newsweek* (July 13, 1942): p. 45.
38. Ayling, *Calling All Women*, p. 107.
39. Ibid., p. 188.
40. "Glory Gals," *American Magazine* (March 1942): p. 83.
41. Ruth Carson, "I Want to Do Something," *Collier's* (September 20, 1941): p. 22.
42. Ayling, *Calling All Women*, p. 111.
43. "African-Americans in the OCD," *The African* (June 1943): p. 10; see also "Here's a New Thing Altogether," *Survey Graphic* (August 1944): p. 358, on USO services to blacks.
44. Minnie L. Maffet, "Mobilize for Victory!," *Independent Woman* (January 1942): p. 1.
45. Ayling, *Calling All Women*, p. 33.
46. "Women in the War Effort," *Current History* (September 1942): p. 29.
47. Furnas, "Are Women Doing Their Share?," p. 12.
48. Ibid.
49. "Ladies in Uniform," *New Yorker* (July 4, 1942): p. 21.
50. Ibid.
51. See especially "The Ladies!" *Time* (January 26, 1942): p. 61, and "Revolt in the AWVS," *Newsweek* (March 16, 1942): p. 46.
52. "Ladies in Uniform," p. 25.
53. Shirley Alexander, "Riding to Trouble," Collier's (October 24, 1942): p. 32.
54. Ayling, *Calling All Women*, pp. 96–97.
55. Bromley, p. 194.
56. "Angels," *American Magazine* (November 1941): p. 93.
57. "WOW Wows 'Em," *Business Week* (May 1, 1943): p. 91. See also I.D. Hays, "The WAMS," *Flying* (June 1943): p. 38. For WIRES, see *American Women in Uniform*.
58. "Let's Face Facts," p. 24.
59. "You're the WINS: Women in National Service," *Ladies Home Journal* (March 1943): p. 24.
60. "Winning on the Home Front," *Ladies Home Journal* (June 1942): p. 31.
61. Ibid.
62. "'No Sam Brown Belts,' Says Mrs. Roosevelt," *New York Times Magazine* (July 27, 1941): p. 6.

63. "Women in Uniform March for a Cause," *Life* (April 27, 1942): p. 39.

64. "The Ladies!," *Time* (January 26, 1942): p. 61.

65. "Ladies in Uniform," p. 26.

66. "No Sam Brown Belts," p. 6.

67. Bromley, "Women on the Home Front," p. 195.

68. "Nursing—A Critical Analysis," *American Journal of Nursing* (January 1943): p. 32.

69. "Ladies!," p. 61.

70. Furnas, "Are Women Doing Their Share?," p. 42.

71. Phillips, *All-Out Arlene*, p. 176.

72. Gorham, *So Your Husband's Gone to War!*, p. 40.

73. Furnas, "Are Women Doing Their Share?," p. 42.

74. Ibid.

75. Ibid. See also "Portrait of a Woman," *House Beautiful* (May 1944): p. 106.

76. Ibid.

77. Ibid.

78. "Ladies in Uniform," p. 29.

15

WARTIME WEDDING

The area of volunteer work that was most eagerly sought was that which gave women direct contact with servicemen. This was the most "real" war work, the most meaningful for those fortunate enough to be in geographical and personal circumstances allowing this choice.

Occasionally, even paid jobs were available. The military employed "hostesses" at some posts even in peacetime, who worked closely with the Chaplain Corps to deal with the personal problems of soldiers. One who served as a surrogate mother to recruits at the Great Lakes Training Station had gotten the job in 1940 when she became a widow. Now, "Mrs. Bailey resists bitterly the attempts to have a uniform designed for her and the assistant hostesses. She thinks they should wear simple and pretty dresses, that men in service are fed up with uniforms."[1]

Their wives and mothers, however, may well have appreciated a uniform which allowed them to distinguish these official women from others like themselves, for the Army hostess did work with wives and mothers, as well as with the men. On a typical day, for instance, Mrs. Bailey explained to one worried wife that her husband "in detention" was not being punished, but was only subject to a health quarantine; she used her "maternal understanding" with a Montana woman "who had driven all alone, day and night . . . on her last tires, to say good-by to her only son,"[2] who, it turned out, had gone to sea 12 hours earlier.

"The senior hostess," wrote an observer, "is an out-and-out twenty-four-hour-a-day slave to a duty which combines diplomacy and discipline, doctor, lawyer, sister, sweetheart, and mother, all in one."[3] After dealing with sometimes complex personal problems in her office all day, she supervised parties and dances in the evening, having recruited the dance partners and chaperones and purchased the food supply. She taught soldiers to do minor sewing tasks on their uniforms and organized the tours of visiting officers. Civilian employees of the Army, hostesses were "not entitled to any . . . special privileges."[4]

More common than these Army employees were those workers—paid and unpaid—in volunteer organizations. While their first obligation was to service the soldier, it was soon apparent to careful observers that if a soldier's loved ones were in need, there was also a negative effect on his morale. For instance, although the director of a Neosho, Missouri USO club was glad to share his opinion that "Army wives frankly were a bother," YWCA workers "strongly defended, brooded over and mothered" the young women who followed husbands there. "All day long," wrote one of these Army brides, "girls climbed the steep hill to Neosha's magnificent U.S.O. club."[5] The women gathered to exchange information, especially about housing and food possibilities; to sing around the piano; play bridge and Ping-Pong; read magazines and books in the library; listen to records; use the sewing machine and ironing board.

We didn't jam the rooms as soldiers did at night, but we used every facility constantly. By the time my daily shift at the reception desk started at five o'clock, the little meter that recorded the number of people entering the building usually read about 200, few of whom by that time of day had been soldiers.[6]

As the war intensified, so did the needs of servicemen's families, and volunteer organizations expanded to do far more. In one small city that was relatively unaffected by the war (Worcester, Massachusetts), the Red Cross Home Service Department handled 1,500 cases per month of families seeking assistance. "The absence of the family breadwinner," wrote a social worker, "has meant real hardships to many families. Households have had to be combined . . . even aged parents have taken jobs again." A typical case was that of a woman whose "dependence on her husband caused her to exert all her energies to get him out of the service rather than to make her own way."[7] Women who had gone from fathers' care to husbands' wrote worried letters, filled with confused details of family finance.

Some soldiers receiving such letters have left their posts without leave. Without doubt many women who write such letters are having a difficult time. But the greatest problem is that many of them are emotionally immature and in the past have leaned heavily on their husbands.

. . . Army life . . . offers a present means of escape for many husbands. This is a very threatening factor to women who are already insecure in their relationships.

The emotional intensity which is centered on the financial problem can be understood only if seen as part of an emotional protest against separation, the bewilderment and fear of being left to manage alone.[8]

Even more serious problems arose, as some women received Dear Jane letters or the news that he had made another woman pregnant; others brought in their pregnant unwed daughters, intent on hunting down the soldier responsible.*

---

* In some places, "requests for services for unmarried mothers" more than doubled in the first two years of the war. Wartime uncertainty also brought a drop in the number of people willing to adopt. See Eleanor S. Boll, "The Child," *Annals of the American Academy of Political and Social Science*, Vol. 229 (1943): p. 77.

"The number of bigamous marriages," reported this worker, "has been surprising. These usually come to light when the Red Cross has occasion to assist the second wife in applying for her allowances."[9]

Most of the time, however, a Red Cross or USO worker was involved in more light-hearted activity, much of it aimed at accommodating a major desire in young men—the opportunity to meet young women. Part of what a man was looking for (whether or not he realized it) was the reaffirmation of his individual worth in this new, conformist world in which he found himself. A perceptive young woman commented:

> When I volunteered to be a dance partner at USO affairs, I was afraid they would turn out to be wrestling matches. Actually, the most illicit proposal I ever received was to slip out between dances for a beer.
>
> What I've found out . . . is that the boy who's going there really wants companionship, a feeling that he's being accepted as a human being. I don't know how many boys have said to me in the middle of a dance, "I'll bet every one of us looks just the same to you."[10]

Organized recreation, however well-intended, did not rescue a boy from longing for his hometown and the girls he knew and who knew him. His life at camp only added to his feeling of being lost in a crowd, for the barracks did not invite the "small, intimate talk about himself" a girl was willing to share. When they tried to find empathetic women, many found themselves playing scenes like this one:

> I see this girl sitting alone in one of the booths, so I move over there with my coffee and sandwich. Her eyes are dull and she's tired and lonely. I think, hell, sister, we're sort of in the same boat even if you don't wear OD's, and I lean over and say, "Have a drink, Miss?" Not fresh or anything, just trying to be friendly.
>
> She doesn't get sore, but she looks at me a minute and says so low I can hardly hear her, "No, thank you." Then I notice her hands, like I should of done in the first place. She's married.
>
> There's only two kinds of girls in Armytown . . . soldiers' wives or anybody's gals . . . Every time I come into town I start to ask myself whatinhell I did it for . . . Some fellas wandering up and down; a few with their gals—the lucky ones—but mostly they've got the paintbrush ready only there's nothing to paint red.[11]

While women generally were eager to don a uniform, men soon discovered that the uniform stereotyped them as unsafe for nice girls. "You would think I had leprosy," summarized one. He considered himself to "know the ropes" of meeting women, but in uniform, he found, everything changed. "You have your choice between a low level of sensual woman . . . and the very professional welfare-conscious attitude of the U.S.O. There isn't anything else."[12]

Though these male classifications of females may well have been as unfair as those that they accused women of unjustly maintaining, the fact remains that Army life was by nature anonymous. "Men in the Army feel strongly their isolation," wrote a male sociologist. "Many privates and minor officers go weeks upon weeks without any female association."[13]

It made a guy very much long for his own girl. If he was lucky enough to have one at home, the chances became better—as more and more were drafted— that folks back home would see him as the boy-next-door rather than the proverbial wolf. If he couldn't get the few available local girls to pay attention to him, perhaps he could persuade one from home to visit him, as even *Good Housekeeping* assured its readers that "Nice Girls Go On Military Weekends."

The experience could be a valuable one, not only for the flagging male ego, but also for the young woman who, probably for the first time, traveled alone to meet a man. While prewar dates were planned and executed largely by the male with the female in a passive role, now she did the planning and traveling. A "proper" girl telegraphed ahead to make arrangements. She was advised to meet her fellow at the USO; cautioned not to expect much from his overcrowded town; and to pay for her own room. "Leave him free to spend his limited funds on food and amusement. . . . Be prepared to stand in line for everything . . . Remember that many places are restricted to officers . . . Sunday morning you'll want to go to church . . ."[14]

Showing his bunkmates that he had another life, and knowing some girl cared enough about him to travel perhaps hundreds of miles to see him was terribly important to a serviceman. It was especially imperative because he knew that any opportunity at all would soon be gone—for once shipped overseas, he could anticipate months of not even seeing a female. If he wanted perfumed letters, now was the time he had to go after them. If he wanted a picture to carry in his pocket or (most especially) a ring on a finger, now was the time. When the notice came to be shipped out, he could be slammed into quarantine without any opportunity to see her again. The military took little note of romantic entanglement; indeed, soldiers who even suspected they were due to be shipped out were warned not to break dates, for a dozen broken dates could tell an enemy spy of an imminent convoy. That this would be hard on a girl's ego (to say nothing of anxiety-producing) was not a military concern.

A soldier who went overseas unattached was very likely to stay that way. Rare indeed was the opportunity for courting one of the few American women abroad, and extremely fortunate was the man who won in such competition. Romance being what it is, however, these exceptions occurred. A Navy lieutenant stationed in North Africa shared his story in *Saturday Evening Post*:

For months we had watched dog-faced G.I.'s leaning over ship rails, so when the nurses arrived they all looked like Grable . . .

246

Courtship wasn't easy. There wasn't any place to go. The officers lounge? But that meant 100 men and a girl. I had a comfortable billet, but Madame had a sign in the lobby, "Ni chat; ni chien; ni femme—no cats; no dogs; no women."

But fate took a hand and she got sick . . . In the hospital, we could talk. "Let's not fall in love," she said, "'cause maybe soon you'll be transferred, or we'll move, or stuff; and if we were in love, it would be tougher."

. . . In July we decided to ask permission to get married. I wrote in quintuplicate, a letter to my commanding officer. He wrote to the admiral . . . [She] also wrote, also in quintuplicate, to her colonel. In duplicate, I wrote, "To whom it may concern . . ." We had to wait three months for what they call, over here, the "cooling-off period."

In August, a call from the executive officer. "Carson, the admiral thinks it's all right for you to get married. There is also a request for you to join the expeditionary force as liaison officer. That means you move."

. . . October: We were at least still in the same theater, 300 miles apart. In triplicate this time, we requested permission to marry, and the answer came. "On or after October 27 . . . permission is hereby granted." [15]

Obtaining the permission of others for a decision so personal as marriage (even for men and women who were college educated military officers) was still an accepted part of societal mores. Older people not only felt free to withhold permission from the young, but were sure to offer plentiful advice along with a decision. "Shall They Marry in Wartime?" was a question that seemed to be addressed by virtually everyone who put a pen to paper. By and large (while acknowledging the inevitable exceptions), it seemed to come down to the male expert saying "no" and the female voting "yes."

Whatever the advice, young people did marry—in historic numbers. War boom cities such as Seattle saw increases in marriage licenses as high as 300%.[16] During the first months after Pearl Harbor, estimates were that more than a thousand brides a day walked down the aisle. One male sociologist complained:

In every section of the country literally hundreds of soldiers, sailors, and their sweethearts are getting married every day . . . This year [1942] will undoubtedly put the 1941 record on the shelf. Everybody seems to be doing his best to hasten the soldier and his girl to church. Department stores are keying their advertising to appeal to the war brides, and many communities are removing the required time lapse between license and ceremony for the benefit of servicemen.[17]

Even more grumpy was the view of another man who deemed these marriages "utterly preposterous, contracted by young people because death was whispering in their ears."[18] Of course the real possibility of death encouraged life-affirming actions, and the moral code of the time made most women insist on

247

marriage prior to sex. While it is true that some of these weddings were impetuous, with partners who had only known each other a few days, it is also true that many had planned to marry anyway and simply moved up the date in response to the war.

There also were other factors to account for the marriage boom. The standards of the time required a man to be able to support a woman in her current fashion. Middle-class fathers often expected a suitor to provide a home with at least one servant; if lacking that, newlyweds lived in hotels. Since it was difficult for young men to meet these requirements during the Depression, a great number of marriages were postponed until the war brought increased prosperity, as well as more democratic standards.

The antimarriage forces found a cold comfort in what they saw as statistical proof of a second reason for increased marriages: draft evasion. It was true that the marriage rate rose significantly after the enactment of America's first peacetime draft in 1940; it rose again after Pearl Harbor made it clear that many more men would be drafted. Since marriage provided at least some protection from the draft, doubtless there were men who hastened their search for a woman willing to wed without extended courtship. Some Selective Service officials believed "that up to December, 1941 . . . about half of the increase in marriages must be traced to barefaced draft evasion."[19]*

A woman might well be ambivalent about the role she was playing in all this. Suspicion could be aroused that her man actually was using her as a pawn for his goals, but even if she as a wife felt secure in his love, there were reasons for turning the issue of the draft in her mind, especially if she worked. If she kept her job, did this increase the likelihood of him being drafted? Should she quit, lest her job be the cause of her loved one's death? She might know "dependent" women who were less dependent on their men both emotionally and financially than she was—women who in fact might be glad to see their husbands out of town—so how could she not feel bitter about these glib governmental decisions on who needed whom more?

Ambivalent or not, hundreds of thousands of women reached the decision to wed, and marriage licenses continued to be issued in record proportions as more and more men saw the deadline of overseas duty. "On Fridays and Saturdays,"

---

* How much protection from the draft marriage offered was debatable even at this time, and as the war worsened, marital status mattered less and less. Since the draft was administered by local boards who sometimes ignored national guidelines, decisions could be arbitrary. Some boards drafted no married men; some drafted married men with working wives; others placed occupational distinctions as more important than marital. Even within the same community, there were irrational distinctions—Cleveland had four draft boards, each with its own set of standards. The view of wives and mothers was not represented in any consistent way, as no women served on these boards.

wrote a New Yorker in mid-1943, "the City Hall area is blurred with running soldiers, sailors, and girls hunting the license bureau, floral shops, ministers, blood-testing laboratories and the Legal Aid Society."[20] The reason for the latter was the complexity of marriage laws in the various states:

> *They are an impressively contradictory patchwork of red tape, racket, . . . and sheer orneriness . . . None of the clauses on [age of] consent is the same. Nearly every state has a different waiting period. Some insist on resident doctors getting the blood business. Civil ceremonies are forbidden in Maryland, Illinois, Iowa, and Kentucky; and West Virginia, whose legislators apparently feared having a flock of old maids on their hands, refuses to grant a license to a girl from another state.*[21]

Legalists and moralists alike insisted on a right to stamp their approval on a couple's decision. New York's Little Church Around the Corner, a legendary place for weddings, saw over 2,000 war weddings by early 1944, but even there couples could be refused a ceremony—some 500 a year were turned down because the minister judged them unfit for his blessing.[22]

The obstacles young people had to overcome certainly had the effect of exhibiting determination to carry out their decision. *Ladies Home Journal* ran the fantastic story of a "Bombardier's Bride" who more than once declared the wedding off because of the difficulties of carrying it out. A Florida woman had planned her wedding for December 19, 1941, but her fiancé got orders to ship out in mid-November. She rushed to him in Salt Lake City and they planned another wedding—when he was given 30 minutes notice to leave for California and foreign duty. She followed him through a snowstorm and car breakdown, and after interminable hassles with two judges over a waiting period partly fulfilled with the Utah license, and partly with the California, they finally were able to marry—in an evening ceremony blacked out by air-raid sirens.[23]

War turned tradition upside down, as brides gave up formalities that their mothers would have thought imperative. One perceptive sociologist observed, "they see essential values more quickly than the older generation, who are only aware that their standards of living are being swept aside."[24] Moreover, the war's booming economy also had a profound effect on values, as families who formerly could not afford middle-class standards rushed to establish these traditions:

> *Watch wedding announcements and one will notice that young people of our most exclusive families are being married hastily . . . and hurrying off to face the problems of living in two rooms near an Army camp, while down near the steel mills the daughter of a factory worker is eagerly planning a large and elaborate church wedding. She is the youngest of eight children and the first to have such a wedding . . .*[24]

Searches commenced to ferret out enough swords for the customary reces-
sional as chapels on military posts saw more weddings than they ever did before,
or would again. Men proudly wore their uniforms rather than tuxedos—and
sometimes women did too. One of the nurses in the Philippines illustrated
clearly how much it meant to these men and women to know their love was
pledged eternal before facing the jaws of death:

> *Everybody in the wedding party, including the bride, was in khaki. I had covered
> my khaki pants with a khaki skirt which one of the nurses had concocted and which
> she loaned to me for my wedding night.*
>
> *There was no ring, no license, no bouquet, no veil, no Mass. It was Lent, a
> season during which Catholics are forbidden to wed . . . Sounds of bombs were
> in the distance . . . Two male witnesses heard us exchange vows.*
>
> *But there was a solemnity and a sacredness about the ceremony, performed in
> the midst of so much tragedy, that made us both feel that ours was no ordinary
> marriage. We had taken vows which can never be broken.*
>
> *We had a six-hour honeymoon before Boots had to return to duty . . .*[25]

Those who advised against marriage often based their arguments on analogy
to World War I, when marriage rates also rose rapidly, and the consequent rise
in divorce after the war. "Due to the separation of the sexes," wrote one woman,
"there is a heightening of sex desire . . . which tends to reduce the amount of
rationality."[26] Young women were warned by older ones to look at these
biological facts candidly, to heed the lessons of the past, to be rational. Her man
might not come back at all and she would be a widow at an early age. With the
future so cloudy, it was a mistake to pledge oneself to faithfulness; her youth
would be lost in waiting. If love was real, they were told, it would be there after
the war, too.

Advice to men implied that marriage was unpatriotic: "These hasty marriages
. . . impair the efficiency of our fighting men—military authorities will tell you
that a bachelor makes a much more determined and fearless fighter than a
married man."[27] War officials believed that the distraction of worrying about a
wife was never overcome by any extra maturity marriage might bring. The war
machine preferred young, single recruits whom it could easily mold; commanders wanted youngsters whose only obligation was the latest order, who had little
desire to get home to someone special, who would not stop to think of a wife
before throwing himself on a grenade. Generals and colonels, of course, were
deemed questionable if they had no wife and children, but the troops were
another matter.

That patriotism sometimes influenced young women in exactly the opposite
direction was not lost on thoughtful observers. It was true that many girls, reared
to a lifetime of vicarious experience, seemed to believe marrying a soldier was

the feminine equivalent of responding to Selective Service's call. But there was more on the minds of these young women—sometimes more than the advice-givers themselves had thought through. One of them, to his credit, acknowledged how glib his counsel had been:

> *During a recent lecture tour I addressed a girls' college in Texas. My subject was the war. When the discussion period ensued, the first question asked was whether I was in favor of war marriages, and almost without thinking, I answered, "No."*
>
> *After a moment of deafening silence, a young woman asked, "But didn't you just say, Mr. Browne, that this war will probably last several years? What are we girls going to do? Many of us are already in our twenties, and if we wait several years we may never get married."*
>
> *For the life of me, I couldn't think of an adequate answer . . .*[28]

Young women who were facing adulthood at this profoundly critical time in history could not walk away from these problems, nor satisfy themselves with pat academic answers, even if those answers contained a wealth of experience. Each had to think it through for herself. "The deciding factor," said one who had pondered the question for months, "was the realization that this topsy-turvy world might not right itself for years . . . It seems to me that the world's chaos and uncertainty are reasons for marriage, not for postponement."[29]

Some responded that the times were not all that extraordinary—"the world has always been at the brink of a precipice and at the beginning of a new era"[30]—but even if this was a particularly crucial historical period, the fact that one faced adulthood during these years was something best accepted with a sort of fatalistic optimism. As one church leader put it, "a young couple might very easily waste their lives away waiting. Economic security such as our grandfathers knew is out of the grasp of all our generation . . . Whether we like it or not, we must adjust our lives to insecurity and uncertainty." If couples were otherwise eligible candidates for marriage, "there is no reason why they should not marry now . . . Any other counsel is one of despair or of a blind and fatuous confidence in the coming back of a dead world."[31]

This was a new and shocking view for most. Young Americans had never before been told that their world was dead and that they must face a future "full of insecurity and uncertainty." Their legacy was supposed to be just the opposite. Nor did this cold comfort take account of practicalities, for assuming that (even with these harsh predictions) a woman was glad to receive permission to marry, how was she to manage living on the government's $50 a month? What about the young woman burdened with a maimed husband or even couples who would develop differently while apart? In a no-divorce world, advice to marry was very risky. The bottom line was that women were expected to simply adopt fatalism as a philosophy and to accept any unknowable sacrifice, even for the rest of their lives.

This passive view of women's role was also inherent in those who gave the opposite, antimarriage advice. Women were usually portrayed as those who simply accepted (or occasionally, refused) a marriage proposal, with the real decision being made instead by the potential groom, who would be taking on the burden of a wife. Even a woman's magazine (*Woman's Home Companion*) posed the question to its readers with the man as the implicit decision maker, asking "should soldiers marry?"*

The common belief was still that men were the ones to decide on marriage while women waited or schemed to manipulate him into "popping the question." Yet one important change war wrought was that the advice givers who wrote for popular magazines and spoke at public lectures finally included at least some men in their audience, for a man could hardly be seen as the ultimate decision maker without some advice being directed straight at him. Often the assumption seems to be that women will be the readers and that they will pass the information on to men (which was the probable case), but much of the advice, especially that against marriage, was aimed directly at the male reader. It may well have been the first time that hundreds of thousands of men considered romantic problems in any systematic form.

The question broke down into about a half-dozen arguments on both sides of the debate. Those against marriage argued that war changes people and the partner might return as a stranger; they worried over the inevitable financial problems and the possibility of widowhood or disability; they scorned many wartime marriages as overly emotional, trend-following decisions and predicted later divorce; they pointed out the military preference for single soldiers and the potential problems of infidelity resulting from separation; they thought that female fears of spinsterhood were silly.

Those in favor of marriage explained that war has a telescoping effect, maturing young people quickly with its drastic impacts; they argued that lives could not be put on hold while waiting for unknowable better times; they claimed marriage was essential as a preventative to illicit sex; they contended that married couples had more invested in the future and each would work harder for their mutual goal; they believed that children, if they came, would only intensify this important stability for the future; and finally that it was better to have loved and lost than never to have loved at all.

---

* Response showed 63% thought it right for soldiers to marry; 30% wrong. On the other hand, they definitely wanted them to marry American women. There was a tie of 47% for each position in response to "should service men be forbidden to marry in foreign countries?" Young women were more liberal than older ones in response to both questions. See Anne Maxwell, "Should Marriage Wait?," *Woman's Home Companion* (November 1942): p. 58.

Ultimately it would be the individuals themselves who would make their decisions, an aspect of democracy reinforced in this battle against fascism. The war against dictatorial ideas, and the experience of many young people in love, strengthened the belief that personal decisions should be made solely by the persons affected and were not the business of the state.

Those coeds mentioned above who brought home to the lecturer his glibness about their lives had good statistical foundation for their premise. Germany's post-World War I surplus of women over men was more than 2,000,000; for France and Britain, it was more than 1,000,000 each. Statistically, more than 4,000,000 women from the nations involved stood no chance of ever marrying, and the casualties from this war could only be worse.* In addition to these historical ghosts, young American women worried also about competition from the more docile, more desperate females that their men would meet overseas.

"The male contemporaries of these girls are being taken, almost in a body for the war," wrote one empathetic woman, acknowledging their anxiety that "those who return won't be interested in 'old hags' of 22 or more . . . but in 18 and 20 year olds . . . [They] fear that a girl who plans to wear a 'Mrs.' in front of her name had better take unto herself a man while the taking is good . . . It's the 'eat, drink, and be married' attitude." Nonetheless, she counseled young women, "believe me, worse things can happen to a girl than to go husbandless all her days."[32]

The few boys left on college campuses are becoming either tremendously conceited or tremendously bored . . . And what it does to the male ego! There'll be no living with one of the creatures.

. . . There will be lots of unmarried men after the war, and by no means will all of them be running after 18-year-olds. They'll include many who are waiting for marriage until they've completed their training for civilian life.

. . . Turn your attention toward shaping the most interesting and satisfying life for yourself that you can contrive. Develop your talents . . . not with the idea of trapping a male, but of making yourself a more vibrant and engaging person.

---

* That some predictions turned out to be grossly exaggerated could not, of course, be foreseen. One sociologist who averred that "no matter what happens, two to five million marriageable women in America are doomed to remain spinsters" was egregiously wrong, since America saw fewer than a half-million war deaths from all causes and without regard to marital status. Given his academic credentials, however, his forecast would certainly have been a justifiable cause of anxiety for young women. (See Samuel Tennyson, "The Fate of Wartime Marriages," *American Mercury* (November 1945): p. 533, quoting Dr. Clifford R. Adams of Pennsylvania State College.)

. . . The girl who takes any job to pass the time away until she can get married may find herself stuck for life in that job. The girl who equips herself for some worthwhile work, on the other hand, often is the one who comes out with a worthwhile husband as well.[33]

Reassurance came also on the question of fears of competition from potential foreign war brides. The military threw up serious obstacles to such marriages during the war itself, and even after peace, its bureaucracy forced a soldier to think through his decision, to be aware of its cultural hazards and to exhibit determination to follow through with paperwork. Many Americans felt marriage to foreigners, especially those from enemy nations, was unpatriotic, and women at home received support for maintaining their differences. Even such a mainstream magazine as *Collier's* encouraged young women:

We take note of numerous letters reaching the public prints from American servicemen overseas, to the effect that American women, by comparison with English, Irish, Australian, etc., women, are too demanding, want men to spend too much money on them before and after marriage, have been unduly spoiled by spineless American men, and had better mend their ways if they know what is good for them.

. . . Were we any American girl, we would discount these complaints heavily . . . Many a smart foreign girl who hoped to marry some American fighting man would naturally try to give . . . the impression that she was a little homebody to whom money . . . meant nothing.

. . . For another thing, . . . ambitious American women have had a great deal to do with pushing the American standard of living to the highest average levels in recorded human history . . .[34*]

Supportive though they might appear of the American woman's economic independence, most were likely to condemn any sexual independence. None-

---

* While many were quick to attribute economic motivations to foreign brides, there also were recurring accusations that some American war brides were primarily interested in their soldier's fortune. "I know this to be true," said one sociologist, "in the mountaineer districts of Appalachia. There, girls can easily live with their parents; meanwhile the family income will rise 300 per cent on account of the marriage of one daughter."

Another wrote that the "most avid huntress is often a divorcee or a woman with children. These mothers have learned that . . . their children . . . become . . . eligible for an allowance . . . For a huntress with three children, $120 per month, tax free, may seem big game . . . [One] married thirteen servicemen and filed for a family allowance from each—without benefit of a single divorce."

See William Cecil Headrick, "To Wed or to Wait?," *Current History* (October 1943): p. 116; Harold M. Wayne, "G.I. Divorce Dangers," *Collier's* (October 21, 1944): p. 80. James H. Bossard, "The Hazards of War Marriage," *Science Digest* (July 1944): p. 1, made the same economic argument.

theless, women were making it known that they wanted sexual standards at least reviewed if not updated. "Old-fashioned moralists shy away from the discussion of such problems," *Ladies Home Journal* editorialist Dorothy Thompson acknowledged, "but it is clear, from the thousands of questions we receive . . . that women want them discussed, and openly, for they are a reality of life."[35]

A double standard was a given in almost all discussions, with male infidelity to be expected. "The strict regimentation of life in the Army," said one male sociologist, "necessitates release in some other department of life, and that release is found in the relaxation of morality, particularly in the field of sex . . . in every war, the family is the first and greatest casualty."[36] Another agreed:

When a man is told to go out and kill or be killed, he isn't likely to be as scrupulous as usual . . . Some of the young men I've talked with recently seem to feel subconsciously that the sacrifices they're ready to make for their country entitle them to special dispensations from their girlfriends. And many girls, in turn, are subject to a romantic urge . . . to go farther—sometimes without, usually with, the sanction of marriage.

A survey on sexual indulgence was made among American soldiers in France during the World War . . . About one third of the men questioned replied anonymously that they took advantage of every opportunity for sexual relations. Another third admitted occasional indulgence. Another third reported they were totally abstinent, and they gave as the reason the fact that they had a girl back home . . .[37]

Women were thus aware that two-thirds of men acknowledged illicit sex in this earlier, more innocent era. The sophistication of the twenties did little to alter this ratio of knowledgeable men to women. "Rage against it if you will," wrote Ethel Gorham, an urbane New York fashion editor, "but the double standard on sex still prevails. You'd be a foolish wife," she warned, "to ask your husband what he does with those leaves of his when he can't get home . . . Don't imagine he remains pure as the driven snow to match your own temperature. Men aren't made that way, but they certainly expect women to be."[38]

The knowledge that male infidelity was more likely than not did not assuage anxiety for either partner. A medical doctor writing on psychological problems reported that one of the "most frequently met is the fearful insecurity on the part of the husband—but often more so on the part of the girl he left behind—about the partner's faithfulness . . . The absent husband or lover imagines that all men are after his girl, and she, in turn, imagines her mate surrounded by glamorous females."[39]

A man was in a far stronger position to see societal enforcement of his woman's virtue, especially if they had married. Women, though aware that the marriage vow offered only slim assurance of male chastity, found other real benefits in marriage, including its enhancement of a woman's importance. She now had a guaranteed status with his family, and the government also now ranked her first in relationship to the soldier. For the man, one of the advantages of marriage was the knowledge that now others would help to see to her fidelity in his absence. This obligation, however, was a worrisome one to many moralists, explaining some of the ambivalence of their advice:

> The churches, which usually favor early marriage, are greatly perturbed about war marriages. This is not because of the risks encountered by the husband, but because they have discovered the demoralizing effect an interrupted marriage has upon a young wife. Her marriage has ended her girlhood, and transferred her from the protection of her parents to the protection of her husband. When he leaves, she is a young married woman, without a man. She is attractive to other men and knows the attraction of men . . .
>
> The greater the woman's capacity for love—the very part of her nature which makes her a loving and devoted wife—the greater her temptation in long periods of separation and loneliness.[40]

Some men were quick to zero in on this loneliness, and it soon became clear that many men found married women more fascinating than single women. Not only was there no threat to the men's marital status, but also they knew that married women were knowledgeable and probably vulnerable. The wolf was often in military clothing, representing himself as the husband's friend. One woman who had dinner with such a friend enjoyed the evening, but "the next day it was cocktails. That was fun too. Then he offered to see about a contract I'd gotten involved with . . . He was helping me find a new apartment, he was phoning me daily at the office, he was getting in my hair." A woman had to be very careful, she acknowledged, to remember that "just because a man is in uniform doesn't mean that you are comforting your husband by proxy."[41]

For whatever complicated and individual reasons, by the end of the war there were reports that more women were emulating men's freer sexual behavior and forgetting promises of purity. Her infidelity, however, was not met with the same equanimity as his:

> In one army division stationed in Europe, an average of five soldiers daily receive word that their wives want to break marital ties or are carrying on affairs, and another division has a "broken hearts club" for men whose wives have jilted them. Incensed by the increasing numbers of infidelity cases brought by returning servicemen, a state's attorney in Illinois has announced that he will vigorously prosecute wives and husbands charged with adultery.
>
> . . . A Newark judge declared, "I am disgusted with the number of cases coming before me of wives who are untrue . . . In the last six weeks I had no less than twenty such cases." And an Army chaplain, shocked by stories of broken marriages, was moved to report, "Our women have failed their fighting men . . . The men come to tell me they are going to divorce their wives . . . After a man has flown seventy to ninety missions . . . and then finds his home has been wrecked by

infidelity, there is little I can tell him to convince him that he should forgive and forget."[42]

The result was that women, understanding that their men were subject to so much psychological stress that paranoia made sense, had to be totally circumspect. For mature women with long-term male friends (often their husband's pals), the situation could be difficult. One woman who wished for occasional nights out pleaded with her husband to write to their maid: "Do I have to go on the rest of my life being kept straight by Fidelia? Will you please write her at once and say it's all right for me to go out to dinner with Tony . . . since I'm practically a grandmother?"[43]

Whether or not it was natural for young women to be socially cloistered during their most active years, and what, if anything, they could do with their leisure that would not arouse gossip and suspicion were questions much debated. A poll of servicemen showed that they understood loneliness, but were also highly aware of the danger represented by other males. By a margin of 3 to 2, they were "in favor of letting the girls date unless they are married . . . One or two liberal husbands felt it was all right for them to go out 'occasionally' or 'with mutual friends.'"[44]

There was, here, a beginning of trust, a glimmer that friendships between men and women did not inherently mean sexual relationships and that a woman who pledged her love to a man need not give up all social activity to exhibit her devotion. Though the double standard remained real, discussion of its unfairness began at least to lift the veil of secrecy and scandal that had surrounded all sexual issues.

One sociologist writing early in the war indeed averred that "the double standard of morals is well on its way out." He was quick to point out, however, that this did not mean "approval of promiscuity."[45] What was developing was a distinction between premarital sex and extramarital relations; it was a lessening of the value placed on virginity, with sex outside of marriage being permissible when there was genuine love. "Moralists still striving to maintain the value of chastity," he continued, "are losing the full force of two of their stock arguments, namely, the fear of pregnancy is diminished by the use of contraceptives and the danger of venereal infection lessened by . . . prophylactics and with the possibilities of cure greatly increased."[46]

Of course this was a view far too sophisticated for many. Indeed, one moralist complained that even marriage was not enough in the case of many war weddings, which he believed were "celebrated on a moment's notice by persons who hardly knew each other . . . They were highly immoral in nature: more immoral, in the view of many church authorities than the cohabitation they were supposed to legitimize."[47]

Such people wanted sexual matters to remain taboo, and the "facts of life" shrouded in mists of secrecy. The Archbishop of Canterbury, for example, "set his face resolutely against" governmental programs to educate soldiers in the prevention of venereal disease, attacking those whom he felt were making a "medical problem [of] what is primarily a moral problem." He also opposed notification of partners who would otherwise be unaware that they were potential victims of venereal disease, saying, "We have enough moral sensitiveness left among us to make the contraction of these diseases a matter of shame."[48]

But much of the public and virtually all of the medical establishment disagreed. Venereal disease could be a life-threatening condition, and war inevitably increased its killing power. The British rate among civilians increased 50% in the first four years of the war, with the military rate up 70%. Despite these appalling numbers, authorities nonetheless said "there is less venereal disease in England than during World War I."[49] Perhaps remembering the horrors of that war, polls of Americans showed that a large majority viewed VD as a medical problem needing a pragmatic approach. Given a choice between two methods of control—weekly VD examinations of prostitutes or police drives to close down prostitution—over 60% said the exams were a more realistic solution.[50]

To some extent, this response may have been influenced by the probability that respondents thought of VD as primarily a problem for the poor and especially the black. Even a black publication acknowledged that "the prevalence of venereal diseases among Negroes, particularly in the South, indicates a relatively high percentage of the men with gonorrhea and syphilis inducted into the Army are Negroes."[51] It was true that these diseases were far more prevalent among black men, who had a shocking syphilis rate more than 10 times higher than that of white males. Among the first 2,000,000 men taking the military's physical exam, whites had a rate of 23 cases per 1,000 men, while blacks had 272 per 1,000.[52]

The Army's initial policy had been to reject infected men, but it soon decided that a treatment program made more sense for both the man and the military. The Medical Corps stayed busy giving "some thirty million tests . . . for syphilis" annually and predicting, because of new methods of treatment for gonorrhea, "quick and certain cure for 95 per cent of patients."[53] Besides the soldier, these programs sought also to treat the prostitute from whom he presumably contacted the problem. "When infected prostitutes are located," reported one expert, "to the extent that facilities are available, every effort is made to treat them and rehabilitate them."[54]

Long before the war began, the War Department was anticipating needs in this area. With other agencies, it requested and received Congressional legislation to control prostitution near military posts and defense plants, and because of this planning, a 1943 investigator reported that "the open practice of prostitution has been curtailed in most military and war-production areas." Curtailment, however, was the best officials hoped for, believing that "it is unreasonable to assume that no prostitution is available to men."[55] One woman, an experienced professional in this ancient field of female employment, reported that while war had increased the number of clients, governmental suppression programs had eliminated competition from novices, leaving life very comfortable for women like herself:

> *The war and its increase in men brought many new girls to Seattle, but the more recent crack-down has forced most of these new ones out of town. The older houses are still running wide open and doing a fine trade. The main difference is that where the girls used to leave Seattle when a large conference or other meeting of men took place in California, there is now plenty of trade here and no changes are necessary.*[56]

The efforts of the military establishment not only did a great deal to lessen a tragic rate of venereal disease, which in earlier times was allowed to kill innocent wives who never even understood the nature of their illness, but it also helped to spread sexual enlightenment in other ways. The military's "social hygiene" lectures became America's first formal sex education program, and the goal of teaching facts openly rather than spreading myths furtively gained public support. Films and posters popularized scientific understanding with these men, and eventually this knowledge filtered back to their women.

Just as importantly, the military's policy of "compulsory use of prophylaxis"[57] increased familiarity with condoms, which soldiers soon discovered could be used for pregnancy prevention as well as VD prevention. Moralists who objected to VD treatment programs, whether or not they said so, probably foresaw this correlation and were actually protesting the long-range implications. They understood, consciously or not, that freedom from sexual fears (VD, unwanted pregnancy or other) would result in the rational control of both the male and female body. It was a basic conflict of old religious and new scientific views, and the triumph of science meant the fundamental freedom for a woman to understand her body and to choose what happens to it.

As planners for VD prevention had based their project on experience from World War I, so did other analysts attempt to draw on that war—with far less success—for lessons on the divorce rate. One of the statistical analogies they noted was that as prosperity brings more marriages, so it also brings more divorce. Nevertheless, even in the midst of the greatest economic depression of the modern world, increasing numbers of Americans continued to cancel their wedding vows.

But with war so much on their minds, it was easy for people to overlook a long-term historical change that had been developing for a century, and instead to blame the war for the increase in marital breakups. The same experts who sang the antimarriage song also led the divorce dirge. One of them, a well-known sociologist, predicted that "two-thirds of this country's 'war marriages' were doomed to break up,"[58] a figure of greatly exaggerated proportions. Other writers repeated his prediction.

A year after the war's end, *Newsweek* confirmed the bad news, announcing in dramatic language that "in 1945 there were 31 divorces for every 100 marriages . . . double pre-war totals."[59] It was not pointed out, however, that not only were these numbers appreciably lower than those predicted, but also that there had been an artificial lull in divorces during the war due to the fact that servicemen were protected by law from civil suit, including divorce cases. Moreover, the most sensational statistics cited were those of known divorce-mill states. Only at the end of the article were these two revealing comments added: "Only 8 per cent of couples with children broke up their homes" and "the majority of divorces were not GI. [A] Chicago Circuit Court Judge . . . states: 'in 324 cases I heard during one month, 266, or 82 per cent, represented pre-Pearl Harbor marriages. '"[60]

In other words, four out of every five of these furor-raising divorces were the ending of marriages that began before the war, rather than one of the much-castigated wartime marriages. Doubtless many of these prewar unions were based on the economic dependence of the wife, and (though this was a point none of these writers pursued) quite possibly the key to the breakup was the new economic freedom women earned with wartime employment opportunities. The fact that "women college graduates were four times as likely to make unsuccessful marriages as men graduates"[61] also went unexplored. The statistical evidence was clear; women who were most likely to be economically independent were also those least dependent on marriage.

Having the financial freedom to end a bad marriage, however, did not imply judicial freedom. "While you're in the process of getting your divorce," *McCall* warned its readers, "you'll fret uselessly at the formidable hurdles that conscientious lawmakers have placed in your path":[62]

> *Nowhere in the United States has divorce by mutual consent been legalized . . .*
> *In most states the . . . proof required varies . . . and if there is a contest you may*
> *find that the courts will deny you a divorce and sometimes will deny it even when*
> *there is no opposition . . . Many states require you to wait varying degrees of time*
> *. . . before remarriage . . . In some states the courts have the power to prohibit the*
> *guilty person from marrying during the lifetime of the innocent spouse . . .*[63]*

---

* Divorce cases were almost always adversarial and bitterly fought, with seekers often establishing "residence" in a state with more liberal law. New York and other states with large numbers of Catholics allowed only the limited grounds of desertion or proven adultery; South Carolina allowed no divorce at all. In others (primarily Nevada,

Reform of divorce laws in fact became one of the first priorities of postwar feminists, a success story so complete that now it is taken for granted that individuals have the right to terminate a marriage they agree is no longer viable. The assumption that the state has a right to contradict the consensual decision of a couple is almost totally gone, with the major function of the state having become the division of assets and custody.

Buried between the lines of many who warned against marriage in wartime is a view of women as—at best—inherently naive and helpless, hopelessly romantic and dangerously beguiling to the male bereft of their advice; or—at worst—fortune hunters callously entrapping soldiers for their money. The war, however, with its increased cracking of social codes, dimmed the defining lines, as "nice girls" did things that previously meant instant loss of respectability. The ancient division of women into whores or saints was less easy. When men danced with women at the USO without intention of future involvement or when they worked next to them in factory and office, they began to see women as real people who were as individually different as men.

The "divorce danger" predicted by antimarriage moralists may be instead largely a fear of the wider social change implicit when the traditionally dependent woman became financially and legally free. These views made it almost impossible for them to even entertain the idea that in some cases, divorce might be a good thing.

As was the case with VD, however, the public was more pragmatic than its so-called opinion leaders. Men and women who fought fascism would not willingly return to a society that refused them permission to make such fundamental decisions as whether or not to be married. If freedom meant anything, it surely meant that personal choices were personal.

SOURCE NOTES

1. Sara Moore Eastman, "Mrs. Neptune of Great Lakes," *Saturday Evening Post* (January 16, 1943): p. 98.
2. Ibid., p. 97.

---

* but also Arkansas, Idaho, Washington and Arizona), divorce was easily obtained, though whether or not the action would be recognized by the *bona fide* home state was up to still other lawyers.

   Nevada and Arkansas allowed divorce "by publication," which meant that "a little two-by-two-inch notice [is published] in the Cherokee Gazette or whatever newspaper is in the area . . . the first notice that the wife receives will arrive when the War Department, Office of Dependency Benefits, in answer to her frantic inquiry, advises that, 'Family allowance has been discontinued. Reason: soldier divorced.'" (Harold M. Wayne, "G.I. Divorce Dangers," *Collier's* [October 21, 1944]: p. 80.)

3. Sgt. Lloyd Shearer, "Army Hostess," *New York Times Magazine* (February 7, 1943): p. 12.
4. Ibid. See also Alma de Coen, "I Am an Army Hostess," *Reader's Digest* (March 1943): p. 80, and "Sister to a Regiment in the Pacific," *Reader's Digest* (October 1943): p. 89.
5. Barbara Klaw, *Camp Follower: Story of a Soldier's Wife* (New York: Random House, 1944), p. 68.
6. Ibid., p. 64.
7. Rose M. Rabinoff, "While Their Men Are Away," *Survey Midmonthly* (April 1945): p. 110.
8. Ibid. See also Donald S. Howard, "American Social Work and World War II," *Annals of the American Academy of Political and Social Science*, Vol. 229 (1943): p. 138.
9. Ibid., p. 111. See also Gretta Palmer, "The Army's Problem Wives," *Reader's Digest* (July 1944): p. 66.
10. Henry A. Bowman, "Should Soldiers Marry?" *American Magazine* (August 1942): p. 74.
11. "Armytown, U.S.A.," *New Republic* (March 20, 1944): p. 375.
12. John F. Cuber, "Changing Courtship and Marriage Customs," *Annals of the American Academy of Political and Social Science*, Vol. 229: p. 36. See also David L. Cohn: "Love—America's No. 1 Problem?" *Science Digest* (August 1943): p. 19.
13. Ibid.
14. Jo Anne Healey, "Nice Girls Go on Military Weekends," *Good Housekeeping* (June 1942): p. 4; see also "Service Sweethearts," *Newsweek* (November 2, 1942): p. 83.
15. Naval Lt. Ralph Carson, "GI Romance," *Saturday Evening Post* (February 5, 1944): p. 6.
16. Katherine Whiteside Taylor, "Shall They Marry in Wartime?," *Journal of Home Economics* (April 1942): p. 213; see also "Marriage Rate Up During War Boom," *Science Digest* (March 1942): p. 58.
17. Bowman, "Should Soldiers Marry?" p. 47. See also William Fielding Ogburn, "Marriages, Births, and Divorces," *Annals of the American Academy of Political and Social Science*, Vol. 229 (1943): p. 22. Ogburn was one of several who estimated 1,000 brides daily.
18. Jere Daniel, "Whys of War Divorces," *New York Times Magazine* (February 3, 1946): p. 18.
19. Gretta Palmer, "Marriage and War," *Ladies Home Journal* (March 1942): p. 110. See also Augusta J. Street, "Hasty Marriage and the Draft," *Journal of Social Hygiene* (May 1941): p. 228; "Marriage Problems in Relation to Selective Service," *The Family* (June 1941): p. 129.
20. Harry Henderson and S. Shaw, "Marriage in a Hurry," *Collier's* (July 17, 1943): p. 22.

21. Ibid., p. 23.
22. "Little Church's War Weddings," *Newsweek* (March 13, 1944): p. 84. See also Randolph Ray, "For Better For Worse," *Atlantic* (March 1944): p. 62; well-known as a marital expert, Ray was rector of the "Little Church."
23. "Bombadier's Bride," *Ladies Home Journal* (September 1943): p. 26.
24. Gladys Gaylord, "Marriage Counseling in Wartime," *Annals of the American Academy of Political and Social Science*, Vol. 229 (1943): p. 40.
25. Engles, "I Was Married in Battle," p. 113. A similar report of a North African wedding is in Martin, "Angels in Long Underwear," p. 11.
26. Taylor, "Shall They Marry?," p. 214; see also Ruth Zurfluh, "The Impact of War on Family Life—Wartime Marriages and Love Affairs," *The Family* (December 1942): p. 304.
27. Bowman, "Should Soldiers Marry?" p. 74.
28. "Will War Marriages Work?," *Reader's Digest* (November 1942): p. 14. The article was a condensation of a radio discussion on "America's Town Meeting of the Air"; the speaker was Lewis Browne, author of *Believing World*.
29. "I Married My Soldier Anyway," *Good Housekeeping* (June 1942): p. 33.
30. Robert G. Foster, "Marriage During Crisis," *Joural of Home Economics* (June 1943): p. 329.
31. Walter John Marx, "What About Marriage?," *Commonweal* (July 10, 1942): p. 270; see also E.M. Phelps, ed., "War Marriage," *University Debaters Annual* (1942–43): p. 159–91, for a summation of the pros and cons of all these arguments.
32. Gladys Denny Shultz, "Must We Ration Husbands?" *Better Homes & Gardens* (November 1944): p. 10.
33. Ibid., p. 68. See also "The National Sex Ratio," *School and Society* (June 2, 1945): p. 362.
34. "Our Demanding Women," *Collier's* (July 1, 1944): p. 70.
35. Dorothy Thompson, "Soldier's Wife," *Ladies Home Journal* (February 1945): p. 6.
36. Palmer, "Marriage and War," p. 110.
37. Bowman, "Should Soldiers Marry?" pp. 74–75.
38. Gorham, *So Your Husband's Gone to War*, p. 74.
39. Erwin O. Krausz, MD, "For the Duration Widow," *Parents* (March 1944): p. 31.
40. Thompson, "Soldier's Wife," p. 6.
41. Gorham, *So Your Husband's Gone to War*, pp. 72 and 76.
42. Samuel Tenenbaum, "The Fate of Wartime Marriages," *American Mercury* (November 1945): pp. 530 and 535.
43. Margaret Buell Wilder, *Since You Went Away* (Garden City, NY: The Sun Dial Press, 1944), p. 118.

44. Anne Maxwell, "Should Marriage Wait?" *Woman's Home Companion* (November 1942): p. 58.
45. Ernest W. Burgess, "The Effect of War on the American Family," *American Journal of Sociology* (November 1942): p. 350.
46. Ibid.
47. Daniel, "Whys of War Divorces," p. 18, quoting Willard Waller. Waller was a well-known sociologist specializing in the family.
48. Willard Waller, "The Family and Other Institutions," *Annals of the American Academy of Political and Social Science*, Vol. 229 (1943): p. 114.
49. Ibid., citing references in the *New York Herald Tribune* (February 1943), and in the *New York Times* (October 30, 1942).
50. Gallup, *The Gallup Poll*, p. 379. Polling date was January 1943. See p. 353 for an earlier poll with similar response.
51. Louis Lauter, "Sidelights on the Negro and the Army," *Opportunity: A Journal of Negro Life* (Winter 1944): p. 7.
52. Ibid.
53. Charles P. Taft, "Public Health and the Family in World War II," *Annals of the American Academy of Political and Social Science*, Vol. 229 (1943): p. 146.
54. Ibid., p. 146.
55. Walter C. Reckless, "The Impact of War on Crime, Delinquency, and Prostitution," *American Journal of Sociology* (April 1943): p. 385.
56. Ibid., p. 386.
57. Burgess, "Effect of War," p. 350.
58. Tenenbaum, "The Fate of Wartime Marriages," p. 530, citing "the late Dr. Willard Waller of Columbia University."
59. "Divorce—The Postwar Wave," *Newsweek* (October 7, 1946): p. 33.
60. Ibid. See also "Divorces: A New High for U.S," *U.S. News* (October 4, 1946): p. 30.
61. Ibid.
62. Jacques W. Bacal and E.B. Foskett, "Divorce—the Lonesome Road," *McCall's* (December 1946): p. 19.
63. Ibid., p. 104.

16

THE WAITING WIFE

Before the year is over, there will be half a million more of us hanging out the blue stars, for no woman with a husband under thirty-eight is sure of keeping him with her much longer. Of course, these young wives and mothers are on the anxious seat. They weep on occasion; they spend sleepless nights . . . Life has become for them an existing from one mail delivery to the next.

. . . For over a year I had been in turmoil . . . The constant dread of my husband's leaving had been making a nightmare of my hours. Like most other American wives, I had not only to contend with the gradual dreaded approach of the draft, but with a husband who was uneasy and itching to get into the fight, as soon as he could decently dispose of me and the home.

But . . . it's lots worse in anticipation than it is in reality . . . And the strangest thing of all is that after it happens, you are conscious of a new pride and distinction you had never imagined. You suddenly find you can face it![1]

Others testified to the drain of endlessly twisted emotions, the all-consuming apprehension of the draft notice. "You go through hell," Ethel Gorham agreed. "Your husband's gloom, his constant irritation; the inability to carry on his job in the old routine fashion; your own restlessness and frustration and inner laceration; the two of you at constant cross-purposes, because . . . you feel your home is at stake if he goes and he feels it is if he doesn't."[2]

A few women found that they couldn't face it, at least not without professional help. *Time* reported in January 1945 (after months of the most bitter battles of the war) that 2,500 servicemen's wives had undergone psychiatric treatment during the past 18 months in San Francisco alone. "Women are paying the same war penalties as men," they wrote, "many of whom crack up long before they reach combat. Women who have followed their husbands to embarkation ports often find themselves spiritually stranded . . . Particularly those recently married or childless develop physiological disturbances, resentment, . . . inability to recall the husband's face."[3] But one of the war's achievements was public acceptance of psychiatry as a legitimate medical field, and with minimal treatment, most of these women "get over their depressions very quickly."[4]

New-found knowledge of basic psychological principles was only one aspect of the huge amounts of information women learned during the war—a phenomenon that, while little noted, was nonetheless a significant achievement. In addition to all of the ideas absorbed about new employment fields, most women learned, usually by osmosis, a great deal about the military. Her husband was taught in basic training that a major outranked a captain in the Army while in the Navy a captain outranked all but admirals—and yet, while no one made the effort to teach her in a systematic way, a wife could be sure that her husband would expect her to know such things.

But the subject that she may well have learned best was geography. School books were dusted off and maps bought in unprecedented quantities as Americans attempted to figure out what was happening where. The tiny, distant islands of the South Pacific soon sounded as familiar as the state next door, and those who had never been out of New England came to appreciate through personal travel what a truly big state Texas is.

Many women learned this by once again disregarding the advice generally given by those older and presumably wiser. If there was frequent advice that marriage in wartime was a bad idea, then there was almost unanimity that following a husband to camp was a foolish notion a wife would live to regret. A columnist for *Ladies Home Journal*, who was both a medical doctor and a retired Naval officer, was typical when he stated:

> *It sounds heartless to say to young people in love that the wife should stay in the home town while her husband is in . . . the United States. But . . . romance does not usually thrive in crowded, miserable quarters, with worry, extra expense, lack of old friends, too much idleness or too much work . . . The tendency in wartime is to grab at every fleeting moment of happiness. This grabbing will bring wives and husbands only a mocking imitation [of the marriage] . . . for which they yearn.*[5]

The magazine bolstered the argument by publishing the results of a questionnaire given to servicemen, which showed "the vote is 4 to 3 *against* wives' living near camps. More than one man speaks of its being an added burden . . . "[6] Yet with or without resolving the ambivalence of their men, women boarded buses and trains in droves.

> *Unofficially, the War Department hints that it won't do—too much strain on transportation and housing facilities . . . Yet, like an army of Ruths, the wives follow, anyway! The extent of these migrations can't be measured. The Army keeps no record. But they cover the map, a very few even slipping overseas or down to South America—of course, in some essential capacity as nurses, newspaper women . . .*
>
> *A sergeant's wife, who has covered 9,000 miles in nine months, says she has learned more geography . . . Practically, the war wife has enriched her storehouse of common sense with a variety of efficiencies—from knowing how to travel to*

knowing how to mine the gold in a new acquaintance in a fifteen-minute conver-
sation . . . Psychologically, she is stronger. She has met the awful loneliness of
virtual solitary confinement in an unfurnished rented room in a strange town . . .
Never again will her emotional horizon be a fireplace mantel nor her mental
summits the idea traffic of one town.[7]

That it was a learning experience and an adventure did not mean that it was
easy. "Lacking any official traveling status," *Time* reported, "the service wife
is at the bottom of the priority heap; even when she can afford better accommo-
dations, she must usually expect to wind up in coach, possibly sitting on her
suitcase in the aisle."[8] Travel, while still available in the United States, was
rationed to the extent that military needs came first. A experienced traveler
wrote of her response:

In time I was to learn the art of waiting—of stretching out little tasks and
insignificant thoughts . . .
I noticed a sign at the train gate, saying, "Servicemen will board all trains
before civilians." A fine idea, no doubt, but multiplied a hundred times—service-
men will get in diners first, servicemen will have first crack at sandwiches sold on
trains, servicemen will have first choice of hotel rooms—it made me feel like an
excessively useless object, or a member of a persecuted class.[9]

For most of these young women, brought up during the Great Depression,
any travel was a new thing, a factor that may well have made uncomfortable
situations more bearable since it did not mean a drop in standards. USO workers
said that they were "frequently stunned by the valor of ignorance shown by some
young wives who have led completely sheltered lives in small towns. They have
had to instruct the girls on how to use dial telephones, how to ride a bus," etc.[10]

Travelers Aid was the lead volunteer organization in this work, handling over
a million cases in the first six months of 1943. They found their clients to be
astonishingly devoted to the cause of staying near their men as long as possible.
Women rocked crying infants in crowded bus stations; changed diapers and
hauled all the paraphernalia of babyhood over thousands of miles without any
assurance of a seat; ate stale sandwiches they brought along because the fare
took every penny they had. One, intending to surprise her man, carried on a
crowded, rocking train all the way from Oregon to Missouri his favorite cake.

They simply gave up on second-guessing the Army with its crazy training
systems that sometimes meant incredible numbers of transfers. Cases were not
uncommon like that of the woman who moved so often that she had seven
prenatal doctors in nine months of care, and another whose six-month old baby
had lived at five Army camps. There were cases, too, that involved more than
mere inconvenience and discomfort.

One "very pregnant" woman "came perilously close to becoming a casualty
in [this] strange, unorganized army of women"[11] when she went into labor after

four days of waiting in a hotel lobby for a phone call from her husband. Another "very young mother with a three-week-old baby in her arms got off to change trains in Jacksonville, Florida, and toppled in a faint." She was in the hospital for two weeks, and then, "with no money and faint prospect of a roof over her head if she did get to Mississippi" where her husband was stationed "she meekly accepted a ticket back home."[12]

The baby's father would be shipped overseas, perhaps to die, without ever seeing his child. Most women were unwilling to allow that possibility and went their own individual ways, ignoring both obstacles and public pronouncements of their foolishness, helped by few but each other. They understood, if the public did not, the deep love motivating a woman with five children who arrived in Corpus Christi at 1:00 A.M. searching for her husband. Though the welfare-conscious professionals tried, "no one has found any way to exorcise the heart-wrenching truth from the simple statement: 'I don't know whether I'll ever see him again.'"[13]

The California port cities from which men sailed to fight the Japanese saw hundreds of thousands of these women arrive, often with no more information than that their men were somewhere in San Diego or San Francisco and would be gone soon. "There is no place to put them," a reporter wrote:

The hotels put out cots in the halls or let them sleep sprawled uncomfortably in the chairs in the lobby. One hotel not only lets them sleep in the lobby but provides the women with pillows, and when the first guests check out in the morning, the stranded ladies are invited up to the vacated rooms, to freshen up and have a bath free of charge.[14]

Yet despite the obvious problems of these overcrowded towns, many women decided to stay on there rather than return home. Asked why she remained, the wife of a submarine sailor responded: "A friend of mine went home to visit her family and she'd no sooner left than her husband got in with forty-eight hours leave, and she missed him. And . . . [when she went] for Christmas, she missed him again. I'm staying right here."[15]

Beyond the possibility of a husband's unexpected leave, there was the more real chance of getting news about him via internal news networks. A woman might see a man who had seen her husband a month before; she might hear where his unit was and how the combat had gone there in a way official broadcasts would never tell her. Particularly for those whose husbands were reported missing in action, being near where his ship or unit was based could offer clues and hope and mostly a feeling that she was doing all that she could.

Probably of overwhelming importance, however, was the empathy she felt with other women in the same situation. No one else could understand in the same way, and their company did a great deal to ease loneliness and anxiety. Often a woman found that she had more in common with others who a week before had been strangers than she did with family and lifelong friends back home. The homebodies now seemed too remote; their lives too narrow; their interests trivial and unreal. These women stayed in Texas or California or Florida, and they started new lives.

They depended on their unofficial support systems for practical help as well as emotional. The wives of career military men were of inestimable assistance to the huge numbers of newcomers to their ranks, capable of giving experienced and precise advice. One wrote:

> *In these uncertain times, the energetic wife who wishes to be with her Navy husband every possible minute follows him to pillar to post as far as finances permit. She does not expect to have a house and often not even an apartment, but she does carry the essentials for the homey touch to be given whatever space she is able to rent . . .*
>
> *Here is a list of things she has found most useful and practical. They can be packed in a trunk and shipped as baggage and unpacked in an hour to give an air to even the least desirable of the places she is likely to find available:*
>
> *A few scatter rugs; her chest of flat silver; some good linens; several pictures and photographs; ash trays and cigarette boxes; an electric coffee percolator and a few cups and plates; an electric plate; a small frying pan and stew pot; salt and pepper shaker; sugar bowl and creamer; a small pillow and good-looking blanket; plus any personal trinkets easy to carry and reminders of home; and always an electric fan in summertime.*[16]

It wasn't long before the media followed with similar advice for readers who chose to ignore the warnings on camp following. Even *House Beautiful* compromised its high standards to acknowledge the housing realities these women faced, offering sensible suggestions. Since a kitchen of one's own was a dream and even kitchen privileges unlikely, one should "take enough electrical appliances so you can get at least breakfast and your lunch in your room." Because it was also difficult to buy new appliances, a new homemaker should "frankly put the problem up to the relatives. They're going to be staying home with a stove, and they can make toast, coffee, and such without special appliances." One might also buy a bolt of fabric—preferably dark green—"because it will 'go with' practically any color scheme . . . You'll need a lot of it to camouflage (by slipcovering) the old horrors you'll meet up with." Finally, brides were reminded that wedding presents were intended to be used. "Only the most beautiful things can rise and shine above the drab and dreary." Using one's "fine possessions" was "little enough to give a man before he goes overseas to a soldier's life."[17]

Some women found, however, that much of this creative advice could not be followed due to obstacles placed by obstinate landlords—and, more often, landladies. The housing shortage in towns near military posts put property owners into positions of tremendous power. With no civil rights laws to curb them, whimsy alone could govern, and landlords refused to rent for any reason or none at all. Women without character references risked being turned away; black women of course could not expect space in any except black establishments; and mothers found their children regarded almost as lepers rather than as the nation's future. One desperate woman placed an ad in a New Orleans paper:

> WANTED BY A NAVAL OFFICER'S WIFE—whose husband is serving overseas—and THREE MONSTERS in the form of my little children—TO RENT—a 2 or 3 bedroom house, apartment, BARN or CAGE or whatever is supposed to serve as shelter when such terrible creatures as children have to be considered . . .[18]

Even after a rental agreement was reached, some owners raised petty despotism to an art form. Many refused to allow tenants to have even a coffeemaker in their rooms; one woman whose landlady prohibited food found an unopened box of candy thrown out. It was common to ban even hand laundry, so women had to carry clothes to expensive commercial places. Many houses lacked telephones, but in others where they were available, renters were not allowed to use them. One landlady allowed only a 15-watt light bulb and pounded on the door at 10 each night for that to be turned out. There were even reports of "landladies meting out the toilet paper, sheet by sheet."[19]

But then again, these tenants might have counted themselves lucky, for there were others whose rent bought no toilet at all. Troops trained disproportionately in the South, where the general poverty was eased only slightly by the power of its Congressional delegations to bring in Army posts. Even if some of these Southern families now had the money for long-awaited plumbing, there was little possibility of buying the materials during the war. In one Ozark town, the USO "thoughtfully excluded the soldiers from the shower room in the basement for two hours every morning, leaving it free for the wives. The girls who lived in unequipped homes met regularly there in the morning, grateful and unembarrassed to use the clean public room with its modern, swift showers."[20]

Yet, like other isolated military posts, the property owners of this town were more than willing to collect unconscionable rents. A woman who moved there from Washington, D.C., found that one room—without closet or dresser and containing only a bed and a straight chair—cost considerably more than her apartment in the nation's capital. In some small towns, rent rose 100% between 1940 and 1942. The Office of Price Administration largely gave up on rent control near military posts where little housing existed, for if they tried to enforce regulations, the rooms were withdrawn from the market and desperate servicemen's wives were forced into the awkward position of trying to bribe someone into giving them shelter. When OPA eventually held hearings, they found that the "flood of tenant complaints" was "not concerned so much with rent as with an accumulated resentment in landlord-tenant relationships."[21]

There was reason for resentment. Just as women munitions workers found that the businesses in towns that were recruiting them as workers were then hostile to their needs as customers, so also did the businessmen of Armytown often see servicemen's wives only as a potential wartime bonanza to be exploited. Women lost weight as they coped with overcrowded, overpriced restaurants serving meager, unappetizing food. Conscious of their appalling diets, many took vitamins. A male USO director, who smugly said that he "had his restaurant at home,"[22] was scornful of these needs until he had to eat out one day. Shocked by reality, in blustering irritation he gave the green light to a luncheon program for Army wives that included fresh vegetables in a healthy menu at reasonable cost, which of course proved tremendously popular.

Doubtless he had to explain his epiphany to the town's restaurant owners, whose creed would be that a quasi-governmental institution should not compete with their free enterprise. On the other hand, some businesses insisted on turning down potential customers; banks, for instance, refused to cash out-of-town checks, leaving that privilege to the USO or other nonprofit groups.

While this sort of grasping materialism contrasted sharply with the ideals taught to people sacrificing their youth for their country, in many military locales it seems obvious that the town got its attitudes from the military leadership. Post commanders did not want the women there and had said so; if women came anyway, the opinion was that they deserved what they got. While a man might see his wife's presence as a boon to his morale and a steadying influence that kept him from prostitutes, drunkenness and gambling, the military's official view was different and axiomatically correct.

The result was the development of attitudes that were sometimes little short of misogyny. One example was that of a gentle, uncomplaining expectant mother whose doctor, anticipating a difficult delivery, "called out to the camp for my husband to come in," but, as the woman concluded sadly, "I guess his C.O. wouldn't let him." In the words of the reporting hospital volunteer, it was another of the "Army's stupid, needless cruelties,"[23] contributing nothing to the war or to national morale, while baldly exhibiting disdain for the supposedly sacred role of motherhood.

———————

Some women who never would have thought of themselves as domestic servants did indeed apply for housework jobs as a way of finding a room. Jobs, like housing, were extremely scarce for military wives, for no employer wanted to hire someone whose reason for being there might soon be gone. "If the wife with money enough to pay her way is unwelcome around the camps," wrote a reporter, "how much sadder is the case of the bride who expects to support herself near her service husband!" Restaurant work was often all that was available, "and girls holding these jobs are viewed askance by the respectable ... The Travelers Aid, lately, was unable to find a room in any respectable home of a large town for a soldier's wife with a waitress job."[24]

The situation was an ironic and infuriating revelation to one woman who, prior to joining her husband at camp, had worked for the Office of War Information entreating women to enter the labor force. The small-minded man she encountered at the U.S. Employment Service was a product of his small town; far from trying to recruit her into war industry, he was arrogantly indifferent and callous, refusing to respond to her inquiries. When she asked about the Crop Corps, he clearly had never heard of it. She "stalked out of the office. I felt like apologizing personally to every person who had ever read my appeals to go to the U.S.E.S."[25] After another week of futile job hunting, she decided to settle for volunteer work.

I registered for a nurses' aide course, which "will get under way any day now," the Red Cross woman told me confidently. The course was still about to get underway six weeks later ...

At first I hated myself for being content, and I was amazed that the days passed so quickly. I still winced when I heard a soldier's wife say, "Oh, I'm doing my share. Gosh, I've given my husband, haven't I?" But I couldn't argue anymore, because I, too, had become one of the fiddlers.[26]

Like millions of bright women before and after the war who were forced by their husbands' careers into military and college towns too small for their abilities, some turned housekeeping into an obsession. The wife of a recent West Point graduate was typical.

She put out her "Mr. & Mrs." towels in the bathroom and her cookbooks in the kitchen of a miniscule apartment near Ft. Monmouth, N.J., promptly took in two boarders, . . . old sidekicks of her husband . . . Housekeeping occupies most of the day, as Mrs. Thompson, with bridelike fervor, experiments with recipes, rearranges the furniture trying to make more room, keeps order in the closet . . .[27]

"The days are very empty," acknowledged a report on the 30,000 women who became temporary San Antonions each year while their husbands trained as air cadets. "Myrtle has a radio in her room and goes to the movies two or three times a week."[28] Like the others, she lived for the weekends, for even though the men could see them for a few hours in the evening, most wives could not afford the bus fare for the long and complex trip out to the base. The excessive leisure of their lives really was a burden, because with it they had to "take the dreary penny pinching of trying to live idly, when jobs prove unavailable, on the $50 . . . of a cadet's pay."[29]

One woman who had worked and supported her husband through college summarized the situation by saying, "All this is just terrible and if it lasts much longer, I think I'd go crazy."[30] Another, lucky enough to find a job, still faced a dilemma:

> When Bob's Pre-flight nine weeks are up, he goes on two days' notice to a second nine-week tour at some Primary Training field. There is none near San Antonio, so June will have to decide whether to up stakes and go along or stick to her present job in hopes that . . . the third nine weeks will bring him back to near-by Randolph Field . . . Advanced Training means still another shift . . .[31]

Only a tremendous lack of official imagination explains the government's failure to work out ways that the labor of these women also could have been used for the war effort. There was no attempt to provide buses, for example, which might have taken them en masse to war plants for assembly-line work that required little training. While WAC quotas went unfilled, no one ever conceived of taking this body of potential recruits and sending them to classes on the same posts as their men in preparation for work that they might then do after he went overseas. Even in the large port cities where many jobs were available and labor shortages acute, the prejudice against hiring military wives remained an obstacle. In one of the few exceptions, a San Diego "feminist" cab-company owner had "fifty or sixty women drivers—half of those on the day shift are women. He is proud of the fact that his was the first cab company . . . to introduce women on a large scale; proud of their low accident record and the way the public likes them."[32] His example encouraged the city to hire over 100 women to drive streetcars and buses.

Most women had no choice except to view their wifely roles as their jobs. They would have agreed with one who said, "When he's sent over, I'll go back and get a job. But until that happens I'm going wherever he goes . . . Our merit badge is a 'Gee, I'm glad you're here, darling!' As long as we get that response I'm afraid no amount of outside moaning about 'selfishness' will hit us very hard."[33]

As the war wore on, other Americans began to review the situation and decided that perhaps they were the selfish ones. *American Home* chastised its readers:

> We open our homes to the men in service and ask them to dinner with the family—let's do as much for the homesick women. Can you begin to imagine what it means to the soldier's wife who has been waiting three months for a letter to be asked in for a cup of tea?
> . . . Our communities are filled with women who have followed their soldier husbands to new bases, or their civilian husbands to war jobs—and with women carrying on alone while their men are overseas . . .[34]

One woman, a volunteer with War Housing, found the numbers of lonely women so great that she resolved, "No sailors, soldiers, WACs or WAVEs for my war work. I've picked the WIVES for my interest."[35] Another, the owner of several guesthouses, refused at first to rent to "cadet wives" until she thought of her own son in India. When she got to know her tenants, however, she found herself changed.

> The lamps burned late while they scrubbed and waxed floors, doing a better job than I could. In the morning they appeared in blue jeans and bandannas, without war paint, ready to go down to the office at the Air Academy to find work. When they returned, they had been fingerprinted and signed up to work from 6:00 P.M. to 2:30 A.M.. They were to wash planes! I was appalled, for working with cold water in a cold hangar on desert winter nights was punishment I could not have taken.
>
> . . . For two weeks these amazing young women worked by night, and by day cleaned, washed and ironed, planned their big turkey dinner, wrapped Christmas packages, and wrote faithful daily letters to their husbands. Then, learning that there were some boys from their home town who would have to spend a lonely Christmas, they invited them . . .
>
> I tried to persuade one of the girls, who looked especially pale, to stay home from work . . . She said simply, "They need me. I'll be all right." She had lost premature twin sons three months before. As the Chevrolet drove off I felt very humble. These misjudged youngsters are earning the better world they deserve.[36]

Even the military showed some sign of reevaluation of its wife-exclusionary dogma. In early 1944, the Army Air Force and the Navy "relented" and leased two "swank" hotels in Miami Beach for the use of wives of officers who returned from overseas for additional training. It was "only the barest kind of relief for the service wives from the housing congestion,"[37] but it was something. The public apparently also grew to appreciate the devotion and difficulties of these women, for when Gallup asked after victory in Europe whether "wives of servicemen should be permitted to visit their husbands who have to stay abroad to police conquered countries," 64% said yes. In response to who should pay for this, 42% thought the government should pick up the tab, compared with 30% who put the burden on the travelers.[38]

In the final analysis, wrote a social worker after the war's end:

> Of all the groups of women involved in the war, the servicemen's wives have been the most inchoate. There was no . . . uniform which would give them a feeling of group unity . . . Sitting up all night on trains, on buses, hushing fretful babies, carrying bags with bottles and diapers, and clutching the older children . . . these tired young women were simply trying to maintain their family life as long as they could . . . Hundreds of thousands of others are still in or near the hospital towns, where the wounded convalesce.

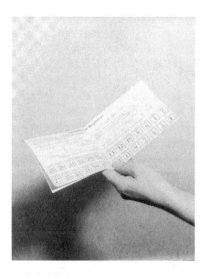

STAMPS IN A SUGAR RATION BOOK, 1942.
U.S. DEPARTMENT OF AGRICULTURE, FARM
SECURITY ADMINISTRATION, PHOTO BY
MARJORY COLLINS; LIBRARY OF CONGRESS.

AN "ALUMINUM FOR DEFENSE"
COLLECTION BIN IN WINDSOR,
VERMONT; AUGUST 1941.
U.S. DEPARTMENT OF AGRICULTURE, FARM
SECURITY ADMINISTRATION, PHOTO BY
JACK DELANO; LIBRARY OF CONGRESS.

WAITING IN LINE FOR THE SUGAR RATIONING BOARD, DETROIT, SPRING 1942.
U.S. OFFICE OF WAR INFORMATION, PHOTO BY ARTHUR SIEGEL; LIBRARY OF CONGRESS.

VICTORY GARDENING IN NEW YORK CITY, JUNE 1944. NOTE THAT THE WOMEN
ARE WEARING DRESSES, WHICH IS INDICATIVE OF THE RADICAL CHANGE
THAT THE ADOPTION OF PANTS IN FACTORY WORK WAS.
U.S. OFFICE OF WAR INFORMATION, PHOTO BY HOWARD HOLLEM; LIBRARY OF CONGRESS.

WOMEN PRESERVING GRAPEFRUIT JUICE IN A COMMUNAL CANNERY IN
HARLINGTON, TEXAS, FEBRUARY 1942.
U.S. DEPARTMENT OF AGRICULTURE, FARM SECURITY ADMINISTRATION, PHOTO BY
ARTHUR ROTHSTEIN; LIBRARY OF CONGRESS.

A COTTON PICKER IN ARKANSAS CROSSING A WAR EMERGENCY PIPELINE THAT DELIVERED EXTRA PETROLEUM FROM TEXAS TO ILLINOIS. THE HEAVY BAG SHE DRAGGED WAS FASTENED AROUND THE NECK TO FREE BOTH HANDS FOR PICKING.
U.S. OFFICE OF WAR INFORMATION, PHOTO BY JOHN VACHON; LIBRARY OF CONGRESS.

A WOMAN MARRIED TO A NAVY OFFICER DOES THE DAILY DIAPER WASHING IN HER CROWDED WASHINGTON APARTMENT, DECEMBER 1943.
U.S. OFFICE OF WAR INFORMATION, PHOTO BY ESTHER BUBLEY; LIBRARY OF CONGRESS.

A FRAME FROM A FILMSTRIP, "VICTORY IN AN EGGSHELL," MADE TO ENCOURAGE FARM PRODUCTION.
U.S. DEPARTMENT OF AGRICULTURE, FARM SECURITY ADMINISTRATION; LIBRARY OF CONGRESS.

A WORKER SOLICITING FUNDS FOR THE
AMERICAN RESCUE SOCIETY, JULY 1943.
U.S. OFFICE OF WAR INFORMATION, PHOTO BY
ESTHER BUBLEY; LIBRARY OF CONGRESS.

CIVILIAN AIRCRAFT SPOTTERS AT WORK
AT A WEST COAST POST. NOTE WHAT
APPEARS TO BE CAMOUFLAGE
PAINT ON THE BUILDING.
U.S. AIR FORCE PHOTO; FROM THE U.S.
NAVAL INSTITUTE PHOTO COLLECTION.

CIVIL AIR PATROL CADETS FIRING CARBINES IN RAPID CITY, SOUTH DAKOTA.
SMITHSONIAN INSTITUTION PHOTO NO. 36730AC.

THE VICTORY CLUB OF FLORIDA STATE
COLLEGE FOR WOMEN FORMS THE
POPULAR WARTIME SYMBOL FOR
VICTORY, TALLAHASSEE, FLORIDA, 1942.
FLORIDA STATE ARCHIVES.

BANDAGE ROLLERS IN A BROOKLYN
RED CROSS UNIT, JUNE 1944.
U.S. OFFICE OF WAR INFORMATION, PHOTO BY
HOWARD HOLLEM; LIBRARY OF CONGRESS.

RED CROSS VOLUNTEERS PACKING BOXES FOR PRISONERS OF WAR.
AMERICAN RED CROSS; LIBRARY OF CONGRESS.

A GREYHOUND GOODBYE IN
CHICAGO, SEPTEMBER 1943.
U.S. OFFICE OF WAR INFORMATION, PHOTO BY
ESTHER BUBLEY; LIBRARY OF CONGRESS.

CROWDED WARTIME WAITING IN
PENNSYLVANIA RAILROAD STATION,
NEW YORK CITY, AUGUST 1942.
U.S. OFFICE OF WAR INFORMATION, PHOTO BY
MARJORY COLLINS; LIBRARY OF CONGRESS.

BLACK WOMEN ENTERTAINING AIRMEN AT A SIOUX FALLS, SOUTH DAKOTA,
USO CLUB, APRIL 1944.
SMITHSONIAN INSTITUTION PHOTO NO. 36290AC.

A MILITARY WEDDING AT CAMP GRANT, ILLINOIS. THE BRIDE WAS IN THE
ARMY NURSE CORPS.
U.S. ARMY CENTER OF MILITARY HISTORY.

YOUNG PARENTS SEEKING CHILD CARE IN WASHINGTON, DECEMBER 1943.
"UNITED NATIONS" REFERRED TO THE ALLIED FORCES, FOR TODAY'S
INTERNATIONAL ORGANIZATION DID NOT YET EXIST.
U.S. OFFICE OF WAR INFORMATION, PHOTO BY ESTHER BUBLEY; LIBRARY OF CONGRESS.

A MOTHER READING A LETTER FROM ONE OF HER THREE SONS IN THE MILITARY. A BLUE STAR IN A WINDOW INDICATED A HOUSEHOLD MEMBER ON DUTY; A GOLD STAR REPRESENTED SOMEONE WHO HAD DIED IN ACTION.
LIBRARY OF CONGRESS.

THE BURIAL OF A MERCHANT MARINE IN BALTIMORE, JUNE 1943.
U.S. OFFICE OF WAR INFORMATION, PHOTO BY JACK DELANO; LIBRARY OF CONGRESS.

THE NETHERLANDS AMERICAN CEMETERY, ESTABLISHED IN NOVEMBER, 1944 NEAR MAASTRICHT, HOLLAND, MARKS THE BURIAL GROUNDS OF OVER 8,000 AMERICANS WHO WERE AMONG THE FIRST TO DIE IN THE ADVANCE ON GERMANY.
AUTHOR'S PERSONAL COLLECTION; DEESE STUDIOS, YBOR CITY, FLORIDA.

... She has had to depart from the American tradition of the husband-supported family which formerly gave her security. The wife of the man in uniform has had to fend for herself, make her own decisions ... The growing ability of women to find and assimilate new experience has, during the war years, been unhappily associated with material discomfort and emotional strain.[39]

When training was over and men moved overseas to do their jobs, then women were hit full force with the reality of separation. An experienced military wife warned that with the final farewell, "there are certain family provisions . . . that must be arranged now." Her "list of essentials" for a safe deposit box included, "Arrangements for allotment of pay; Power of attorney; Original and copy of last will . . . ; Original marriage certificate and one true copy, certified . . . ; Original birth certificates of wife and children and one certified copy . . ."[40]

Legal complexities certainly encouraged anxiety and doubtless, for some, denial. Although it might have been easier to evade such foreboding considerations, most waded into the military's regulatory maze to figure out the answers. Common questions were: "Does my husband have to take out Army life insurance?" (no, but he should since the premiums are small); "How long after a man is reported missing until the insurance payments start?" (a year, generally); "Will we lose our house if we can't keep up the payments?" (probably not, because of federal protections); "Can I be evicted if I can't pay the rent on our reduced income?" (maybe or maybe not, depending on the amount of rent); "Are the back taxes we owe suspended?" (a state matter, but the court will probably find in your favor); "Should my husband sign the house and furniture over to me?" ("It would save many complications in case of his death.") "Is it necessary for me to have the safe-deposit box in my name if I want to open it?" (An emphatic yes. The military has "had millions of furious requests from the wives of plain Joes who've locked up their little secrets and gone to war. And what can you do about it? Not a thing, lady, not a thing.")[41]

Apprehensions could not be allayed with certainty on anything, especially on where and when a soldier was going. Some left without any advance notice to their families at all, as indicated by this series of frantic notes from a woman to her husband, whom she believed to be in Miami:

If there isn't a letter or wire when I get home this afternoon I'll phone you ...
In case I can't reach you, though, before this does, wire me the instant you get it. I don't care if you're not supposed to talk, you can at least say "yes" or "no" ... I'd have to hock the furniture or car to get some cash, I suppose, and there might be delay on the plane reservations ...
Oh, where are you? The operator tried to get me a line for three hours this evening, and when she finally did reach the hotel all they could say was that you

hadn't left any forwarding address, that they were under the impression you . . .
were just moving on orders . . .

It's silly to be writing letters when I can't get you by phone or wire. But just
doing something helps . . .

Still no word from you . . . Thank heaven it's Saturday so I can stay near the
phone . . . I'm trying to keep it from getting too grim for the kids. They've been
watching me anxiously, and every hour or so they just come up and pat me . . .

It's still too unreal. I can't believe it. I keep walking around . . . saying, "What
was it I was going to do? Oh, yes get ready for Christmas" . . . I keep thinking
how terrible those last few minutes must have been for you . . . being ordered
directly to the point of embarkation—and knowing you wouldn't be allowed to
communicate . . . that it had to come so suddenly, without seeing you again, without
one last Christmas together, is the worst part.[42]

Once a man was gone, anxiety centered around the daily mail. Nothing could
be expected at first, and even after he was settled two and three months could
go by without a word—and then perhaps a dozen letters would arrive at once.
Delivering ships were torpedoed and planes were shot down, with precious
letters destroyed forever. Moreover, women usually were not told where a man
was going. "I don't even know where he is," said a typical bride, "except that
he sailed from an Atlantic port and the Army issued tropical clothing . . . It's
nearly two months since he left and I haven't had a word from him yet."[43]

Although the setting was different, once again a woman's chief problem
(especially for a young bride) became how to fill up the days; how to keep busy
enough to prevent paralyzing worry. Work was unanimously recommended as
a mental health preservative. According to "a new national club called War
Brides of America," the "best cure for loneliness is a full-time war job. Other
tips: go to the movies, cooking classes, church affairs, look up old girlfriends,
start hobbies."[44]

Leisure activities were essential, for even a full-time job could not wipe out
the lonely evenings and empty weekends. "If Sundays are bad," wrote one
experienced wife, "holidays are immeasurably worse . . . Watch out for them;
don't let them come upon you without plans . . . How desolate it is to . . . spend
Thanksgiving feasting on soup and crackers!"[45] Planning ahead was essential,
as was occupying one's mind. "One of the things you will discover," she
continued, "is how much you value the friendships of women . . . You are going
to find that intelligent women add as much vigor to an evening as intelligent
men. Often more, because you can talk more openly and freely and much more
honestly than you can with men."[46]

Women were told to visit the library; to develop systematic reading lists
(usually centered around their husbands' interests); or to take courses (usually
cooking or some other vocational activity). Though colleges saw their male
enrollments virtually wiped out and were desperate for students, it was almost
never suggested that women might fill these years with getting a college

education. Indeed, one of the few writers to specifically address the possibility came down largely against it, concluding: "Will she, four years hence, with a B.A., unconsciously begin to feel that she is superior? . . . A college education may be just the thing for her, or it may end by wrecking her marriage."[47]

A great deal was written on the question of where and how the temporarily single woman should live. Probably most would have agreed with the writer who said, "It is, on the whole, wiser to try and stay on in the same fashion you did before the war. Perhaps in a less spacious, cheaper house, but with intrinsically the same set-up, the same furniture, you as the mistress of the house." This was particularly so if children were involved, for in most families, "taking the children back to Grandma, even if you find you have to work, is only a limited solution."[48]

For many women, however, this better idea was a financially impossible one. With housing scarce, rents high, and husbandless incomes low, many young families had no choice except to give up their separate home and move in with the grandparents. *House Beautiful* assumed even its upper class audience would be facing this dilemma, advising young women on how best to face it:

> *Back in the room that was yours before you were married, you're brought up short by the startling realization that you are not the same person . . . You are not a guest and you are no longer an intrinsic part of the family.*
>
> *. . . You've been used to planning your own meals, entertaining when and whom you chose . . . and basking in the independence of a young married woman. But now you find yourself transplanted into another woman's domain.*
>
> *. . . Make a hard and fast rule to maintain your privacy and independence by converting your old bedroom into a bed-sitting-room . . . Be sure to hang up your clothes. Make a point of emptying ash trays at night . . . make your bed, and help with the dishes . . . Be sure to watch your share of the telephone bill . . . Don't mope![49]*

A reader in this situation responded with tips for keeping busy. During time off from her war plant job, she said: "I'm using those hours now to get . . . the things we hadn't had time for, or money either." She was monogramming towels for her postwar dreamhouse and needlepointing covers for future dining room chairs. "Saturday afternoons I spend in second-hand stores looking at china . . . I'm going to book sales, looking for good editions."[50]

Adding a sitting room to a bedroom was commonly suggested for easing the awkwardness of a two-family household. One who had done it reminded others:

> *Do not forget to use this privacy once you have contrived it. Sit there when you are home evenings. This obviates the necessity of compromise on radio programs, reading aloud, and so forth. And try eating a tray breakfast in your room . . . Contacts are avoided in the difficult just-waking part of the day when many people's tempers are short . . .*

277

If you are fortunate enough to have two bedrooms at your disposal . . . perhaps your bed and your child's crib will fit into one bedroom, and the other can house all your living room furniture. Then you will be able to entertain friends in your own quarters.

. . . It is necessary to get entirely out of the home situation frequently, regardless of how happy that home situation may be. If you have no children, the solution is obvious—get a job. But if you do have children, then evenings when they are asleep and the family is at home are your opportunity . . . Plan something special for weekends. The week has focus then . . .

Why not try doing something in the evening that pertains to your married future? My scheme was to work out plans for the home that we hope to have . . . I got books from the library . . . [and] sent him pictures of rooms . . . It may mean learning more about good books or history . . . If you can grow in this period of separation, you will have a great deal more to give as an individual.[51]

This woman lived with her husband's parents, but circumstances were probably even more difficult for those young women forced to return to their own parents' homes. Anxiety about husbands often turned into depression that could "sap energy and initiative,"[52] making it likely that both mother and daughter would revert to previous relationships that neither really wanted. Young women were warned not to regress into girls who expected mother to look after them.

This was particularly important if there were children involved. Young mothers should "remember it has been years since Mother's house has had to cater to infant care. Respect her neat kitchen."[53] Emotional problems were likely to cause deeper conflict than the practical, however, as new mothers felt their roles usurped and older ones felt their experience ignored. Most of the advice, however, was directed to the young:

You are likely to resent Mother's role as the heavy suggestion-maker in things pertaining to Baby.

Take it gracefully. She doesn't mean to be bossy. And remember that Dad and Mother aren't cold-storage octogenarians and it actually hasn't been eons since they safety-pinned you . . . Share Baby with them.

Don't make sister Sue feel that you expect her to assume responsibility for your darling. She'll love doing it if it isn't an obligation.

. . . Regardless of trivial upsets, never forget that the family is pulling with you and praying for that day when Johnny'll come marching home.[54]

Many women found that a better alternative to living with parents or parents-in-law was to live with each other. The empathy of two young women in the same unhappy situation could develop into a level of unspoken communication and deep understanding similar to that of husband and wife. Two young Navy wives, for example, were rewarded for their "weeks of pavement pounding" with "an attic apartment just completed in one of the oldest houses" near Great

Lakes Naval Station. It had "everything they had dreamed of within their Navy wives' budget. A typical steep attic stairway leads to a delightful four-room suite" with two bedrooms, a small kitchen, living room and bath. They felt that their "joint venture has proved women can live together very congenially and comfortably . . . Their duration home is the product of ingenuity, some skill at sewing, . . . cast-offs, and above all, an appreciation of friendship."[55]

It was an especially good solution for those with children, for their position as mother was unchallenged. Since affordable nurseries were uncommon and in-home care by a responsible person even more unlikely, it was a sound idea to "join up with some other young mother in similar circumstances. One of you can work while the other tends the home."[56] One with an infant son and a "mounting stack of bills" needed to work and yet did not like the idea that "someone else would feed Billy and sun him, would enjoy his smiles . . . while I came home in time to put him to bed." A swing-shift job was her solution, with her college roommate moving in and being available to the child while she worked. "As Sue and I figure it," she summarized, "we are two persons with three jobs. Our extra half-job apiece takes the place of the time we used to spend with our husbands and keeps us busy so we can't worry and brood."[57]

<hr/>

Brooding returned again and again to the mail. Problems that would be magnified with foreign complications were revealed already before a man left America, for the written word often gave more opportunity for misunderstanding than the spoken. Margaret Wilder's first letter to her husband, for example, showed how profoundly she missed him: "I came back from the station in the rain . . . It wasn't till I picked up the shirt you'd worn this morning that the feel of you was unbearable . . . That you, the best natured and most tolerant person in the world, should have to learn to hate and kill . . . still seems incredible to me . . ."[58]

Yet it wasn't long before she had to soothe his hurt feelings by explaining why letters were no longer rainy-day depressed:

No, my darling, we're not "having a gay time" . . . I just wanted you to think of us as busy and more and more self-sufficient so you wouldn't worry. Evidently I was wrong . . . I should have known you'd want to share the dull days and bad breaks with us too . . .

Sometimes I've felt like a magpie, sorting over the news till I found a shiny bead or two to send you. And I got so tired of being a magpie . . . Especially as I often felt like the droopiest of crows.[59]

The longer the separation, the more likely it was that women (ever cautioned not to worry soldiers nor to sound shrewish) went over their everyday lives for the "shiny beads," thereby creating a version of the civilian world that looked more and more heavenlike in his harsh reality. As time passed, each wrote "to a conception of the other which is unreal."[60] Men and women alike portrayed themselves differently in letters than they naturally were; each fantasized the other into images of patient sainthood or manly heroism.

It was hard to tell whether personalities had in fact changed, or whether unreality was simply the result of the only available mode of communication. "It's one of the few letters I've had from *you*," Margaret Wilder responded to one, "not from that somewhat frightening lieutenant who's been writing to us lately . . . I'd begun to think that most of the things we did and thought would bore him. That maybe he was really glad to be away . . ."[61]

Doubtless some men were rather bored by letters they received, especially from those other than wives and lovers. A mother who included in letters to her son "all the countless small ties" certainly intended to make him feel an on-going part of a family. Yet in his daily reality of death and danger, reports of "when we laid the linoleum, when the cat had her kittens, and the day the tractor got stuck" might well seem petty and parochial.[62]

On the other hand, it was possible that communication improved in cases in which people discovered they could say on paper things that they could not put into spoken words. "His letters carry a warmth he was never able to give me before," said one woman. "And, in return, I find myself writing things I never dreamed I could say . . . We are much more sympathetic to each other . . . more revealing."[63]

Regardless of the effectiveness of the communication, simply getting a letter in itself was tremendously important. To be lined up for mail call and receive nothing was public humiliation, a notification to a man's peers that no one cared about him. Men hung around post-office windows "as if they were handing out reprieves." Soldiers testified that letters were "the best hold the girls have on us. You want to be as nice as you can to them when you're out on leave so you can get them to write to you."[64]

While the judgments of others usually were not so painful in the civilian world, women too had their version of mail call. Nell Giles wrote of her coworkers:

If a girl doesn't hear from her man overseas for a long time, the whole factory knows about it. She is comforted by the other girls and is even offered their own letters to read, if that will help. One girl, who hadn't had a letter since March, suddenly got one the other day. The news spread like a war extra. The girl who told me about it didn't even know the "war widow's" name—she was just "the girl who hasn't heard since March."[65]

The government and other morale boosters reminded the public constantly how important letters were. Posters and other forms of publicity encouraged people to write not only to their most immediate loved ones, but also to the boy down the street or even strangers. Postage was kept a Depression-era bargain, and women were advised to keep stamps, as well as paper and envelopes, handy for quick notes.

In addition to caring that people wrote, the government also cared about what they wrote. The censors' rules were many:

> *Don't identify by name or location factories and facilities engaged in war work. In particular, don't describe new plants . . . Don't tell where a war factory is shipping its product . . . Don't describe new products.*
>
> *. . . Don't identify the country where your soldier is stationed . . . That's why you address mail for overseas delivery to an Army Post Office ("APO" number) in the United States . . . Keep the geography anonymous. Don't inquire about the Scottish landscape or the Egyptian climate. Don't identify the unit or branch of service of friends.*
>
> *. . . Don't write detailed reports of the weather over here . . . Last summer hundreds of letters in the overseas mail were held up while the censors deleted accounts of towns isolated and power plants put out of commission by a storm in the South.*
>
> *. . . Don't write letters in private codes, jargon, shorthand. Yes, it's all in fun. But the censor doesn't take chances.*
>
> *. . . Don't repeat rumors and "inside stories." . . . Don't be abusive about the government, the Army, or our allies.*[66]

Despite censorship delays and transport difficulties, tremendous amounts of mail got through, as the public obviously took to heart its obligation to correspond. A year before D-Day (long before the real action of the war) 20,000,000 pieces of mail, including newspapers, parcels, etc., were being received overseas each week, an average of 14 pieces of mail for each soldier. "Mail is so important to troops," *Time* reported, "that a shipment is included on every ship and available plane leaving the U.S."[67]

Some wives dropped as many as three notes a day to their husbands. Said one, "Right now we have to build our marriage on paper, so letters overflow . . ."[68] For the time being, sending her love in a letter was all a woman could do beyond hoping and praying and working for the end of the war.

SOURCE NOTES

1. "You Can Face It," *American Home* (January 1944): p. 4.
2. Gorham, *So Your Husband's Gone to War!*, p. 8.
3. "Heartsickness," *Time* (January 29, 1945): p. 65.
4. Ibid. See also Ann Maulsby, "War Wives: The Four Types," *New York Times Magazine* (April 22, 1945): p. 45.

5. Leslie B. Hohman, MD, "Don't Follow Your Husband to Camp," *Ladies Home Journal* (September 1943): p. 109.
6. Louise Paine Benjamin, "Orders For the Girls at Home," *Ladies Home Journal* (November 1944): p. 118.
7. Nancy MacLennon, "Gypsy Wives—Army Style," *New York Times Magazine* (December 27, 1942): p. 19.
8. "Whither Thou Goest," *Time* (August 30, 1943): p. 66.
9. Klaw, *Camp Follower*, p. 13.
10. "Whither Thou Goest," p. 66.
11. Ibid., p. 65.
12. Helen Huntington Smith, "G.I. Babies," *Collier's* (December 4, 1943): p. 11.
13. "Whither Thou Goest," p. 68.
14. Helen Huntington Smith, "Port of Navy Wives," *Collier's* (February 20, 1943): p. 74.
15. Ibid.
16. Clella Reeves Collins, *Navy Woman's Handbook* (New York: Whittlesey House, 1943): p. 158; see also Mary Ellen Green and Mark Murphy, "No Mamma's Girls," *Saturday Evening Post* (April 3, 1943): p. 20.
17. Elizabeth Gordon, "The Triumph of Little Things," *House Beautiful* (May 1943): pp. 100–1, and 104.
18. "Whither Thou Goest," p. 68.
19. Klaw, *Camp Follower*, p. 163.
20. Ibid., p. 67.
21. Edmund N. Bacon, "Wartime Housing," *Annals of the American Academy of Political and Social Science*, Vol. 229 (1943): p. 131.
22. Klaw, *Camp Follower*, p. 119.
23. Ibid., pp. 83–84.
24. Palmer, "Marriage and War," p. 111.
25. Klaw, *Camp Follower*, p. 37.
26. Ibid., p. 44.
27. Martha Stout, "War Wives," *Good Housekeeping* (October 1942): p. 49.
28. "Meet Three Army Air Corps Wives," *Ladies Home Journal* (April 1943): p. 126.
29. Ibid., p. 123.
30. Ibid., p. 126.
31. Ibid., p. 125.
32. Smith, "Port of Navy Wives," p. 75.
33. Helen B. Sweedy, "I'm Following You," *New York Times Magazine* (October 3, 1943): p. 32.
34. "Old Fashioned Neighborliness," *American Home* (September 1944): p. 4.
35. Ibid., p. 6.
36. Muriel Van Tuyl Trigg, "Twenty-Nine Palms," *Atlantic Monthly* (May 1945): p. 104.

37. "Services Relent," *Business Week* (February 5, 1944): p. 36.
38. Gallup, *The Gallup Poll*, p. 515.
39. Pearl Case Blough, "The Waiting Wife," *Survey Midmonthly* (January 1946): p. 7.
40. Clella Reeves Collins, *The Army Woman's Handbook* (New York: Whittlesey House, 1942): p. 9.
41. Nell Giles, "That Army-Navy Pay Check," *Ladies Home Journal* (March 1944): p. 4.
42. Wilder, *Since You Went Away*, pp. 169, 171, 173, and 175.
43. Paul Popenoe, "If You're a War Bride," *Ladies Home Journal* (September 1942): p. 24.
44. "Brides They Left Behind Them," *American Magazine* (February 1943): p. 108; see also "Soldier's Wife at Work," *Life* (September 7, 1942): p. 39.
45. Gorham, *So Your Husband's Gone to War!*, p. 64.
46. Ibid., p. 70. See also "Lonely Wife," *Life* (December 21, 1942): pp. 71–78, a photo summary of Gorham's book.
47. Popenoe, "If You're a War Bride," p. 70.
48. Gorham, *So Your Husband's Gone to War!*, p. 19.
49. Patricia Davidson Guinan, "Back Home to Mother," *House Beautiful* (August 1943): pp. 17–18, and 55.
50. Letters to the editor, *House Beautiful* (October 1943): p. 49.
51. Jeanette G. Imlay, "Double-Family Living," *Parents* (June 1944): pp. 107–8.
52. Ibid., p. 39.
53. Billie Maye Eschenburg, "While His Address is A.P.O.," *Better Homes & Gardens* (February 1944): p. 64.
54. Ibid.
55. "Attic Home for Two Navy Wives," *American Home* (October 1944): p. 54.
56. Gladys Denny Shultz, "If Daddy's Gone to War," *Better Homes & Gardens* (October 1943): p. 14.
57. Jane Lynott Carroll, "Raising a Baby on Shifts," *Parents* (October 1943): pp. 20 and 80; see also "Tripling Up," *Life* (December 13, 1943): p. 69.
58. Wilder, *Since You Went Away*, pp. 1–2.
59. Ibid., p. 60.
60. James H. Bossard, "The Hazards of War Marriage," *Science Digest* (July 1944): p. 2.
61. Wilder, *Since You Went Away*, p. 60.
62. Letter to the editor, *Parents* (October 1944): p. 77.
63. Gorham, *So Your Husband's Gone to War!*, p. 192.
64. Ibid., p. 194.

65. Giles, *Punch In, Susie!*, p. 114.
66. Jonathan Wake, "The Censor Reads Your Letters," *Good Housekeeping* (November 1942): p. 117; see also "How I Wonder Where You Are," *Woman's Home Companion* (September 1943): p. 19, which dealt with geographical censorship and guessing games.
67. "Mail Call," *Time* (June 7, 1943): p. 61.
68. Alexander Woollcott, "To Loving Young People Apart," *Reader's Digest* (December 1942): p. 2.

17

"THE WAR DEPARTMENT REGRETS . . ."

There were brides for whom war dominated life so completely that they had never seen their husbands in civilian clothes; as victory appeared and reunion neared, they wondered "what he will look like."[1] Even women who had known their men many years had to expect changed appearance. "Your husband is going to look younger, slimmer, more dashing than he has in years," women were told. While that might have been happily anticipated, the next thought was less cheering: "If you don't want to be taken for the dowdy elder sister, or even—heaven forbid—for his young-looking mother, you'll have to follow a regime to compensate for his."[2]

Couples quite naturally felt like strangers around each other at first—her new hair style and clothes, his stronger muscles and weather-worn face—all caused judgments and reappraisals. It was possible that they would feel again the excitement of their courting days and fall in love once more; it was also possible that the spouse would seem disappointing, particularly when compared with the fantasy each had likely created while separated.

A man especially brought a "fresh eye to bear upon his beloved, . . . an eye made even more critical by his new man-in-the-mass life, where women are appraised and approached via the once-over and yoo-hoo techniques." The more a man had passed up opportunities to consort with available females while gone, the more likely it was that he had fantasized about his wife being a dream goddess that she could not possibly be. One thoughtful writer cautioned:

> The piling up of erotic desire makes for a phantasy life of unrealistic proportions which cannot be matched by reality. The image of the beloved becomes a model of perfection . . . Reunion with the real person frequently brings a jolt.
> . . . Because of the impossibility of making those who have not shared their suffering really feel what they have been through, they are apt to consider everyone, including their own sweethearts and wives, shallow and sentimental.

... And many young wives, eager for a zestful life after a period of deprivation, may not really want to devote themselves to either physical or psychic nursing, and the result will be heartache and suffering on both sides.[4]

All men changed in personality and value systems, for even the "good" ones saw that moral codes were relative to time and place. All were exposed to drinking, gambling, cursing and illicit sex. Even if they did not condone such behavior, it was so common that they could not help but become inured. They would never again be so easily shocked as were those who spent their lives in communities where virtually everyone lived by the rules of the local Baptist church.

A man's attitudes were also apt to be complicated by the likelihood of unacknowledged ambivalence about his military experience. While most complained loudly, eagerly averring their distaste for Army life, in fact they had become more accustomed to it than they themselves knew. After the first homecoming, a man was apt to assess his civilian world and even his family as petty and parochial. "He may unconsciously miss the very things he has hated and longed to get away from," said one expert. "He may feel . . . that the buddies who fought with him have more reality than his own family."[5]

Often, and without being aware of it, he had become handicapped in dealing with others, for the military trained men in the psychological techniques of avoidance and denial. The seemingly inane scheduling of camp life was actually devised to fill in the corners of the mind, to prevent men from having time to dwell on why they were there and what might happen to them and the military's ultimate purpose of killing or being killed:

An arduous calendar of routine and special trainings sufficiently occupies a man's mind. Fatigue takes care of the night. The problem of military morale is largely a problem of leisure.

. . . Coldbloodedly, . . . the U.S.O. and field entertainment and recreation programs, all represent efforts to prevent men from being alone with their thoughts.[6]

These methods were essential for military ends, but the psychological mechanisms of avoidance and denial that were thereby drilled into a man's subconscious are almost always damaging in personal relationships. Meanwhile, their women had an experience that was in almost direct contrast, for women's lives were not rearranged to avoid their fearsome thoughts. Most women, instead of learning to deny problems, were forced to face them. They dealt with the solitude; they lived with the unknown and the continual anxiety that not knowing brings. A woman was—whether she liked it or not—responsible for her own life, while every action her husband took was directed by a commander above. It may be argued that many men did not learn true bravery nor develop the self-reliance that their wives did.

286

A wife's experience, however, was somehow invalid in the common public view. Far more frequent was commentary such as:

> He may see his comrades shot to pieces. His perspective has changed. His values are different . . . A great many servicemen have opportunities for personal development much greater than do their wives. Many of them are receiving considerable instruction, both technical and cultural. Some are made officers and placed in charge of other men . . . Travel, in war as in peace, is a great educator.
> Meanwhile, the wife remains at home on the Tennessee farm, in the Carolina mill town . . . Her mental horizon remains the same, changing only with the slower tempo of her home community.[7]

That she might have also traveled—and without the privileges and special arrangements made for him—was not considered. That she also may have had training and have worked in new fields under difficult conditions was not mentioned. If a woman earned a living for herself and her children, that too was not noteworthy, except possibly as a difficulty in a husband's readjustment if a wife considered herself independent. Attention focused almost exclusively on the veteran* and his readjustment problems.

One of those problems was that of his position as father. Many men had never met their children, and often the little ones whom they did know no longer knew them. Mothers, following both their natural inclinations and expert advice, had spoken continually of the wonderful person that Daddy was:

> She talked of things that Daddy would do for them and with them when he returned. Frequently she labeled a task "Daddy's job" . . . When Susan put her pennies in the piggy bank, Jinny told her about "Daddy's big bank" downtown . . . She built Bill up to Susan as the head of the house and a person of authority, as well as someone with whom they would have fun.[8]

It would not be surprising if Bill soon found that he could not live up to Susan's ideal of him as a superhero. Clashes were inevitable as fathers—though unaware of individual likes and dislikes, fears and joys—tried to quickly take control of youngsters' lives, often imposing the sort of discipline they had learned in the military. Children naturally ran to their mothers for protection; wives tried to explain; husbands and children misunderstood; tempers flared and tears flowed. This was not the way anyone wanted it to be, but it was the most likely scenario even when forethought was given to the reunion. In many families, women lacked the necessary psychological skills; in most families, men had given no thought whatever to potential problems.

---

* See Chapter Seven for comparison with the problems of female veterans.

Even if a husband continued to leave child supervision to his wife for a while, there was always the understandable awkwardness of a child meeting a stranger—and in this case, a stranger whom the child was supposed to love. A wise father waited for love to come naturally:

> *When he met Linda he longed for the touch of tiny arms about his neck and the quick rush of affection of which he had dreamed for the many months while in the Pacific. He was dismayed and heartbroken at first because he was treated as an outsider and a stranger. Linda was shy and offish.*
>
> *She thought men in uniform were called "daddy"—but this particular man meant no more than any other. Bud was upset emotionally, as what father would not have been? . . . But Bud waited, although he frequently had to hold tightly to himself, and in due course Linda began to show signs that she approved of him.*[9]

Readjustment to the world of civilian work held its difficulties also, for once again, military training was sometimes at odds with effectiveness in the real world. Men who had come to take seriously the Army attitude of doing nothing unless ordered found themselves failures at work, especially any work requiring initiative and a competitive spirit. Men who had lived in tents and foxholes, their "bodies hard from rigorous training," discovered "that the office chair galls them more than the lurching tank."[10] Many found themselves consumed with a restlessness they did not understand, experiencing great difficulty in concentrating on tasks that seemed ridiculously insignificant in comparison with their former work.

The nature of the work a veteran did mattered in other ways, too. Loud noises could trigger remembrance of bombs and artillery, and employers were told "unless you are sure he has overcome this dread, don't put him at riveting." But as the work could not be too loud, neither could it be too quiet: "This man needs to work with other men. Put off by himself, he may have too much time for brooding." Best of all was "a job that has a steady pace" rather than "one which has peaks of frenzied activity followed by dull spells."[11]

That was assuming, however, that the returned man could work at all. Even before the war was over, more than a half million disabled veterans were receiving pensions, "many of whom have wives and families they may be unable to support unaided, or may not be able to support at all."[12] Disability payments, of course, were paid directly to the veteran and were based on the percentage of disability—unlike dependency allotments or widows' pensions, which were based on the number of persons financially dependent on a soldier. The mathematics of the matter indicated the lowly status of women in officialdom's view, for total disability paid $115 a month, which was more than twice as much as the $50 paid to a widow or dependent wife.*

Although the mathematics of the situation dictated that a wife would have to work to support the family, in fact the usual premise was that she would instead become a full-time nurse to her wounded husband. She was assumed to have tremendously deep love for her man, and great reserves of empathy, which she would need to cope with the profound change in her life that his injury meant:

> The first question that occurs to the soldier who has been badly hurt and somehow saved, will be to ask himself how his wife or his sweetheart will take it, if she can still love him. And his concern over her opinion of his appearance may far outweigh any feeling he has for himself. He will want more to be reassured, by her eyes and her hands and her lips than by all the doctors and nurses in the world, that she does not care, that to her he is as lovable as he was.
>
> . . . [You are] dealing with the fragile stuff of human character; heartbreak and bitterness and hopelessness and sometimes a desire for suicide.
>
> . . . The healing of his mind and heart will take weeks and months and years . . . those who have facial wounds have it hardest . . . For it is . . . connected with the basic desire in all of us to be attractive to the opposite sex . . . Since the wounded have been defeated on the physical level, it is on the physical level, and on that alone, that they can be wholly reassured . . . There is still the deep hunger in them—the now exaggerated hunger—for the reassurance that finally counts most with them.[13]

Women were warned that disfigured men would not want to see anyone; that children, with their unintentional ruthlessness, would be hardest of all to handle; that after one look in the mirror a man seemingly on the mend might descend again into days of despair. The permanently injured "will not ever be able to be carefree . . . All their anxieties and fears, felt only partially before, will become greatly exaggerated."[14] Those less seriously injured needed aid and understanding in convalescence, especially a watchful wife who, with marvelous diplomatic skill, would not let visitors overtax him or allow him to overestimate his strength and plunge himself into relapse. Once again, wives were asked to have the wisdom of Solomon and the patience of Job for the task assigned:

> Be gentle with the wounded man you love, then. But not too gentle. Demand of him all that he has the strength to do and to give. Start him in on little things . . .

---

* A widow with children was paid a maximum of $100 a month, no matter how large her family; the wife of a serviceman on active duty received a maximum of $120. If it is assumed that the $115 paid to the totally disabled veteran was in replacement for the food, clothing and shelter the military had given him free of charge, then it becomes clear that in this mathematical scheme there is no choice except for the veteran's wife to support herself and the children alone.

and lead him on to bigger and bigger adventures until he is used to his new self
... Only those with the vision of love can force him to help himself when it would
have been so much easier to help him.[15]

Yet coping with these physical problems was simple compared with those faced by the woman whose man's injuries were not visible, whose wounds were of the soul rather than the body. In an era when those with mental problems were often termed "crazy" and dismissed, much of the public lacked basic understanding and willingness to empathize with the psychological casualty. Doctors began family education by explaining that if a man was discharged by the Army as neurotic-psychotic, or NP, it "does NOT mean crazy; it doesn't even mean queer or odd."

It does not mean that the man is a coward or that he has not made an effort. And since it is not insanity, it is neither inherited nor passed along to children except by example and environment. Neither does it mean unintelligent or stupid.

If a man is mentally too ill to fit into civilian life he will not be discharged. Therefore, the N.P. who comes home is not dangerous . . . He is an invalid, recovering from strain . . .

In war . . . the pace is so swift and so strange that it leaves him no time to adjust, and when he reaches the limit of his endurance, his mind and emotions become ill. They refuse to allow him to function further.[16]

It could hit a man anywhere. His ears could hear bombardment that was not there; his legs could become paralyzed and refuse to carry him into further danger; his stomach could end his misery by no longer nourishing him. That was what happened to one man who could not "eat a mouthful" for 15 days after crawling out of combat "all dead and numb" in the abdomen. "Distressingly skinny" a year later, "his appetite still ranged from absent to finicky." When he mentioned an interest in Brussels sprouts, his wife "tramped all over town till she found them—at seventy-five cents per quart . . . only to see him push his plate away and go into the living room supperless."[17]

A young woman who had looked forward to the fun of going out again when her husband returned found that instead she had to shield him from social contact. The war and his comrades still in battle "prey on Ed's mind," she said. "Some nights he can't eat a mouthful. I try to keep him cheerful and never mention the war. Then some stupid friend has to ask him how many Germans he killed!"[18] She turned off the radio news not only to protect his fragility, but also to preserve herself, for her twin had been recently killed in Germany and two more brothers remained overseas. Her young life, so unfairly anxious and sad, demanded tremendous skill to keep up the prescribed cheerfulness.

Women like her received little help with their terrible problems. This was not an area in which the media trumpeted advice, for the topic was so depressing that it was easier to avoid it. Nor were women likely to get assistance from the medical establishment; instead they were forewarned that "there is neither time nor personnel available to give each man the psychiatric help he needs . . . Also, there are wide areas of our country in which no psychiatric clinics are available and in which psychiatry itself is regarded with fear and suspicion." This article that told women to be ever cheerful around their men ended with the demoralizing forecast that "in spite of whatever good we can accomplish we have to face the fact that some—perhaps many—psychoneurotic casualties won't be reclaimed. Many need continued psychiatric help, which they won't get . . . They may turn to alcohol or drugs . . . They may be unfit for any sort of work."[19]

But at least he was home. At least her dreams had not ended with the nightmare of a telegram from the War Department regretting that he would never come home. Never before in our national history had "such large numbers of women found themselves faced with the identical problems of enduring the illness of grief, making homes without men, supporting themselves and their children," sympathized one writer. "Some have become widows before they were really wives."[20]

It was true for a young Air Corps widow whose marriage had been an extended honeymoon of hotel life until she became pregnant. As soon as her husband knew a baby was on the way, "he made out a will, took out more insurance. We rented an apartment and started to furnish it. We lived in it just two weeks."[21]

Many war widows like her would be profoundly grateful that they had ignored the expert advice and followed their husbands' military trail—or they would have had no memories to treasure at all, but only bitterness and regret. Though married four years, another widow who never enjoyed a real home was terribly grateful for the temporary ones, saying amid her grief, "We had so much. Much more than some people get in all their lives." As newlyweds, they lived with her family while awaiting his call to duty, during which time a son was born. Then "Dee began to move."

First Tennessee. Then Santa Ana, then Tucson. . . . Then Lemoore, California; Stockton, California; and Albuquerque. Dianne was born there. Bill was able to be with Dee there until a month before Dianne arrived. He went to El Paso then . . . Although Dee had a pretty bad time with Dianne—four transfusions—she insisted on getting down to Bill. Her mother drove . . .

Those last two months . . . she'd wake up at night and listen to Bill breathe, telling herself that he was alive—he was so alive that he could never die . . . Well, he did die, at not quite twenty-four.

Now there are just the children . . . And all the other things. The house they were going to build . . . Bill would get his job back . . . and go to law school at night . . . Both the children were to go to the University of Illinois . . .[22]

Death was no easier for those with long-established marriages, or even for career military wives who had lived with the low-level fear all of their lives. A colonel's wife whose husband was part of the D-Day invasion of France explained:

This is the way the news came to me. It was on a hot July day in Washington . . . Nan and I had just returned from the market. The boys were playing in the yard . . .

I heard the screen door slam as Robin clattered in and shouted, "Mail's here, Mother!"

"Letter from Daddy?" Nan called . . .

"No." Robin ruffled through the letters with his grubby small-boy hands. "Who's this APO from, Mom—Uncle Bill?"

I took the letter from him and recognized Bill's handwriting . . .

"Dear Carol," I began, "I hasten to write this before you receive an official communication . . ." The words froze on my lips . . .

"He was on a mission when his party drew enemy fire . . . We have made several searches on the spot . . . He hasn't been found. We all believe he was taken prisoner and not killed, for if he were dead the Germans would not have carried off his body . . ." [23]

After two weeks of fear and hope and anxiety, she got a telegram. The letter that followed explained it had taken some time to "clean out the German resistance" in the area sufficiently to conduct a proper search, but her husband's body was found "in the high grass along the river." He had been shot through the head. "His death was instantaneous," she was assured. "Wednesday evening, July 5, at 9:00 PM, your husband was buried in the VII Corps Cemetery No. 2, southwest of Ste. Mere Eglise . . ."

"I think of the morning we said good-bye," she went on, recalling the details of breakfast and last minute packing, the minutiae of life that canceled out the larger question: "How can you let him go—how can you? I will tell you. It is because you know that what happens in war to other men—to the husbands and lovers and sons of other women—can never happen to him." [24]

But of course it can and it does. A career officer's wife was likely to have absorbed the same attitudes of denial that made it possible for her husband to do his work, but the for-the-duration military wife was less protected by this shield of pretense. Beyond that, of course, the front-line troops were in fact far more likely to die than their commanders to the rear. But if she was not to become bitter, both the private's wife and the general's could have her grief assuaged only by believing that his death was meaningful.

World War II, with its unanimity, clear justice, and inescapable need—which became even more real after Nazism's horrifying truth was revealed at the end—made this belief genuine. Widows might, however, see the significance in somewhat different ways. For the professional military man's wife, there was the comfort of pride in her husband's organization and the support of comrades who understood. Such women might rear their sons to replicate the values that killed their fathers, as this little Robin was introduced as a potential West Pointer at ceremonies honoring his father. "Duration" widows would be more likely to believe that while this war was sadly inevitable, all war and warring institutions were essentially wrong. They would agree with the camp-following young mother: "If Billy is going to grow up to face the same situation that took Bill . . . then there will be nothing left . . . to believe in."[25]

The military did what it could to encourage this essential belief that the cause was meaningful. While wives of high-ranking officers understandably got more personal attention from their husbands' friends, the military had developed procedures intended, within the limits of war resources, to reach out to widows. Occasionally, personal notification for deaths "in action" was made by Red Cross or military officials, but the prevailing practice was notification from the War Department in Washington by a brief telegram with "Letter Follows." Telegraph messengers and, in rural areas, mail carriers who delivered telegrams sometimes exercised personal judgment to ease the pain they knew their message would bring.

The letter that followed was usually written by a man's commanding officer; with dubious frequency such letters assured families that their loved one died quickly and painlessly. Probably the greatest comfort was any word that might be possible from an eyewitness, and a letter from a known buddy was far more cherished than any official communication could be. The Red Cross made itself helpful in garnering as much follow-up information as feasible, for families almost always wanted to know every detail they could about the circumstances of the death. An officer returned personal possessions if they were accessible, and the flag used to cover the soldier's casket at burial was sent home. To the extent that combat made it possible, bodies were returned for burial at home. Obviously, the military did not encourage this use of precious shipping resources, and in many cases, especially in the Navy and Air Corps, recovering the body was impossible.

Never having her husband come home in any form, however, made the process of grief much harder for a widow; the lack of a burial for some meant that the death was a chapter never closed. In 1977, a woman wrote to Ann Landers about her experience with this delayed mourning. Her husband had been declared missing in France on June 10, 1944; in January 1945 he was declared dead, but she refused to believe it. He was buried in France and a flag sent home to her, but she continued to see news items that gave her false hope. Finally, two decades later she took her son to France to find the grave. "When the kindly custodian asked us whose grave we had come to see my throat closed," she wrote. "I couldn't speak or eat for 48 hours. I grieved as if my husband had just died . . . I realize I suffered all that agony because I had never witnessed the final farewell. I should have requested that my husband's remains be sent home . . ."[26]

If death was difficult for adults to resolve, how much harder it was for children who did not fully understand either the concept of death or that of Daddy. Little Billy, the Air Corps widow's son, kept inquiring, "Daddy?" when planes flew over, breaking his mother's heart anew each time. He was simply too young to understand, but other, older children had the tragic news kept from them by mothers who apparently could not bring themselves to say the needed words. One mother of two who "thought it best not to tell them anything at all" allowed her boy to develop a morass of confusion:

> *For weeks after we had received the War Department's message Jimmy kept posting his letters in our front porch mailbox and almost every day he would ask Mr. Kaufman, our mailman, when he was going to bring us a letter.*
>
> *When V-E Day came, Jimmy wanted to know, "Isn't Daddy coming home now?" I told him his daddy had been hurt and had gone to heaven. Not long afterward I was telling a friend how Shel had been killed at Aachen by German artillery fire. I didn't know Jimmy was standing behind my chair . . .*
>
> *"Now that Daddy's in heaven," he said defiantly, "the Germans can't kill him."*[27]

To the extent that this difficult topic was addressed at all, the advice was as it had been when dealing with war in general—to tell youngsters the truth. "Death is a fact to be faced, and children can be helped to face it," wrote one child specialist. "We should not try to keep the knowledge from them . . . Remember that a child may feel hurt and resentful when there is secrecy about death and he feels shut out." It was important to help them to sort out their feelings, being aware that a child's first reaction was likely to be that "father, whom he dearly loves, cares so little for him that he has gone away."[28] Often children found a way to blame themselves; sometimes they felt unloved when mother was obviously engulfed by her own grief. A child might focus on a neighbor or friend and try to make that person into a substitute father; grief could easily be concealed in psychosomatic illness or regression into babyish behavior.

A mother simply had to pull herself out of her own mourning to deal with all this. Moreover, soon she had to face the trial of how her family was to live. Most discovered, as had a long line of earlier widows, that despite all the expressions of sympathy, ultimately one could depend only on herself. Death was not a subject that others wanted to dwell on, nor was widowhood an area in which advice was handed out as it had been in other areas of her life. "A generation whose psychologists have spent so much time on the problem of how to make marriage last," said one thoughtful observer, "has only barren cliches for its ending."

> *It has kept "widow" one of the pathos words of its language . . . The law still speaks of "relicts," the leftovers of marriage. Yet the woman widowed is the same*

person she was before, with the same needs for a place to live, a way of living, for companionship and sexual fulfillment.[29]

The latter was a need some men were willing to meet long before the widow was even beginning to think again about the possibility. "The wolf angle is one with which every personable widow I know, with *no* exceptions, has to contend," wrote one. "Always the tune is the same: You must miss your husband and here am I, the hero, willing to make up for that loss."[30]

Although certain men paid them too much attention, many widows soon discovered that too little attention was paid by other women, as even lifelong friends now placed them in a different caste. Invitations that had been routine for years were no longer issued, and in social as well as business situations many a woman discovered to her shock that earlier status she thought belonged to her was actually dependent on her husband. Wives who at first offered their husbands' services for household needs soon made clear their insincerity, and former male friends hesitated to be seen with her. After the initial shock of death was over, widowhood even became the subject of nervous jocularity:

"Hold your husbands, girls, here comes the merry widow." I laughed too at this sally a few years ago . . . But now—a widow myself—I know . . . the disapproval associated with the word "widow"—in jest or in reality—is virtually a form of persecution.

. . . Whether we like it or not our role in life is fixed—we are predatory females on the prowl for a second husband. We cannot talk to a man without learning (friends will tell us) that we have a new boyfriend.

. . . Full of these new experiences, I asked other widows I know why they had never mentioned them. One plain-looking woman remarked succinctly, "And if we did, as a married woman what would your reaction have been?"

And then I understood why widows don't talk much about this phase of their lives. I certainly would not have believed her. I would have thought she was an extreme egotist or that sorrow had caused her imagination to run wild.[31]

Besides overcoming this social/sexual hurdle, the other great obstacle society threw before widows was financial. "I have never known a widow—and I include my mother, sister, and myself," said one, "who has not been tested to find out whether she's going to stand on her own feet in a business deal or let people push her around."[32] Even if no one attempted to take advantage of her vulnerability, however, a widow's monetary state was almost by definition assumed to be a dire one. This was even true for the career military man's wife, a woman who by all the chivalric codes should have been most secure:

The "officer's lady" has many privileges, much respect, and a world of protection during her husband's lifetime . . . This protection, sweet as it is, becomes a handicap when she is forced to take up the management of her own affairs.

... If taps is blown for her husband ... one becomes a civilian overnight ...
A new set of rules is needed, and the protection of as much income as can be got
together during that charmed period of married life ...
   The pension is all that you, as a widow, can expect from the government as
regular income. It is inadequate in most cases ...[33]

The pension—no matter what the husband's rank or years of service or the family's need—was "$50 for a widow, $65 if she has one child, and $13 for each additional child up to a maximum of $100." Even government economists agreed that it was woefully meager: "According to standard budgets, a woman living alone needed [annually] for adequate living expenditures, excluding taxes ... at least $1,370, ... compared to the $600 provided by the pension."[34]

By June 1945 (before the war was over), more than 50,000 widows had completed the paperwork and were collecting "death benefits." Many of them also received the life insurance that was issued at low cost by the government to soldiers, but even if a husband took out the maximum amount, the monthly payment would be $55.10 and still insufficient to meet standard budget estimates of family expenses.

Nor was it possible to collect this life insurance in a lump sum. Though government officials were surely mindful of the principal saved and the interest earned by the Treasury rather than by the widow, this arrangement was presented as protective paternalism: "Knowing that few women have ever had the disposal of four digit sums, the government ... doles out the money, month by month, for 20 years to women under 35, for 10 years to those beyond that age."[35]

A lump-sum insurance payment might have been used to give a renting widow the financial advantages of home ownership, but that was not to be. It could have enabled her to buy a business, for the "middle-aged woman must, of course, recognize that ... her employability will decrease with the years."[36] But that sort of independence for a widow also was not envisioned. Instead, the general assumption was that her financial dilemma would be solved through remarriage.

The younger she was, the greater the statistical probability of remarriage. At age 25, a widow had an 80% chance of marrying again; five years later, at age 30, chances dropped to 60%; after that, marriage became increasingly less likely.[37]* No actuarial or financial mathematics meant much, however, to widows dealing with the personal question of whether or not to remarry.

More important factors were the feelings of her children and herself and (a special consideration) those of her parents-in-law whose son had died. It was a terribly difficult thing for parents-in-law to face, for understandably they might

---

* Divorcees married at a somewhat higher rate (94%) and never-married women at a much lower rate. The never-married woman at age 25 had only a 48% chance of ever marrying—something that has changed significantly today.

hate to see their son replaced as a father figure to their grandchildren. Occasionally, parents-in-law made financial help for grandchildren dependent on mothers remaining single, but most were more understanding. Very often a widow concluded that remarriage, if offered by an acceptable man, was a beneficial thing for all the family, and especially for children who needed a father.

Sometimes a widow saw that she herself needed a relationship with a man again if her mental health was to be fully restored. A Denver mother of two, who dropped to 92 pounds after her mother died within months of her husband's death in combat, recognized that she had become "crabby and irritable" until her brothers insisted that she start going out. "Now, a year and a half after his death," she said, "I don't believe I can ever stop loving [him] . . . But . . . I am beginning to feel alive again. I don't want to spend the rest of my life alone. I want to love and be loved again."[38]

It was a 20th century, democratic assumption that life should go on and that a widow should live according to her individual choice. Cultures throughout the ages had different assumptions, with many holding a fundamental belief that a woman's life effectively ended when her husband's did. Even Civil War America, less than a century earlier, expected that a woman would wear her widow's weeds of black for years. Grief was formal, defining rigid roles for the mourner's life, and the rules were stricter for women than for mourning men. Much had changed in the 80 years since America's terrible internal bloodletting, and the status of widows was an excellent index to the status of women generally. On that front, all the news was good.

Over 125,000 American men were taken as prisoners of war. At the beginning of 1946, 44,000 others were still officially "missing in action." Since many death notices were preceded by missing notices, hundreds of thousands of women— lovers, wives, mothers—lived in a state of indefinite suspension during the war, not knowing what had happened to the one they loved.

Notification of a man's POW or missing status* was for many even more difficult than a death notice, for it would be followed by potentially years of anxiety—of terrifying dread alternating with timid hope, of sleepless nights and nightmarish days. One expert observed that even though many bereaved people experienced denial when notified of a death, "refusal to accept the actual as real does not represent a preference for uncertainty."[39] Nothing seemed as bad as not knowing.

And yet there was ambivalence, because uncertainty did allow for hope. Naturally families were inclined to exaggerate that hope, to cling to any straw.

---

* "MIA" was not in common usage during World War II.

Official procedure encouraged this sad stress when missing notification preceded death notification by weeks, even when the military had every reason to believe that survival was impossible. Families convinced themselves that loved ones were "prisoners of war even when the servicemen are casualties at sea. They will explain in very plausible detail that the man might be stranded on an island . . ."[40] They held firm to the belief that he had been confused with another man in his unit who had the same name; they saw newspaper pictures they were positive showed the lost loved one. Sometimes, in their blind devotion and terrified hope, they "make this identification from a picture showing only a serviceman's back."[41] A Red Cross worker added:

> When a boy has been reported missing in action, the conflict between hope and fear produces an almost unendurable tension which frequently finds expression in ceaseless effort to secure more information about him. The shock from the news that he is considered dead at least brings a certain kind of relief from the uncertainty of not knowing. A happier kind of relief comes with the notification that a son or husband is a prisoner of war . . . [But this] brings other worries about nutrition, disease and possible abuse.[42]

Women who lived through months and years of uncertainty found comfort in believing that their enforced state of ignorance was helpful to the military, and therefore to their loved ones. The military kept secret the torpedoing of ships and the annihilation of aircraft, for it did no good to tell the enemy which of its methods was successful. Often the news of a sinking ship, with hundreds of lives lost, was not acknowledged until months after the men had gone to their watery graves. A woman did not know if the cessation of letters from her man meant simple delivery difficulty or if in fact she had become a widow.

In one of the most famous cases in the war, there were seven months of worry between the missing notification and the death notification for Iowa's Sullivan family, who had five young men aboard the USS *Juneau*. It was even longer since their first inkling that something was wrong, for informal news sometimes spread faster than the official. Mrs. Sullivan wrote:

> The way the news first came to me was through a neighbor who had received a letter from her son in the Navy saying, "Isn't it too bad about the Sullivan boys? I heard that their ship was sunk."
>
> . . . About a week after . . . someone knocked at our door at 7 o'clock in the morning . . . We all went down in our bathrobes . . . I think we all had a premonition of what the news was going to be . . .
>
> Genevieve turned white and Katherine Mary looked as if she were going to collapse. I could hardly hold back the tears, but I wouldn't let myself cry in front of the three men . . . I particularly wanted to comfort [daughter-in-law] Katherine Mary. It was terribly hard on her, with [baby] Jimmy.

. . . In my first blind grief, it seemed as if almost everything I had lived for was gone. I couldn't eat or sleep . . . I did find comfort in one thing they told me. I learned that everything had happened so fast that the boys must have died quickly and easily, without anguish or pain.[43]

The Navy, which normally did not assign family members to the same ship but which had acceded to the Sullivan's request, used this tragedy in a way that some felt was both exploitative of that family and offensive to others. The Navy persuaded them to tour defense plants talking of their loss and of the need for war production. The visits did have good effect on productivity statistics, and, on a more significant level for women, the conservative, modest Mrs. Sullivan became one of many who advocated employment as necessary to mental health. "I met some mothers," Mrs. Sullivan wrote, "who . . . were doing something to carry on the work their sons had begun." She observed that those who were able to sublimate their pain into a war job "were in much better spirits than those who grieved and worked alone." For women with no option but continued housework, she believed, "your grief remains very sharp, for there is nothing else for you to think about."[44]

Though the Navy clearly thought their production campaign worthwhile, there was speculation that the publicity given to this family was damaging to the morale of others. "We do not know," wrote one sociologist, "whether such exceptional attentions help or embitter other mothers, who have lost, for example, an only son, or only three sons; or wives whose men die as Merchant Marines."[45]* Grief was not a subject easily quantified by sociologists, and mourning was not a popular topic for sponsored research. Women faced this trial largely alone, with few expressing any concern as to what comforted or what made tragedy only more barbed and embittering.

Mothers were the women most likely to feel alone and ignored. Of the little written about combat death, most was aimed at widows. Yet, devastating as their lot was, mothers faced much greater odds of loss. Not only did almost every widow have a mother-in-law who had lost a son, but also, because of the military's predilection for single men, mothers as a group were four times more likely to be bereaved than wives were.

Widows were the more romantic subject and the more hopeful one, since the bottom line for them could be that life would go on. For mothers, however, life was closer to over. Age discrimination being the actuality it was, advice on how to get a job and rebuild one's life was largely meaningless. Most painful of all

---

* Merchant Marines, though they were not militarized, did some of the most dangerous and important work of the war in getting supply ships through enemy lines. Because no public relations officers looked out for them, their heroic deaths went unnoticed, and their families did not receive the comfort of medals, ceremonial funerals and other consolations offered by the military.

to a mother—a hurt she could not acknowledge, lest she be termed bitter and selfish—probably was the fact that she had invested twenty years or more of her life in loving this young man and bringing him to adulthood, while the widow may have known him for mere months. The aching pain of a bereaved mother of an only child could not be concealed when she wrote of her reluctance to bring her grandchildren to live nearby: "I made so many plans for him and lived through him so much that I haven't the heart to take it up again, even where the boys are concerned."[46]

For the widow, this sad time of her youth would become an aberration fading into dim memory—but for the mother, the future held no similar promise. The years she spent with her child could become the highpoint of her life, the treasured memories her sole comfort.

Her memories ranged from infancy to adolescence. During this latter time, many mothers faced years of turmoil over the possibility of their sons' being drafted, another subject on which there was virtually no public discussion or aid offered. Many a woman would understand from the mid-1930s on that she might well be raising her son as a lamb for the slaughter. She might secretly hope for physical defects that would keep him safe; she might well rage against teenage bravado hurrying him into a manhood that could be cut down before it truly was.

Ultimately, there was little that a mother could do except to swallow any personal objections and aver, as her son doubtless did, the public pride in his uniform and her Blue Star. She might well enlist in one of several organizations of mothers. Most notable were Blue Star Mothers of America, MOMS (Mothers of Men in Service), Navy Mothers of World War II, and the unique American WAC Mothers. While most of these women acted as support for each other, some well-located, well-organized groups emulated the USO and ran clubhouses for service members. The Navy Mothers Club of Chicago had five hundred boys each week "stop in for dinner . . . or just talk to mothers." Said one sailor of them, "There are plenty of spots in this town were you can go to the movies, get a drink or dance with a girl, but this is the only place where you can forget the war and pretend you're home with your mother. And believe me, it's sure swell."[47]*

---

* There were a half-dozen right-wing organizations that used the word "mother" to attract support for their anti-Semitic, anti-British, anti-Russian, and anti-Roosevelt views. They were centered primarily in the midwest, where isolationism had a long history. Most were formed prior to Pearl Harbor by women genuinely opposed to a peacetime draft, and they lost membership once the United States entered the war.

Their leadership seemed made up of sick women with ties to outstanding male bigots such as Father Coughlin and Gerald L.K. Smith. The astonishingly insensitive president of the Mothers of Sons forum, for instance, exhibited "with pride a letter which the group had mailed to all the parents of American boys who died when the destroyer *Reuben James* was sunk . . . advocating that the President and the Secretary of the Navy be sued as private citizens for the lives lost . . . I don't need to stress," concluded the reporter, "the effect such a letter would have on the mother of a son who had died for his country."

As mothers were more likely than wives to be bereaved, so also were mothers more likely to be called on to assume the care of men who came back blinded or crippled or mentally doomed. Though this burden would become harder to bear as age caused a woman to need care herself, doubtless many mothers felt their lives made new because they were needed. This was particularly true when a mother's love proved more powerful than professional care, as *Time* was pleased to report of a Texas woman:

> *Army doctors fought to save what the Japanese had left of Jim Newman—one of the saddest cases they had seen of starvation, beri beri, tuberculosis. Other survivors of the prison camps gained weight and strength; Jim Newman did not.*
> *A fortnight ago the doctors gave up, flew him home to Fort Worth. He would die, they said, in a day or so. But this week Corporal Newman still lived, . . . thumbed his nose at death, and took . . . some more of his mother's biscuits.*[48]

But there were hundreds of thousands of mothers who had no opportunity to bake powerful biscuits, for their sons never came home. These women lived out their lives with the Gold Star of his memory shining from their front doors, carefully filling up their days with enough detail to numb, and weeping their quiet tears alone decades after everyone else had forgotten. On Memorial Day of 1989—almost a half-century after the war—Erma Bombeck wrote of visiting a Gold Star Mothers meeting in Arizona "a couple of years ago":

> *As the white-haired warriors, most of them approaching 90 years of age, stood at attention, their hands over their hearts, their eyes on the flag, reciting the Pledge of Allegiance, I felt I was seeing the last bit of unashamed patriotism . . .*
> *A few days ago, I called . . . and asked if the Gold Star Mothers were going to meet this Memorial Day.*
> *"Oh no, dear, we're not meeting anymore. We're all so old and we can't drive. It doesn't mean there's a day goes by that our sons aren't on our minds . . ."*[49]

SOURCE NOTES

1. Ray E. Baber, "Marriage and the Family After the War," *Annals of the American Academy of Political and Social Science*, Vol. 229 (1943): p. 167.
2. Gorham, *So Your Husband's Gone to War!* p. 146.
3. Ibid.
4. Taylor, "Shall They Marry?" p. 218.
5. George D. Stoddard and Toni Taylor, "A Father Comes Home," *McCall's* (March 1945): p. 92.

6. Thomas D. Eliot, ". . . of the Shadow of Death," *Annals of the American Academy of Political and Social Science*, Vol. 229 (1943): p. 97.

7. Bossard, "Hazards of War Marriage," p. 3. See also Leslie B. Hohman, "Married Strangers," *Ladies Home Journal* (October 1944): p. 61, for another example of male authors considering the experience of women invalids. Though the article features the readjustment of a Navy couple where the wife "had lived through months in a Japanese concentration camps, had borne her child in a Jap-controlled hospital, and then had to nurse the little redheaded daughter through a devastating attack of diphtheria," he goes on to focus almost exclusively on the man.

8. Stoddard and Taylor, "Father Comes Home," p. 92.

9. Hohman: "Married Strangers," p. 62.

10. Baber, "Marriage and the Family," p. 173.

11. Toni Taylor, "If Your Man Is an NP," *McCall's* (July 1944) : p. 80.

12. "Effect of War Casualties on Economic Responsibilities of Women," *Monthly Labor Review* (February 1946): p. 181. Figures were as of June 1945.

13. Betsey Barton, "Those Who Did Not Die," *McCall's* (January 1945): p. 17.

14. Ibid., p. 118.

15. Ibid.

16. Taylor, "If Your Man Is an NP," p. 14.

17. J.C. Furnas, "Meet Ed Savickas, a Victim of Combat Fatigue," *Ladies Home Journal* (February 1945): p. 141.

18. Ibid., p. 142.

19. Taylor, "If Your Man Is an NP," p. 80.

20. Zelda Popkin, "A Widow's Way," *McCall's* (November 1945): p. 60.

21. Gladys Denny Schultz, "Cited for Courage," *Better Homes & Gardens* (May 1944): p. 44.

22. Elizabeth Janeway, "Meet a War Widow," *Ladies Home Journal* (January 1945): p. 97 and 120.

23. "Next of Kin," *Atlantic* (June 1945): p. 59.

24. Ibid.

25. Janeway, "Meet a War Widow," p. 120.

26. Ann Landers, *Chicago Tribune* syndicated column, January 1977. Grateful acknowledgment for permission to reprint is made to Ann Landers Creators Syndicate.

27. Lilian Rixley, "Shall I Remarry?" *Life* (April 15, 1946): pp. 107–8.

28. Catherine MacKenzie, "Children Must Be Told Father Will Never Come Home," *New York Times Magazine* (June 17, 1945): p. 27.

29. Popkin, "Widow's Way," p. 60; see also Maxine Davis, "Women Without Men," *Good Housekeeping* (March 1942): p. 30.

30. "Pity the Merry Widow," *Woman's Home Companion* (November 1946): p. 34.

31. Ibid., pp. 34 and 174.
32. Ibid., p. 34.
33. Collins, *Army Woman's Handbook*, p. 6.
34. "Effect of War Casualties," p. 181.
35. Popkin, "Widow's Way," p. 66.
36. Ibid.
37. Ibid., pp. 17 and 68. See also "Your Chances of Remarrying," *Science Digest* (May 1944): p. 9; "Attitudes and Ideas of High-School Youth in Regard to Marriage," *School and Society* (September 12, 1942): p. 221.
38. Lilian Rixley, "Shall I Remarry?" p. 107.
39. Eliot, ". . . of the Shadow of Death," p. 95.
40. Ibid., p. 94.
41. Ibid.
42. Rabinoff, "While Their Men Are Away," p. 112.
43. Mrs. Thomas Sullivan, "I Lost Five Sons," *American Magazine* (March 1944): pp. 17 and 92.
44. Ibid., p. 93.
45. Eliot, ". . . of the Shadow of Death," p. 94.
46. Rixley, "Shall I Remarry," p. 113.
47. Patricia Lochridge, "The Mother Racket," *Woman's Home Companion* (July 1944): p. 21.
48. "Never Say Die," *Time* (July 29, 1945): p. 26.
49. Erma Bombeck, *Los Angeles Times* syndicated column, May 30, 1989. Grateful acknowledgment for permission to reprint is made to Erma Bombeck and the Aaron M. Priest Literary Agency.

PART V

AFTERWARD

AFTERWARD

Long before the war was over—indeed, before it was scarcely underway—worry began over whether or not women would relinquish the gains they were making. At the same time that the headlines pleaded for women to join the war industries, they also warned women not to take this call too seriously. The invitation was intended, it should be understood, for the duration only.

Headlines appeared: "16,000,000 Women; What Will Happen After?" asked the *New York Times Magazine* in 1943; "Watch Out for the Women," cautioned a 1944 *Saturday Evening Post*; "Getting Rid of the Women," was *Atlantic*'s blunt summary after European victory. Women's magazines joined in, with a 1943 *Woman's Home Companion* title, "Give Back the Jobs," indicating typical attitudes.

A postwar economic crash was widely expected. Many who formed their economic views in the twenties and thirties were fatalists who believed that depression was the capitalistic norm and prosperity the exception. "Post-war America will not be a land of limitless opportunity," predicted a popular speaker. "Jobs will be scarce . . . Even at our peak of prosperity, millions lived on the very brink of starvation."[1]

Prewar commerce often assumed that jobs should be meted out according to worker need, and the corollary of this maxim was that men, as presumed heads of households, were axiomatically most deserving. The war replaced this hiring precept with another based instead on the need of industry, and for a few years those excluded from the hiring lines had an opportunity to earn. War, for them, meant a chance to pay off the mortgage and save against the depression they knew would come. Prosperity was an aberration in this view, and good times were a blessing possible only with the sacrifice of young lives.

Advocates for women and other excluded groups first had to challenge these pessimistic tenets. "We are afraid," said one Rooseveltian believer, "as well we may be if we think of our economy in the old terms."[2] The old views and its analogy to World War I was no longer valid, for Democratic planners had taken care to see that history would not repeat itself. Many shock absorbers that were built into the economy by the Roosevelt presidency were not present during World War I: there was unemployment insurance;* retirement incentives

---

* Unemployment compensation, though indeed a real boon to postwar readjustment, did not see women as genuine workers who were entitled to the return of the money they paid in. "If a woman is married, she isn't eligible . . . for the law assumes . . . she forthwith took over household duties." (See "Getting Rid of the Women," *Atlantic* (June 1945): p. 82; Gladys L. Palmer, "Women in the Post-War Labor Market," *Forum* [October 1945]: p. 134.)

through the new Social Security system; and enforcement of child labor laws to prevent competition with adult wages. Unions were more powerful in dealing with layoffs; the U.S. Employment Service provided services that were unavailable earlier. The Great Depression need not be repeated.

Eleanor Roosevelt, in a 1943 speech to the Business and Professional Women's Clubs, foretold this optimistic future.[3] Though the details were not yet clear even in her own prescient mind, what the First Lady was envisioning would turn out to be the Marshall Plan—which, by providing former allies and enemies with the money to buy from the United States, rebuilt Europe while surging the American economy forward in a way undreamed of in 1943. Such assurances, though, had to be repeated many times before even a portion of the public was diverted from the seeming World War I portent.

At the beginning of World War II, most women accepted the economics of scarcity and docilely intended to go along with postwar disemployment plans, but surveys showed that experience changed their minds. Originally, "as many as 95 per cent of women war workers planned to quit as soon as victory was certain," but when that time came, "polls began to reveal that the percentage ... was dropping sharply. The trend has been steady, until now every one of the 80,000 women working in Chicago radio plants wants to stay on."[4]

At the same time, women and men responding to other polls gave traditional views, agreeing that married women "should not be allowed to hold jobs."[5] The key to this confusion seemed to be whether or not the questions were personalized, for discussion of women's proper place meant one thing when viewed as an abstraction and quite another when viewed as a personal decision. Men were willing to see opportunity for women when they saw those women as wives, but when they viewed women as simply women (and marketplace competitors), they were quick to say their place was at home. That this abstract woman at home was ultimately a man's wife (whom he wished to see treated fairly in the workplace) was a contradiction unresolved.

But whether or not workers wanted it, war production was shutting down; in the first nine months after VE Day, women's numbers dropped by four million—down from 19,500,000 to about 15,500,000.[6] What made this plunge somewhat less dramatic, though, was that men also were undergoing a readjustment to the postwar economy. When factories retooled from making bombers to making appliances, both sexes were temporarily idled, making it easier for all workers to feel that unemployment was neither indicative of personal failure nor a permanent situation.

The two-thirds or more of women who told pollsters that they intended to keep working did in fact continue to work or seek work, and over the years the number of women in the labor force steadily rose. At the same time, however, women echoed the platitudes about need to work, and most justified employment in their individual cases as adhering to this principle. Women could not yet bring themselves to say that they worked for any reason other than the needs of their families, but they did redefine family needs to include items not considered necessities during their own youth.

The genie was indeed let out of the bottle. "There is no example," said *Ladies Home Journal*'s Dorothy Thompson, "in which a class or group of people who have once succeeded in expanding the area of their lives is ever persuaded again to restrict it."[7] It would take decades to achieve the individual liberations implied, but the essential movement began with the recognition, as Eleanor Roosevelt suggested, that the key lay in redefinition of the economy itself.

What was needed was expansion of ideas on suitable jobs for women, for even in the depressed thirties there was agreement that certain occupations naturally belonged to women. The first steps towards permanent expansion of women's employment came in the postwar period when women with teaching and nursing skills found tremendous demand for them, with no questions asked on need to work. As the postwar economy transformed itself from a manufacturing one to a service one, more and more jobs would be seen as naturally suited to women.

Rosie the Riveter did not vanish with victory; she simply transformed herself into Wendy the White-Collar Worker. In part, this was because she understood that in any contest between herself and GI Joe for a factory job, she would be the loser. The veteran's right to a job was as inviolate as was the soldier's right to a seat on the train. But because Johnny marched home did not mean that she had to accept the kitchen for the rest of her life. If she couldn't have the factory, then she would take the office. In doing so, she entered a segment of the economy that would boom, while he, unknowingly, was more likely to go for the one that would stagnate in the postindustrial society.

It had been both a blue- and a white-collar war, and afterwards, women would take over office jobs so completely that soon it would be forgotten that prior to the war women had little chance of even pink collar ghetto jobs. Bookkeeper, bank teller, ticket reservationist—all of these sorts of jobs were largely held by men in the thirties and before. The change, accelerated by the war, was part of a long-term transformation of ideas on suitable jobs for women. In most of the 19th century, those women who had to earn were primarily domestic workers; manufacturing was the great leap forward of the late 19th and early 20th century; and the switch to pink-collar predominance came with World War II.

Nowhere was this trend more obvious than in government employment. Even in Hoover's conservative FBI, for instance, five times as many women were employed after the war as before.[8] Federal employment was particularly meaningful for black women; by April 1944, about 200,000 black women worked for the nation, compared with fewer than 60,000 in 1940.[9] But while women began looking to Uncle Sam for jobs, they were very slow to demand federal protection for equal opportunity in either private or political arenas.

"American women have the right to vote," wrote a man in *Good Housekeeping* midway through the war. "They can be expected to impress that fact on legislators."[10] That such a conservative source would so early point out the latent political power of women showed how great the potential was, but it was a potential that did not come close to being exercised in the immediate postwar period. Real opportunities for political success were resoundingly ignored.

For instance, House Labor Chairman Mary Norton and Senator Claude Pepper introduced legislation at the war's end to "make it an unfair labor practice for an employer to discriminate against women by paying them lower wages or by laying them off in favor of men."[11] Despite qualifying language that included exemptions for "sound reasons," seniority systems and veterans' preference, the bills went nowhere. But this was not surprising in view of the total failure of the women's press to urge political action in support of this or any other proposal. Not even *Independent Woman*, the era's most tireless advocate for women, ran any campaign in support of the legislation, presumably because it would have benefited blue-collar workers more than its white-collar audience. Class cleavage continued in women's ranks, promoting only political impotence.

The leaders who failed to lead might have taken a lesson from a handful of Detroit women whose political philosophy may have been inchoate, but who understood political action. When their local union agreed with management on a plan to cancel out their seniority, they "invaded" the AFL-CIO session and gained their point.[12] This sort of tough-girl act could have become the rule instead of the exception had there been appropriate leadership from either the unions, which were accustomed to political battle, or from women's organizations, had they dropped their cripplingly polite style.

Women who had themselves gained the right to vote should have remembered that men will accede to the demands of organized women whose cause is just. That right to vote came as a direct result of the roles women played in World War I, during which their activity was far shorter and less sacrificial than that of World War II. Women might well have claimed similarly significant benefits after that war—if only they had tried.

War had changed women's image in ways beyond those of the employment world. "Once upon a time," wrote a man just after Pearl Harbor, "it may have been all right for a man to marry an ornament . . . Today John wants a wife who can make herself useful."[13] Veterans returning from the horrifying seriousness of war were unlikely to view girlish giddiness as admirable. What young men told pollsters they wanted in a wife was essentially a young, only slightly updated version of Mom.

That "her specialty must be homemaking"[14] was a given for most. In one survey of servicemen, none of a list of mutual interests such as books, travel and sports was high in their estimation—except for children, with "a wife who has a fondness for kids" rated at the top. Only 8% wanted a "brainy girl who keeps up with world problems;" just 7% wanted a "business girl who could take care of herself."[15] Both women and men told pollsters that they wanted large families, though not as large as families had been prior to Planned Parenthood. Three or more children was the ideal of 77%.[16]

While women in their childbearing years also approved of this image of themselves at home with several kids, nonetheless both sexes agreed that the assigned female role was harder than the male role. Gallup found that men by 47% to 30% thought that women's lives were harder than their own; women were more adamant, with only 18% saying that men's lives were more difficult.[17] Women's postwar perception of unfairness and consequent discontent, echoed in the opinions of their men, pointed to fundamental contradictions and to something disturbingly wrong.

That any gains in the status of women were tenuous had been made clear by Hitler, who demonstrated how open women's lives are to institutional manipulation. Americans found "the fascist concept of women" despicable, for the image of the German female whose "life's work is to breed and feed"[18] was seen as a repulsive triumph of technocratic eugenics over humanist values. Indeed, so intent was Germany on keeping women bound to *kinder, kirche* and *kuchen* that it was even slow to allow its women a share of production, let alone offer them military-service opportunity. The majority of women who toiled in the German war machine were slave laborers, who justifiably worked as little as possible and sabotaged when they could.

The te●logical destiny that fascism assigned to women was not compatible with American ideas of individual worth—and yet it seemed easy for many to talk of the national birth rate in terms that also emphasized woman as reproducer of the race. The baby boom at the war's end was a happy affirmation of the future by young people feeling fortunate to have survived, but the long-term trend soon showed this boom to be a temporary blip on a downward chart. As the nation continued to urbanize, nostalgia for the big family of one's youth was replaced by the practicalities of providing decent care in a nonfarm economy in which children became a liability rather than an asset. America opted for quality, not quantity, and moreover, its women opted for space in their lives for activities other than motherhood.

It was not surprising that eventually women would want to emphasize other aspects of their lives, for the first antimother whisperings that began during the war would increase to a furor in the fifties and sixties.* One immediate cause of wartime criticism was working mothers,** but—in another of the confusing contradictions—some psychologists found wartime evidence for exactly the

---

* Philip Wylie's 1945 novel, *Generation of Vipers*, was widely discussed late in the war. Wylie's succinct summary of its thesis: "Mom is a jerk."

** See Chapter 11.

opposite case against mothers. Far from being negligent, in this view, American mothers were excessively indulgent.

Fuel for this fire came from the nation's high rate of young men emotionally unequipped for military life. "Of the more than 25,000 men who are being discharged each month as psychiatric casualties, the largest number do not crack up as a result of combat," said an expert. "They meet their Waterloo during training, and often near the beginning."[19] Many psychologists saw this as the fault of their women, especially their mothers:

> ... More than 50% of our casualties at present haven't a scratch on them, and yet they are unfit for military service.
>
> ... *When he is bawled out by a tough sergeant and ridiculed by other men for mistakes, he cannot turn to a sympathetic, over-protective mother or wife ... Many of our men are not emotionally grownup.*
>
> ... *Some women consciously or unconsciously overuse their power ... Outside the home most American boys continue to be raised mostly by women ... Relatively few boys have consistent training by men until they get to high school and meet the coach. The average American father has a very casual relationship with his children.*[20]

Yet painful and unfair though some of the antimother literature was, the release of vituperative tension eventually improved family relations. With mother treated as a real person, in time emotions would move to a middle ground preferable to the limited love/hate options of an earlier era.

Seeing mother as an individual in her own right was one of many changes in the family begun during the war; it was one of several steps in diminishing patriarchal values and replacing them with a democratized unit. Migration from old homesteads, housing shortages that allowed only small groups; new experiences for young people not shared by the old; freer sexuality—all these and more promoted individual freedom. Uncle Sam gradually replaced earlier patriarchs, as the government intervened on behalf of families in housing, food supply and health care. Schools assumed more parental functions, and through Social Security and other subsidies, the government replaced the extended family as the ultimate provider in need. These changes encouraged families that were based on ties of love rather than those of economics.

Creation of more democratic families meant, however, a long and painful transitional stage. The instability inherent in that transformation exhibited itself in its most obvious way during the telescoped years of the war. The rootlessness of millions of moving people, the rising divorce rate and especially the adoption of roles other than motherhood by women—all signaled change that many found frightening.

Men in military camps were not the only ones dreaming of home, for women, too, spent the war holding tight to a peacetime dream home. They emphatically agreed with *Ladies Home Journal*'s forecast that "it will be the aim of every American to have a *home* for his family—not a series of shifting apartments."[21]

The craving for a place of one's own was strongly affected by wartime crowding. Cabs had to be shared, trains and buses were packed, even restaurant booths were divided; men living in barracks went years without any space of their own larger than a bed. People longed for privacy—space and a single-family home.

Dreaming was encouraged by advertisers, and there was little note of the irony that most modern conveniences would be available only after the period of greatest need of them was past. Women's war years were still dominated by the weather on wash day, but they were supposed to see beyond to a pin-up plan for the future: "She looks at it when she leaves . . . and again when she returns wearily from the war plant. *It's her dream kitchen.*"[22]

Dream houses cut across class lines—everyone wanted a share of space, and moreover, believed they were entitled to it. Once materials were available, an army of construction workers hit the land, applying production techniques learned during the war to housing. Instead of past craftsmanship and architectural ornamentation, simple but affordable homes were quickly built. "Subdivision" was added to the American vocabulary, with all its implications for changes in family life. Single-family homes and new suburban communities reinforced the nuclear family, segregated people by age as well as race and class, and isolated housewives. A generation passed though, before these negatives were considered; during the war, dream homes remained an unalloyed joy.

The price of the dream home meant that, after a few years of postwar rest and baby birthing, women went back into the labor market to earn a higher standard of living for their families. First, though, there was a time of experimentation while men attempted to support these more elaborate homes on a single income, and then—and probably more important—a time during which business made its surprisingly slow discovery of women as consumers.

The wartime view of most businessmen towards women never varied much from the traditional. While some were forced to see women in new employee roles, few were capable of envisioning a future greatly different from the past. "I am opposed," said a typically unimaginative man, "to the peacetime employment of women with husbands on payrolls—who just want money for nonessentials."[23] This Depression view of jobs as charity, to be granted or withheld on the basis of need, blinded business to the fantastic potential of "nonessential" sales. They did not see that if women had jobs—and families had discretionary income—endless yet-to-be-invented items would become needs rather than luxuries.

In their apprehensive concern for returning women to the kitchen, some proposed a "campaign to glorify the American homemaker. We will have to . . . sell them on the idea of the home, just as we sold them the idea of going into war work."[24] Without stating such a baldly manipulative aim, the advertising announcing new marvels rolling off of postwar assembly lines had exactly this effect—women did indeed see themselves as homemakers, happily running these new homes. But the sales ploy succeeded beyond the intent of its creators, working so well that ultimately it went full circle and negated any aim of making the majority of women into full-time homemakers, for women and their families wanted these "nonessentials" enough that they went back to work to pay for them.

Because women were still working on behalf of their homes (only in a different way), many individuals were able to make this transition without changing their rhetoric on women's proper place. Business meanwhile, expanding on wartime familiarity with working women, began to see them as essential in certain jobs—and all of this could be and often was done with the person treating his or her case as an exception, while retaining cherished prejudices on working women.

It was indeed a revolution, but a revolution without manifesto and without declaration, and accomplished so quietly and gradually and ambivalently that even the victors did not know they had won. It was a revolution in fact, but not in philosophy. Those who dared to dream of this change were scorned as believing in science fiction. Historians who had never seen societal transformation at the rate needed for implementation in the lifetimes of those who lived through World War II were skeptical:

> They paint dream pictures of huge low-cost housing projects . . . There the home duties all but disappear. The children are cared for by nursery experts. Shopping and transportation difficulties vanish . . . No longer will women waste their skills . . . Upon the joint income of a man and his wife, higher living standards will be achieved.
> . . . This portrayal of a new world seems at the moment far in the future.[25]

And yet within a decade after the war, the "dream pictures" of millions of new homes had come to be; within two decades, the interstate highway system was just part of a transportation revolution; within three decades shopping became as much an entertainment as a chore with the development of malls.

All of these changes were dependent on women as earners, buyers and taxpayers, as well as homemakers and mothers. The war gave an opportunity to demonstrate that a woman was capable of doing many things, doing them simultaneously and well. During the postwar period, she would finally be recognized as a producer as well as a consumer, and a full human being.

Creating a dreamhome was the major task assigned to postwar women, but homebuilding included worldwide implications. A brutal male history of warfare had been brought to its most appalling level during this war, and women understood that "a Nazi victory would have frightful consequences" for their sex.[26] This was not a war to be evaded with platitudes on peace; women instead had to get on with the job of defeating the threat.

Those who did that most effectively, of course, were the extraordinary women of the Resistance. Throughout occupied France, Scandinavia, the Low Countries and the Balkans, there were women who blew up Nazi trains, planted explosives in bunkers, and carried vital espionage. When caught, they were beaten, tortured, hung, and shot, dying like men, except for the additional anguish of rape.

While little could be written about the Resistance during the war, Americans did read about our women allies in the Soviet Union. They discovered that women made up 75% of their work force, doing many jobs closed here. They read about the Moscow engineer who raced her explosive-laden train out of the city while German planes bombed; about the elderly aircraft spotter found dead on her roof, her frying pan useless as a helmet; about the small-town mayor, who, left naked and presumed dead by an execution squad, crawled to safety, dragging a dying man with her.

Everyone knew about the heroic women of Stalingrad who, though starving under siege, defended their city's barricades in house-to-house warfare. WASPs were fascinated by Russian women pilots who also had to fight for the right to fly, but ultimately were awarded the highest medals for hundreds of Nazi "kills." Americans could scarcely comprehend the grief of Soviet women, who were far more likely to be widowed—their men died at a rate of 1 out of every 22, compared with 1 out of 450 for us.[27]

Because of eased communication, more was published on our nearest sister, Britain. Mid-way through the war, over a thousand members of the Women's Voluntary Services alone were dead in action in their homeland, "killed as they strove to save life, to help others." During one horrible night in May, 1941, 278 WVS women were bombed out of their homes, but only one was late for duty the next morning.[28] There was no chivalry in the military codes of Nazi warriors; the "Battle of Britain" was aimed at civilians, and during 1940–41 it was more dangerous to be a child in southern England than to be a soldier abroad. Before the war's end, London housewives would be slain in their own kitchens by manless V-2 rockets. No more could combat be called an area for males only.

While Americans read of these civilians killed in open warfare, what they did not read about was the millions systematically put to death by Nazi genocide. Only in leftist and Jewish publications did hints of what was happening appear; the mainstream media rarely picked up these threads. That the land of Beethoven and Bach had descended to such unheard of depths was hard to credit, and editors cautioned themselves with remembrance of the hyperbolic Hun propaganda of World War I. Those with personal experience of pogroms could not talk about the fearful possibilities of this war in a way that did not make them sound crazed with paranoia. Even leftist publications prepared to believe the worst of Germany's right could not quite repeat the information they got without a hint of incredulity.

When the war ended and American troops liberated the concentration camps, the actuality of what we had been fighting hit home. The outrage could only be comprehended by seeing it, but ever since the invention of the camera there had been a gentleman's agreement that war's reality would not be shown in its totality. *Life* and others who made the decision to publish atrocities in full detail forced many a flag waver to come to grips with the truth of war, as well as with the terrifying implications of racial prejudice.

Women were at the forefront among those working to change these ancient racial tenets. Pearl Buck topped best-seller lists for years with her sympathetic interpretation of Asians. She was joined by other women who spelled out the dangers of cherishing hatreds, with Eleanor Roosevelt awakening Southern Democrats to black inequality, and Republican Clare Booth Luce pointing out that while we fought the Japanese, other Asians were our staunch allies. Old female warhorses, those who had formed the Women's International League for Peace and Freedom after World War I, came back for another stab at world sanity. Elderly Emily Greene Balch* reported of the league's first postwar meeting, "We found each other again; . . . we were resolved to go on working together."[29]

Working for peace became another task assigned to postwar women, but that this mandated political involvement was largely seen as a necessary evil. It was something a woman was supposed to do, not because she would enjoy politics or because she might think of a career there, but rather because it was her duty. Like homebuilding, it was justified as innate. "Women have generally a stronger instinct for creating and preserving life," wrote Virginia Gildersleeve, the only woman appointed to the first U.S. delegation to the United Nations. "War, with its destruction of life . . . they instinctively hate."[30] Women's political action, in this view, was emotionally based.

Political effectiveness would be better built on numerical strength and power, but at least this was a beginning; at least there was the development of an understanding that peace would not come of its own accord and that it was inextricably bound up with politics. And if they were novices in the political world, it must be remembered that women had only been voting for 25 years. Older women, many of whom had opposed enfranchisement, had never developed the habit of casting a ballot. Moreover, the women's media was of almost no help in forming political consciousness or the necessary skills, for while peace-promoting articles were written, how peace was to be accomplished was left nebulous.

---

* Dr. Balch worked and studied in Europe prior to the first world war. Her first book, *Our Slavic Fellow Citizens*, became an early sociological classic.

The same writer, for instance, who told women to "stand up and be counted" also said that "the days of a Militant Sisterhood . . . are away behind us" and that women "will not increase their influence by organizing a female pressure bloc." Instead, presumably, the path to power lay in meekness, for "women should make a study of how not to annoy men in public meetings and discussions."[31] Such naive advice did not see that no sweeping social change occurs without anger on the part of those demanding it. Male politicians had a long history of inciting anger, but the cultural limitation on a woman's right to show anger—while she was encouraged to exhibit other emotions—remained a political handicap.

It was not as though there were not women who could have spelled this out, for alternative leadership did exist. Besides the stellar Eleanor, there was Frances Perkins, the first woman Cabinet member. There were other female political insiders such as Anna Rosenberg, who became a postwar Assistant Secretary of Defense. There were women in Congress, some of them quite powerful. There was Daisy Harriman, ambassador to Norway when the Nazis overran it, who helped the Norwegian royal family escape. Besides these Democrats, there was Republican Frances Bolton, who organized women to stun the male power structure of Ohio, while Margaret Chase Smith of Maine ran against "most of the money in the state . . . and won."[32]

Yet somehow these were not the women featured in the media or by those whose ostensible aim was political education. In all the interminable articles on postwar unemployment, for example, the views of the female chairman of the House Labor Committee were never included in a publication aimed at women. It was as though these opinion makers thought of politics as either boring or perhaps too dirty for their audiences. The same was true of the politics of peace, for the agenda and methodology remained undefined.

Everyone was for peace. No one wanted its fragility to come apart and the world to return to war, but therein lay the problem. Even the Women's International League for Peace and Freedom found that good feelings were not enough. Though no one from Germany, Russia or Japan was able to participate, the others still had difficulty reaching conclusions. Despite the strong motivation of these women, "certain resolutions proposed—on the Nuremberg trials and on treatment of vanquished peoples—were painful and unacceptable to some delegates.[33]"

Peace was not an easy matter, and yet individual women worked at it in ways that were very different from prewar American isolationism. They expanded their new global awareness with increased reading and attendance at serious lectures—more than 25,000,000 people paid admissions at local auditoriums to ponder world questions in 1945.[34] They showed generosity in deed as well as thought, as they gave huge amounts of money to both allies and enemies, took displaced persons into their homes and sent care packages to impoverished Europeans for years after the war was over.

But in a sense that sort of humanitarianism, tangible and precious though it is, is easy compared with understanding the distinctions between Austria and Albania or India and Indonesia. Comprehension of world events required almost Orwellian adjustment, as our enemies in Japan and Germany quickly became our friends, and our ally, the Soviet Union, became our enemy.

Yet if the details were overwhelming, the spirit for peace was still there; most women felt strongly that something hopeful must result from all the world had suffered. They put tremendous faith in the infant United Nations, and, almost orphanlike after the death of the only President many had known, they watched the UN for signs of hope and wisdom.

To protect the homes they built, women had no choice except to work for peace. To make those homes worth living in, they had to work for freedom as well. Authoritarianism took many forms and often disguised itself as benign, but the roots of the gestapo and those of the patriarchal home were the same. The end of totalitarianism must necessarily lead to the end of paternalism, for there was no longer a place for anyone who claimed the right to force others to live his way. Only with freedom and fairness would there be lasting peace.

SOURCE NOTES

1. Ray, "For Better, For Worse," p. 64.
2. Mary Anderson: "16,000,000 Women; What Will Happen After?" *New York Times Magazine* (July 18, 1943): p. 18. See also Dorothy Thompson, "The Stake for Women in Full Employment," *Ladies Home Journal* (April 1944): p. 6.
3. "America's First Lady Speaks," *Independent Woman* (December 1943): p. 359. See also Gladys F. Gove: "Just Around the Postwar Corner," *Independent Woman* (February 1944): p. 45.
4. "Getting Rid of the Women," *Atlantic* (June 1945): p. 79. See also Ruth Young and Catherine Filene Shouse, "The Woman Worker Speaks," *Independent Woman* (October 1945): p. 274; and Constance Roe, "Can the Girls Hold Their Jobs in Peacetime?" *Saturday Evening Post* (March 1944): p. 28; Herbert E. Fleming, "Women War Workers Look Ahead," *Survey Graphic* (October 1944): p. 415; Ellen D. Ellis, "What Chance for Women?," *Forum* (March 1946): p. 590; and "Third of Women to Work," *Science News Letter* (August 24, 1946): p. 123.
5. "The Fortune Survey," *Fortune* (August 1946): p. 5. See also a continuation of the survey's results in the next month's issue, also p. 5; "Women War Workers' Post-War Job Plans," *Monthly Labor Review* (September 1944): p. 589; "Women Will Stay," *Business Week* (March 11, 1944): p. 46; Lucy Greenbaum, "Women Who Need to Work," *New York Times*

Magazine (April 29, 1945): p. 16; and Gallup, *The Gallup Poll*, p. 372. A February 1945 Gallup question to all working women (not just war plant workers) found 61% intending to continue working. Ibid., p. 487.

6. Frieda S. Miller, "What's Become of Rosie the Riveter?," *New York Times Magazine* (May 5, 1946): p. 21. See also by the same author, "Women and Their Jobs," *Survey Graphic* (May 1943): p. 182. In *Independent Woman*, see I. Parsons, "We Lay Our Plans for Postwar Jobs," (May 1944): p. 148; Margaret A. Hickey, "The Task Ahead for Women," (August 1945): p. 213; also by Hickey, "What Next for Women?" (August 1946): p. 221; Josephine Skinner, "Postwar Employment of Women," (September 1944): p. 278; Pauline Arnold, "Where Will the Postwar Chances Lie?," (October 1944): p. 303; and George F. Devanel, "When Johnny Comes Marching Home," (July 1945): p. 182.

7. Dorothy Thompson: "Women and the Coming World," *Ladies Home Journal* (October 1943): p. 6.

8. Henry Charles Suter: "Uncle Sam's G-Women," *Independent Woman* (December 1946): p. 358.

9. "Negro Women Bridge Manpower Gap," *Service* (September 1945): p. 13, and "Effect of 'Cutbacks' on Women's Employment," *Monthly Labor Review* (September 1944): p. 585. See also "Women at War," *Brown American* (Summer 1943): p. 5; Frieda S. Miller, "Negro Women Workers," *Opportunity: Journal of Negro Life* (Fall 1945): p. 207; and in the same publication, Ida Coker Clark, "Negro Woman Worker, What Now?" (Spring 1944): p. 93; and "Women in De.↔nse Industry," (April 1943): p. 86.

10. Cecil Brown, "What's Going to Happen to Our Women Workers?," *Good Housekeeping* (December 1943): p. 42.

11. "Women in the Labor Force," *Business Week* (December 29, 1945): p. 93. See also Rebekah S. Greathouse, "The Effects of Constitutional Equality on Working Women," *American Economic Review* (March 1944): p. 227.

12. "Women's Exit," *Business Week* (July 18, 1945): p. 104.

13. Howard Whitman: "What Makes Females So Useless?," *Good Housekeeping* (February 1942): p. 46. Other articles on the image of women are: "Women Have Changed," *New York Times Magazine* (March 10, 1946): p. 24; Ray Josephs, "My, How You've Changed!," *Woman's Home Companion* (February 1946): p. 4; Raymond Knight, "A Lass—but Still a Lack," *Independent Woman* (October 1942): pp. 299–300; and Harold Ickes, "Watch Out for the Women," *Saturday Evening Post* (February 22, 1944): p. 19. (Ickes was the nation's Secretary of the Interior.) On black women, see: "The Women Behind the Men Behind the Guns," *The African* (May 1943): p. 10; "African- American Women Warriors," *The African* (August 1943): p. 10; and Joseph V. Baker, "To a Brown Lady," *Brown American* (Fall 1943): p. 1.

14. Ibid.

15. Louise Paine Benjamin: "What is Your Dream Girl Like?" *Ladies Home Journal* (March 1942): p. 114. See also D.L. Cohn, "Love—America's No. 1 Problem," *Science Digest* (August 1943): p. 19.
16. Gallup, *The Gallup Poll*, p. 524. See also J.C. Furnas, "Baby Boom," *Ladies Home Journal* (February 1943): p. 35; "Motherhood Boom," *Time* (May 11, 1942): p. 22; Henry Pratt Fairchild, "Family Limitation and the War," *Annals of the American Academy of Political and Social Science*, Vol. 229 (1943): p. 79; Winifred Hayes, "Woman's Place in the Future World Order," *Catholic World* (August 1943): p. 482.
17. Gallup, *The Gallup Poll*, p. 576. Polling date was April 1946. See also "The Fortune Survey," August 1946, p. 5; Ferdinand Lundberg and Marynia F. Farnham, "Men Have Lost Their Women," *Ladies Home Journal* (November 1944): pp. 23 and 133. See especially Margaret Mead, "What Women Want," *Fortune* (December 1946): p. 220.
18. Anthony, *Out of the Kitchen*, p. 244.
19. Taylor, "If Your Man Is an NP," p. 76.
20. Ibid. See also Howard Mumford Jones, "Mother Love is Not Enough," *Saturday Review* (October 28, 1944): p. 16; Ernest R. Mowrer, "War and Family Solidarity and Stability," *Annals of the American Academy of Political and Social Science*, Vol. 229 (1943): p. 100.
21. Dorothy Thompson, "The New Woman in the New America," *Ladies Home Journal* (January 1945): p. 6. See also Elizabeth Gordon, "What People Want in Postwar Houses," *House Beautiful* (September 1944): p. 86; and Marion Gough, "Home Should be EVEN MORE WONDERFUL Than He Remembers It," *House Beautiful* (January 1945): p. 29.
22. Ad by Briggs, a Detroit plumbing company, *House and Garden* (Spring 1944): p. 67. See also "Plan Your Postwar Home," *Parents* (October 1944): p. 38.
23. "Pay Women Equal Wages?" *Rotarian* (September 1943): p. 26.
24. Brown, "What's Going to Happen," p. 59. See also Margaret Culkin Banning, "Will They Go Back Home?," *Rotarian* (September 1943): p. 28; Dorothy Canfield Fisher, "From Lathe to the Hearth," *New York Times Magazine* (December 3, 1943): p. 46; Elinore Herrick, "What About Women After the War?," *New York Times Magazine* (September 5, 1943): p. 7; Edith M. Stern, "Brains in the Kitchen," *The Nation* (January 22, 1944): p. 95; Mildred Welch Cranston, "The Modern Woman's Place in the Home," *Atlantic* (July 1946): p. 106; Nell Giles, "What About the Women?," *Ladies Home Journal* (June 1944): p. 23; and "High School Girls Deny That 'Woman's Place is in the Home,'" *Scholastic* (March 5, 1945): p. 26. Only a bare majority of boys (56%) agreed.
25. Colston E. Warne, "The Reconversion of Women," *Current History* (March, 1945): p. 203. See also in this publication, Gladys L. Palmer, "Women's Place in Industry" (January 1944): p. 22.

26. Dorothy Thompson, "The Stake for Women," *Ladies Home Journal* (April 1944): p. 6.

27. The engineer and aircraft spotter are featured in Irina Skariatina, "The Fearless Women of Russia," *Collier's* (November 7, 1942): p. 15; the mayor in Quentin Reynolds, "Three Russian Women," *Collier's* (July 3, 1943): p. 13. See also, in that publication, Alice Leone Moats, "Russian Women at War" (October 18, 1941): p. 18. On women pilots, see especially Madelin Blitzstein, "How Women Flyers Fight Russia's Air War," *Aviation* (July 19, 1944): p. 116.

   In the *New York Times Magazine*, see Ralph Parker, "Moscow Hails Tanya" (March 22, 1942): p. 11, and by the same author, "Women Workers of the Russian Miracle" (February 14, 1943): p. 18; W.H. Lawrence, "Russia's New Woman" (November 5, 1944): p. 22; and Oriana Atkinson, "Weaker (?) Sex of Russia" (March 3, 1946): p. 15.

   See also Fannina W. Halle, "Free Women of Russia," *Woman's Home Companion* (February 1943): p. 29; Rose Maurer, "Those Russian Women," *Survey Graphic* (February 1944): p. 109; and Joseph B. Phillips, "A Typical Woman of Postwar Moscow," *Newsweek* (November 4, 1946): p. 52.

28. Birdwell, *Women in Battle Dress*, p. 83. See also Frances Blackwood, *Mrs. England Goes on Living* (New York: Creative Age Press, 1943): p. 286.

29. Emily Greene Balch, "Women for Peace and Freedom," *Survey Graphic* (October 1946): p. 358. See also Dorothy Thompson, "A Call to American Women," *Ladies Home Journal* (August 1945): p. 6; Anne O'Hare McCormick, "The Woman with a Broom," *Reader's Digest* (June 1945): p. 37; Florence E. Allen, "Women's Obligation for Peace," *Independent Woman* (September 1946): p. 274; Agnes E. Meyers, "A Challenge to American Women," *Collier's* (May 11, 1946): p. 15; and Ethel McCall Head, "The Magnificent Challenge," *American Home* (July 1945): p. 18.

30. Virginia C. Gildersleeve, "Women Must Help Stop Wars," *Woman's Home Companion* (May 1945): pp. 32–33. See also Major George Fielding Eliot, "Women and a People's Peace," *Independent Woman* (May 1943): p. 131; and Alma Lutz, "Woman's Hour," *Christian Science Monitor* (August 24, 1946): p. 2.

31. Margaret Barnard Pickel, "There's Still a Lot for Women to Learn," *New York Times Magazine* (November 11, 1945): p. 14. See also by the same author and in the same publication, "A Warning to the Career Women" (July 16, 1944): p. 11, and "How Come No Jobs for Women?" (June 27, 1946): p. 20. See also a very progressive article by Pennsylvania's U.S. Senator Francis J. Myers: "Don't Take It Out on the Women," *Woman's Home Companion* (January 1946): p. 13; and "The American Woman," *Life* (October 21, 1946): p. 26.

32. Eleanor Roosevelt and Lorena A. Hickok, *Ladies of Courage* (New York: G. P. Putnam's Sons, 1954), p. 177.

33. Balch, "Women for Peace and Freedom," pp. 359–360. See also "Shall We Have Compulsory Military Training After the War?," *Parents* (October 1944): p. 16.

34. Ray Josephs, "My How You've Changed!," *Woman's Home Companion* (February 1946): p. 4.

BIBLIOGRAPHICAL NOTE

As is clear in the Notes, the primary source for this history was the current and widely read information of that time. There were two main objectives in selecting sources: The first was to use material that reflected the mainstream of the era's thought, with only occasional asides to the fringes of both left and right. The second was to write a book based as much as possible on the perceived reality of the times, rather than using wartime memories that may have unconsciously altered with age. Therefore the reader will find very few dates in the Notes that are not between 1940 and 1946, with most of them in fact being the crucial years between 1942 and 1945. The Notes include over 750 periodical sources of this era.

Women were news during the war, and the newsmagazines alone produced more than 135 cited articles related to women. The greatest number came from the *New York Times Magazine* (*NYTM*) with both *Time* and *Newsweek* as very close competitors. Unlike the latter two, the *NYTM* usually published signed articles with more complete analysis of a single topic. Among its best reporters were Nancy MacLennon, Elizabeth Hawes, Nona Baldwin, Lucy Greenbaum, and Nancy McInerny. Catherine Mackenzie published a half-dozen excellent *NYTM* articles on child-care issues, some of which are not cited because of the elimination of a planned chapter titled "Children and the War." The daily *New York Times* also served as a clarifying source in several cases of sparse information, especially on military matters. Finally, the *Christian Science Monitor* offered work that was similar to the *NYTM* in format, but far less of it. Their most helpful writers were Alma Lutz and Josephine Ripley.

The publications that are called "mass magazines" in publishing lingo were of tremendous importance in this era before television. The mass magazines, especially *Life*, gave readers the vivid picture views of war news that television would later supply. These publications paid a good deal of attention to women in the war: almost 100 articles are cited from *American Magazine, Collier's, Life, Reader's Digest*, and *Saturday Evening Post*. Except for the nonpictorial *Reader's Digest*, all of these would suffer from the introduction of television, but they were very popular in their day and did much to acquaint the masses with the changing roles of women.

Their opposite type, those magazines we might term "intellectual," in fact wrote far less on women's issues. The Notes contain citations for approximately 20 such publications, yet all of these combined produced only about 50 articles that merited inclusion. The largest number were published by *Current History* and *New Republic*, but their citations number only a half dozen each. *Atlantic, Harper's*, and *The Nation* were responsible for some truly outstanding articles but only a very few. *Harper's* piece by A.G. Mezerik, "The Factory Manager Learns the Facts of Life," was especially thoughtful, as was Edith Stern's "America's Pampered Husbands," in *The Nation. Atlantic* also presented some perceptive work, including Mildred Cranston's "The Modern Woman's Place in the Home," but such topics were far more the exception than the rule in these publications.

If these "liberal" periodicals did not see women's concerns as valid, then it is hardly surprising that more conservative publications would also ignore the area. Literary magazines such as *Saturday Review* and *American Mercury* apparently thought their audiences unconcerned with war and women's rights, and what little they did publish on the topic was generally unsympathetic to change. *American Mercury*, for example, featured only Ruth Peters' elitist opinions in "Why I Don't Join the WACS," and Samuel Tenenbaum's morose predictions in "The Fate of Wartime Marriages." *Forum, Commonweal, Christian Century*, and *Catholic World* similarly could be depended on for regressive views when they chose to deal with women's issues at all.

Though women's increased travel and global awareness was a significant wartime change, *Travel* published just one article on women's new activities and *National Geographic* only two (both by LaVerne Bradley and both excellent). Other special interest magazines similarly failed to reflect change; as indicated in the text, *Gourmet* dealt with wartime dietary adjustment by simply ignoring reality. Other sophisticated magazines, such as the *New Yorker*, generally followed the same rule, with the result that feminists looking for new ideas were far more likely to see them in literature aimed at the masses than in publications with better-educated audiences.

Though disdained by many feminists today, it was in fact *Ladies Home Journal (LHJ)* and *Woman's Home Companion (WHC)*, which, despite their Victorian-sounding names, published the most valuable information on the wide range of women's wartime roles. More than 40 *LHJ* and 30 *WHC* articles are cited in the Notes. The work of *WHC* writers Anne Maxwell, Doris Fleeson, and Patricia Lochridge was especially worthwhile. *WHC* also opened its pages to more political personalities than most publications and endorsed feminist legislation editorially.

LHJ supported an even larger group of regular writers with definite (and sometimes differing) views. Though primarily a beauty editor, Louise Paine Benjamin managed to turn out some truly interesting articles. Nell Giles, Joseph Chamberlain Furnas (who signed his name "J.C."), and, late in the war, young Elizabeth Janeway were especially good writers published by *LHJ*. Columnist Leslie B. Hohman regularly offered conservative views, and met his monthly match in editorialist Dorothy Thompson. A brilliant woman who presaged much current feminist thought, Thompson deserves to be more widely read.

The third popular women's magazine that merits attention is *McCall's*. Although scorned by the indexers of *Reader's Guide* at the time and thus somewhat inaccessible, several articles in *McCall's* explored sensitive areas untouched elsewhere. Betsey Barton's "Those Who Did Not Die," Zelda Popkin's "A Widow's Way," and Toni Taylor's "If Your Man is an NP" were unparalleled in their analysis of difficult problems that more conventional publications forced women to face alone.

If women in general were slighted by the publishing world, black women were all but ignored. There was no national magazine aimed at black women during this era, and those for blacks in general reveal their tenuous financial circumstances with irregular publication dates. The citations from black periodicals are therefore limited to about two dozen from *The African, Brown American, Pulse, Service,* and, the most helpful, *Opportunity: Journal of Negro Life*.

Scholarly journals were often better sources for information on black women, as well as on women in general. *Survey Graphic* and *Survey Midmonthly,* related publications for social workers and sociologists, provided valuable analyses of wartime change, particularly by contributors Rose Rabinoff, Katherine Glover, and Frieda S. Miller. *Hygeia* and *American Journal of Public Health* published an impressive number of articles concerning women, ranging from maternity costs to the nursing shortage. The most important source of information on the nursing profession was, of course, the *American Journal of Nursing*. While the *American Journal of Sociology* offered disappointingly few worthwhile articles, the *Annals of the American Academy of Political and Social Science* published an extremely helpful volume midway through the war, with more than a dozen articles that are listed in the Notes.

Beyond the social sciences, "hard" science publications also wrote a good deal about women in science fields. The Notes show upwards of 30 articles from seven sources, of which *Science News Letter* and *Flying* (on women pilots) were the most frequently cited. Virtually all of this publicity was positive, and the same is refreshingly true of business publications.

Business Week published over three dozen cited pieces, almost all of which were supportive of women as employees or as customers dealing with rationing. Though offering little during the war, *Fortune* in the immediate postwar period paid for and published two remarkably thorough and unusual polls on relationships between men and women, and also featured an important work by Margaret Mead, "What Women Want." Finally, the federal government's *Monthly Labor Review* was an invaluable source of detailed economic information related to women, with almost 30 of its reports cited.

Wartime changes were reflected in eight home-related publications, which account for almost 50 cited articles. *Good Housekeeping* was especially likely to move away from housework into other aspects of women's lives, while

American Home probably made the most suggestions for dealing with wartime shortages. The *Journal of Home Economics* also published several worthwhile articles. Similar publications aimed at parents and educators account for another four dozen sources; *Parents* and the federal government's *Education for Victory* were especially beneficial.

Finally, by far the most valuable periodical used was *Independent Woman*. The official organ of the Business and Professional Women's (BPW) Clubs, it (unlike the League of Women Voters' publication) devoted little space to internal organizational news, and instead paid a great deal of attention to the range of contemporary women's issues. Approximately 70 articles from this publication served as sources, an average of 1.5 items per issue for the 46 months of the war. *Independent Woman* published many popular writers and political figures, as well as commentary on current issues by BPW presidents Margaret Hickey and Dr. Minnie Maffett. Probably the single most creative article written by a man, Laurence Hammond's "Kitchen Lore Speeds War Production," appeared in *Independent Woman*.

In addition to these and other periodicals and government documents, about 35 books, virtually all of them published during the war, were useful sources. The Notes reveal that Colonel Julia Flikke's *Nurses in Action* (New York: Lippincott, 1943) was especially significant for Part I. Mattie Treadwell's 800-plus- page postwar history of *The Women's Army Corps* (Office of the Chief of Military History, Department of the Army, 1954) was of incomparable importance in Part II. Personal accounts of military women added greatly to understanding their experience, and almost a dozen are cited in the Notes. Most were published during the war and were clearly intended to be used as recruiting tools. Wartime publishers also produced quickly written books designed to encourage women into industry, and almost a dozen of these are listed in the Notes for Part III. Similar books aimed a recruiting volunteers were important to Part IV. In addition, several midwar publications by soldiers' wives were also of tremendous benefit, especially for Chapter 16.

Since these books were written with a specific, short-term purpose in mind, all are now out of print and many are difficult to locate. For the preservation of such obscure and seemingly ephemeral writing that is nonetheless vital in bringing back the immediacy of the times, several libraries deserve thanks. The Library of Congress, of course, was the terminus for difficult research questions and sources that could not be located elsewhere. The book's early research, however, was done during summers at Brown and Princeton universities and owes much to those libraries. The Providence Public Library and the Boston Public Library served as especially good sources for nonscholarly publications. The Tampa Public Library provided additional popular sources (especially the incomparable *Independent Woman*), while the University of South Florida, its interlibrary loan system, and its always knowledgeable and interested librarians are owed the deepest debt of gratitude.

INDEX